An Encyclopaedic Dictionary of Ancient Indian Hisotry

A SERIES OF AN ENCYCLOPAEDIC DICTIONARY OF INDIAN HISTORY AND CULTURE

An Encyclopaedic Dictionary of

ANCIENT INDIAN HISTORY

2700 BC—1192 AD

Edited by :

A.N. Kapoor
V.P. Gupta
Mohini Gupta

RADHA PUBLICATIONS
NEW DELHI 110 002

First Published 2003

ISBN 81-7487-287-6

Published by

RADHA PUBLICATIONS
4378/4-B, Ansari Road,
Daryaganj,
New Delhi 110002
Phones: 3261839, 3254306

PRINTED IN INDIA

Published by Nitin Garg for Radha Publications, Lasertypeset by Jitendra Kumar Singh, Delhi-94, and printed at Tarun Offset Press, Delhi.

Dedicated to
my esteemed friend
Dr. S.P. Bhatnagar
and his devoted wife
Dr. Shrimati Susheela Bhatnagar

Preface

The present work *An Encyclopaedic Dictionary of Ancient India* is the second publication under the ongoing series *An Encyclopaedic Dictionary of Indian History and Culture*. The first volume of the series is on the Indian mythology and the subsequent volumes deal with Medieval India, Modern India, Freedom Movement and Contemporary India.

An Encyclopaedic Dictionary of Ancient India aims to be a handy reference manual for understanding ancient Indian history and culture. Traces of human activity found in India go back to the interglacial period between 400,000 and 200,000 B.C. The Harappa culture flourished from, 2700 to 1500 BC. The people of Indus Valley had commercial relations with contemporary Mesopotamia and Egypt. The period from 1500 BC to 1000 BC makes the age of the Vedas. It was around 600 BC that Buddhism and Jainism arose and opposed the dominating role of rituals and animal sacrifice. Alexander of Macedonia raided north western India in 326 BC. The kindgom of Magadha expanded into a vast empire. The Mauryan dynasty produced emperors like Ashoka (269-232 BCE) who sent missions to neighbouring kingdoms in West Asia, Burma and Lanka. High levels of artistic and economic activity were attained during his reign.

The period 300-700 AD has been hailed as the classical age of Hindu civilization. The Gupta Dynasty rose in Magadha and held its sway, over the Indo-Gangetic Plains, Kashmir and the Deccan. Several Chinese Buddhist pilgrims came to India during this period. Their accounts testify to the all-round prosperity of the people. The political hegemony of the Gupta rulers was shattered by a series of Huna invasions in the fifth and sixth centuries.

Islam came to India in the 8th century. Sultan Mahmud of Ghazni (979-1030) launched a series of attacks on north Indian temples. He was followed by Muhammad Ghori who after occupying Multan in 1176, Punjab and Sindh in 1186 defeated Prithvi Raj Chauhan at the battle of Tarain in 1192 resulting in the establishment of the Muslim power in India.

In the course of its evolution India has given birth to four world religions—Hinduism, Buddhism, Jainism and Sikhism. The country has witnessed a large number of sects within these established religions. Islam came to India in the 8th century and is the second most populous religion of India after Hinduism. Historically Hinduism is the oldest religion of India. The basic tenets of Hinduism are found in the four Vedas, Upanishads, Bhagvadgita, six systems of philosophy, the two epics *Ramayana* and *Mahabharata*, Dharmashastras, Puranas and Smriti-books.

The social structure of India is a unique blend of diverse elements. India has been a hospitabile land for numerous immigrants. The social and cultural patterns of these aliens have been interwoven with the native culture. The caste-system, the joint family system, unity amidst diversity and an amazing degree of toleration have been some of the major traits of India's social evolution. The foundations of all these tracts were laid in ancient India.

There were regular trade relations between India and the rest of the world during the first half of the first millennium B.C. As a result of the invasion of Alexander India came into close contact with the Hellenic world. Kautilya's *Arthashastra* furnishes a vivid account of the economic conditions during the times of Chandragupta Maurya. It was indeed India's wealth which attracted foreign invaders.

The enormous wealth of the country led to the development of art and architecture during the Gupta age. The stupas and rock-cut temples were built with striking novelty. The caves at Ajanta were carved out with grandeur. During the six hundred years following the Gupta age we find remarkable development in architecture. The Kailash temple at Ellora has been hailed as one of the most singular and interesting monuments of architectural art in India.

The Gupta period saw the highest development of the art of sculpture in India. The figures found at Sarnath and other places, show a fully developed form. The famous iron pillar at Delhi, near the Qutub Minar, is a marvel of metallurgical skill.

Dance in India has an unbroken tradition of about 2000 years.

The sage Bharat in his *Natya Shastra* has laid down the basic principles of dance.

A drama tells a story by means of action and speech. Kalidas was a great dramatist. His *Shakuntala* and *Vikramorvasi* are great dramatic works. Aswaghosa, Bhasa, Sudraka, Bhavbhuti, Vishakhdutt and Rajshekhar were outstanding dramatists.

Indian music tradition goes back to the Vedas. During the course of time it developed into an integrated system.

The beginning of the Sanskrit literature can be traced to Rigvedic poetry. The two major epics of India are the Ramayana and the Mahabharata. Kalidasa, Bharavi, Bhatti, Magha are considered to be great epic poets. Sanskrit has rich scientific literature in mathematics, astronomy and medieval science.

The book is divided into four sections. *Section One: Historical Perspecitves* presents a rapid survey of Indian history from paleolithic age to the establishment of the Muslim authority in India in 1192.

Section Two constitutes the main Dictionary and contains more than five hundred entries drawn from the diverse areas of ancient Indian history and culture such as administration, architecture, arts, battles, concepts, costumes, dynasties, events, institutions, language, literature, movements, personalities, philosophy, polity, religion, sciences, scriptures, sects and sculpture. While *Section Three* describes major dates and events of the period, *Section Four* furnishes an exhaustive bibliography of more than 200 titles covering the entire subject matter.

An understanding of India's past is necessary to understand India's present and anticipate its future. It is hoped that the compendium would be found useful by the general public as well as the scholars.

Editors

Contents

Section Three
The Chronology

Section Four
The Bibliography

Section One
Historical Perspectives

1

Geographical Setting

Introduction

India emerged as a State on August 15, 1947, as a result of the dissolution of the British Empire in South Asia. It was given the status of a dominion within the British Commonwealth of nations but granted itself the status of a republic on January 26, 1950, while retaining its membership in the Commonwealth. The republic is often referred to in Hindi as "Bharat". The Constitution of India defines it as a "sovereign socialist secular democratic republic", with a parliamentary system of government. New Delhi is the capital of India.

India is a union of 28 States and seven Union Territories. Each unit enjoys specific powers and responsibilities, and residuary power is vested in the union government. In the Seventh Schedule of the Constitution of India, these powers have been exclusively allocated between the Union government and the State government. There is also a list of powers concurrently shared by the State and Union governments.

Objects of National Identity

A national flag was adopted in the Constituent Assembly of India on July 22, 1947, and its use and display are regulated by the Indian Flag Code. The national emblem is an adaptation of the Saranath Lion Capital of Ashoka.

The song *Jana-gana-mana,* originally composed in Bengali by poet Rabindranath Tagore, was adopted, in its Hindi version of the first stanza, by the Constituent Assembly as the national anthem of India on January 24, 1950. The song *Bande Mataram,* originally composed in Sanskrit by Bankim Chandra Chatterjee, has an equal status as the national anthem and is the national song of India.

A calendar based on the *Shaka* era with *Chaitra* as the first month and a normal year of 365 days was adopted as the national calendar on March 22, 1957. This, together with the Gregorian calendar, is used to date all official communications.

The national animal of India is the tiger (*Panthera tigris*) and the national bird is the peacock (*Pavo cristatus*). Both are protected under the Wildlife (Protection) Act of 1972. The national flower is the lotus.

Location of India

India is the largest country of South Asia. It has an area of 3,287,263 sq km, of which the island chains of Amindivi, Minicoy, and Lakshadweep in the Arabian Sea and the Andaman and Nicobar Islands in the Bay of Bengal together cover a total area of 8,281 sq km. The mainland comprises the rest of the area. India is the seventh largest country of the world and accounts for slightly more than 2 per cent of the Earth's land surface. It contains more than one-sixth of the world's population, ranking second to China.

India has common land boundaries with the countries of Pakistan, Afghanistan, China (Tibet), Nepal, Bhutan, Myanmar (formerly Burma), and Bangladesh. The narrow Palk Strait and the Gulf of Mannar separate India from Sri Lanka. India has a land frontier of about 15,200 km. The coastline of the mainland and the islands is about 7,517 km.

Physical Configuration

In a very broad sense, there are five major types of landforms in India. The first type is made up of a cluster of plateaus of very ancient origin, constituting peninsular India and some parts in the northeast, which account for more than half the total area of the country. The next important type of landform, in size, is the alluvial plain of North India, formed in very recent geologic time by three major rivers: the Indus, the Ganga, the Brahmaputra, and their tributaries. The main valley of the Indus River falls mostly within Pakistan. Before meeting the Bay of Bengal, the Ganga and the Brahmaputra together form the largest delta of the world, which falls partly within Bangladesh. Young folded mountains constitute the third type of landform, extending along the northern and eastern boundaries of the country. Among these, the Himalaya extend along the full length of the northern boundary and include several of the highest peaks of the world. The fourth type of landform is found along the flanks of peninsular India, bordering the Arabian Sea and the Bay of Bengal in the shape of narrow and disjointed coastal plains. These have formed through the combined processes of marine transgression and riverine alluviation. Some of the rivers have formed deltas, particularly along the littoral tracts of the Bay of Bengal, including the Cauvery, the Krishna, the Godavari, and the Mahanadi. The islands represent the fifth type of landform. The Arabian Sea islands are coral formations upon submarine ridges. The Bay of Bengal islands are peaks of submerged folded mountains of recent origin.

Climate

India provides the world's most pronounced example of a monsoon climate. The wet and dry seasons of the monsoon system, along with annual temperature fluctuations, produce three general climatic periods over much of the country. From about mid-June to the end of September, the weather is hot and wet. From early October to February, the weather remains generally cool and dry. From about March to mid-June, the weather turns hot and dry, with increased atmospheric humidity. The actual time of occurrence of these types of weather may vary by several weeks, not only from one part of the country to another but also from year to year. Regional differences, which are often considerable, result from a number of factors, such as local relief, altitude, and proximity to bodies of water.

The changes in weather conditions in India are primarily the product of the seasonal variations in the direction of prevailing winds. This is commonly referred to as the monsoon system, which is essentially a gigantic land-and-sea breeze system operating over seasons rather than between the hours of the day. This change takes place under the influence of the latitudinal shift of the midday sun between months and the consequent replacement in the summer of the normal high-pressure system in the tropics by a low atmospheric pressure system. With the change in pressure systems, reversals in the direction of winds take place between the summer and winter months. During summer, moisture-laden sea breezes come from the southwest. In winter, the winds blow from northeast or northwest.

Over most parts of India, the major wet season starts from about mid-June and continues till early October, when winds from the Indian Ocean carry moisture-laden air across the subcontinent, causing heavy rainfall. About three-fourths of the country's total annual precipitation usually falls during these months. During the winter months, generally from November through February, this pattern is reversed, as dry air from the Asian interior moves across India towards the ocean. This period is referred to as the period of retreating monsoon, when winds blow from the northeast across the Bay of Bengal and pick up a significant amount of moisture, which is subsequently released, on the southern part of the peninsula. October and also March through May, by contrast, are the periods of transition with no strong prevailing patterns.

Another feature of the summer months is fierce tropical cyclones that hit the coasts of Andhra Pradesh, Orissa, and West Bengal. These originate from the Bay of Bengal. The depressions also cause tidal waves to hit the east coast of India. Storms originating in the Arabian Sea hit Gujarat and often move into southern Rajasthan. These are the periods of unusually heavy showers.

Another type of rainfall occurs in northern India during winter. Weak depressions originating from the Mediterranean Sea reach northwest India and cause rain in the plains and snowfall on the mountains.

The annual range of temperature (difference between minimum and maximum) varies widely in India. It tends to be significantly lower along the coastal plains and decidedly higher in the interiors. The temperature range also tends to increase with latitude. Temperatures are moderate wherever elevations are significant as in many resort towns on the Himalayan range.

Soils

In India, a wide range of soils is found. On the basis of the natural environmental processes that produce them these can be broadly divided into two groups, *in situ* soils and transported soils (formed by transportation of eroded material). The *in situ* soils get their distinguishing features from the parent rock.

The *black soil* found in the lava-covered land is the most conspicuous. These are often referred to as *regur* but are popularly known as black-cotton soil since, cotton has been the prevailing traditional crop on such soils. These are poor in humus yet highly moisture-retentive, responding well to irrigation. Black soils are primarily found in peninsular India where the underlying rock is basalt, as in Maharashtra, Karnataka, Gujarat, and Madhya Pradesh.

Red *in situ* soils called *lateritic soils*, are generally found over extensive tracts of peninsular India that are composed of acidic rocks such as granite, gneiss, and schist. Lateritic soils develop through leaching of soluble minerals, particularly the chemically basic constituents, and enrichment from oxidized iron, which imparts the reddish hue. Heavily leached red soils are found in the high-rainfall areas of the Western Ghats, western Kathiawar peninsula, eastern Rajasthan, the Eastern Ghats, the Chota Nagpur plateau, and other upland tracts of northeastern India. Less-leached red soils occur in areas of low rainfall immediately east of the Western Ghats in the dry interior of the Deccan plateau. Red soils are poor in humus; but in forested tracts, humus concentration and the recycling of nutrients help restore fertility in the topsoil. However, humus-rich forest soils are found on all forest-clad mountainous tracts even though the *in situ* soils of those tracts are not of the same type.

Alluvial soils occur widely in India: in all river valleys, deltas, and coastal plains. The mineral composition of these transported soils differs according to the source materials. The grain-size distribution also varies according to the distance travelled. The tracts close to the Himalaya have a coarse-grained alluvium with large annular space, known locally as *bhabbar* soil. As these are further sifted and carried some distance, coarse sand particles are gradually replaced by fine sand, with corresponding increase in clay. Hence the permeability of the alluvial soils and correspondingly, their water-holding capacity vary between tracts. In the plains, newer alluvium, locally called *khadar*, is found on the floodplains. This newer alluvium is uniform in texture and extremely fertile. In some of the old alluvium on the slightly elevated terraces, which is termed *bhangar*, patches of alkaline efflorescence called *usar* are found. These make the soil infertile.

Plant Life (Vegetation)

Currently available data on plant diversity places India as the tenth most botanically varied region in the world and the fourth in Asia, although enumeration has not yet been completed. Publications of the Botanical Survey of India, Calcutta, indicate that there are

49,000 species of plants within 70 per cent of the geographical area of India surveyed so far. The total floral wealth of the country includes the flowering trees and shrubs as well as nonflowering plants such as ferns, liverworts, algae, and fungi. The vascular flora, which forms conspicuous vegetation, comprises over 15,000 species, of which more than 35 per cent is native and has so far not been reported anywhere else in the world. The flora of India largely reflects the regionally varied climate, especially the temperature range and seasonal distribution of rainfall. Latitude and altitude are the other attenuated variables.

Approximately 75 million hectares, or some 22 per cent of India's geographical area, is officially classified as forest. The actual amount of forested area, however, is lower. Expanding agriculture, urban-industrial development, and lack of effort to renew consumed resources has resulted in depletion of forest cover. The severity of the problem is clear from the fact that several Indian plants are facing extinction. About 20 species of higher-order plants are believed to be already extinct, and some 1,336 species are considered endangered. The limitation of identifying floral zones based on enumeration of species found in the existing forests is therefore obvious.

The most important are the *tropical evergreen and mixed evergreen-deciduous forests*. These generally occupy areas with more than 2,032 mm of annual rainfall, mainly in upper Assam, the Western Ghats (especially in Kerala), parts of Orissa, and the Andaman and Nicobar Islands. Common trees in these tall, multi layered forests include species of *Mesua, Toona ciliata, Hopea,* and *Eugenia,* as well as *gurjun (Dipterocarpus turbinatus)*, which grows to over 50 m on the Andaman Islands and in Assam. The mixed evergreen-deciduous forests of Kerala and the Bengal Himalaya have a large variety of commercially valuable hardwood trees, of which *Lagerstroemia lanceolata,* East Indian, or Malabar, kino *(Pterocarpus marsupium)* and rosewood *(Dalbergia latifolia)* are well known.

The *tropical-moist deciduous forests* represent the next important zone. These generally occur in areas with 1,524 to 2,032 mm of annual rainfall, such as the northern part of the Eastern Ghats, east-central India, and western Karnataka. Dry deciduous forests, which grow in places receiving less than 1,524 mm of precipitation, characterize the subhumid and semiarid regions of Gujarat, Madhya Pradesh, eastern Rajasthan, central Andhra Pradesh, and western Tamil Nadu. Teak, sal, axlewood, tendu, ain, and *Adina cardifolia* are some of the major deciduous species. Among the important commercial species, teak *(Tectona grandis)* and sal *(Shorea robusta)* are raised in some State-controlled reserved forests as plantations. Teak, the foremost furniture timber, is largely confined to the peninsula. Sal, a widely used construction timber, is confined to the lower Himalaya, Uttar Pradesh, Bihar, Assam, and Madhya Pradesh. Other species with commercial uses are the fragrant and precious sandalwood *(Santalum album)* and the evergreen rosewood used for carving and furniture.

Tropical thorn forests, is the third zone which occupies various parts of the country, mainly in the northern Gangetic plain and southern peninsular India. These forests generally grow in areas with less than 610 mm of rain but are also found in more humid areas, where deciduous forests have been degraded because of unregulated grazing, tree felling, and slash-and-burn agriculture. In such areas, xerophytic (drought-tolerant) trees such as species of *Acacia* (babul and catechu) and *Butea monosperma* predominate.

Deltaic areas, for example, are fringed with *mangrove forests*, in which the dominant species, *sundri* and *Avicinia*, are characterized by respiratory roots that emerge from the tidal water. Conspicuous features of the tropical landscape are the palms, which are represented in India by some 100 species. Coconut and betel nut (the fruit of which is chewed) are cultivated mainly in coastal Karnataka and Kerala. Among the common, majestic-looking trees found throughout much of India is the mango *(Mangifera indica)*, a major source of fruit. Similarly, three species of *Ficus (Ficus officinalis, F. religiosa,* and *F. benegalensis)* grow in most parts of India. Many types of bamboo (members of the grass family) also grow over much of the country, with a concentration in the rainy areas.

Vegetation in the Himalaya can be generally divided into a number of altitude zones. It can also be classified as western and eastern Himalayan types. Mixed evergreen-deciduous forests dominate the foothill areas. Above these, subtropical forests make their appearance, followed by moist-temperate forests, then by Alpine shrubs, then Alpine meadows, and finally lichens and moss. Zones overlap considerably with wide transitional bands. The altitudes at which these floral zones are encountered vary between the western and eastern Himalaya, the former being cooler and drier than the latter. Major contrast in floral mix is discernible in the temperate zone. In the western Himalaya, the common varieties of trees of the temperate zone are chir and pine. In the eastern Himalaya, oaks, laurels, maples, rhododendrons, alder, and birch are prevalent.

The Zoological Survey of India, with headquarters in Calcutta and 16 regional stations, has been studying the faunal resources of the country. Data collected so far indicate the great variety in India's fauna. Insects account for some 60,000 species; the next important group is the molluscs with about 5,000 species. At the turn of the twentieth century, 372 species of mammals, 1,228 species of birds, 446 species of reptiles, 204 species of amphibians, and 2,546 species of fish had been identified.

Expansion of area for agriculture, surface-irrigation systems, mining, and urban-industrial development has resulted in depletion of vegetative cover and consequent habitat destruction. Added to these are the destructive processes of nature, such as cyclones, floods, and droughts. More than 77 species of mammals, 72 species of birds, 3 species of amphibians, 2 species of fish, and a large variety of butterflies, moths, and beetles are considered vulnerable and endangered.

Population

The second most populous country in the world, India is home to 16 per cent of the global population. Very little of India's surface area is uninhabited. Only in the rugged mountain terrain are there any substantial continuous areas not in use by humans. In 1901 nationwide population density was a mere 77 persons per sq km. In 1991 it stood at 273 persons, excluding the area of Jammu and Kashmir. It was highest (6,352 persons per sq km) in the Union Territory of Delhi and lowest (10 persons per sq km) in Arunachal Pradesh. The 10 most heavily populated tracts of India are Calcutta, Chennai (formerly Madras), Greater Mumbai (formerly Greater Bombay), Hyderabad, Delhi, Chandigarh, Mahe, Howrah, Kanpur, and Bangalore. More than three-fifths of the total population live either on the fertile alluvial soils of the Indo-Gangetic Plain and the deltaic regions of the eastern coast or on the mixed alluvial and marine soils along India's western coast. Within these agriculturally productive areas, for example, in parts of the eastern Gangetic Plain and in the State of Kerala, population densities exceed 750 persons per sq km.

An organized census of the Indian population was first attempted in 1872. From 1881, the census had been carried out regularly at an interval of 10 years. However, comparable statistics on population are available for each decade only from 1901 onwards. In 1971 no enumeration in Assam could be carried out. Similarly, in 1991, enumeration for Jammu and Kashmir failed due to disturbed conditions. Based on interpolation, the total population of India in 1991 stood at 846,302,688 with 439,230,458 males and 407,072,230 females.

Records indicate an increase in population during each decade of the twentieth century except for 1911-1921, when an absolute decline in numbers took place. Between 1921 and 1931, the average annual exponential growth rate stood at 1.04 per cent. It increased steadily to a maximum of 2.22 per cent between 1971 and 1981. In 1981-1991, it declined to 2.14 per cent for India as a whole. However, this rate varied in different parts of the country. In most States, the rate declined in comparison with that of the previous decade. However, the States of Andhra Pradesh, Arunachal Pradesh, Madhya pradesh, Maharashtra, Nagaland, Tripura, and West Bengal, and the Union Territories of Daman and Diu, Lakshadweep, and Pondicherry (which together account for one-third of the country's population), recorded an increase in the growth rate. Nagaland registered the highest growth rate and Kerala the lowest. Regionally varying patterns of migration, the spread of literacy, improvements in the morbidity profiles, and general increase in life expectancy are among the many factors to be taken into account for such variations. It is important to consider that a marked reduction in the birth rate in the foreseeable future could be inhibited by the increasing proportion of females attaining and living through their child-bearing years.

According to the 1991 census, there are 927 *females* per 1,000 *males* in India taken as a whole. This ratio, however, varies between regions. The territories having a larger number of females than males are Kerala, Himachal Pradesh, Andhra Pradesh, Goa, Karnataka, Manipur, Orissa, Tamil Nadu, Dadra and Nagar Haveli, Daman and Diu, and Pondicherry. Chandigarh has the lowest ratio. Dominance of male migration to urban places is common across the country.

For the purposes of the census, a person is declared *literate* if she or he can read and write in any language with understanding. Recent data on literacy is not strictly comparable with earlier information because in 1991 only persons aged seven years and older were enumerated, while before that the lowest limit of the range was five years of age. Nevertheless, from a dismal figure of 18.33 per cent in 1951, the literacy rate has steadily increased, reaching 52.21 per cent in 1991. Female literacy has remained significantly lower than that of males. In 1991 the male literacy rate stood at 64.13 per cent, while that for females was 39.29 per cent.

A considerable regional variation in literacy is seen in India. In terms of the total population, it is highest in Kerala (89.81 per cent) and lowest in Bihar (38.48 per cent). Rajasthan has the lowest female literacy at 20.44 per cent as against 54.99 per cent for males. Literacy in the urban areas has been consistently higher than in the rural tracts.

2

The Dawn of Indian History

From the Palaeolithic Period to the decline of the Indus Civilization

The earliest periods of Indian history are known only through reconstruction from archaeological evidence. In the late twentieth century, much new data emerged, allowing a far fuller reconstruction than was formerly possible. Traditional and textual sources, transmitted orally for many centuries, are available from the closing centuries of second millennium BC, but their use depends largely upon the extent to which any passage can be dated or associated with archaeological evidence.

For the rise of civilization in the Indus Valley and for contemporary events in other parts of the subcontinent, the archaeological evidence is still the principal source of information. Even when it becomes possible to read the short inscriptions of the Harappan seals, it is unlikely that they will provide much information to supplement other sources.

The Early Prehistoric Period: The Indian Palaeolithic Age

The oldest artefacts yet found on the subcontinent, marking what may be called the beginning of the Indian Lower Palaeolithic age, come from the western end of the Shiwalik Hills, near Rawalpindi in northern Pakistan. These quartzite pebble tools and flakes date to about two million years ago, according to palaeomagnetic analysis. They represent a pre-hand-axe industry of a type that appears to have persisted for a very long period thereafter. The artefacts are associated with extremely rich sedimentary evidence and fossil fauna, but so far no correlative hominid remains have been found. In the same region, the earliest hand axes (of the type commonly called Acheulian, after an early find in France) have been dated palaeomagnetically to about 500,000 years ago.

The Great India (Thar) Desert, straddling what is now the southern half of the India-Pakistan border, supplied significant archaeological materials in the late twentieth century. Hand axes found at Didwana, Rajasthan, similar to those from the Shiwalik Hills, yield slightly younger dates of about 400,000 years ago. Examination of the desert soil strata and other evidence has revealed a correlation between prevailing climates and the successive levels of technology that constitute the Palaeolithic age. A prolonged humid phase, for example, as attested by reddish-brown soil with a deep profile, appears to have commenced some 140,000 years ago and lasted until about 25,000 years ago, roughtly the extent of the Middle Palaeolithic Period. During this time the area of the present desert provided a rich environment for hunting. The earliest rock paintings yet discovered in the region date to the Upper Palaeolithic age.

Other important Palaeolithic sites under excavation in the 1990s included ones at Hunsgi in Karnataka State and in the Vindhya Range separating the Gangetic basin from the Deccan Plateau.

Mesolithic Hunters

The progressive diminution in the size of stone artefacts that began in the Middle Palaeolithic period reached its climax in the small parallel-sided blades and microliths of what has been called the Indian Mesolithic. A great proliferation of Msolithic cultures is evident throughout India, although they are known almost exclusively from surface collections of tools. Cultures of this period exhibited a wide variety of subsistence patterns, including hunting and gathering, fishing, and, at least for part of the period, some herding and small-scale agriculture.

Thus, chronologically, the Mesolithic cultures cover an enormous span. In caves of the Hindu Kush in northern Afghanistan, evidence of occupation dating to between 15,000 and 10,000 BC represents the so-called Epipalaeolithic stage, which may be considered to fall within the Mesolithic age. The domestication of sheep and goats is thought to have begun in this region and period.

Many of the caves and rock shelters of central India contain rock paintings depicting a variety of subjects, including game animals and such human activities as hunting, honey collecting, and dancing. This art appears to have developed from Upper Palaeolithic precursors and reveals much about life in the period. Along with the art have come increasingly clear indications that some of the caves were sites of religious activity.

Neolithic Agriculture in the Indus Valley

The group of sites at Mehrgarh (now in Pakistan) provides evidence of some five or six thousands years of occupation comprising two major periods, the first from the eighth through the sixth millennium BC and the second from the fifth through the fourth (and possibly the third) millennium.

Phase 1A, dating to the eighth-seventh millennium BC, was an aceramic (lacking pottery) Neolithic occupation. The main tools were stone blades. A relatively small number of ground stone axes have been found. Domestication of wheat and barley apparently reached the area some time during this phase, as did that of sheep and goats, although the preponderance of gazelle bones among the animal remains suggests continued dependence on hunting. Houses of mud brick date from the beginning of this phase and continued throughout the occupation. Accompaniments to the simple burial of human remains included shell or stone-bead necklaces, baskets, and occasionally young caprids (both sheep and goats) slaughtered for the purpose.

Phase 1B, dating to the seventh-sixth millennium, is characterized by the emergence of pottery and improvements in agriculture. By the beginning of Phase 1B, cattle (apparently *Bos indicus*, the Indian humped variety) had come to predominate over game animals, as well as over sheep and goats. A new type of building, the small regular compartments of which identify it almost certainly as a granary, first apeared during this phase and became prevalent in Period II, indicating the frequent occurence of crop surpluses. Burial took a more elaborate form—a funerary chamber was dug at one end of a pit, and, after inhumation, the chamber was sealed by a mud brick wall. From the latter phase of Period I also come the first small, hand-modelled female figurines of unburned clay.

The Period I evidence at Mehrgarh provides a clear picture of an early agricultural settlement exhibiting domestic architecture and a variety of well-established crafts. Striking changes characterize Period II. It appears that some major tectonic event took place at the beginning of the period (c. 5500 BC), causing the deposition of great quantities of silt on the plain, almost completely burying the original mound at Mehrgarh.

The Rise of Urban-life in the Indus Valley

From about 5000 BC, increasing numbers of settlements began to appear throughout the Indo-Iranian borderlands. These, as far as can be judged, were village communities of settled agriculturalists, employing common means of subsistence in the cultivation of wheat, barley, and other crops and in the keeping of cattle, sheep, and goats; there was a broadly common level of technology based on the use of stone for some artefacts and copper and bronze for others. Comparison and contrast of the high-quality painted pottery of the period suggest distinct groupings among the communities.

At a somewhat later date, probably towards the middle of the fourth millennium BC, agricultural settlements began to spread more widely in the Indus Valley itself. The earliest of these provide clear links with the cultures along or beyond the western margins of the Indus Valley. In the course of time, a remarkable change took place in the form of the Indus settlements, suggesting that some kind of closer interaction was developing, often over considerable distances, and that a process of convergence was under way. This continued for approximately 500 years and can now be identified as marking a transition towards the full urban society that emerged as Harappa and similar sites around 2600 BC. For this reason, this stage has been named the Early Harappan or Early Indus culture.

Early Harappan Settlements

One of the most significant features of the Early Harappan settlements is the evidence of a hierarchy among the sites, culminating in a number of substantial walled towns. The first site to be recognized as belonging to the Early Harappan period was Amri in 1929. In 1948 Sir Mortimer Wheeler discovered a small deposit of pottery stratified below the remains of the mature Indus city at Harappa. The next site to be excavated with a view to uncovering the Early Harappan period was Kot Diji in Sind. A stone rubble wall surrounded this settlement, which appears to date to about 3000 BC. An even earlier example is Rehman Dheri, near Dera Ismail Khan (now in Pakistan), which appears to have achieved its walled status during the last centuries of the fourth millennium. Here the roughly rectangular, grid-patterned settlement was surrounded by a massive wall of mud brick. Early Harappan Kalibangan (Kali Banga) in Rajasthan resembled Rehman Dheri in form. It later served as the basis for an expanded settlement of the mature Indus civilization. Still farther east in Haryana and the eastern Punjab are many other Early Harappan sites. Among them several have been excavated, notably Banawali and Mitathal. Another example of a walled settlement of the period is Tharro in southern Sind. This was probably originally a coastal site, although it is now many miles from the sea. Here the surrounding wall and the extant traces of houses are of local stone.

3

The Indus Valley Civilization

Character and Significance

While the Indus (or Harappan) civilization may be considered the culmination of a long process indigenous to the Indus Valley, a number of parallels exist between developments on the Indus and the rise of civilization in Mesopotamia. It is striking to compare the Indus with this better-known and more fully documented region and to see how closely the two coincide with respect to the emergence of cities and of such major concomitants of civilization as writing, standardized weights and measures, and monumental architecture. Yet, nearly all the earlier writers have sensed the Indianness of the civilization, even when they were largely unable to articulate it. Thus, V. Gordon Childe wrote in his *New Light on the Most Ancient East* that:

"India confronts Egypt and Babylonia by the third millennium with a thoroughly individual and independent civilization of her own, technically the peer of the rest. And plainly it is deeply rooted in Indian soil. The Indus cuvilization represents a very perfect adjustment of human life to a specific environment. And it has endured; it is already specifically Indian and forms the basis of modern Indian culture."

The attention paid to domestic bathrooms, the drains, and the Great Bath at Mohenjodaro can all be compared with elements in the later Indian civilization. The bullock carts with a framed canopy, called *ikkas,* and boats are little changed to this day. The absence of pins and the love of bangles and of elaborate nose ornaments are all peculiarly Indian. The religion of the Indus also is replete with suggestions of traits known from later India. The significance of the bull, the tiger, and the elephant; the composite animals; the seated yogi god of the seals; the tree spirits and the objects resembling the Shiva *linga* (symbolic of the god Shiva) of later times—all these are suggestive of enduring forms in later Indian civilization.

The evidence of widespread trade in many commodities, the apparent uniformity in weights and measures, the common script, and the uniformity—almost common currency—of the seals all indicate some measure of political and economic control and point to the great cities, Mohenjodaro and Harappa, as their centres. The presence of the great granaries on the citadel mounds in these cities and of the "citadels" themselves suggests the existence of priest-kings, or at least of a priestly oligarchy, that controlled the economy and civil government. The intellectual mechanism of this government and the striking degree of control implicit in it are still matters of speculation. Nor can scholars yet speak with any certainty regarding relations between the cities and surrounding villages. Much more research needs to be done, on many such topics, before the full character of the Indus civilization can be revealed.

The End of the Indus Civilization

Among the causes of the breakdown of Harappan urban society, the first is gradual environmental change, such as a shift in climatic patterns and consequent agricultural disaster, perhaps coinciding with rapid population growth. Second, was more precipitous environmental changes, such as tectonic events leading to the flooding of Mohenjodaro, the drying up of the Sarasvati River, or other such calamities. Third, was growth of human activities such as influx of tribal people from the hills to the west of the Indus Valley. Perhaps even Indo-Aryans, contributed to the breakdown of Indus external trade links or more directly disrupted the cities. The fourth was occurrence of an epidemic. The Vedic civilization flourished in the region much earlier along the banks of the Sarasvati River. When this river dried in a later period, the population gradually shifted westwards towards the Indus, and eastwards towards and along the Ganga, and to the south. Whatever may have been the cause, it appears likely that some complex of natural forces compromised the fabric of society and that subsequent human intervention hastened its complete breakdown.

Post-Harappan developments

The urban society broke down between about 2000 and 1750 BC. The collapse of the urban system does not necessarily imply a complete breakdown in the lifestyle of the population in all parts of the Indus region, but it seems to have involved the end of whatever system of social and political control had preceded it. After this date the cities, as such, and many of their distinctively urban traits—the use of writing and of seals and a number of the specialized urban crafts—disappear. The succeeding era, which lasted until about 750 BC, may be considered as post-Harappan or perhaps better as "post-urban".

In the Sarasvati valley, the early post-urban stage is associated with the pottery known from the so-called Cemetery H at Harappa. This coincides with a major reduction in both the number and size of settlements, suggesting a deterioration in the environment. In the eastern Punjab, too, there is a disappearance of the larger, urban sites but no comparable reduction in the number of smaller settlements. This is also true of the settlements father east in the Ganga-Yamuna valleys. It is probably correct to conclude that, in each of these areas during the post-urban period, material culture exhibited some tendency to develop regional variations, sometimes showing continuations of features already present during the pre-urban and urban phases.

The Arrival and Spread of Indo-Aryan Speakers

Scholars generally agree that the arrival and spread of people speaking Old Indo-Aryan dialects of the Indo-Iranian branch of the Indo-European language family took place during the late third and second millennia BC. Probably these people came from the steppes to the north and east of the Caspian Sea, moving first southwards into the southern parts of Central Asia and from there fanning out across the Iranian plateau. This movement may already have begun during the life-span of the Indus civilization. One hypothesis is that between about 2000 and 1500 BC a continuing spread of Indo-Aryan speakers occurred, carrying them much farther into India, to the east and south, and coinciding with a growing cultural interaction between the native population and the new arrivals. From these processes a new cultural synthesis emerged, giving rise by the end of the second millennium to the conscious expressions of Aryan ethnicity found in the Rigveda, particularly in the later hymns.

Towards the end of the second millennium in the period from about 1200-800 BC there appears to have been a further deterioration in the environment throughout the Indus system. Many of the post-urban settlements seem to have been abandoned, and traces are found of temporary settlements that were probably associated with nomadic pastoral groups and distinguished by the poverty of their material culture. In the Sarasvati valley there is further evidence of the drying up of the Derawar oasis, with a further decline in the number and size of settlements. Temporary encampments of pastoral nomads indicate a general deterioration in the standard of living.

To the north, in Punjab, Haryana, and the upper Ganga Valley, such deterioration is less apparent, perhaps because the proximity of the Himalaya produced a more consistent level of rainfall. It is in this area that the expansion of settlements associated with the pottery known as painted gray ware emerged. This characteristic ceramic accompanied a spread of settlements towards the east into the upper Ganga-Yamuna valleys and constitutes a distinguishing feature of the process of development that, by the second quarter of the first millennium BC, gave rise to the first cities of the Ganga system.

4

The Vedic Age

From about 2000 BC there appears to have been a general expansion of the early settlements. It is sometimes suggested that this expansion may have been in some way a result of the end of the Indus civilization and that large numbers of "Harappans" migrated to the south.

The Development of Indian Civilization from c. 1500 BC to c. AD 1200

The urban economy was crucial to the rise of civilization in the Indus Valley (c. 2600-2000 BC). Later, the first millennium BC saw an urban civilization in the Ganga Valley and still later in coastal South India. The emergence of towns was based on administrative needs, the requirements of trade, and pilgrimage centres.

The structure of Indian society was characterized by caste. The distinguishing features of a caste society were endogamous kinship groups *(jatis)* arranged in a hierarchy of ritual ranking, based on notions of pollution and purity, with an intermeshing of service relationships and an adherence to geographic location. There was some coincidence between caste and access to economic resources. Although ritual hierarchy was unchanging, there appears to have been mobility within the framework. Migrations of peoples both within the subcontinent and from outside encouraged social mobility and change. The nucleus of the social structure was the family, with the pattern of kinship relations varying from region to region. In the more complex urban structure, occupational guilds occasionally took on *jati* functions, and there was a continual emergence of new social and professional groups.

Religion in early Indian history did not constitute a monolithic force. Even when the loyalty attempted to encourage certain religions, the idea of a State religion was absent. In the main, there were three levels of religious expression. The most widespread was the worship of local cult deities vaguely associated with major deities, as seen in fertility cults, in the worship of mother goddesses, in the Shakta-Shakti cult, and in Tantrism. Less widespread but popular, particularly in the urban areas, were the more puritanical sects of Buddhism and Jainism and the *bhakti* tradition of Hinduism. A third level included classical Hinduism and more abstract levels of Buddhism and Jainism, with an emphasis on the major deities in the case of the first and on the teachings of the founders in the case of the latter two. It was this level, endorsed by affluent patronage, that provided the base for the initial institutionalization of religion.

By about 1500 BC an important change began to occur in the northern half of the Indian subcontinent. The Indus civilization had declined by about 2000 BC (or, perhaps as late as 1750 BC), and the stage was being set for a second and more lasting urbanization in the Ganga Valley.

Early Vedic Period

The earliest literary record of Indian culture were the Vedas. Composed in archaic, or Vedic, Sanskrit, generally dated between 1500 and 800 BC, and transmitted orally, the Vedas comprise four major texts—the Rigveda, Samaveda, Yajurveda, and Atharvaveda. Of these, the Rigveda is the earliest. The texts consist of hymns, charms, spells, and ritual observations current among the Indo-European-speaking people known as Aryans (from the Sanskrit arya, "noble").

The early Vedic period was a transition from nomadic pastoralism to settled village communities intermixing pastoral and agrarian economies. Cattle were initially the dominant commodity, as indicated by the use of the word *gotra* ("cowpen") to signify the endogamous kinship group and *gavisti* ("searching for cows") to denote war. A patriarchal extended family structure gave rise to the practice of *niyoga* ("levirate"), which permitted a widow to marry her husband's brother. A community of families constituted a *grama*. The term *vish* is generally interpreted to mean "clan". Clan assemblies appear to have been frequent in the early stages. Various categories of assemblies are mentioned, such as *vidatha, samiti,* and *sabha,* although the precise distinctions among these categories are not clear. The clan also gathered for the *yajna,* the Vedic sacrifice conducted by the priest, whose ritual actions ensured prosperity and imbued the chief with valour. The chief was primarily a war leader with responsibility for protecting the clan, for which function he received a *bali* ("tribute"). Punishment was exacted according to a principle whereby the social rank of a wronged or slain man determined the compensation due to him or his survivors.

Later Vedic Period (c. 800-c. 500 BC)

Samaveda, Yajurveda, and Atharvaveda (mainly ritual texts), the Brahmanas (manuals on ritual), and the Upanishads and Aranyakas (collections of philosophical and metaphysical discourses) are the principal literary sources from this period.

Associated with the corpus are the *sutra* texts, largely explanatory aids to the other works, comprising manuals on sacrifices and ceremonies, domestic observances, and social and legal relations. Because the texts were continually revised, they cannot be dated accurately to the early period. The Dharmasutra texts of this period became the nuclei of the sociolegal Dharmashastras of later centuries.

5

The Historical Period

The Beginning of the Historical Period (c. 500-150 BC)

For this phase of Indian history a variety of historical sources are available. Besides the Buddhist canon the Brahmanic sources and Jain sources, there are secular writings on political economy and accounts of foreign travellers. The most important sources, however, are inscriptions of the third century BC.

Magadhan Ascendancy

Political activity in the sixth-fifth century BC centred on the control of the Ganga Valley. The States of Kashi, Kosala, Magadha, and the Vrijjis battled for this control for a century until Magadha emerged victorious. Magadha's success was due, in part, to the political ambition of its king, Bimbisara. He conquered Anga, which gave him access to the Ganga Delta—a valuable asset in terms of the nascent maritime trade. Bimbisara's son Ajatashatru implemented his father's intentions within about 30 years.

Campaigns of Alexander the Great

The northwestern part of India witnessed the campaign of Alexander of Macedonia, who in 327 BC, in pursuing his campaign to the eastern extrêmities of the Achaemenian Empire, entered Gandhara. He campaigned successfully across the Punjab as far as the Beas River, where his troops refused to continue fighting. The vast army of the Nandas is referred to in Greek sources, and some historians have suggested that Alexander's Greek soldiers may have mutinied out of fear of this army. The campaign of Alexander made no impression on the Indian mind, for there are no references to it in Indian sources.

The Maurya Empire

The accession (dated to c. 325-c. 321 BC) of Chandragupta Maurya was significant because it inaugurated the first Indian empire. The Maurya dynasty was to rule almost the entire subcontinent (except the area south of present-day Karnataka), as well as substantial parts of present-day Afghanistan. Chandragupta Maurya, according to Jain sources, became a Jain towards the end of his reign. He abdicated in favour of his son Bindusara, became an ascetic, and travelled with a group of Jain monks to South India, where he died in the orthodox Jain manner by deliberate slow starvation. Bindusara, the second Maurya emperor, came to the throne about 297 BC. Bindusara was succeeded by his son Ashoka, either directly in 272 BC or, after an interregnum of four years, in 286 BC (some historians say c. 265 BC). Ashoka's reign is comparatively well documented. He issued a large number of edicts, which were inscribed in many parts of the empire and were composed in Prakrit, Greek, and Aramaic, depending on the language current in a particular region. Greek and Aramaic inscriptions are limited to Afghanistan and the trans-Indus region.

Ashoka ruled for 37 years. After his death a political decline set in, and half a century later the empire was reduced to the Ganga Valley alone. Tradition asserts that Ashoka's son Kunala ruled in Gandhara. Epigraphic evidence indicates that his grandson Dasharatha ruled in Magadha. Some historians have suggested that his empire was bifurcated. In 185 BC the last of the Mauryas, Brihadratha, was assassinated by his Brahmin commander-in-chief, Pushyamitra, who founded the Shunga dynasty.

The disintegration of the Maurya Empire was an aftermath of Ashoka's policies and actions and that his pro-Buddhist policy caused a revolt among the Brahmins. Ashoka's insistence on nonviolence resulted in the emasculation of the army, which was consequently unable to meet the threat of invaders from the northwest. A weakening of the economy acted as an economic pressure on the empire.

The Shunga Kingdom

Magadha was the nucleus of the Shunga kingdom, which succeeded the Maurya. The kingdom extended westwards to include Ujjain and Vidisha. The Shungas came into conflict with Vidarbha and with the Yavana, who probably were Bactrian Greeks attempting to move into the Ganga Valley.

Southern Indian Kingdoms

Significantly, historically arrested contact between the north and the Tamil regions can be reasonably dated to the Maurya period. Evidence on the early history of the south consists of the epigraphs of the region, the Tamil Sangam literature, and archaeological data.

Northern India in AD 300-750

The Guptas

Gupta period (c. 320-540) regarded as the classical age of India, the period during which the norms of Indian literature, art, architecture, and philosophy were established. It was also thought to have been an age of material prosperity, particularly among the urban elite, and of renascent Hinduism. The Gupta realm, although less extensive than that of the Mauryas, did encompass the northern half and central parts of the subcontinent. The Gupta period also has been called an imperial age, but the administrative centralization so characteristic of an imperial system is less apparent than during the Mauryan period.

The Guptas, a comparatively unknown family, came from either Magadha or eastern Uttar Pradesh. The third king, Chandra Gupta I, took the title of maharajadhiraja. Chandra Gupta appointed his son Samudra Gupta to succeed him about AD 330.

Samudra Gupta was succeeded in about 380 by his son Chandra Gupta II, though there is some evidence that there may have been an intermediate ruler. Chandra Gupta II's major campaign was against the Shaka rulers of Ujjain, the success of which was celebrated in a series of silver coins.

The first hint of a fresh invasion from the northwest came in the reign of Chandra Gupta's son and successor, Kumara Gupta (c. AD 415-455). The threat was from the Huns, a branch of the Hephthalites. Skanda Gupta (c. 455-467), who succeeded Kumara Gupta, and his successors all had to face the full-fledged invasion of the Huns. Skanda Gupta managed to rally Gupta strength for a while, but after his death the situation deteriorated. Dissensions within the royal family added to the problem. Gupta genealogies of this period show considerable variance in their succession lists. By the mid-sixth century, when the dynasty apparently came to an end, the kingdom had dwindled to a small size. Northern India and parts of central India were in the hands of the Huns.

In the early eighth century, a new power base was established briefly with the arrival of the Arabs in Sind. Inscriptions of the western Indian dynasties speak of controlling the tide of the *mleccha*, which has been interpreted in this case to mean the Arabs; some Indian sources use the term *yavana*. The conquest of Sind marked the easternmost extent of Arab territorial control. A local chronicle from Sind, the *Chach-nama*, gives an account of these events.

Northern India in AD 750-c. 1200

The Rajputs

In Rajasthan and central India there arose a number of small kingdoms ruled by dynasties that came to be called the Rajputs. The name was assumed by royal families that claimed Kshatriya status and linked their lineage either with the Suryavanshi or the Chandravanshi, the royal lineages of the *itihasa-purana* tradition, or else with the Agnikula (fire lineage) based on a lesser myth in which the eponymous ancestor rises out of the sacrificial fire. The four major Rajput dynasties—Pratihara, Paramara, Chauhan, and Chalukya—claimed Agnikula lineage.

The Cholas

The Cholas were by far the most important dynasty in the subcontinent at this time, although their activities mainly affected the peninsula and Southeast Asia. The nucleus of Chola power during the reign of Vijayalaya in the late ninth century was Thanjavur, from which the Cholas spread northwards, annexing in the tenth century what remained of Pallava territory. To the south they came up against the Pandyas. Chola history can be reconstructed, in considerable detail, because of the vast number of lengthy inscriptions issued not only by the royal family but also by temple authorities, village councils, and trade guilds. Parantaka I (907-953) laid the foundation of the kingdom. He took the northern boundary up to Nellore (Andhra Pradesh), where his advance was stopped by a defeat at the hands of the Rashtrakuta king Krishna III. Parantaka was more successful in the south, where he defeated both the Pandyas and the Gangas. He also launched an overlapping reigns that did not strengthen the Chola position. Then there followed two outstanding rulers who rapidly reinstated Chola power and ensured the kingdom its supremacy. These were Rajaraja I and Rajendra.

Section Two
The Dictionary
Entries from A to Z

A

Abhinavagupta, eleventh-century Indian philosopher, ascetic, and aesthetician. Abhinavagupta was a great writer on philosophy and aesthetics. Among his most well-known philosophic works are the *Ishvara-pratyabhijna-vimarshini* and the more detailed *Ishvara-pratyabhijna-vivrti-vimarshini*, both commentaries on *Ishvara-pratyabhijna* ("Recognition of God"), by Utpala, an earlier philosopher of the *pratyabhijna* school. He was an outstanding representative of the "recognition" (*pratyabhijna*) school of Kashmiri Shaivite monism, which conceived of the god Shiva, the individual soul, and the universe as essentially one; *pratyabhijna* refers to the way of realizing this identity.

Advaita, the most influential of the schools of Vedanta, a central philosophy of India, its historical beginning was with the seventh-century thinker Gaudapada, author of the *Mandukya-karika*, a commentary in verse form on the Mandukya Upanishad.

The philosopher Shankara (c. 700-750) built further on Gaudapada's foundation, principally in his commentary on the Vedanta Sutras, the *Shariraka-mimamsa-bhashya* ("Commentary on the Study of the Embodied Self"). Shankara argued that the Upanishads teach the nature of Brahman (the absolute). According to Shankara only the nondual Brahman is ultimately real. Shankara had many followers who continued and elaborated his work, notably the ninth-century philosopher Vachaspati Mishra. Advaita literature is extremely extensive, and it plays a major role in Hindu thought.

The basic premise of *advaita* is of nonduality. There is only one reality—it does not allow for an individual self or soul (*jiva*); only the ultimate self (*atman*) exists. The mind, awake or dreaming, moves through illusion (*maya*); and only *advaita* is the final truth.

Ajanta Caves, Buddhist rock-cut cave temples and monasteries celebrated for their wall paintings. They stand near Ajanta village, Aurangabad district, north-central Maharashtra State, western India. The temples are hollowed out of granite cliffs on the inner side of a 20 m ravine in the Wagurna River valley, 105 km northeast of Aurangabad. Although the sculpture, particularly the rich ornamentation of the *chaitya* pillars, is noteworthy, it is the murals that are the chief interest of Ajanta. These superb frescoes and sculptures depict scenes from the Buddha's life and illustrate the popular Jataka stories about the Buddha's previous lives. There are other images, as well, of various Buddhist deities.

These are remarkable and world-famous man-made cave temples and monasteries. The group of some 30 caves were accidentally discovered and were excavated between the first century BC and the seventh century AD. There are two types of caves, the *chaityas* ("sanctuaries") and *viharas* ("monasteries").

Ajatashatru, king of the Indian kingdom of Magadha, son of Bimbisara, Ajatashatru strengthened the defences of the Magadhan capital, Rajagriha, and built a small fort on the Ganga at Pataligrama, which was to become the famous capital Pataliputra (Patna). He then attacked and annexed the neighbouring States of Kashi (Banaras) and Koshala, but his attempt at subduing the confederacy of Vrijji State turned out to be a protracted affair lasting 16 years. Ultimately the Vrijjis, including the important Lichhavi clan, were overthrown, having been weakened by a minister of Ajatashatru, who was able to sow dissension in the confederacy.

Ajivika, ascetic sect that emerged in India about the same time as Buddhism and Jainism, it was founded by Goshala Maskariputra (also called Gosala Makkaliputta), a contemporary of Mahavira.

After a period of acceptance during the Maurya dynasty (third century BC), the sect apparently dwindled, although followers lived on until the fourteenth century in what is present-day Karnataka. In latter-day developments of the sect, the founder Goshala came to be worshipped as a divinity, and the tenet of *niyati* developed into the doctrine that all change was illusory and everything was eternally immobile.

The Ajivikas believed that the universe was governed by a cosmic force called *niyati* (which in Sanskrit means "rule" or "destiny"), which determined all events—and consequently, man's fate—to the last detail; therefore, any efforts to change or accelerate improvement would prove futile. Accordingly, the Ajivikas practised austerities not for any purposeful goal but because their *niyati* had determined them to do so.

Alexander the Great (b. 356 BC, Pella, Macedonia; d. June 13, 323 BC, Babylon), also known as Alexander III or Alexander of Macedonia, king of Macedonia (336-323 BC), he overthrew the Persian Empire, carried Macedonian arms to India, and laid the foundations for the Hellenistic world of territorial kingdoms.

In 327 BC Alexander left Bactria with a reinforced army consisting of 35,000 men under a reorganized command. After crossing the Hindu Kush, probably by Bamian and the Ghorband Valley, Alexander divided his forces into two. Half the army, led by Hephaestion and Perdiccas—both cavalry commanders—was sent through the Khyber Pass, while he himself led the rest through the hills to the north. In his advance through Swat and Gandhara he stormed the almost invincible pinnacle of Aornos (modern day Pir-Sar, Pakistan), a few kilometres west of the Indus and north of the Buner River. It was an impressive feat of siegecraft. In the spring of 326 BC, he entered Taxila after crossing the Indus near Attock. Taxiles, the ruler of Taxila, furnished elephants and troops in return for support against his rival Porus, who ruled the lands between the Hydaspes (Jhelum) and the Acesines (Chenab) rivers. In June, Alexander fought his last great battle on the left bank of the Hydaspes. He founded two cities there, Alexandria Nicaea and Bucephala, and Porus became his ally.

Alexander was anxious to press on farther than Hyphasis (modern Beas) when his army mutinied, refusing to go farther in the tropical rain. They were weary in body and spirit, and Coenus, one of Alexander's four chief marshals, acted as their spokesman. On finding the army adamant, Alexander agreed to turn back.

He erected 12 altars to the 12 Olympian gods on the Hyphasis, and on the Hydaspes he built a fleet of 800 to 1,000 ships. Leaving Porus, he then proceeded down the river and into the Indus, with half his forces on shipboard and half marching in three columns down the two banks. The fleet was commanded by Nearchus while Alexander's own captain was Onesicritus. Both later wrote accounts of the campaign. The march was attended with much fighting and heavy, pitiless slaughter; at the storming of one town of the Mali near the Hydraotes (Ravi) River, Alexander received a severe wound that left him weakened. On reaching Patala, located at the head of the Indus delta, he built a harbour and docks and explored both arms of the Indus, which probably then ran into the Rann of Kutch (Kachchh). He planned to lead part of his forces back by land, while the rest in 100 to 150 ships, under the command of Nearchus made a voyage of exploration along the Persian Gulf. Local opposition led Nearchus to set sail in September (325 BC), and he was held up for three weeks until he could pick up the northeast monsoon in late October. In September Alexander too set out along the coast through Gedrosia (modern Baluchistan).

He was forced to turn inland because of the mountainous country and, in the process, failed to establish food depots for the fleet. Craterus, a high-ranking officer, had already been sent off with the baggage, the elephants, and the sick and wounded, together with three battalions of the army. The route Craterus took was through the Mulla Pass, Quetta, and Kandahar (Qandahar) into the Helmand Valley. From there he was to march through Drangiana to rejoin the main army on the Amanis (modern Minab) River in Carmania. Alexander's march through Gedrosia proved disastrous. The waterless desert and shortage of food and fuel caused great suffering, and many, especially women and children, perished in a sudden monsoon flood while encamped in a valley. Finally, he was rejoined by Nearchus and his fleet at the river Amanis (modern Minab). The fleet led by Nearchus had also suffered greatly.

From age 13 to 16 he was taught by Aristotle, who inspired him with an interest in philosophy, medicine, and scientific investigation; but he was later to advance beyond his teacher's narrow precept that non-Greeks should be treated as slaves. In 336 BC, on the assassination of his father and reigning monarch Philip II, Alexander was acclaimed by the army and succeeded without opposition. He at once executed the princes of Lyncestis, alleged to be behind Philip's murder, along with all possible rivals and the whole of the faction opposed to him. He then marched south, recovered a wavering Thessaly, and at an assembly of the Greek League at Corinth was appointed generalissimo for the forthcoming invasion of Asia, already planned and initiated by Philip.

Amaravati Sculpture, style of Indian scultpture that flourished in southeastern India from about the second century BC to the end of the third century AD, during the rule of the Satavahana dynasty, it is known for its superb reliefs, which are among the world's finest examples of narrative scultpure.

A depiction of the monument in London on a railing slab gives an indication of the appearance of the *stupa* at the end of the second century AD. The slab shows a low drum with a hemispherical dome, the railings and drum covered with carvings, and the whole surrounded by an elaborate and richly carved railing. The four cardinal points are marked by groups of five pillars, while free-standing columns topped by lions are set up at the four entrances, replacing the *torana* (ceremonial gateway) of earlier *stupas*.

The reliefs, carved on the greenish white limestone characteristic of the region, mostly depict events of the Buddha's life and his previous births (*Jataka* stories). The four centuries over which the style developed were also a period of change from aniconic to iconic representations of the Buddha. At Amaravati both methods of depiction appear together on one slab—the iconic being represented by images of the seated and standing Buddha, and the aniconic by an empty throne symbolizing his presence.

The Amaravati *stupas* was begun about 200 BC and underwent several renovations and additions. One of the largest *stupas* built in Buddhist India, it was about 50 m in diameter and about 30 m high, but it has been largely destroyed, much of the stone having been used by local contractors during the nineteenth century to make lime mortar. Many of the surviving narrative reliefs and decorative plaques are in the Government Museum in Chennai, and the British Museum in London.

In addition to the ruins of the great *stupa*, or relic mound, at Amaravati, the style is also seen in the *stupa* remains at Jaggayyapeta, Nagarjunakonda, and Goli, in Andhra Pradesh State, and as far west as Ter, Maharashtra State. The style also spread to Ceylon (now Sri Lanka), as seen at Anuradhapura, and to much of Southeast Asia.

Ananda, a first cousin of the Buddha, and one of his principal followers, known as his "beloved disciple" and devoted companion he flourished sixth century BC.

Buddha's intimate disciples, Ananda alone had not attained Enlightenment when the Buddha died. He attained it, however, just beofre the first council (c. 544 or 480 BC), at which he repeated the "Basket of Discourse" (*Sutta Pitaka*). He is said to have created a collection of verses in the *Theragatha*. He is believed to have lived to the age of 120 years.

Ananda entered the order of monks in the second year of the Buddha's ministry and in the twenty-fifth year was appointed his personal attendant. According to the *Vinaya Pitaka* texts, he persuaded the Buddha, much against the Buddha's own inclination, to allow women to become nuns.

Ancestor Worship, religious beliefs and practices concerned with the spirits of dead persons regarded as relatives, some of whom may be mythical. Although far from universal, ancestor worship existed in societies at every level of cultural development. Ancestors venerated by elaborate rites are those persons who in their lifetimes held positions of importance, such as heads of families, lineages, clans, tribes, kingdoms, and other social groups.

Characteristically, in Hinduism, funeral rites are very elaborate and have many motifs of supernaturalism, among which is attention to ancestral spirits. The practices relating to ancestors reflect ideas concerning reincarnation and the system of castes, which are in turn closely intertwined. One of the purposes of the funeral rites is to guide the spirits of the deceased during the perilous time between death and rebirth. The idea that a person's moral behaviour in life determines his fate in the next life is also connected with caste affiliation. Sinful behaviour will bring rebirth in a low caste. Among some castes and in some regions of India, annual rites are performed in honour of the spirits of the ancestors of the male heads of household, who are believed to give spiritual aid in promoting the growth of crops and in other important matters of everyday life.

The core of ancestor worship is the belief in the continuing existence of the dead and in a close relation between the living and the dead, who continue to influence the affairs of the living.

All societies give ritual attention to death or to the souls of the dead, but not all of these practices may appropriately be called ancestor worship. If death itself, rather than the ancestral relationship, is the focus of attention, the name "death cults" is more appropriate.

Apabhramsha Language, literary language of the third and final phase of the Middle Indo-Aryan languages, Apabhramsha shows developments that must have taken place in the dialects spoken in northern India. The Middle Indo-Aryan languages showed several phonological and morphological departures from Sanskrit. The conservative grammarian branded all cases of such departures as *apabhramsha,* which means "departure from correct speech", or "deviance". In early times, this usage was considered corrupt.

Even now Apabhramsha is known only as a language of poetry, there being no prose or plays in the language. Most of the extant literature is based on Jain mythology and legends. Some of the classics in this language are *Paumachariu*, a Jain version of the Ramayana, written by Svambhudeva in the eighth century; *Mahapurana* (based on the lives of 63 Jain legendary figures) and *Nayakumarachariu* by Pushpadanta from the tenth century; *Bhavisattakaha* by Dhanpala, tenth century, and *Pasanahachariu* by Padmakirti, belonging to the eleventh century.

Doha verses, each complete in itself and embodying an independent concept, are a popular literary form in Apabhramsha. Some noteworthy collections of *dohas* are: *Paramappayasu* and *Yogasara* written by Yogideva seventh century, *Savaya-dhammadoha* by Devasena in the tenth century, and *Dohakosha* by Kanha in the eighth century.

Shauraseni Prakrit is considered to be the early phase of Apabhramsha. When Prakrit was formalized by literary use, its dialectal variations came to be called Apabhramsha. In his *Natyashastra*, a treatise on dramaturgy, the sage Bharata of the third century AD mentions two types of vernacular languages, the Prakrits (Bhashas) and their corruptions (Vibhashas). The seventh-century poet Dandin refers to poetic languages like Abhira as "Apabhramsha". It could thus be concluded that in the third century there were certain dialects called Apabhramsha, and these gradually rose to a literary level. Bhamaha, in the sixth century, classifies poetry as Sanskrit, Prakrit, and Apabhramsha. By the sixth century, Apabhramsha was recognized as a literary language, and it continued in a stereotyped form, coexisting even with New Indo-Aryan languages.

Aranyakas, later development of the Brahmanas, or expositions of the Vedas, these were composed in India in about 700 BC. They contain information on secret rites to be carried out only by certain persons, and more philosophic speculation. The Aranyakas are given over to secret explanations of the allegorical meaning of the ritual and to discussion of the internal, meditative meaning of the sacrifice, as contrasted to its actual, outward performance. The philosophic portions, more speculative in content, are sometimes called Upanishads. Thus they were intended to be studied only by the initiated, by which might have been meant either hermits who had withdrawn into the forest and no longer took part in ritual sacrifices, or pupils who were given instruction by their teachers in the seclusion of the forest, away from the village.

Ardhanarishvara, composite male-female figure of the Hindu god Shiva, together with his consort Parvati.

The symbolic intent of the figure according to most authorities is to signify that the male and female principles are inseparable. A popular explanation, as given in a collection of myths known as the Shiva-Purana, is that Brahma created male beings and instructed them in turn to create others, but they were unable to do so. When Shiva appeared before him in an androgynous form, Brahma realized his omission and created females. Yet another narrative has it that the sage (*rishi*) Bhringi had vowed to worship only one deity and so failed to circumambulate and prostrate himself before Parvati. She tried to force him to do so by asking to be united with her lord and then taking the form of half male and half female.

As seen in many beautiful Indian and Southeast Asian sculptures, the right (male) half of the figure is adorned with the traditional ornaments of Shiva. Half of the hair is piled in a hairdress of matted locks, half of a third eye is visible on the forehead, a tiger skin covers the loins, and serpents are used as ornaments. The left (female) half shows hair well combed and knotted, half of a *tilaka* (mark) (vermillion round or elongated dot) on the forehead, the eye outlined in black, one well-developed breast, a silk garment caught with girdles, an anklet, and the foot tinted red with dye.

Arhat, in Buddhism, a prefected person, one who has gained insight into the true nature of existence and has achieved Nirvana (spiritual Enlightenment), the *arhat,* having freed himself from the bonds of desire, will not be reborn again. The state of an *arhat* is considered in the Theravada tradition to be the proper goal of a Buddhist. Except under extraordinary circumstances, a man or woman can become an *arhat* only while living in a monastery. Mahayana Buddhists criticize the *arhat* ideal on the grounds that the *bodhisattva* is a higher goal of perfection, for the *bodhisattva* vows to remain within the cycle of rebirths, even though capable of Enlightenment, in order to work for the good of others. This divergence of opinion continues to be one of the basic differences between the Theravada and Mahayana traditions.

Arishtanemi, also called Neminatha, twenty-second of the twenty-four Tirthankaras, of Jainism, Arishtanemi is said to have lived 84,000 years before the coming of the next Tirthankara, Parshvanatha; he is also said to have been a contemporary of the Hindu god Krishna, who was his cousin. In paintings he is always shown black in colour (in paintings of the Digambara sect, he is blue) and his symbol is the conch.

On his marriage day, Arishtanemi heard the cries of the animals that were to be slaughtered for the marriage feast and immediately renounced the world. He attained *moksha* (release from earthly existence) on the Girnar Hills in Kathiawar (western India), which has become a place of pilgrimage for the Jains.

Artha Shastra, singularly important Indian manual on the art of politics, it is attributed to Kautilya (also known as Vishnugupta or Chanakya), the chief minister to King Chandragupta (c. 300 BC), the founder of the Maurya dynasty. Although it is unlikely that all of the text dates to such an early period, several parts have been traced back to the Mauryas.

The *Artha Shastra* is a primary source of the theory and practice of political economy in ancient India. It is entirely practical in purpose.

It presents no overt philosophy but in fact displays complete scepticism concerning human nature and its corruptibility; the ways in which the king—and his trusted servant—can take advantage of such human weakness.

The author of the *Artha Shastra* wrote, keeping in mind the central control by the king of a kingdom of fairly limited size. He speaks of the way the State's economy is organized, how ministers should be chosen and war conducted, and how taxation should be arranged and distributed. Great emphasis is placed on the importance of a network of runners, informers, and spies, which, in the absence of a ministry of public information and a police force, functioned as surveillance corps for the king, focussing particularly on any external threats and internal dissidence.

Unstated but apparent is the paradox that a king has to have complete confidence in the minister who is ruling his State.

Aryabhata I (b. 476; d. 550), Indian astronomer and mathematician of the fifth century AD, he lived and worked in Kusumapura near present-day Patna (Bihar). According to some scholars he was the *Kulapa* (vice-chancellor) of the famous Nalanda University. His greatest work is *Aryabhatiya*, which he wrote in 499 when he was 23 years old. *Aryabhatiya* is a scholarly treatise in Sanskrit on mathematics and astronomy. Using the Sanskrit alphabet, he invented on ingenious system to express numbers on the decimal-place value model. This allowed him to give astronomical constants and numerical data in a highly condensed form so that they could be easily memorized.

Aryabhata was the first Indian astronomer to state that the Earth is spherical and rotates on its axis. He explained that the apparent daily east-west motion of the Sun, Moon, planets, and stars are due to the rotation of the Earth from west to east. He introduced two systems for reckoning time: (1) the *audayika* system, from sunrise to next sunrise, and (2) the *ardharaatrika* system, that is, midnight to midnight (sidereal time). He gives the time for one sidereal rotation of the Earth as 23h 56m 4.1s (modern value: 23h 56m 4.091s).

The mathematical part of *Aryabhatiya* deals with important topics like geometrical figures and their properties, arithmetic progression, and geometrical progression, as well as simple, simultaneous, and quadratic equations. It also gives rulers and methods for construction of trigonometric sine tables in which sine and cosine are known as *jya* and *koti-jya*. Aryabhata gave an accurate approximation for pi (3.1416), and introduced into trigonometry the versed sine function (that is, 1 minus the cosine of an angle).

He formulated the rules for extraction of square and cube roots by the arithmetical method which are the rules used even today all over the world. Aryabhata was responsible for the Indian mathematical renaissance. The pattern and tone set by him in mathematical investigations were emulated by generations of mathematicians to follow.

Aryan, a people, who in prehistoric times, settled in Iran and northern India, are presumed to be tribal people speaking Aryan (Indo-European) languages. It is assumed that these people originated in central Asia and settled in Iran and India. The Vedas and the Ramayana and the Mahabharata are the major sources used by historians to map the spread of the Aryan civilization in India. There is reference to the Indo-Gangetic plains as Aryavarta, or the country of the Aryans, and to their first king as Bharata, after whom the name Bharat is derived for India.

During the nineteenth century there arose a notion—propagated most assiduously by the Comte de Gobineau and later by his disciples—of an "Aryan race", those who spoke Indo-European languages, who were considered to be responsible for all the progress that mankind had made and who were also morally superior to "Semites", "yellows", and "blacks". The Nordic, or Germanic peoples came to be regarded as the purest "Aryans". This notion, which had been repudiated by anthropologists by the second quarter of the twentieth century, was seized upon by Adolf Hitler and the Nazis and made the basis of the German government policy of exterminating Jews, Gypsies, and other "non-Aryans".

In the nineteenth century, the term was used as a synonym for "Indo-European" and also, more restrictively, to refer to the Indo-Iranian languages. It is now used in linguistics only in the sense of the term Indo-Aryan languages.

Ashoka (d. 238? BC, India), last major emperor in the Maurya dynasty of India, whose vigorous patronage of Buddhism during his reign (c. 262-238 BC) furthered the expansion of that religion throughout India. Following his successful but bloody conquest of Kalinga on the East coast, Ashoka renounced armed conquest and adopted a policy that he called "conquest by *dharma* (principles of right life)".

A sample quotation that illustrates the spirit that guided Ashoka is: "All men are my children. As for my own children I desire that they may be provided with all the welfare and happiness of this world and of the next, so do I desire for all men as well."

According to his own accounts, Ashoka conquered Kalinga (the modern State of Orissa) in the eighth year of his reign. The sufferings that the war inflicted on the defeated people moved him to such remorse that he renounced armed conquests. It was at this time that he came in touch with Buddhism and adopted it. He resolved to live according to, and preach, the *dharma* and to serve his subjects and all humanity.

Ashoka understood the *dharma* as being the energetic practice of the sociomoral virtues of honesty, truthfulness, compassion, mercifulness, benevolence, nonviolence, considerate behaviour toward all, "little sin and many good deeds", nonextravagance, nonacquisitiveness, and noninjury to animals. He did not speak of any particular mode of religious creed or worship, or of any philosophical doctrines. He never thrust Buddhism on anyone.

He adopted a policy of respect towards all religious sects and guaranteed them full freedom to live according to their own principles, but he also urged them to exert themselves for the "increase of their inner worthiness". He encouraged respect for the creeds of others, praise for the good points of others, and refraining from vehement adverse criticism of the viewpoints of others.

To practise the *dharma* actively, Ashoka went out on periodic tours preaching the *dharma* to the rural people and relieving their sufferings. He ordered his high officials to do the same, in addition to attending to their normal duties. He asked administrative officers to be constantly aware of the joys and sorrows of the common folk and to be prompt and impartial in dispensing justice. A special class of high officers, called "*dharma* ministers", was appointed to help relieve sufferings wherever found and look to the special needs of women, of people inhabiting outlying regions, of neighbouring peoples, and of various religious communities. It was ordered that matters concerning public welfare were to be reported to him at all times. The only glory he sought, he said, was for having led his people along the path of *dharma*.

Among his works of public utility were hospitals founded for men and animals and to supply medicines. Trees and groves were planted on roadsides, wells were dug, watering sheds and resthouses constructed. Orders were also issued to prevent cruelty to animals. With the death of Ashoka the Maurya Empire disintegrated and his work was discontinued. His memory survives for what he attempted to achieve and for the high ideals he held before himself.

Ashoka popularized his teachings by means of oral

announcements and also had them engraved on rocks and pillars at suitable public sites. These inscriptions—the rock edicts and pillar edicts (for example, the lion capital of the pillar found at Sarnath, which has become India's national emblem)—mostly dated in various years of his reign, contain statements regarding his thoughts and actions and provide information on his life and acts. He built a number of *stupas* (commemorative burial mounds) and monasteries and erected pillars on which he got inscribed his understanding of religious doctrines. He took strong measures to suppress chasms within the order (the Buddhist religious community) and prescribed a course of scriptural studies for adherents. Tradition recorded in the Ceylonese chronicle *Mahavamsa* says that, when the church decided to send preaching missions abroad, Ashoka helped them enthusiastically. He sent his own son and daughter as missionaries to Ceylon (now Sri Lanka). It is as a result of Ashoka's patronage that Buddhism spread throughout India and subsequently beyond the frontiers of the country.

Ashram, "ascetic's dwelling", or "place or mode of life associated with religious exertion"), in Hinduism represents any of the four stages of life through which the "twice-born" Hindu ideally will pass. The stages are those of: (1) the student (*brahmachari*), who is devoted and obedient to the teacher; (2) the householder (*grhastha*), who works to sustain the family and to help support priests, while also fulfilling duties towards gods and ancestors; (3) the hermit (*vanaprastha*), who withdraws from concern with material things and pursues ascetic and yogic practices; and (4) the homeless mendicant (*sannyasi*), who renounces all possessions to wander and beg for food, concerned only with the eternal. In the classical system, the vigorous pursuit of *moksha* (liberation of the self from attachment to the world) is reserved for persons in the last two stages of life. In practice, however, many *sannyasis* have never married, which shows that even as an ideal the four-ashram system has been questioned.

In a second meaning, the term *ashrama*, familiarly spelt *ashram* in English, denotes a place of refuge, especially one removed from urban life, where spiritual and/or yogic disciplines are pursued. Often these ashrams are associated with the presence of a central teaching figure, a guru, who is the object of common adoration on the part of other ashram residents. The guru may or may not belong to a formally constituted order or spiritual community.

Ashtadhyayi, Sanskrit treatise on grammar, which became basic to Sanskrit education of the time was written by the eminent grammarian Panini, in fifth or sixth-century BC. The text summed up the science of phonetics and grammar evolved in the Vedic religion.

Ashvaghosha (b. AD 80?, Ayodhya, India; d. 150?, Peshawar), philosopher considered the father of Sanskrit drama and also the greatest poet of India before Kalidasa (fifth century), he popularized the style of Sanskrit poetry known as *kavya*.

A brilliant orator, Ashvaghosha spoke at length on Mahayana (Greater Vehicle) Buddhist doctrine at the fourth Buddhist council, which he helped organize. His fame lay largely in his ability to explain the intricate concepts of Mahayana Buddhism. Among the works attributed to him are the *Mahayana-shraddhotpada-shastra* ("The Awakening of Faith in the Mahayana"), the *Buddhacharita* ("The Life of Buddha") in verse, and the *Mahalankara* ("Book of Glory").

While in Varanasi (formerly Banares), where Gautama Buddha had preached his first sermon, Ashvaghosha saw the city conquered by the Kushan emperor Kanishka, a devout Buddhist. A huge war indemnity was demanded, and the ruler of Varanasi handed over instead, a symbolic tribute, a begging bowl said to have been used by both the Buddha and Ashvaghosha. Apparently the philosopher rose to the position of spiritual counsellor in Kanishka's court at Peshawar.

Ashvaghosha was born a Brahmin. Legend obscures the man, but it is known that he was an outspoken opponent of Buddhism until, after a heated debate with a noted Buddhist scholar on the relative merits of the Vedantic (Hindu) religion and the middle path (Buddhism), he accepted the value of Buddhism and became a disciple of his earlier opponent.

Ashvalayana (400 BC), author of the Ashvalayana-shrauta-sutra, a Vedic manual of sacrificial ceremonies composed for the use of the class of priests called *hotar*, or *hotr*, whose main function was to invoke the gods. Ashvalayana is mentioned as a teacher as well as a sage in Vedic litanies and in the one text is invoked along with Indra and the "sons of Brahma". Belonging to the "forest tradition" of hermits and wandering holy men rather than to the priesthood, he is described as a student of Shaunaka, who composed many texts.

Ashvamedha, Ashwamedha, "horse sacrifice", the grandest of the Vedic religious rites of ancient India, was performed by a king to assert his authority and supremacy.

In historical times the practice was condemned by the Buddha and seems to have suffered a decline, but it was revived by

Pushyamitra Shunga (reigned 187-151 BC). He is said to have defeated, while protecting his horse, Greek warriors who had reached the Punjab. Samudra Gupta (c. AD 330-c. 380) issued coins in the commemoration of his successful completion of an *ashvamedha*, and the rite is mentioned in connection with other Gupta and Chalukya monarchs. It may have continued into as late as the eleventh century, when it is said to have taken place in the Chola Empire.

The ceremony is described in detail in various Vedic writings, particularly the Shatapatha Brahmana. An especially fine stallion was selected and was allowed to roam freely for a year under the protection of a royal guard. If the horse entered a foreign country, its ruler had either to fight or to submit. If the horse was not captured during the year, it was victoriously brought back to the capital, accompanied by the rulers of the lands it entered, and then sacrificed at a great public ceremony, which was accompanied by much feasting and celebration. The wandering horse was said to symbolize the sun in its journey over the world and, consequently, the power of the king over the whole earth. On successfully carrying out a horse sacrifice, the king could assume the title of *chakravartin* (universal monarch). The rite served not only to glorify the king but also to ensure the prosperity and fertility of the entire kingdom.

Atman, one of the most basic concepts in Hindu philosophy, describing that eternal core of the personality that survives after death and that transmigrates to a new life or is released from the bonds of existence *atman* is that which makes the other organs and faculties function and for which indeed they function; *atman* underlies all the activities of a person, as Brahman (the absolute) underlies the workings of the universe. So fundamental was *atman* deemed to be that certain circles identified it with Brahman. Of the various systems (*darshans*) of Hindu philosophy, the schools of Samkhya and Yoga (which use the term *purusha* to convey the idea of *atman*) and the orthodox school of Vedanta particularly concern themselves with *atman,* though the interpretation varies in accordance with each system's general worldviews.

While in the early Vedic texts it occurred mostly as a reflexive pronoun (oneself), in the later Upanishads it is more of a philosophic topic.

Audambaras, one of the tribal republics it occupied the watershed between the Indus and Ganga river valleys, and between present-day Punjab and Rajasthan States. The politically most important tribal republics were the Audambaras, Arjunayanas,

Malavas, Yaudheyas, Shibis, Kunindas, Trigartas, and Abhiras.

Avalokiteshvara, Chinese Guanyin, Japanese Kannon, the *bodhisattva* ("Buddha-to-be") of infinite compassion and mercy, possibly the most popular of all Buddhist deities, beloved throughout the Buddhist world, he exemplifies the *bodhisattva*'s resolve to postpone his own Buddhahood until he has helped every being on earth achieve emancipation.

The virtues and miracles of Avalokiteshvara are accounted in many Buddhist *sutras* (scriptures). Avalokiteshvara is the only Mahayana Buddhist deity commonly worshipped in Theravada Buddhist countries that base their worship on the Pali canon and do not normally recognize the concept of *bodhisattvas*. In Sri Lanka he is known as Natha-deva (often mistakenly confused with Maitreya, the Buddha yet to come).

Avalokiteshvara is the earthly manifestation of the self-born, eternal Buddha, Amitabha, whose figure is represented in his headdress. He guards the world in the interval between the departure of the historical Buddha, Gautama, and the appearance of the future Buddha, Maitreya. Avalokiteshvara protects against shipwreck, fire, assassins, robbers, and wild beasts. He is the creator of the fourth world, which is the actual universe in which we live.

His name has been variously interpreted as "the lord who looks in every direction" and "the lord of what we see" (that is, the actual, created world). In Tibet he is known as Spyan-ras gzigs (With a Pitying Look) and in Mongolia as Nidu-ber ujegci (He Who Looks with the Eyes). The title invariably used for him in Indochina and Thailand in Lokeshvara (Lord of the World).

According to legend, his head once split with grief at realizing the number of wicked beings in the world yet to be saved. Amitabha Buddha caused each of the pieces to become a whole head and placed them in three tiers of three, then the tenth, and topped them all with his own image. Sometimes, the 11-headed Avalokiteshvara is represented with thousands of arms, which rise like the outspread tail of a peacock around him. In painting he is usually shown white in colour (in Nepal, red). His consort is the goddess Tara. His traditional residence is the Tibetan mountain Potala, and his images are frequently placed on hilltops.

B

Bahubali, also called Gommateshvara, according to Jain legends, is the son of Rishabhanatha, the first Tirthankara (or saving teacher).

Several sculptures depict Bahubali, including an outstanding ninth-century bronze in the Prince of Wales Museum in Mumbai. A colossal tenth-century sculpture stands on top of a hill at Shravana Belgola, a centre of the Digambara sect in Karnataka. Carved out of a single rock, the figure is 17.5 m tall, one of the largest freestanding images in the world. Every 12 years, the entire statue is ceremonially bathed in curd, milk, and ghee.

Bahubali is said to have stood immobile, his feet facing forward and arms at his side, for an entire year, meditating. He was so unmindful of the world around him that vines and creepers grew up his body and anthills rose around his feet.

Bana, also called Banabhatta, one of the greatest masters of Sanskrit prose who flourished first half of seventh century, he was principally famous for his chronicle, *Harshacharita* ("Deeds of Harsha"), depicting the court and times of the Buddhist emperor Harsha (reigned c. 606-647) of northern India.

Bana's biography of Harsha provides valuable information about the period, though with some obvious exaggeration in the emperor's favour. Written in the ornate *kavya* style, involving extremely lengthy constructions, elaborate descriptions, and poetic devices, the work has great vitality and a wealth of keenly observed detail. His second great work, the prose romance *Kadambari,* describes the affairs of two pairs of lovers through a series of incarnations. Both works were left unfinished. The second was completed by the author's son, Bhushanabhatta.

Bana gives some autobiographical account of himself in the early chapters of the Harshacharita. He was born into an illustrious family of Brahmins; his mother died when he was a small child, and his father raised him with loving care. His father died, however, when Bana was 14, and for some years he travelled adventurously, visiting various courts and universities with a colourful group of friends (including his two half brothers by a lower-caste woman, a snake doctor, a goldsmith, a gambler, and a musician). At last he returned home and married. Then one day he was called to the court of Harsha. Though the Emperor gave him a cool reception at first, possibly due to some gossip about his wayward youth, in time he won the Emperor's high regard.

Basava, Basavanna, twelfth-century Hindu religious reformer, teacher, theologian, and administrator of the royal treasury of the Chalukya king Bijjala I (reigned 1156-67), Basava is the subject of the Basava Purana, one of the sacred texts of the Hindu Virashaiva (Lingayat) sect.

Basava helped to spread the Virashaiva sect by teaching and by dispersing funds to Virashaiva guilds. His uncle, the prime minister, arranged his appointment as chief of the treasury, and for several years he and his faction enjoyed a great deal of popularity. But other factions at court were apparently resentful of his power and the flourishing of Virashaiva mendicants under his patronage. As a result of their accusations, he fled the kingdom, dying soon thereafter. His poetry to Shiva as "Lord of the meeting rivers" has earned him a place at the front rank of Kannada literature and the literature of Hindu devotion (*bhakti*) generally.

According to tradition, he was the actual founder of the Virashaivas, but study of Chalukya inscriptions indicates that he in fact revived an existing sect.

Bhadrabahu (d. 298 BC, India), Jain leader and philosopher who, after a 12-year famine, is said to have led an exodus, in 310 BC, from the Jain stronghold in northern India to Shravana Belgola in the State of Karnataka, Bhadrabahu, was a monk who became the spiritual head of the Jains. He is believed to have been the author of three of the Jain sacred books as well as of *Niryuktis,* short commentaries on 10 of the 12 original sacred books. Some authorities say that, after the famine, Bhadrabahu retired to seclusion to Nepal; others say he remained in Mysore. He is reputed to have died by realizing the Jain ideal of starving to death.

Bhagavadgita, one of the most important and profound Hindu scriptures, it forms part of Book VI of the Mahabharata and is written in the form of a dialogue between the warrior prince Arjuna, and his friend and charioteer, Krishna, who is also an earthly form of the god Vishnu.

The dialogue takes place on the battlefield of Kurukshetra, just as the great war between the Pandavas and the Kauravas is about to begin. The two armies stand opposing each other, and, on seeing many of his friends and kinsmen among those lined up on the other side, Arjuna hesitates. He considers whether it would not be better to throw down his arms and allow himself to be slain by the enemy rather than to engage in a just, but cruel, war. He is recalled to his sense of duty as a warrior by Krishna, who points out to him that the higher way is the dispassionate discharge of his duty (*dharma*), performed with faith in God and without selfish concern for personal triumph or gain.

The Bhagavadgita is composed separately from major parts of the Mahabharata and was probably written in the first or second century AD. The poem consists of 700 Sanskrit verses divided into 18 chapters.

The importance of the Bhagavadgita is evident from the many commentaries, glossaries, and expository books written on it in both ancient and modern times. The earliest commentary that has come down is that of the great philosopher Shankara. Other important commentaries of ancient times are those of Bhaskara, Ramanuja, Madhva, Nilakantha, Shridhara, and Madhusudana; and outstanding modern commentaries are those of B.G. Tilak, Sri Aurobindo, Mahatma Gandhi, and Sarvepalli Radhakrishnan. The Bhagavadgita has been translated into many languages.

The Bhagavadgita goes far beyond the ethical question with which it begins, to consider broadly the nature of God and the means by which man can know Him. The greatness of the scripture lies in its description of both the end and the means. It gives a synopsis of the religious thought and experience of India through the ages. The three paths of the Hindu religious tradition leading to union with God are all described as different aspects of a single way of approach.

Bhagavata-Purana, the most celebrated text of a variety of Hindu sacred literature in Sanskrit known as the Puranas, this specific text is regarded as supreme by the Bhagavata sect. The Purana is made up of some 18,000 stanzas divided into 12 books; but it is book 10, which deals with Krishna's childhood and his years spent among the cowherds of Vrindavan, that accounts for its immense popularity with Vaishnavas throughout India. The Bhagavata-Purana was probably composed about the tenth century, somewhere in South India; its expression of *bhakti* ("religious devotion") is akin in its emotional fervour to that of the South Indian devotional poets, the Alvars. The attempts on Krishna's life made by his wicked uncle Kamsa, the childhood pranks he played on his foster mother Yashoda, his love for the *gopis* (the wives and daughters of the cowherds), and their devotion and spiritual surrender to him are treated with endearing charm and grace.

The Bhagavata-Purana, in translation and in inspiration, has resulted in an enormous body of related vernacular literature. Its scenes have been carved in stone on temple walls and have been illustrated in beautiful miniatures by Rajasthani and Pahari painters of the seventeenth and eighteenth centuries.

Bharavi, sixth-century Indian writer, Bharavi probably hailed from the south during the reign of the Pallava dynasty. He took up a Mahabharata theme in his poem *Kiratarjuniya* ("Arjuna and the Mountain Man"), recounting to Pandava prince Arjuna's encounter and ensuing combat with a wild mountaineer who in the end proves to be the god Shiva. Bharavi's language and style are more difficult than Kalidasa's but the poem is highly respected in Indian literary tradition.

Bharhut Sculpture, early Indian sculpture of the Shunga period (mid-second century BC) it decorated the great *stupa*, or relic mound, of Bharhut, in Madhya Pradesh State. The *stupa* is now largely destroyed and most of the existing remains—railings and entrance gateways—are now in the Indian Museum in Calcutta.

The stone railing is decorated with medallions and lotus ornaments, some of them centred by the head of a man or woman. *Jataka* stories (legends of the Buddha's previous births) and events of the Buddha's life are also depicted on the *stupa* and the railings. Since these are labelled, Bharhut sculpture is indispensable for an understanding of Buddhist iconography. As in all early Indian sculpture before the first century AD, the Buddha is represented by a symbol such as a wheel, empty throne, or umbrella, never in human form. The composition is simple, even naive, with overlapping figures used in an attempt to distinguish planes. Animals appearing in the sculptures are treated with the sympathetic understanding characteristic of Indian art at all periods.

The detailing of the ornamentation and the stiffly posed figures suggest that this style began in wood and was later continued in stone. Some of the uprights bear in relief standing figures of *Yakshas* and *yakshis* (male and female nature deities); a frequent motif is the woman embracing a tree.

Although it appears primitive at times, the Bharhut style marks the beginnings of a tradition of Buddhist narrative relief and decoration of sacred buildings that continued for several centuries. Sculptures closely similar to the Bharhut remains are located throughout northern India, suggesting that the Bharhut site is the only survivor of a once widespread style.

Bhasa, earliest-known Sanskrit dramatist, many of whose complete plays have been found he flourished in third century AD, India. His best work, *Svapnavasavadatta* ("The Dream of Vasavadatta"), depicts a king losing and then regaining his kingdom from a usurper. The majority of his dramas are ingenious adaptations on themes of heroism and romantic love borrowed from India's two great epics, the Ramayana and the Mahabharata. Bhasa deviated from the accepted dramaturgy of the time by portraying battle scenes and killings on the stage. His influence is seen in the works of the great fifth-century dramatist Kalidasa, who consciously imitated and improved upon some of Bhasa's literary motifs.

In 1912 an Indian scholar discovered and published the texts of 13 of Bhasa's dramas, previously known only by the allusions of ancient Sanskrit dramatists.

Bhaskaracharya II (b. 1114, Biddur, India; d. 1185, probably Ujjain), also called Bhaskara II or Bhaskara the Learned, eminent twelfth-century Indian astronomer and mathematician he wrote the first work with full and systematic use of the decimal number system. He was born into a talented and respectable family as the son of Maheshwara, a saintly and scholarly person.

He invented the Chakravala (cyclic) method for solving the so-called pellian equations of the type: NX2 + 1 = Y2. This method was examined by Elas-olof Selenius of the University of Uppsala, who observed "the cyclic method is the absolute climax of the Indian mathematics. In my opinion, no European performance at the time of Bhaskara, nor much later, came up to this marvellous height of mathematical complexity."

Bhaskara also had knowledge of the concepts of calculus. In his mathematical work he has used a method analogous to integration to determine the volume of a sphere. Similarly, in determining the instantaneous velocity (*tatkaliki gati*), he describes methods analogous to differentiation. Bhaskaracharya II represents the culmination point in astronomical and mathematical studies in ancient and medieval India.

Bhaskara wrote his celebrated mathematical-astronomical work, *Siddhanta Shiromani*, in Sanskrit in AD 1150, when he was 36 years of age. His treatise consists of four parts: *Lilavati, Bijaganita, Grahaganita,* and *Goladhyaya*. The *Lilavathi* deals with arithmetic, elementary algebra, and geometry. The *Bijaganita* is a treatise on advanced algebra. The *Grahaganita* is devoted to astronomy and the *Golaganita* to the study of spherical trigonometry.

In *Lilavati,* Bhaskara combines his poetical imagination and remarkable mastery over language with his mathematical ingenuity to compose the text. He introduces birds, animals, and absorbing anecdotes from the epics to illustrate mathematical examples and problems. Bhaskara, in his arithmetical and algebraic texts, has discussed in detail, operations with zero. He also correctly noted that the division of a finite number by zero would be equal to infinity. Bhaskara anticipated the sign convention (plus, minus) and the use of letters to denote unknown quantities in algebra.

Bhavabhuti (AD 700), Indian dramatist and poet his dramas, written in Sanskrit and noted for their suspense and vivid characterization, rival the oustanding plays of Kalidasa.

He is best known as the author of three plays. *Mahaviracharita* ("Exploits of the Great Hero") gives in seven acts the main incidents in the Ramayana up to the defeat of Ravana and the coronation of Rama. *Malati Madhava* is a domestic drama in 10 acts abounding in stirring, though sometimes, improbable, incidents. *Uttararamacharita* ("The Later Deeds of Rama"), continues the story of Rama from his coronation to the banishment of Sita and their final reunion. This last play, though containing far less action than the other two, shows Bhavabhuti at the height of his power in characterization and in presenting suspense and climax.

A Brahmin of Vidarbha (the part of central India later called Berar), Bhavabhuti passed his literary life chiefly at the court of Yashovarman of Kanauj.

Bimbisara (b. c. 543 BC; d. 491 BC), one of the early kings of the Indian kingdom of Magadha, his annexation of the kingdom of Anga to the east, is considered to have laid the foundations for the later expansion of the Maurya Empire. He is also known for his cultural achievement and was a great friend and protector of the Buddha. He was succeeded by his son Ajatashatru, who murdered his father to obtain power.

Bindusara, second Maurya emperor, who came to the throne in 297 BC. This name perhaps reflects a successful campaign in the Deccan, Chandra Gupta having already conquered northern India. Bindusara's campaign stopped close to Karnataka. This was probably because the territories of the extreme south, such as those of the Cholas, Pandyas, and Cheras, had good relation with the Mauryas.

Greek sources refer to him as Amitrochates, the Greek for the Sanskrit *Amitraghata,* meaning "destroyer of foes".

Bo Tree, also called bodhi tree, is the the pipal tree (*Ficus religiosa*) under which the Buddha sat when he attained Enlightenment (*bodhi*) at Bodh Gaya (near Gaya, west-central Bihar). In early Buddhist art the Bo tree was often used to represent the Buddha. A living pipal at Anuradhapura, Ceylon (now Sri Lanka), is said to have grown from a cutting from the Bo tree sent to that city by emperor Ashoka in the third century BC.

Bodhisattva, in Buddhism, this term refers either to the historical Buddha, Gautama, prior to his Enlightenment, or other individuals who are destined to become Buddhas in this or in another life. Just as the number of Buddhas in the world is theoretically limitless, so also the number of possible *bodhisattvas* is infinite. The title has been frequently applied to great scholars and teachers and, in Southeast Asia, it was a conventional title honouring Buddhist kings.

Celestial *bodhisattvas* are manifestations of the eternal Buddhas. They are the great saviour figures who—particularly in East Asia—often eclipse the historical Buddha in the personal devotion they inspire. Foremost among the celestial *bodhisattvas* is the compassionate and merciful Avalokiteshvara, who is associated with the eternal Buddha, Amitabha. In China the most widely worshipped *bodhisattvas* are Manjushri (representing wisdom), Kshitigarbha (the saviour of the dead), Samantabhadra (representing happiness), and Avalokiteshvara (known in China as Guanyin). In Tibet, Avalokiteshvara, Manjushri, and Vajrapani (who holds the thunderbolt) form a popular trinity. Maitreya, represented both as a future Buddha and as a *bodhisattva*, is the only *bodhisattva* honoured by Theravadins (followers of the Way of the Elders and continuers of the early Hinayana teaching) as well as by Mahayanists.

In Mahayana Buddhism the decision of the *bodhisattva* to postpone his own final entrance into Nirvana in order to alleviate the suffering of others is given special valuation. The ideal of the *bodhisattva* supplants the earlier, Theravada goal of the *arhat*, or disciple, who perfects himself by following the Buddha's teachings, and of the *pratyeka* Buddha, or self-enlightened Buddha, both of whom are criticized by Mahayana as concerned solely with their own personal salvation. The *bodhisattva* concept elevates the virtue of compassion (*karuna*) to equality with wisdom (*prajna*). The *bodhisattva* exercises his compassion by transferring his own merit to his devotees.

Once the *bodhisattva* declares his intention, he enters the first of 10 spiritual stages (*bhumi*) and henceforward is reborn only in the world of men or of gods. The aspirant *bodhisattva* must be a male but (according to Japanese schools) may live the live of a householder and need not be a monk.

Brahmacharya, in Hinduism, it is the discipline of the pupil apprenticed to a preceptor (guru) for a period of religious study during the second phase of life. The pupil has to be chaste, abstemious, and obedient to his guru. More generally, the term denotes the endeavour by monks and nuns as well as lay devotees to live a moral life, as a way to end suffering and to reach Enlightenment. Lay followers are asked not to kill any living being, not to steal, to avoid improper sexual intercourse, not to lie, and to avoid intoxicants. Novices, monks, and nuns must obey these same rules, observe complete chastity, refrain from eating after noon, avoid all musical and theatrical enjoyments, refrain from wearing jewellery or cosmetics, sleep only in a very simple bed, and refuse gifts of gold or silver. In Buddhism, *brahmacharya* in its strictest sense refers to the practice of sexual chastity.

Brahmagupta (b. AD 598), one of the most accomplished of the ancient Indian astronomers and mathematicians, he is said to be one of the greatest scientists of his race and the greatest of his time.

Brahmagupta lived and worked in the town called Bhillamala, situated near the northern border of Gujarat. His monumental works are *Brahmasphuta Siddhanta* and *Khandakhadyaka*.

Both the texts *Brahmasphuta Siddhanta* and *Khandrakhadyaka* were translated into Arabic in AD 770 by Muhammad ibn Ibrahim al-Fazari and Yaqub ibn Tariq with the assistance of Hindu pandits. The translations were called *Sindhhind* and *Al-Arkand*, respectively. This paved the way for the introduction of new mathematics-based astronomy among Arabs.

The *Brahmasphuta Siddhanta* is a voluminous work comprising 100 verses and is divided into 24 chapters. The first 10 chapters deal with topics concerned with astronomy: planetary conjunctions, solar and lunar eclipses, position of planets, and lunar phases. The twenty-second chapter deals with instruments used in astronomy. The twelfth chapter is devoted to arithmetic, and the eighteenth chapter is devoted to algebra and geometry. Brahmagupta composed this book when he was 30 years old. The second text, *Khandakhadyaka*, was composed by him in the year AD 665, when he was 67 years of age.

The *Khandakhadyaka* is a *karana* text (practical manual) based on Aryabhata's *ardharatrika* system. It contains eight chapters and a small appendix called *uttara khandakhadyaka*. The text deals only with astronomical topics and was very useful in astronomical calculations and computations. It was popularly used for several centuries.

Brahman, Sanskrit term used in the Upanishads it refers to the supreme existence or absolute, the font of all things, as eternal, conscious, infinite, and omnipresent. It is the spiritual source of the universe. Marked differences in the interpretation of Brahman characterize the various sub-schools of Vedanta, the orthodox system of Hindu philosophy based on the writings of the Upanishads.

Brahmana, is any of a number of prose commentaries attached to the Vedas, the most ancient Hindu sacred literature. The

Brahmanas belong to the period 900-700 BC, when the gathering of the sacred hymns into Samhitas ("collections") had acquired a position of sanctity. They present a digest of accumulated teachings, illustrated by myth and legend, on various matters of ritual and on hidden meanings of the sacred texts. Their principal concern is with the sacrifice, and they are the oldest extant sources for the history of Indian ritual. Appended to the Brahmanas are chapters written in similar language and style, but with a more philosophic content, which specifically instruct that the matter of these chapters should be taught only in the forest, away from the village. These later works, called Aranyakas, served as a link between the Brahmanas and the Upanishads. The Brahmanas explain the significance of the Vedas as used in the ritual sacrifices, and the symbolic import of the priests' actions. The word *brahmana* may mean either the utterance of a Brahmin (priest) or an exposition on the meaning of the sacred word; the latter view is more commonly accepted by scholars.

Brahmanism, religion of ancient India that evolved out of the Vedas, it is different from the classical Hinduism that succeeded it. The biggest point of difference is the enhanced significance given in classical Hinduism to individual deities, such as Shiva and Vishnu, and to devotional worship (*bhakti*). It takes its name both from the predominant position of its priestly class, the Brahmins, and from the increasing speculation about, and importance given to, Brahman, the supreme power.

Brahmarshi-Desha, land of the *rishi*, or sages, Brahmarshi-desha was occupied before 1000 BC and is associated with the Vedic commentaries of the Brahmanas as well as the Upanishads. The Sanskrit term used to describe the area eastward from Sirhind, including the tract between the Yamuna (Jumna) and Ganga rivers as far south as Mathura, it included Indraprastha (Delhi), the capital of the Pandavas, and Kurukshetra, the legendary battlefield of the Kurus and the Pandavas, whose struggle is the main theme of the Hindu epic the Mahabharata.

This region is to be distinguished from the Brahmavarta, or Holy Land, which covered the seven rivers from the Indus to the Sarasvati and the town of Sirhind.

Brahmi, ancient writing system ancestral to all Indian scripts except Kharoshti, it is derived from Aramaic and can be traced to the eighth or seventh century BC, when it may have been introduced to Indian merchants by people of Semitic origin.

Brahmi is semialphabetic, each consonant having either an

inherent sound pronounced after it or a diacritic mark to show another vowel. Initial vowels have separate characters. In most cases Brahmi and its derivatives are written from left to right, but a coin of the fourth century BC, discovered in Madhya Pradesh, is inscribed with Brahmi characters running from right to left. Among the many descendants of Brahmi are Devanagari (used for Sanskrit, Hindi, and other Indian languages), the Bengali and Gujarati scripts, and those of the Dravidian languages.

Brahmin, is highest ranking of the four *varnas*, or social orders, in Hinduism. The elevated position of the Brahmins goes back to the late Vedic period, when the Indo-European-speaking settlers in northern India were already divided into Brahmins, or priests, warriors (of the Kshatriya order), traders (of the Vaishya order), and labourers (of the Shudra order). The Brahmins still enjoy esteem as the learned and sacerdotal members of society, though their claim to tangible privileges is no longer officially admitted. The basis of the veneration of Brahmins is the belief that they alone are capable of mediating between humans and gods and of performing the most important and effective ritual actions. The study and recitation of the sacred scriptures was traditionally reserved for the Brahmins, and for centuries Indian scholarship was in their hands.

The ritual superiority of the Brahmins is maintained through the observance of numerous taboos, many of which relate to diet and contact with lower castes. Most Brahmin castes are strictly vegetarian, and their members must abstain from certain occupations. They may not plough or handle any impure material, such as leather or hides, but they may farm and do such agricultural work as does not violate these specific restrictions. They may also accept employment as domestic servants; many well-to-do Hindus have Brahmin cooks, who are valued because members of all castes may eat the food that they prepare.

The Brahmins are divided into 10 man territorial divisions, 5 of which are associated with the north and 5 with the south. The northern group consists of Sarasvati, Gauda, Kannauj, Maithil, and Utkal Brahmins, and the southern group comprises Maharashtra, Andhra, Dravida, Karnata, and Malabar Brahmins.

Brahmin influence extended into worldly affairs, because of their learning and the prestige that went with it. There were many Brahmin advisers and ministers in precolonial governments, and many Brahmin leaders in the nationalist movement. In some parts of India, Brahmin influence in the Congress Party generated a reaction. In southern India, where Brahmins were particularly influential, an anti-Brahmin movement gathered considerable strength. This did not, however, affect their traditional position as priests, ministering both in temples and at domestic rites. The Brahmin family priest (*purohit*) continues to officiate at weddings, funerals, and other ceremonial occasions.

Brihaspati, in Vedic mythology, the instructor of the gods, the master of sacred wisdom, charms, hymns, and rites, and the age counsellor of Indra in his war against the titans, or *asuras*, Brihaspati is the heavenly prototype of the caste of Brahmins and, most particularly, of the earthly *purohit*, or family priest. A hymn in the Rigveda is attributed to him. An ancient sage and a founder of a heretical sect also bear his name. He is the regent of the planet Jupiter.

Buddha, original name (Sanskrit) Gautama, or (Pali) Gotama, also called Siddhartha, was the founder of Buddhism that flourished sixth-fourth century BC.

Siddhartha was born in the sixth or fifth century BC in the kingdom of the Sakyas, on the borders of present-day Nepal and India. As the son of Suddhodana, the king, and Maha Maya, the queen, the Buddha thus came from a Kshatriya (warrior) family. He was raised in luxury by an adoring father who sought to protect him from the sight and knowledge of evil. He married early and had a son while he was still a youth. The turning point in the prince's life came when he was 29 years old. One day, while out driving with his charioteer, he saw an aged man, a sick man, and a dead body.

Shocked by these sights, Gautama decided to discover the true meaning of life, and the cause of suffering. He renounced the world, and sought to gain insight into life's meaning. Gautama first went to two gurus, Alara Kalama and Uddaka Ramaputra, who would instruct him. What he learnt from them, however, was not enough: Gautama was seeking Nirvana. For six years he practised severe austerities but ultimately realized that such self-mortification could not lead him to what he sought. Finally, as he meditated in solitude under the Bo tree, which Buddhists call the "tree of wisdom", Gautama experienced a spiritual awakening (Enlightenment).

Once Gautama was awakened to the truth about life, he became the Buddha and devoted his life to sharing his teachings with others. The Buddha preached his first sermon (ar Sarnath) to only five followers. In it, he set forth his beliefs. A man who has left home and gone forth should not follow two extremes, namely self-indulgence and self-mortification. Avoiding these two extremes, the Tathagata ("He Who Has Thus Attained"—that is, the Buddha) has discovered the middle path leading to vision, knowledge, calmness, awakening, and Nirvana. This middle path is known as the Noble Eightfold Path. It consists of right view, right thought, right speech, right action, right mode of living, right endeavour, right mindfulness, and right concentration.

The term Buddha ("Awakened One" or "Enlightened One") is not a proper name but rather a title, such as messiah (the Christ). Thus, the term should be accompanied by an article, as in "the Buddha" or "a Buddha" (because of a belief that there will be innumerable buddhas in the future as there have been in the past). The Buddha was born into the Gautama clan and is often referred to as Gautama. When the term "the Buddha" is used, it is generally assumed that it refers to Gautama the Buddha.

According to almost all Buddhist traditions, the Buddha lived many lives before his birth as Gautama. These previous lives are described in stories called *jatakas* that play an important role in Buddhist art and education. The following account, however, focusses on the Buddha's "historical" life from his birth as Gautama to his death some 80 years later.

The Buddha taught Four Noble Truths. The First Noble Truth is that man's existence is *dukkha*, full of conflict, dissatisfaction, sorrow, and suffering. The Second Noble Truth is that all this is caused by man's selfish desire—craving, or *tanha* (thirst). The Third Noble Truth is that there is emancipation, liberation, and freedom for human beings from all this, which is Nirvana. The Fourth Noble Truth is the Noble Eightfold Path, which is the way to this liberation.

At the end of the sermon, these five ascetics, the Buddha's first disciples, were admitted by him as *bhikkhus* (monks) and became the first members of the *sangha* ("community", or "order"). For the next four decades, he trained learned, well-disciplined followers. Considering his mission fulfilled, he died at the age of 80.

Buddhacharita, Buddhacharita-Kavya-Sutra, poetic narrative of the life of the Buddha by the Sanskrit poet Ashvaghosha, it is considered one of the finest examples of Buddhist literature. Ashvaghosha's work also reflects a vast knowledge of Indian mythology and of pre-Buddhist philosophies, as well as a court poet's interest in love, battle, and statecraft. Though only the first half of the *Buddhacharita* remains intact in Sanskrit, all 28 chapters are preserved in Chinese (fifth century) and Tibetan translations. The author, who lived in northern India in the first to second century

AD, created a loving account of the Buddha's life and teachings. In contrast to other treatments such as the *Mahavastu* ("Great Story") and *Lalitavistara* ("Full Description of the Play [of the Buddha]"), it is both artistically arranged and restrained in its description of miracles.

Buddhaghosha, Indian Buddhist scholar he is famous for his *Visuddhimagga* ("Way to Purity"), a summary of current Buddhist doctrines and flourished early fifth century AD. Scholars do not agree about Buddhaghosha's birthplace, but it is known that he travelled to Anuradhapura, Sri Lanka, where he discovered many Sinhalese Buddhist commentaries which he translated into Pali and communicated to his countrymen.

Buddhism, a religion and philosophy that developed from the teachings of the Siddhartha Gautama. Buddhism played a central role in the spiritual, cultural, and social life of the Eastern world and, during the twentieth century, spread to the West.

Many people in India were no longer content with the external formalities of Brahminic sacrifice and ritual. In northwestern India there were ascetics who tried to go beyond the Vedas (Hindu sacred scriptures); there was a new emphasis on renunciation and transcendental knowledge. But northeastern India, which was less influenced by the Aryans who had developed the main tenets and practices of the Vedic Hindu faith, became the breeding ground of many heterodox sects. Society in this area was troubled by the breakdown of tribal unity and the expansion of several petty kingdoms. Religiously, this was a time of doubt, turmoil, and experimentation.

Buddhism came into being in northeastern India during the period from the late sixth century to the early fourth century BC, a period of great social change and intense religious activity. There is disagreement among scholars about the dates of the Buddha's birth and death. Most scholars in Europe, the United States, and India believe that the historical Buddha lived from about 563 to about 483 BC. Many others, especially in Japan, believe that he lived about 100 years later (from about 448 to 368 BC).

Buddhism, like many of the sects that developed in northeastern India at the time, was constituted by the presence of a charismatic teacher, by the teachings this leader promulgated, and by a community of adherents that was often made up of renunciant members and lay supporters. In the case of Buddhism this pattern became the basis for the Triratna—the "Three Jewels" of Buddha (the teacher), *dharma* (the teaching), and *sangha* (the community)—

in which Buddhists have traditionally taken refuge.

In the centuries following the founder's death, Buddhism developed in two directions: Theravada (the Way of the Elders) remained relatively faithful to what it considered to be the true tradition of the Buddha's teachings. The other is called Mahayana, "the means of salvation available to a larger number of people", by its followers, who call the first school Hinayana, "the means of salvation restricted to a smaller number of people" (or simply the greater and lesser vehicles).

In its spread, Buddhism influenced the currents of thought and religion in other countries. In response to the diverse religious aspirations of the various Buddhist communities, the strict law of *karma* was modified to accommodate new emphases on the efficacy of ritual actions and various forms of devotional practice. Finally, there developed in India a movement called Vajrayana, or esoteric Buddhism, the aim of which was to obtain liberation more speedily. This movement was influenced by gnostic and magical currents pervasive at that time.

Expansion of Buddhism: During the first several centuries after the Buddha's death, the story of his live was remembered and embellished, his teachings were preserved and developed, and the community that he had established became a significant religious force. Many of the followers of the Buddha who were wandering ascetics began to settle in permanent monastic establishments (*vihara*) and to develop the procedures needed to maintain large monastic institutions (*mahavihara*). During the first century of its existence, Buddhism spread from its place of origin in Magadha and Kosala throughout much of northern India, including the areas of Mathura and Ujjayani (Ujjain) in the west.

The Maurya emperor Ashoka's reign in the third century BC helped greatly in spreading the religion through the subcontinent. The archetypal Buddhist king, Ashoka attempted to establish in his realm a "true *dharma*" based on the virtues of self-control, impartiality, cheerfulness, truthfulness, and goodness. By the first century BC, Buddhism had succeeded in maintaining and even expanding its influence. Buddhist monastic centres and magnificent Buddhist monuments such as the great *stupas* at Bharhut and Sanchi were established throughout the subcontinent, and these institutions often received royal patronage. In the early centuries AD, Buddhism was especially flourishing in northwestern India, and from there it spread rapidly into Central Asia and China.

Buddhism under the Guptas and Palas: The revival of Brahminic religion and the rising tide of *bhakti* had begun affecting Buddhism by the time of the Gupta dynasty (AD 320-600). During this time, some monasteries joined together to form monastic centres (*mahaviharas*) that functioned as universities. The most famous of these, located at Nalanda, had a curriculum that went far beyond the bounds of traditional Buddhism. Nalanda soon became the leading centre for the study of Mahayana, which was rapidly becoming the dominant Buddhist tradition in India. Though Buddhist institutions seemed to be faring well under the Guptas, various Chinese pilgrims visiting India between AD 400 and 700 could discern an internal decline in the Buddhist community and the beginning of the reabsorption of Indian Buddhism by Hinduism. Among these pilgrims were Fa-hsien, Sung Yun, Hui-Sheng, Hsuan Tsang, and I-ching (Yijing).

After the destruction of numerous Buddhist monasteries in the sixth century AD by the Huns, Buddhism revived, especially in the northeast, where it flourished for a time under the Buddhist Pala kings (eighth-twelfth century AD). These kings continued to protect the *mahaviharas*, building such new centres as Odantapuri, near Nalanda, and establishing a system of supervision for all such institutions. Under the Palas, Vajrayana or Tantric Buddhism became the dominant sect. During this period, the University of Nalanda became a centre for the study of Tantric Buddhism and the practice of Tantric magic and rituals. With the collapse of the Pala dynasty in the twelfth century, however, Buddhism suffered another defeat, and this time it did not recover. Though some pockets of Buddhist influence remained, the Buddhist presence in India became so negligible that it could hardly be noticed.

At the beginning of the twentieth century Buddhism was virtually extinct in India. In the early 1900s, however, a significant Buddhist presence began to be reestablished. In the early decades of the twentieth century a number of Buddhist societies were organized by Indian intellectuals who found in Buddhism an alternative to a Hindu tradition that they could no longer accept; an alternative that was, in addition, part of the cultural heritage of India. Following the Chinese conquest of Tibet in the late 1950s, there was an influx of Tibetan Buddhist community in northern India. In addition, the incorporation of Sikkim in 1975 into the Republic of India brought into the modern Indian nation a small Himalayan society with a strong Buddhist tradition related to the Vajrayana Buddhism of Tibet.

The major component in the twentieth-century resurgence of Buddhism in India has, however, been the mass conversion of large numbers of people from the so-called Scheduled Castes (formerly called untouchables). This conversion movement, originally led by Bhimrao Ramji Ambedkar, began in the 1950s. In October 1956 Ambedkar and several thousand of his followers converted to Buddhism, and—although accurate figures are difficult to determine—the group has continued to grow. Some estimates indicate that the number of converts is as high as four million. This group, which in the past has tended to favour the Theravada version of Buddhism, is developing its own distinctive patterns of Buddhist teaching and practice.

Sri Lanka and Southeast Asia: The first clear evidence of the spread of Buddhism outside India dates from the reign of King Ashoka (third century BC). According to his inscriptions, Ashoka sent Buddhist emissaries not only to many different regions of the subcontinent but also into certain border areas. It is certain that Ashokan emissaries were sent to Sri Lanka (Ceylon) and to an area called Suvarnabhumi that many modern scholars have identified with the Mon country in southern Myanmar (Burma) and central Thailand.

Sri Lanka: According to the Sinhalese tradition, Buddhism took root in Sri Lanka with the arrival of Ashoka's son Mahendra and his six companions. Sent at missionaries by the Maurya emperor, these travellers converted King Devanampiya Tissa and many of the nobility. Under King Tissa, the Mahavihara monastery was built, an institution that was to become the centre of Sinhalese orthodoxy.

In the first century BC, the Pali canon was first written down under King Vattagamani Abhaya. This king also built the Abhayagiri monastery, the main centre of the various Mahayana movements in Sri Lanka. Under Shri Meghavanna, the "Tooth of the Buddha" was brought to Abhayagiri and made the national palladium.

During the first millennium AD in Sri Lanka, the ancient Theravada tradition coexisted with various forms of Hinduism, Mahayana Buddhism, and Buddhist Tantrism. Beginning in the tenth century Buddhism was declining in India, Sri Lanka became a major locus of a Theravada Buddhist revival. As a result of this revival, Sri Lanka became a Theravada kingdom, with a *sangha* that was unified under Theravada auspices and a monarch who legitimized his rule in Theravada terms. The new Theravada tradition that was established spread from Sri Lanka into Southeast Asia, where it exerted a powerful influence.

The monastic community in Sri Lanka is now divided into three major bodies: (1) the Siam Nikaya, founded in the eighteenth century, a conservative and wealthy sect that admits only members of the Goyigama, the highest Sinhalese caste, (2) the Amarapura sect, founded in the nineteenth century, which has opened its ranks to members of lower castes, and (3) the reformed splinter group from the Siam Nikaya called the Ramanya sect. Among the laity several reform groups have been established. Among these the Sarvodaya community headed by A.T. Ariyaratne is especially important. This group has established religious, economic, and social development programmes that have had a significant impact on Sinhalese village life.

Since Sri Lanka attained its independence from the British in 1947, the country has been increasingly drawn into a conflict between the Sinhalese Buddhist majority and the Tamil Hindu minority. Many Sinhalese Buddhists, including some monks, have closely associated their religion with the political agenda of the more militant Sinhalese nationalists. A few Buddhist leaders have, however, tried to adopt a more moderate position and to encourage a negotiated solution, the traditional basis for Sri Lankan political formation.

The Himalayan kingdoms: Tibetan Buddhism has also exerted a considerable influence in the Himalayan kingdoms situated along Tibet's southern border. In Nepal, Buddhism has been influenced by both India and Tibet. Though the Buddha was born in the southern part of the area that is now Nepal, at Lumbini, about 24 km from Kapilavastu, Buddhism seems to have been actively propagated only later, probably under Ashoka. By the eighth century Nepal had fallen into the cultural orbit of Tibet. A few centuries later, as a result of the Muslim invasions of India, both Hindus and Buddhists took refuge in the country. In modern times Buddhist prayer wheels and flags are reminders of the direct influence of Tibetan Buddhism. The Indian heritage is especially evident in the caste system that embraces Buddhists and non-Buddhists alike.

In Bhutan a Tibetan lama introduced Buddhism and a Tibetan style of hierarchical theocracy in the seventeenth century AD. The Buddhism practiced in Bhutan has been influenced by the Tibetan Bka'-brgyud-pa sect, which has stressed the magical benefits of living in caves and has not enforced on its clergy the discipline of celibacy. Buddhism in Bhutan, like Buddhism in Nepal, is coming into increasing contact with modernizing forces that are beginning to undermine many of its traditional practices.

It may be said that the Buddha based his entire teaching on the fact of human suffering. Existence is painful. The conditions that make an individual are precisely those that also give rise to suffering. Individuality implies limitation; limitation gives rise to desire; and, inevitably, desire causes suffering, since what is desired is transitory, changing, and perishing. It is the impermanence of the object of craving that causes disappointment and sorrow. By following the "path" taught by the Buddha, the individual can dispel the "ignorance" that perpetuates this suffering. The Buddha's doctrine was not one of despair. Living amid the impermanence of everything, and being themselves impermanent, human beings search for the way of deliverance, for Enlightenment.

The belief in rebirth, or *samsara*, as a potentially endless series of worldly existence in which every being is caught up, was already associated with the doctrine of *karma* (Sanskrit: *karman*; literally "act", or "deed") in pre-Buddhist India, and it was generally accepted by both the Theravada and the Mahayana traditions. According to the doctrine of *karma*, good conduct brings a pleasant and happy result and creates a tendency toward similar good acts, while bad conduct brings an evil result and creates a tendency toward repeated evil actions. This furnishes the basic context for the moral life of the individual.

Some *karmas* bear fruit in the same life in which they are committed, others in the immediately succeeding one, and yet others in future lives that are more remote.

The teaching attributed to the Buddha was transmitted orally by his disciples, prefaced by the phrase "evam me sutam" ("thus have I heard"); therefore, it is difficult to say whether his discourses were related as they were spoken. They usually allude, however, to the place, time, and community where he preached; and there is concordance between various versions. An attempt was made by Buddhist councils in the first centuries after the Buddha's death to establish his true and original teachings.

The Four Noble Truths: formulated by Buddha cover fundamental realities the truth of misery; the truth that misery originates within us from the craving for pleasure and for being or non-being; the truth that this craving can be eliminated; and the truth that this elimination is the result of a methodical way or path that must be followed.

Hence, the Buddha formulated the law of dependent origination (*pratitya-samutpada*), whereby one condition arises out of another, which in turn arises out of prior conditions. Every mode of being presupposes another immediately preceding mode from which the subsequent mode derives, in a chain of causes.

The Eightfold Path: How one may escape the continually renewed cycle of birth, suffering, and death. Here ethical conduct is important.

It is not enough to know that misery pervades all existence and to know the way in which life evolves; there must also be a purification that leads to the overcoming of this process. Such a liberating purification is effected by following the Noble Eightfold Path constituted by right views, right aspirations, right speech, right conduct, right livelihood, right effort, right mindfulness, and right meditational attainment. The term "right" (true, or correct) is used to distinguish sharply between the precepts of the Buddha and other teachings.

Nirvana: The aim of religious practice is to be rid of the delusion of ego, thus freeing oneself from the fetters of this mundane world. One who is successful in doing so is said to have overcome the round of rebirths and to have achieved Enlightenment, the final goal. Though Nirvana is often presented negatively as "release from suffering", it is more accurate to describe it in a more positive fashion: as an ultimate goal to be sought and cherished.

The Buddha left indeterminate questions regarding the destiny of persons who have reached this ultimate goal. He even refused to speculate as to whether such purified saints, after death, continued to exist or ceased to exist. Such questions, he maintained, were not relevant to the practice of the path and could not, in any event, be answered from within the confines of ordinary human existence.

The role of the Sangha: Buddhists of all times and places have recognized the importance of community life, and over the centuries there has developed a distinctive pattern involving a symbiotic relationship between monks (and in some cases nuns) and the lay community.

The *sangha* is the assembly of Buddhist monks that has, from the origins of Buddhism, authoritatively studied, taught, and preserved the teachings of the Buddha. The early Buddhist monks (Pali: *bhikkus*; Sanskrit: *bhikshus*) wandered from place to place, retreating in communities only during the rainy season. They would gather fortnightly at the time of the full and new moons to recite the *Patimokkha* (Sanskrit: *Pratimoksha*), or declaration of their steadfastness in observing the monastic discipline (contained in the *Vinaya Pitaka*). This ceremony was called the *uposatha*.

Within the first several centuries after the Buddha's death, the *sangha* came to include two different groups of monks. One retained the wandering mode of existence; this group has been a very creative force in Buddhist history and continues to play a role in contemporary Buddhism, particularly in Sri Lanka and Southeast Asia. The other, much larger group gave up the life-in-the-forest and settled in permanent monastic settlements (*viharas*). These monasteries were democratic in nature.

In the Theravada countries—Sri Lanka, Myanmar, Thailand, Kampuchea, and Laos—the Buddhist monastic community is composed primarily of male monks and novices, white-robed ascetics (including various types of male and female practitioners who remain outside the *sangha* but follow a life more or less of renunciation), and laymen and laywomen. The order of nuns died out in the Theravada world more than a millennium ago, and contemporary efforts to reestablish it have met with only minimal success. In the Mahayana and Vajrayana countries of China and Tibet there was traditionally a stage of one year before the aspirant could become a novice. This was a year of probation when the aspirant did not receive tonsure and remained subject to governmental taxation and service, while receiving instructions and performing menial tasks within the monastery. At the end of this one-year probationary period, the aspirant had to pass a test, including the recitation of part of a well-known *sutra*—the length depending upon whether the applicant was male or female—and a discussion on various doctrinal questions. In China, one usually did not progress beyond the novice stage unless he or she was of exceptional character or was affiliated with the government.

According to *vinaya* (monastic discipline) rules, entry into the *sangha* is an individual affair, dependent upon the wishes of the individual and his family. In some Buddhist countries, however, ordination was often under the control of the state, and the state conducted the examinations to determine entry or advancement in the *sangha*. In certain situations, ordination could be obtained not only through such examinations but also by the favour of high officials or through the purchase of an ordination certificate from the government. This selling of ordination certificates was at times abused by the government in order to fill its treasury.

Early Buddhist schools: The early councils: The Buddha did not, as was the custom among the teachers of his time, designate a human successor. Instead, he taught that each monk should strive to follow the path that he had preached. The early Buddhist councils, therefore, were concerned largely with the purity of the faith and with practice of the monastic community. Unfortunately, the councils pose an enormous problem to the historian because each major sect has its own account and opinion of them.

The first council, held at Rajagriha (modern Rajgir, Bihar), is said to have taken place in the first rainy season following the Buddha's death. Compilations were made of the Buddha's rules of *vinaya*, under the monk Upali, and of the *sutras* (instructive aphorisms), under monk Ananda. The entire assembly of 500 monks then recited the approved texts. Many scholars, however, deny that the Council of Rajagriha took place.

More scholars are prone to accept the historicity of the second council held at Vaishali (Bihar), a little more than a century after the Buddha's death. It was called to settle a dispute regarding the relaxed rules of discipline followed by the monks of Vaishali. Many scholars believe this council to have been closely associated with the controversy that led to the open division between two segments of the early community—the Mahasanghika school, which displayed a more liberal attitude, and the Sthaviravada (Theravada) school, which took a more conservative and elitist stance. The list of 10 disputed practices differed in various accounts of the council but apparently dealt with such questions as the storing of salt, eating or begging after the prescribed hours, taking the practices of one's tutor as precedent for one's actions, and accepting gold and silver as alms.

The third council, held during the reign of the emperor Ashoka at his capital, Pataliputra (modern Patna), in the mid-third century BC, may have been confined to an assembly of the Theravadas. By then the faithful had divided into schools and subschools holding different interpretations of monastic discipline; it thus became difficult for monks of separate schools who presided together to hold the fortnightly *uposatha* ceremony, which required prior confession by monks of any breach of discipline. This difficulty may have prompted the convening of the third council. Those monks who failed to declare themselves Vibhajyavadins (adherents of the "doctrine of analysis", presumably Theravadins) were turned out of the assembly.

The chronicles of the Sarvastivada ("Doctrine that All is Real") school do not mention the Council of Ashoka. The third council was held during the reign of Kanishka at Jalandhara or, according to other sources, in Kashmir. The uncertainty of Kanishka's dates makes the dating of the council equally difficult, but it may have been held around AD 100.

The eighteen schools and their successors: During the first several centuries of Buddhist history a number of different schools took form and developed particular traditions regarding the Buddha's teaching and its proper interpretation.

According to later Buddhist tradition, eighteen such schools emerged during the first few centuries of Buddhist history. (These are the schools that the practitioners of the Mahayana, or "Greater Vehicle", grouped together and dubbed the Hinayana, or "Lesser Vehicle".) Among these so-called eighteen schools there are a few about which some reasonably certain statements can be made. In some cases it is possible to trace connections between the early schools and similarly oriented traditions that played a significant role in the later phases of Buddhist history.

Sthaviravada/Theravada: Many scholars trace the emergence of a specific "School of the Elders" (Sthaviravada in Sanskrit, Theravada in Pali) to the second century following the Buddha's death. Whether or not this is true, it is clear that the Theravada was one of the earliest of the early Buddhist schools, and from a historical point of view, was the most successful. The Theravada school ultimately became, and has remained, the predominant Buddhist school in Sri Lanka and much of mainland Southeast Asia.

Mahasanghika/Lokottaravada: According to traditional accounts, the Mahasanghikas ("Adherents of the Great Order, or Assembly") split off from other Buddhists in the fourth or third century BC, in what may have been the original schism. Their emphasis was on a more open community, a less strict version of the discipline, and a metaphysical view of the Buddha—all of which were later appropriated by the Mahayana. In the developed form of their teaching, they focused not on the historical Buddha and his teachings, but on the transcendents Buddha. In their view, the Buddha is *lokottara* ("transcending the world"), indestructible, completely devoid of all worldly impurities, with stainless karma. In their views on the nature of the Buddha, the Mahasanghikas were the precursor of the Mahayana. The Mahavastu is the only surviving part of the Mahasanghika canon.

Sarvastivada (P'i-t'an, Chu-she/Kusha): This group detached itself from the Sthaviravada school around the time of Ashoka and spread from Mathura into Kashmir. Taking a different tack from that of the Sthaviravada/Theravada monks, the Sarvastivadin scholastics developed their own set of "canonical" Abhidharma texts. (The Abhidharma texts are systematizations of the teaching in the early *sutras* that were composed by the monks of the various schools.) The name Sarvastivada refers to the doctrine that everything exists (*sarvam asti*). *Karma* exists, as do the component elements that constitute a human person (the five *skandhas*). Matter has aspects, hence characteristics, and therefore is definable. The other components have characteristics, and therefore they too are knowable. What does not exist is an *atman, pudgala* or any other kind of underlying self or person.

A branch of this school, the Mula-Sarvastivada, was widely diffused in India, Central Asia, Myanmar, Thailand, Kampuchea, and Indonesia.

Theravada (Sthaviravada): Adherents of Theravada accept as authoritative the Pali canon of ancient Indian Buddhism and trace their lineage back to the Sthaviras (Pali: Theras, "Elders"), who followed in the tradition of the senior monks of the first Buddhist *sangha.* During the reign of the emperor Ashoka (third century BC), the Theravada school travelled to Sri Lanka, where it divided into three subgroups, known after their monastic centres as the Mahaviharavasi, the Abhayagiriviharavasi, and the Jetavanaviharavasi. The Mahavihara form of the Theravada tradition became dominant in Sri Lanka about the beginning of the second millennium AD and gradually spread eastward, becoming established in Myanmar in the late eleventh century, in Thailand in the thirteenth century, and in Kampuchea (Cambodia) and Laos by the fourteenth century.

Theravada Buddhism tends towards a conservative, orthodox interpretation of Buddha's teaching. The ideal Theravada Buddhist is the arhat (Pali: *arahant*), or perfected saint, who attains Enlightenment as a result of his own efforts. Theravadins profoundly revere the historical Buddha as a perfected master but do not pay homage to the numerous celestial Buddhas and *bodhisattvas* that are worshipped in Mahayana temples.

Human existence is a privileged state because only as a human being can a *bodhisattva* become a Buddha. Theravadins insisted that Nirvana was beyond the realm of empirical reality and that the Buddha who had founded the religion could be distinguished from the *dharma* he taught.

The state of the Buddha, the perfectly Enlightened One, is Nirvana—an attainment from which one does not return. It is beyond death, not caused, not born, not produced; it is beyond all becoming and devoid of all that makes up a human person.

The Buddha has been given many other names, the most common of which are Arahant and Tathagata ("He Who Has Thus Attained"). The Theravadin scriptures, in the later stages, express a belief in previous Buddhas before Gautama (six in one list, more in others) and also in a future Buddha, Maitreya (Pali: Metteyya), who presently dwells in the Tusita Heaven and who will come into the world when the proper time *arrives*.

Theravada literature: The earliest systematic and most complete collection of early Buddhist sacred literature is the Pali Tipitaka ("The Three Baskets"; Sanskrit: Tripitaka). Its arrangement reflects the importance that the early followers attached to the regulations of the monastic life (Vinaya), to the discourses of the Buddha (Sutra), and subsequently to the interest in scholasticism (Abhidharma). Written in Pali, the Vinaya Pitaka is an authoritative compilation of the regulations relating to the conduct of monks and nuns, ordination, and instruction. By far the largest of the three "baskets" is the Sutra Pitaka ("Basket of Discourse"), which consists of five collections *(nikayas)* containing the discourses attributed to the Buddha. The third "basket", the Abhidharma Pitaka ("Basket of Scholasticism"), comprises seven works that, although based on the contents of the Buddha's discourses, deal with selected and specific topics which form the basis for the later philosophical interpretations.

The noncanonical literature of Theravada Buddhism largely consists of commentaries on the Tipitaka texts but also includes independent works. Two texts which are held in high esteem are the *Milinda-panha* ("Questions of Menander"), said to have been compiled by Nagasena, and Buddhaghosha's *Visuddhimagga* ("Way to Purify"). Written in the form of a dialogue between the author and King Menander, Milinda-panha presents a profound and comprehensive exposition of Buddhist doctrine, ethics, and psychology. Buddhaghosha, who belonged to the fifth century AD, is undoubtedly the most prolific and important writer in the Pali language. His first work, *Visuddhimagga,* is a compendium of Theravada teaching that has been greatly revered by his successors.

Mahayana: Mahayana Buddhism emerged in about the first century AD from the ancient Buddhist schools as a more liberal and innovative interpretation of the Buddha's teachings. Arising in India, the Mahayana version of Buddhism spread to Central Asia, China, Japan, mainland Southeast Asia, Java, Sumatra, and even Sri Lanka (Abhayagiri monastery). It became the Pan-Asiatic form of Buddhism and involved basic shifts in doctrine and approach for which, however, there were precedents in earlier schools. It taught that neither the self nor the dharmas exist. It substituted the *bodhisattva*—an individual who postpones his entry into Nirvana in order to help others achieve salvation. In Mahayana, love for creatures is exalted to the highest; a *bodhisattva* is encouraged to offer the merit he derives from good deeds for the good of others.

In the Mahayana tradition, the Buddha is viewed not merely

as a human master and model but also a supramundane being. He multiplies himself and is reflected in a pentad of Buddhas: Vairochana, Akshobhya, Ratnasambhava, Amitabha, and Amoghasiddhi.

As Mahayana developed, a great deal of literature called *Buddhavachana* (Revelation of the Buddha) was circulated, but it went far beyond the ancient canons; it was proposed as the highest revelation, superseding prior texts. In this literature the teaching is viewed not as merely of one kind but as one comprising various levels, each adapted to the intellectual capacity and karmic propensities of those who hear it. The Buddha is no longer simply the historical sage of the Shakyas but is now supramundane *(lokottara)*. Even the sangha is of two types: that of this world and that beyond it.

In Mahayana Buddhism, the decision of the bodhisattva to postpone his own final entrance into Nirvana in order to alleviate the suffering of others, is given special valuation. The ideal of the bodhisattva supplants the earlier, Theravada goal of the arhat, or disciple, who perfects himself by following the Buddha's teachings, and of the pratyeka Buddha, or self-enlightened Buddha, both of whom are criticized by Mahayana as concerned solely with their own personal salvation. The bodhisattva concept elevates the virtue of compassion *(karuna)* to equality with wisdom *(prajna)*. The bodhisattva exercises his compassion by transferring his own merit to his devotees. The essential premise of the *bodhisattva* ideal is to generate in one's own self the thought of Enlightenment and to fulfil the vow to become a Buddha, foregoing entrance into Nirvana in order to remain in the world as long as there are creatures to be saved from suffering.

The three Buddha bodies: The doctrine of the Buddha's threefold nature *(trikaya)* rooted in Theravada teachings assumes central significance. The dharmakaya (body of essence), the unmanifested mode, represents the supreme state of absolute knowledge; the sambhogakaya (body of enjoyment), the heavenly mode; and the nirmanakaya (body of transformation), the earthly mode, the Buddha as he appeared on earth. This could be in any form: for instance, as a bodhisattva, a king, a painting, or a lotus. Mahayana, thus, considers the historical Buddha, Siddhartha Gautama, as only one manifestation of the Buddha.

The Mahayana schools and their texts: The main Mahayana schools are: *Madhyamika, Yogachara (Vijnanavada), Saddharmapundarika,* Pure Land, and *Dhyana* (Ch'an in China, Zen in Japan).

Madhyamika (San-lun/Sanron): The Madhyamika ("Doctrine of the Middle Way"), also known as Shunyavada ("Theory of Negativity [or Relativity]"), system—which held both subject and object to be unreal—is the systematized form of the doctrine of shunyata (cosmic emptiness) contained in the Prajnaparamita literature. The most famous exponent of this system was the Indian philosopher Nagarjuna (AD 150-250), the presumed author of the voluminous *Mahaprajnaparamita-shastra* ("The Great Treatise on the Perfection of Wisdom"). Nagarjuna attempted to prove that all worldly thought is empty (shunya) or relative. He believed that the true path is that of the middle, the path that is between or, more correctly, above extremes.

Yogachara/Vijnanavada (Fa-hsiang/Hosso): The Yogachara (or Vijnanavada) school is traditionally ascribed to the brothers Ashanga and Vasubandhu (fifth century AD), to whom may be added Sthiramati (sixth century). Yogachara explored and propounded the basic doctrines that were to be fundamental in the future development of Mahayana and that influenced the rise of Tantric Buddhism. Its central doctrine is that only consciousness is real, that thought or mind is the ultimate reality. External things do not exist; nothing exists outside the mind. The special characteristics of Yogachara are its emphasis on meditation and a broadly psychological analysis. This contrasts with Madhyamika where the emphasis is on logical analysis and dialectic.

Saddharmapundarika (T'ien-t'ai/Tendai): The T'ien-t'ai / Tendai school is one of the most important developments in Chinese and Japanese Buddhism; it is significant not only for its doctrines, but also for its practical devotional influence. Its doctrines and practices are focused on the Indian or Central Asian Saddharmapundarika-sutra ("Lotus of the True Law Sutra"), or Lotus Sutra. This sutra is one of the best known and most popular of Mahayana Buddhist texts. The Lotus Sutra's main purpose is to establish the one way ("vehicle", or "career") for attaining salvation (Buddhahood). It claims to be the definitive and complete teaching of the Buddha, here presented as a transcendent eternal being, preaching to myriad arhats, gods, bodhisattvas, and other figures using all sorts of sermons, lectures, imaginative parables, and miracles. Religious merit is attributed to preaching, reciting, and hearing the sutra, which is not merely a statement of the nature of things but also a central object of devotion.

Pure Land (Sukhavati/Ching-t'u/Joho, Shin, and Ji): The main text of the Pure Land schools is the *Sukhavativyuha-sutra* ("Pure Land

Sutra") written in northern India probably before the beginning of the second century AD. This sutra tells of a monk, Dharmakara, who heard the preaching of Lokeshvararaja Buddha many aeons ago and asked to become a Buddha. After millions of years of study, Dharmakara promised to fulfill a number of vows if he finally attained Buddhahood. He vowed to establish a Pure or Happy Land (Sanskrit: Sukhavati; Chinese: Ching-t'u; Japanese: Jodo), also known as the Western Paradise. In this Pure Land no evil would exist, the people would be long-lived, they would receive whatever they desired, and from there they might attain Nirvana. Dharmakara then revealed in a number of vows the means by which this Pure Land can be reached. Several of these vows emphasize meditation and good works on earth as a prerequisite, but the eighteenth one (a famous vow in the later development of Pure Land schools) states that if one merely calls the name of the Buddha at the moment of death, one will be reborn in the Pure Land.

The basic doctrines of the Pure Land sects differ considerably from the doctrines of the early Buddhists. The Pure Land's leaders have generally taught that a person reaches salvation from this earth not by individual effort or the accumulation of merit but through faith in the grace of the Buddha Amitabha. The main practice of those who follow the Pure Land teachings is not the learning of the texts nor meditation on the Buddha but rather the constant invocation of the name Amitabha. Furthermore, in Pure Land Buddhism, the attainment of Nirvana is not the primary goal; it is rather to be reborn in the Pure Land of Amitabha.

Dhyana (Ch'an/Zen): The Dhyana school of Buddhism emphasizes meditation as the way to immediate awareness of ultimate reality, an important practice of Buddhism from its origin in India, and derives its name from the Sanskrit term for meditation, dhyana. Ch'an, with its special training techniques and doctrines and its Taoist influence, however, is usually considered a specifically Chinese product.

Esoteric and Mystical Practices: Mystical practices and esoteric sects are to be found in all forms of Buddhism. Buddhist mysticism (including the philosophical school of Dhyana), like other forms of mysticism, insists on the ineffability of the mystical experience, because it defies expression in terms that are intelligible to anyone who has not had analogous experience. The knowledge involved is never merely intellectual but is a kind of felt knowledge in which things are seen in a different perspective and take on a new significance.

The earliest Buddhist mysticism was concerned with the emptying of one's subjective being, considered to be the greatest obstacle to the individual's spiritual growth. This passing into a new dimension of reality was described in terms of a flame going out: it was merely extinguished; it could not be said that it had gone somewhere.

Vajrayana Buddhism: Vajrayana ("Diamond Vehicle"), or Mantrayana ("Path of the Sacred Formulas"), also known as Tantric Buddhism, first gained prominence in various parts of India and Sri Lanka. Although Vajrayana texts describe numerous yogic or contemplative stages that an aspirant must experience before achieving Enlightenment; rather than elaborating doctrines, they hold the Mahayana identification of Nirvana and samsara as a basic truth. Adherents of the Vajrayana tradition believe that as all things are in truth of one nature—the void—the physical-mental processes can be used as a vehicle for Enlightenment. In the Kalachakra Tantra it is written that the Buddha taught that in this age of degeneration Enlightenment must be achieved through one's own body, which contains the whole cosmos. This doctrine is taught in all the tantras.

Vajrayana Buddhism involves mudras (meditative gestures and postures), mantras (sacred syllables and phrases), and icons. A mandala (a symbolic diagram which represents the universe) is used as an aid to meditation.

Vajrayana literature: Vajrayana Buddhism has its own authoritative texts, called tantras, that are primarily manuals of ritual and esoteric lore. While the sutras can be said to represent the theoretical and speculative aspect of Buddhism, the *tantras* express Buddhism as individually lived. The tantras are essentially individually oriented works that apply to larger groups of people because of the similarity of the experiences described in them. Because of their symbolic character, the tantras have usually been kept secret, and a literalist interpretation of such texts has usually failed to make any sense out of them.

The earliest known written tantra is the Guhyasamaja-tantra ("Treatise on the Sum Total of Mysteries"), also known as the *Tathagataguhyaka* ("The Mystery of Tathagatahood [Buddhahood]"), is the earliest known written tantra. It is by tradition ascribed to Ashanga, a renowned fourth-century-AD scholar from India; he was the propounder of the Yogachara philosophy. Usually the tantras do not give an explanation of the technical or symbolic terms, as this explanation is left to the teacher, but the Guhyasamaja-tantra devotes a very long chapter to the elucidation of these terms. Other important tantras are the Hevajra-tantra and the Mahavairochana-tantra. One of the last Sanskrit works to have been written in Central Asia was the Kalachakra-tantra (tenth century AD).

Vajrayana Buddhism in Tibet: During the period Tibet was being converted to Buddhism (seventh to eleventh centuries), the most dynamic form of Buddhism in India was Vajrayana. Thus, it was this Buddhist tradition that became established in Tibet. Among the various Vajrayana schools of Tibet and neighbouring regions are Rnying-ma-pa, Sa-skya-pa, Bka'-brgyud-pa, the Bka'-gdams-pa, and the Dge-lugs-pa. The Dalai and Panchen lamas are members of the Dge-lugs-pa.

Buddhism in the contemporary world: The nineteenth and twentieth centuries have been challenging times for Buddhism. As modern ideas began asserting themselves, the Buddhists' response was twofold. They came to associate Buddhism with the religious and cultural identity that they sought to preserve and reassert in the face of Western domination. In addition, they sought to initiate reforms that would make Buddhism a more appealing and effective force in the modern world.

They attempted to strengthen the Buddhist cause through the initiation of Buddhist missions, including missions to the West. Organizations such as the World Fellowship of Buddhists (founded 1950) and the World Buddhist Sangha Council (1966) were established to promote cooperation among Buddhists from all countries and denominations.

In the religiopolitical sphere, many Buddhist leaders sought to associate Buddhism with various nationalist movements that were struggling to achieve political, economic, and cultural independence. Where these leaders and the nationalist causes with which they associated themselves have been successful, Buddhism has retained a central role in political life. Where they were superseded by other forces (as in China), Buddhism has been relegated to the periphery.

Three emphasis have been especially important in the various reform movements. *First,* many Buddhist leaders have put forward a highly rationalized, Protestant-type interpretation of Buddhism that de-emphasizes the supernormal and ritualized aspects of the tradition and focuses on the supposed continuity between Buddhism and modern science, and on the centrality of ethics and morality. A *second,* closely related emphasis that has been prominent among modern Buddhist reformers represents Buddhism as a form of religious teaching and practice that provides a basis for social, political, and economic life in the modern world. *Finally,* Buddhist reformers have initiated and supported movements that give the Buddhist laity (and in some cases, Buddhist women) a much stronger role than they have had in the past. In the Theravada world, lay societies have been formed, and lay-oriented meditation movements have enjoyed great success.

For more than two millennia Buddhism has been a powerful religious, political, and social force, first in India, its original homeland, and then in many other lands. It remains a powerful religious, political, and cultural force in many parts of the world today.

Buddhist Council, any of the several assemblies convened in the centuries following the death of the Buddha to recite approved texts of scriptures and to settle doctrinal disputes.

The *first council,* held at Rajagriha (modern Rajgir, Bihar), is said to have taken place during the first rainy season following the Buddha's death. Compilations were made of the Buddha's rules of Vinaya (monastic discipline), under the direction of the elder Upali, and of the sutras (instructive aphorisms), under the direction of the disciple Ananda. Many scholars, however, deny that the Council of Rajagrha took place.

The *second council* was held at Vaishali (Bihar) a little more than a century after the Buddha's death. Virtualy all scholars agree that this council was a historical event. It was called to settle a dispute regarding the relaxed rules of discipline followed by the monks of Vaishali. The list of 10 disputed practices differs in various accounts of the council but apparently dealt with such questions as the storing of salt, eating or begging after the prescribed hours, taking the practices of one's tutor as precedent for one's actions, and accepting gold and silver as alms.

The *third council,* held during the reign of the emperor Ashoka at his capital, Pataliputra (modern Patna), about 247 BC, may have been confined to an assembly of the Theravada. By then the faithful had divided into schools and sub-schools holding different interpretations of monastic discipline.

The council that they speak of as the third—and about which the Theravadas, in turn, are silent—was held during the reign of Kanishka at Jalandhara (or, according to other sources, in Kashmir). The uncertainty of Kanishka's dates makes dating of the council equally difficult, but it may have been held in about AD 100. The renowned scholar Vasumitra was named president of thc council;

and, according to one tradition, commentaries on the scriptures were composed under his direction and copies were enclosed in stupas (reliquaries).

In the *modern era,* a notable Buddhist council was the *sixth,* which convened in Yangon (Rangoon) from May 1954 to May 1956 to commemorate the 2,500th anniversary (according to Theravada chronology) of the death of Gautama Buddha. The entire text of the Pali Theravada canon was reviewed and recited by the assembly of monks from Myanmar (Burma), India, Sri Lanka, Nepal, Cambodia, Thailand, Laos, and Pakistan.

C

Chaitya, in Buddhism, a sacred place or object, it was originally said to be the natural home of earth spirits and was most often recognized in small stands of trees or even in a single tree.

It appears that over the years these meditation and pilgrimage groves became the sites for more permanent, probably wooden, structures that housed the people visiting them. From the second century BC to the eighth century AD, chaityas were carved directly into the rock bluffs of the Western Ghats in a style that clearly alludes to wooden prototypes. For example, "beams" were carved into the roofs of the caves. These permanent chaityas characteristically consist of a central rectangular nave, separated from aisles at either side by two pillars that support the roof. Often, small meditation rooms line the periphery of the space, and a semicircular apse stands at one end of the room. Frequently this apse holds a stupa, a solid-domed structure that generally enshrines relics or serves a similar memorial-funerary function and often serves as a focus of Buddhist worship. An outstanding example of a classical chaitya is the magnificent Karli chaitya-hall from the late first century AD near Pune in Maharashtra.

According to Jain and Buddhist texts, from about 200 BC, wandering Indian ascetics often gathered near chaityas to pay homage to the resident deities and to beg alms from local religious pilgrims. Later, the term chaitya assumed the distinctive meaning of a meeting place or meditation grove for mendicant renunciates and a pilgrimage centre for the laity.

Chakravartin, the ancient Indian conception of the world ruler, derived from the Sanskrit chakra, "wheel", and vartin, "one who turns", may be understood to refer to a ruler "whose chariot wheels roll everywhere", or "whose movements are unobstructed".

Buddhist and Jain sources distinguish three types of secular *chakravartin: chakravala chakravartin,* a king who rules over all of the continents covered by ancient Indian cosmography; *dvipa chakravartin,* a ruler who governs only one of those continents and is, therefore, less powerful than the first; and *pradesha chakravartin,* a monarch who leads the people of only a part of a continent, the equivalent of a local king. The first reference to a secular king who achieved the status of a universal monarch, chakravala chakravartin, is to King Ashoka (third century BC). Ashoka does not take the title of *chakravartin* in his inscriptions. He is described as such in later texts. Buddhist and Jain philosophers of this period merged the notion of the universal monarch with the idea of a king of righteousness and maintainer of moral law. The chakravartin was considered to be the secular counterpart of a Buddha, with whom he shared many attributes.

The turning of the wheel can also relate to the wheel of righteousness and moral authority—*dharma*—as in Buddhism. The Buddha's Sarnath sermon is the turning of the wheel of law, and a chakravarti is supposed to ensure the turning of the wheel of righteousness in his kingdom.

Chalukya Dynasty, either of two ancient Indian dynasties, the western Chalukyas ruled as emperors in the Deccan (peninsular India) from AD 543 to 757 and again from about 975 to 1189. The eastern Chalukyas ruled in Vengi (in eastern Andhra Pradesh) from about 624 to 1070.

Between 641 and 647 the Pallavas ravaged the Deccan and captured Vatapi, but the Chalukyas recovered it by 655. They even extended their power in Gujarat. By 660 they had acquired land in Nellore district. Vikramaditya I (reigned 655-680) took Kanchipuram (ancient Kanchi), then the Pallava capital, in about c. 670. Vikramaditya II (reigned 733-746), again captured, but spared, the city in 742. His successor, Kirtivarman II, was replaced by the Rashtrakuta dynasty in 757.

When the last Rashtrakuta fell, in 975, Taila founded the second Western Chalukya dynasty. He named Kalyani as the capital since it was more central. His great achievement was to subdue the Paramara dynasty of Malwa.

The Chola king, Rajaraja I, invaded south Deccan in 993 for the first time. Repeated Chola invasions of the plateau occurred until about 1021. After many tribulations the Chalukya dynasty was supplanted by the Kalachuri family under Bijjala, who usurped the throne in about 1156 and reigned until 1167. The Chalukya dynasty was restored in the person of Someshvara IV, who lost the empire in 1189 to the Yadavas (or Sevunas) of Devagiri, the Hoysalas of Dorasamudra, and the Kakatiyas of Warangal.

The descendants of Kubja Vishnuvardhana constantly had to fight for the riches of Vengi and were pawns in the struggle between the Deccan emperors and the Chola kings. The Cholas eventually adopted the family, and the two countries were united under Kulottunga I (Rajendra II), whose reign began in 1070.

The dynasty was founded by Pulakeshin I, a petty chieftain of Pattadakal in the Bijapur district. His reign began in 543, when he took and fortified the hill fort of Vatapi (modern Badami). He also seized control of the territory between the Krishna and Tungabhadra rivers and the Western Ghats. His son Kirtivarman I (reigned 566-597) secured the valuable Konkan coast. The family then turned its attention to the fertile coastal regions lying northwest and east of the peninsula. Pulakeshin II (reigned c. 610-642) acquired parts of Gujarat and Malwa and defied the North Indian ruler Harsha of Kannauj. The boundary between them was fixed on the Narmada (Narbada) River. In about 624, Pulakeshin II took the kingdom of Vengi from the Visnukundins and gave it to his brother Kubja Visnuvardhana, the first Eastern Chalukya ruler.

Chandela, Rajput clan of Gond origin it ruled Bundelkhand in north-central India for some centuries and fought against the early Muslim invaders.

The Chandela Raja Nanda, or Ganda, assisted Jaipal at Lahore in his campaigns against the Muslim Turks and shared in the great defeat of 1001 near Peshawar by Mahmud of Ghazna (Ghazni). In 1023 the Chandelas lost Kalinjar, which was thereafter an object of contention between Hindus and Muslims. In 1082 they were reduced to slavery by Ajmer. Chandela rule was replaced eventually by that of the Bundelas.

The first Chandela is thought to have ruled early in the ninth century AD. The Chandela kingdom extended from the River Jumna (Yamuna) in the north to the region of Saugor (Sagar) and from the Dhasan River to the west to the Vindhya Hills. Their strongholds were the famous fortress of Kalinjar, together with Khajuraho, Mahoba, and Ajaigarh.

Chandra Gupta I (reigned 320-c. 335), Indian king, founder of the imperial dynasty of the Guptas he was the grandson of Sri Gupta, the first known ruler of the Gupta line. Chandra Gupta I became a local chief in the kingdom of Magadha (in modern Bihar). The suggestion that Chandra Gupta I conquered the Scythians is probably without foundation. Nor is it likely that he overcame the Lichchhavis by killing their king or that he was murdered by his heir. The tradition generally accepted is that the king held an assembly of councillors and royal family members at which Prince Samudra Gupta was was formally nominated to succeed his abdicating father. Not much is known about his early life. He increased his power and territory by marrying, in 308, Princess Kumaradevi of the Lichchhavi tribe, then controlling north Bihar and perhaps Nepal. Towards the close of the third century AD, India consisted of a number of independent states, both monarchical and nonmonarchical. It is highly probable that the Guptas and Lichchhavis ruled over adjoining principalities. Their union by marriage enhanced the power and prestige of the new kingdom. Special gold coins depicted the king and queen on one side and the Lichchhavis on the other. The chronology of the Gupta era, dating from AD 320 and used in India for several centuries, is believed to be based on the date either of his coronation or of his marriage. By the conclusion of his reign, his kingdom probably extended west to the present city of Allahabad and included Ayodhya and south Bihar. These regions were assigned to him by the Puranas (ancient chronicles of early Sanskrit literature). His dominions must have been sufficiently large to justify his assumption of the imperial title *maharajadhiraja*—"king of kings". It also enabled his son Samudra Gupta to begin the conquest that led to the founding of the Gupta Empire.

Chandra Gupta II, also called Vikramaditya (reigned c. 380-c. 415), powerful emperor of northern India, was son of Samudra Gupta and grandson of Chandra Gupta I. A strong and vigorous ruler, Chandra Gupta II was well qualified to govern an extensive empire. Some of his silver coins bear the title Vikramaditya ("Sun of Valour"). Although the emperor generally resided at Ayodhya, which he made his capital, the city of Pataliputra (Patna) also achieved prosperity and grandeur. A benevolent king under whom India enjoyed peace and relative prosperity, he also patronized learning. Among the scholars at his court were the astronomer Varahamihira and the Sanskrit poet and dramatist Kalidasa. The Chinese Buddhist pilgrim Fa-Hsien, who spent six years (405-411) in India during his reign, spoke highly of the system of government, the means for dispensing charity and medicine (the emperor maintained free rest houses and hospitals), and the goodwill of the people. But he never visited the emperor or his court. Chandra Gupta II was a devout Hindu, but he also tolerated the Buddhists and the Jains.

During his reign, art, architecture, and sculpture flourished, and the cultural development of ancient India reached its climax. Chandra Gupta II supposedly achieved power by assassinating a weak elder brother. Inheriting a large empire, he continued the expansion policy of his father Samudra Gupta. He extended his control over neighbouring territories, whether by military or peaceful means. From 388 ro 409 he subjugated Gujarat and Saurashtra, in western India, and Malwa, with its capital Ujjain. These territories were ruled by Shaka chiefs, whose ancestors were Scythian tribes from the regions around Lake Balqash (in Kazakstan). To strengthen his southern flank he arranged a marriage between his daughter Prabhavati and Rudrasena II, king of the Vakatakas. When Rudrasena died, Prabhavati acted as regent for her sons, therey increasing Gupta influence in the south. The emperor may also have made a matrimonial alliance with a dynasty in Mysore. He is also the King Chandra eulogized in the Sanskrit inscription on the iron pillar in the Quwat-ul-Islam mosque in Delhi.

Chandragupta Maurya, (reigned 321-297 BC), founder of the Maurya dynasty, he was the first emperor to unify most of India under one administration.

Chandragupta was born into a family left destitute by the death of his father in a border conflict. He was chief of the migrant Mauryas. His maternal uncles left him with a cowherd who brought him up as his own son. Later, he was sold to a hunter to tend cattle. Purchased by a Brahmin politician, Chanakaya (also called Kautilya), he was taken to Taxila (now in Pakistan), where he received an education in military tactics and the aesthetic arts. Legend goes that while he slept, following a meeting with Alexander the Great, a lion began licking his body, gently waking him and prompting in him hopes of royal dignity. With Chanakya as his adviser, he collected mercenary soldiers, secured public support, and ended the autocracy of the Nanda dynasty in a bloody battle against forces led by their commander-in-chief, Bhaddasala.

Credited with saving the country from maladministration and freeing it from foreign domination, he fasted to death in sorrow for his famine-stricken people.

Chandrakirti (flourished AD 600-650), principal representative of the Prasangika school of Buddhist logic, Chandrakirti wrote the Prasannapada ("the clear-worded")—a well-known commentary on the thoughts of the Buddhist sage Nagarjuna. Although there were several earlier commentaries explaining Nagarjuna, Chandrakirti's became the most authoritative, and it is the only one that has been preserved in its original Sanskrit (other commentaries are available only in Tibetan translation).

Charvaka, also called Lokayata, quasi-philosophical Indian school of materialists who rejected the notion of an afterworld, the authority of the sacred scriptures, the Vedas, and the immortality of the self. Although Charvaka doctrine had disappeared by the end of the medieval period, its onetime importance is confirmed by the lengthy attempts to refute it found in both Buddhist and orthodox Hindu philosophical texts, which also constitute the main sources for knowledge of the doctrine.

Of the recognized means of knowledge (pramana), the Charvaka recognized only direct perception (anubhava). They advocated a policy of total opportunism and are often described in literature as addressing princes, whom they urged to act exclusively in their own self-interest, thus providing the intellectual climate in which a text such as Kautilya's Arthashastra ("Handbook of Profit") could be written.

Chauhan or Chahamana, a clan of Rajputs who claim descendance from an ancient sacrificial fire and who rose to political power in northern India during the early medieval period. The Rajputs were on the fighting edge of an expanding Turk-Islamic frontier along the northwest of the Indian subcontinent for centuries, and Prithviraj's victory against Muhammad Ghor at the first battle of Tarain was much celebrated. Unfortunately, he did not alter his military tactics or form alliances to meet renewed attacks. He was defeated and killed by Muhammad Ghor at the second battle of Tarain in 1192.

A Chauhan Dynasty ruled part of Rajasthan with Ajmer as its capital for many centuries and took control of Delhi in the twelfth century. Prithviraj, or Rai Pithora, was the most famous ruler of that dynasty. A great soldier, he defeated the Chandella King and his deeds of valor and of love—especially his elopement with the daughter of a rival Rajput ruler, Raja Jaychandra of Kanauj, in 1175—continue to be recited by bards to the present day.

Chera Dynasty, one of the three major chiefdoms of Tamilakam, centred on the Malabar Coast and the hinterland. The other two were the Pandyas (Madurai) and the Cholas (Thanjavur and the Kaveri Valley). Chera inscriptions of the second century AD referring to the Irrumporai clan have been found near Karur (Tiruchirappalli district).

Sangam literature mentions the names of Chera chiefs who have been dated to the first century AD. Among them, Nedunjeral

Adam is said to have attacked the Yavana ships and held the Yavana traders to ransom. His son Senguttuvan, much eulogized in the poems, is also mentioned in the context of Gajabahu's rule in Sri Lanka. Since there were two rulers called Gajabahu, this can be dated to either the first or last quarter of the second century AD, depending on whether he was the earlier or the later Gajabahu.

Chola Dynasty, South Indian Tamil rulers of unknown antiquity, antedating the early Sangam poems (probably AD 200), the dynasty originated in the rich Cauvery Valley, Uraiyur (now Tiruchirappalli [Trichinopoly]) being its oldest capital.

Chola kings and emperors bore the titles Parakesharivarman and Rajakesharivarman, alternately. Their chronology is difficult. Vijayalaya (reigned 850-870) began the occupation of the territory of the Pallavas, which was extended under Aditya I (reigned 870-907). Parantaka I (reigned 907-c. 953), known as the destroyer of Madurai (the capital city of the Pandyas), defeated Sinhalese invaders and united the lands of the Cholas and the Pandyas between 926 and 942. He took Nellore from the Rashtrakutas in about 940, but their king, Krishna III, seized Tondaimandalam.

Rajaraja I, who reigned from 985 to 1014, was an able administrator. He protected Vengi (the Godavari districts) and occupied the Gangavadi territory (Karnataka State), annihilating the western Ganga. By 996 he had conquered Kerala (the Chera country) and acquired northern Ceylon (now Sri Lanka). With the booty thus acquired he built the great Brihadishvara temple at Tanjore (now Thanjavur). By 1014 Rajaraja had acquired the Laccadive (now Lakshadweep) and Maldive Islands.

His son Rajendrachola Deva I (reigned 1014-1044) outdid Rajaraja's achievements. He placed a son on the throne at Madurai and completed the conquest of Ceylon. He then overran the Deccan in 1021. In 1023 he sent an expedition to the north that brought the Ganga water to the new capital, Gangaikondacholapuram. He conquered portions of the Malay Peninsula and Archipelago.

Rajadhiraja (reigned 1044-1054) fought the Pandyas and Cheras and defeated the Western Chalukya ruler Someshvara I in 1046, but he was killed at the Battle of Koppam against the Chalukyas in 1054. The Chola ruler Virarajendra (reigned 1063-69) attempted to overcome the Chalukya Empire in the Deccan, but his death enabled Vikramaditya Chalukya to dabble in Chola family quarrels.

Kulottunga I (reigned 1070-1122), who inherited both the Chola and Eastern Chalukya crowns, wisely abandoned the Deccan and concentrated on uniting the eastern coast. Intrigues concerning the right to the Pandya throne embroiled the Cholas, Pandyas, and Ceylon (which by then had recovered its independence) from 1166 onward.

The legendary king Karikalan was the common ancestor through whom small Deccan and Andhra families called Chola, or Choda, claimed a connection with the Uraiyur family. The Chola country (Coromandel) stretched from the Vaigai River in the south to Tondaimandalam, the capital of which was Kanchi (Kanchipuram), in the north. Much of Tamil classical literature and the greater Tamil architectural monuments belong to the Sangam period. This period also saw a revival of Shaivism (worship of Shiva) and the development of southern Vaishnavism (worship of Vishnu). Revenue administration, village self-government, and irrigation were highly organized under the Cholas.

While the Hoysala kings acquired lands in the Chola country from 1216, former Chola feudatories threw off their allegiance. At the same time, northern powers intervened. The ensuing chaos facilitated the Pandya conquest of the Chola country in 1257. The Chola dynasty ended in 1279.

D

Dandin, Indian writer of Sanskrit prose romances and expounder on poetics, he flourished in late sixth and early seventh centuries. The *Dashakumaracharita,* translated in 1927 as *The Adventures of the Ten Princes,* and the *Kavyadarsha* ("Mirror of Poetry") are the two important works generally attributed to him with certainty.

The *Dashakumaracharita* relates the vicissitudes of 10 princes in their pursuit of love and royal power. The work is imbued both with realistic portrayals of human vice and with supernatural magic, including the intervention of deities in human affairs.

The *Kavyadarsha* is a work of literary criticism defining the ideas of style and sentiment appropriate to each genre of *kavya* (poetry).

Dasa, Dasyu, members of an aboriginal people in India encountered by the incoming Aryan settlers of India c. 1500 BC, they were a dark-skinned, harsh-spoken people who worshipped the phallus. They lived in fortified places from which they sent out armies. They may be considered the original Shudras, or labourers, who served the three higher classes of Brahmins (priests), Kshatriyas (warriors), and Vaishyas (merchants), but from whose ritual communion they were excluded.

Devadasi, caste of women connected originally with the great temples in southern India, they dedicated themselves to the service of each temple's patron god.

The caste appears to date from the ninth and tenth centuries, the great period of temple building in South India. In 1800 there were about 100 *devadasis* attached to the main temple of Kanchipuram (in Tamil Nadu). The sons and daughters of a *devadasi* had equal rights of inheritance, an unusual custom among Hindus at the time.

Traditionally, young girls were "married" to the temple deity. These *devadasis* then spent the rest of their lives attending the god, fanning the idol, honouring it with lights, and singing and dancing for the god's amusement.

Devadasis played an important role in preserving the cultural heritage of the region, but since their occupation also involved temple prostitution, they came to be held in low social regard. Following a ban on temple prostitution the caste began to disappear.

Devadatta, Buddhist monk who sought to reform the *sangha* by imposing upon it a stricter code of life, he was a cousin of the Buddha.

Devadatta is said to have joined the *sangha* along with Ananda, who was possibly his brother, in the twentieth year of Gautama Buddha's ministry. Fifteen years later, strengthened by his friendship with the crown prince of Magadha, Ajatashatru, Devadatta proposed formally at a meeting of the *sangha* that the Buddha retire and hand over the leadership to him. This proposal was rejected, and Devadatta is said to have successfully instigated Ajatashatru to execute Bimbisara, his aged father, the king of Magadha, and to have made three abortive attempts to kill the Buddha—by hiring assassins, by rolling a rock off a mountainside at him, and by arranging for a mad elephant to be let loose in the street at the time of the collection of alms.

Sensing popular approval, Devadatta proposed stricter ascetic rules for the *sangha*. When these were refused, he persuaded some 500 of the Buddha's followers to join in a secession. Nothing further is known about Devadatta's movement, but it may possibly be referred to under the name of the Gotamakas in the Anguttara Nikaya (a canonical text), for Devadatta's family name was Gotama (Gautama). The Chinese pilgrim Hsuan-tsang recorded that in the seventh century monks of a monastery in Bengal were following a certain regulation of Devadatta's.

Dhammapada, probably the best-known book in the Pali

Buddhist canon and the most quoted in other Buddhist writings, it is an anthology of basic Buddhist teachings (primarily ethical teachings) written in a simple, proverbial style. The book is popular in Buddhist countries of both Theravada and Mahayana traditions. In Sri Lanka it has been used for centuries as a manual for novices, and it is said that every monk can recite it from memory. The Dhammapada contains 423 stanzas arranged in 26 chapters. It also appears in somewhat different versions in Prakrit, Sanskrit, and Chinese, and there are translations in other languages. More than half the verses are excerpted from other canonical texts and include many of the most famous Buddhist sayings; others come from the storehouse of pithy sayings drawn upon by much of Indian literature.

Dhanvantari, Dhanwantari, in Hindu mythology is the physician of the gods. According to legend, the gods and the demons sought the fluid of immortality (*amrita*) by churning the milky ocean, and Dhanvantari rose out of the waters bearing a cup filled with the elixir. Ayurveda, the foremost system of traditional Hindu medicine, is also attributed to him. The name has also been applied to other semilegendary and historical physicians and to a legendary king.

Dharma, is a key concept with multiple meanings in Hinduism, Buddhism, and Jainism.

In Buddhism, *dharma* is the universal truth common to all individuals at all times, as discovered and proclaimed by Gautama Buddha. *Dharma*, the Buddha, and the *sangha* (the Buddhist monastic order) make up the *triratna*, or "three jewels", the primary sources of Buddhist doctrine and practice. In Buddhist metaphysics the term in the plural (*dharmas*) is used to describe the interrelated elements that make up the empirical world.

In Hinduism *dharma* is the religious and moral law which governs individual and group conduct; it is one of the four ends of life. One of its distinctive features is its contextual sensitivity. Although certain aspects of *dharma* are regarded as universal and perennial, others are to be followed according to one's class, status, and station in life. *Dharma* constitutes the subject matter of the Dharmasutras, religious manuals that are the earliest source of Hindu law, and in the course of time was extended into lengthy compilations of law and custom, the Dharmashastras. The best-known Dharmashastra is the *Manusmriti*, which had become authoritative by the early centuries AD, but it remains a question whether it ever functioned in actual judicial practice until British authorities integrated certain aspects of it into colonial law.

In Jain philosophy, *dharma*, in addition to being commonly understood as moral virtue, also has the meaning—unique to Jainism—of an eternal "substance" (*dravya*), the supporting medium that allows beings to move.

Dharmapala, in Tibetan Buddhism, any one of a group of eight divinities who, though benevolent, are represented as hideous and ferocious in order to instil terror in evil spirits, the *dharmapalas* are worshipped in the *mgon khang*, a subterranean room, the entrance to which is often guarded by stuffed wild yaks or leopards. Priests wear special vestments and use ritual instruments often made of human bone or skin. Worship includes the performance of masked dances ('cham).

The *dharmapalas* are shown in painting, in sculpture, and in masks used by dancers as scowling figures with a third eye and dishevelled hair, wearing crowns of skulls and garlands of severed heads; they are depicted treading on human beings or animals, usually in the company of their female consorts. They are worshipped singly or in a group called the "Eight Terrible Ones", which most commonly includes the following: (1) Lha-mo (Tibetan: "Goddess"; Sanskrit: Shri-devi, or Kala-devi), fierce city goddess of Lhasa and the only feminine divinity in the group; (2) Tshangs-pa Dkar-po (Tibetan: "White Brahma"; Sanskrit: Sita-Brahma); (3) Beg-tse (Tibetan: "Hidden Sheet of Mail"); (4) Yama (Sanskrit; Tibetan: Gshin-rje), the god of death, who may be accompanied by his sister, Yami; (5) Kubera, or Vaishravana (Tibetan: Rnam-thos-sras), god of wealth and the only one among the eight who is never represented in a fierce form; (6) Mahakala (Sanskrit: "Great Black One"; Tibetan: Mgon-po); (7) Hayagriva (Sanskrit: "Horse Neck"; Tibetan: rta-mgrin); and (8) Yamantaka (Sanskrit: "Conqueror of Yama, or Death"; Tibetan: Gshin-rje-gshed).

Worship of *dharmapalas* was initiated in the eighth century by the magician-saint Padmasambhava, who is said to have conquered the malevolent deities in Tibet and forced them to take an oath promising to protect Buddhists and the Buddhist faith. Many of the *dharmapalas* can be linked to Hindu, Bon (the indigenous religion of Tibet), or folk deities.

Dharmashastra, ancient Indian body of jurisprudence that is still fundamentally the family law of Hindus living in territories outside India (for example, Pakistan, Malaysia, and East Africa) and is in force, subject to legislative modification, in India. Dharmashastra is not primarily concerned with legal administration but with the right course of conduct in every dilemma.

Dharmashastra is equal in age to Jewish law (or older, if its roots do indeed go back to the Vedas), but its sources are more accessible, more varied, and less codified. It differs from Roman law in these respects but especially in its greater continuity and longevity. The British colonial administration in India affected the system of Hindu law by applying the traditional rules in a hard-and-fast way and by introducing the concept of precedent. Rapid social change, following foreign rule, required many adjustments to India's body of Hindu law. For example, there was no provision in the Dharmashastra for the development of judicial divorce or the allotting of equal shares in their fathers' estate to daughters along with sons at the father's death. This would have necessitated inventing new texts, which was impossible. Hence legislation, initially piecemeal and later (in 1955-1956) comprehensively, altered the system of Indian law administered in the courts. Gradually, as judges lost familiarity with Sanskrit, the ancient texts began to be replaced with contemporary, cosmopolitan juridical, and social concepts.

Dharmashastra literature, which is written in Sanskrit, exceeds 5,000 titles. It can be divided into three categories: (1) *sutras* (terse maxims); (2) *smritis* (shorter or longer treatises in stanzas); and (3) *nibandhas* (digests of *smritis* verses from various quartesr) and *vrittis* (commentaries upon individual continuous *smritis*). The *nibandhas* and *vrittis* are judicial works intended for legal advisers and exhibit considerable skill in harmonizing divergent *sutras* and *smritis*.

The techniques of Dharmashastra are mainly to state the ancient text, maxim, or stanza and to explain its meaning, to reconcile deviating traditions, if necessary by use of the traditional science of interpretation (*mimamsa*). Dharmashastra permits custom to be enforced if it can be ascertained and if its terms are not offensive to the principles of life as understood by Brahmins (the priestly class). Brahmin ethics have given Dharmashastra its intensity and provided a test under which many customs of the Hindu people could be administered by Hindu kings. Courts and their procedures are dealt with comprehensively too. Most Hindus brought up in a traditional environment are familiar with some basic principles of Dharmashastra. These include the beliefs that duties are more significant than rights, that women are under constant guardianship of their closest male relatives, and that the king (the State) must protect the subjects from all harm, moral as well as material.

This ancient Hindu legal practice was introduced to the West by Sir William Jones, the eighteenth-century British Orientalist and jurist. Many who followed him, for example, Sir Henry Maine (1822-1888), believed Dharmashastra was a kind of priestcraft, intended to keep the lowest castes, the Shudras and the "untouchables", under the control of the higher castes. The close study of the Dharmashastra by German and Italian scholars, principally G. Buhler, Julius Jolly, and Giuseppe Mazzarella, showed its psychological and sociological potential.

Dharmasutra, any of several manuals of human conduct that form the earliest source of Hindu law, they consist chiefly of strings of terse rules containing the essentials of law relating to man and his fellow beings and to man and the State. The maxims deal with the practical rules of caste and of human beings in their social, economic, and religious relations. Formulated in prose, they were intended to be committed to memory and expounded orally by teachers—thus forming, as it were, epitomes of class lectures.

Eventually these rules came to be interspersed with verses in various metres, each generally giving the meaning of the rule immediately preceding it. The verses themselves became increasingly popular and ultimately led to the appearance of works entirely in verse. These melodic versions of previously existing Dharmasutras came to be called Dharmashastras. In modern times that term is more commonly used to denote the whole body of customary rules and observances governing Hindu religious and social life.

Dhyani-Buddha, in Mahayana and Vajrayana (Tantric) Buddhism, any of a group of five "self-born" Buddhas, they have always existed from the beginning of time. The five are usually identified as Vairochana, Akshobhya, Ratnasambhava, Amitabha, and Amoghasiddhi.

The five are almost identically represented in art—all dressed in monastic garments, seated with folded legs, with the same hairdress and long-lobed ears—but are distinguished by characteristic colours, symbols, poses of hands, and the directions they face.

According to the full exposition of this scheme, most of the other deities in the vast Buddhist pantheon are related to one of the five Buddhas as members of his "family"; reflect his distinguishing characteristics, such as colour, direction, and symbol; and when represented in art often carry an image of the "parent" Buddha in their crown. Each of the self-born Buddhas is also said to have manifested himself as an earthly Buddha and as a *bodhisattva* ("Buddha-to-be"). Each has his own consort, mount, sacred syllable, natural element, particular sense organ, special sense perception, and symbolic location in the human body.

In order to encounter any tendency toward polytheism suggested by the fivefold scheme, some sects elevated one of the five, usually Vairochana, to a position of an Adi-Buddha (first, or primal, Buddha). Sometimes a sixth deity is worshipped as the Adi-Buddha. The Lamaist sects of Tibet identify the Adi-Buddha as Vajradhara; some sects of Nepal give this position to Vajrasattva.

Scholars in recent years have pointed out that the term Dhyani-Buddha does not appear in the original texts, but the term continues to be commonly used, particularly in describing groups of images composed of five meditating Buddhas—as in *mandalas* (ritual meditation designs), on the four sides and top of votive *stupas* (commemorative monuments), or on the terraces of the great monument at Borobudur in Indonesia.

Digambara, in Jainism, it is one of the two principal sects, whose male ascetics wear no clothes and shun all property. The ascetics of the other sect, the Shvetambara ("White-Robed"), wear white robes.

Besides monastic nudity, the other beliefs of the Digambaras with which the Shvetambaras differ include the following: (1) the perfect saint (*kevalin*) does not need food to stay alive; (2) Mahavira never married; (3) no woman can reach *moksha* without being reborn as a man; and (4) al Tirthankaras, when rendered as images, must be portrayed as naked, without ornaments, and with downcast eyes. The Digambaras do not recognize the Shvetambara canon of religious texts but maintain that the early literature was gradually forgotten and lost completely by the second century AD.

Some time at the beginning of the Common Era, the Digambaras and Shvetambaras finally separated over the issue of whether it was possible for a monk who owned property (even clothes) to attain *moksha* (release from earthly existence). Although the interpretation of the philosophical doctrine of Jainism by the two groups did not differ significantly, variations in their rituals, mythology, and literature appeared over time and, many disputes have arisen, lasting to this day, over ownership of holy places.

The split that gave rise to the two sects is traditionally said to have taken place when the Jain monks migrated southward from the Ganga River or from Ujjain to Karnataka during a serious famine in the reign of Chandragupta Maurya. Bhadrabahu, the leader of the emigrants, insisted on the men wearing no clothes, thus following the example set by Mahavira, the last Tirthankara, or saving teacher.

Sthulabhadra, the leader of the monks who remained behind in the north, allowed the wearing of white garments.

The Digambara influence in southern India during the medieval period was considerable, but it diminished in importance in that area as Hindu devotional Shaivism and Vaishnavism grew. The sect continues mainly in southern Maharashtra, Karnataka, and Rajasthan States with about one million followers.

Dvija, in the Hindu social system, it is a characteristic of the members of the three upper *varnas,* or social orders—the Brahmins (priests and teachers), Kshatriya (warriors), and Vaishya (merchants)—whose sacrament of initiation is regarded as a second or spiritual birth. The initiation ceremony (*upanayana*) invests the male caste members with a sacred thread, a loop worn next to the skin over the left shoulder and across the right hip. The lowest Hindu *varna,* the Shudra (the artisan and labouring class), has no initiation ceremony, and its members are considered to be non-Aryan in origin.

E

Eightfold Path, Pali *Atthangika-magga,* Sanskrit *Ashtangika-marga,* it is a doctrine taught by Gautama Buddha in his first sermon at the deer park near Banaras (Varanasi).

The Eightfold Path consists of: (1) *right understanding*—which implies belief in the Four Noble Truths as the basis of all existence; (2) *right thought*—which is the resolve to practice the faith; (3) right speech—or the avoidance of falsehoods, slander, or abusive speech; (4) *right action*—which means abstaining from taking life, stealing, and improper sexual behaviour; (5) *right livelihood*—rejection of occupations not in keeping with Buddhist principles; (6) *right effort*—which means the avoidance of bad and development of good mental states; (7) *right mindfulness*—the awareness of the body, feelings, and thought; (8) *right concentration*—which means meditation.

Together with the Four Noble Truths, of which it forms a part, the Eightfold Path sums up the whole of Buddhist teaching. It is also called the Middle Path, as it steers a course between the sensual pleasures of the materialists and the self-mortification of the ascetics. Those who follow the noble Eightfold Path are freed from the suffering that is an essential part of human existence and are led ultimately to Nirvana, or Enlightenment. Some Buddhist teachings have held that to enter this path in itself implies an experience of Nirvana.

Ellora Caves, series of magnificent rock-cut temples of the seventh and eighth centuries, they are situated near the village of Ellora, central Maharashtra State, western India, 29 km northeast of Aurangabad town. Excavated out of rock cliffs overlooking a plain and being of Buddhist, Hindu, and Jain origins, the most remarkable of the monuments is the monolithic Kailash Temple, 50 m long and 29 m high, cut from a single outcropping of rock. It is extensively carved with exceptionally vigorous sculptures of Hindu divinities and mythological figures, many in erotic poses. The temple, dedicated to the god Shiva, was built in the eighth century during the reign of the Rashtrakutas. Ellora attracts many thousands of tourists annually.

F

Fa-Hsein, Fa-hien, original name Sehi, Chinese Buddhist monk whose pilgrimage to India in AD 402 initiated Sino-Indian relations and whose writings give important information about early Buddhism.

Sehi, who later adopted the spiritual name Fa-hsien ("Splendour of Religious Law"), was born at Shansi during the fourth century AD. Living at the time of the Eastern Chin dynasty, when Buddhism enjoyed an imperial favour seldom equalled in Chinese history, he was stirred by a profound faith to go to India, the "Holy Land" of Buddhism, in order to visit the sites of the Buddha's life and to bring back Buddhist texts that were still unknown in China.

In northwestern India, which he entered in 402, Fa-hsien visited the most important seats of Buddhist learning: Udyana, Gandhara, Peshawar, and Taxila. Above all, however, he was attracted by eastern India, where the Buddha had spent his life and had taught his doctrines. His pilgrimage was completed by visits to the most holy spots: Kapilavastu, where the Buddha was born; Bodh Gaya where the Buddha acquired the supreme Enlightenment; Banaras (Varanasi), where the Buddha preached his first sermon; and Kushinagara, where the Buddha attained Nirvana. Everywhere Fa-hsien was amazed at the extraordinary flowering of the Buddhist faith.

Then he stayed a long time at Pataliputra, conversing with Buddhist monks, studying Sanskrit texts with Buddhist scholars, and transcribing the Vinaya of the Mahasanghika school. He also acquired another version of the Vinaya, worked out by the Sarvastivada school—an early Buddhist group that taught the equal reality of all mental states (past, present, and future)—and the famous Mahaparinirvana-sutra.

When he had deepened his knowledge of Buddhism and was in possession of sacred texts that were not yet translated into Chinese, he decided to go back to China. Instead of once more taking the overland route, however, Fa-hsien took the sea route, first sailing to Ceylon (Sri Lanka), at that time one of the most flourishing centres of Buddhist studies. There, by securing the Mahishasaka Vinaya—a recension of the Hinayana Vinaya—and a selection of the Sarvastivada canon, he added to the number of Buddhist texts that he had collected.

After a two-year stay in Ceylon, Fa-hsien set sail for China, but the perils of the sea were as great as the hardships and dangers of the desert and mountains he had faced in coming to India. A violent storm drove his ship onto an island that was probably Java. He took another boat bound for Canton. Instead of landing at the south China port, Fa-hsien's ship was driven astray by another storm and was finally blown to a port on the Shantung Peninsula. In all, Fa-hsien spent more than 200 days at sea. After returning to his homeland, Fa-hsien resumed his scholarly tasks and translated into Chinese the Buddhist texts he had taken so much trouble to bring back.

The historical importance of Fa-hsien is twofold. On the one hand, a famous record of his journeys—*Fo Kuo Chi* ("Record of Buddhist Kingdoms")—contains valuable information, not found elsewhere, concerning the history of Indian Buddhism during the early centuries AD. Because of the fairly detailed descriptions of Fa-hsien, it is possible to envision Buddhist India before it was reconquered by the counter reforms of Hinduism and eclipsed by the Muslim invasion. On the other hand, he strengthened Chinese Buddhism by helping provide a better knowledge of Buddhist sacred texts. After studying them for 10 years in India, he brought back to China a great number of copies of Buddhist texts and translated them from Sanskrit into Chinese. Among them, two of the most important were the Mahaparinirvanasutra, a text glorifying the eternal, personal, and pure nature of Nirvana (Enlightenment)—on which the Nirvana school in China then based its doctrines—and the Vinaya (rules of discipline for the monks) of the Mahasanghika school, which thus became available for the regulation of the numerous monastic communities in China.

Four Noble Truths, the essence of Buddhist religious doctrine, these four truths are universally recognized by all Buddhist schools.

The causes of suffering are expressed in a formula of 12 interdependent stages (*pratitya-samutpada*) that form an infinitely repeating cycle of coming and becoming. The breaking of this cycle constitutes cessation of suffering and freedom from rebirth. Expounded by Gautama Buddha in his first sermon at the deer park near Banaras (Varanasi), India, shortly after his having attained Enlightenment, the four truths are: (1) existence is suffering (*dukkha*); (2) this suffering has a cause (*samudaya*); (3) it can be suppressed (*nirodha*); and (4) there is a way (*magga*) to acomplish this, the noble Eightfold Path.

G

Gahadavala Dynasty, one of the many ruling families of North India on the eve of the Ghorid conquests in the twelfth-thirteenth century AD, its history, ranging between the second half of the eleventh century and the mid-thirteenth century, illustrates all the features of early medieval North Indian polity—dynastic hostilities and alliances, feudal-state structure, absolute dependence on Brahminical ideology, and vulnerability in the face of external aggressions.

The family most probably originated in the Varanasi-Ayodhya area in Uttar Pradesh. Later it came to be associated with Kannauj, which had become a key political centre in India. Most of the Gahadavala epigraphic records were discovered in Uttar Pradesh and issued from Varanasi. Dynastic power became gradually consolidated in the reign of the first three rulers: Yashovi-Graha, Mahichandra, and Chandradeva (c. 1089-1103). By the period of Chandradeva, the Gahadavalas had taken control of Varanasi, Ayodhya, Kannauj, and Indrasthaniyaka (modern Delhi) and expanded all over Uttar Pradesh. The Gahadavalas sought to ward off the growing menace of Muslim invasions by advantageous alliances and the payment of tributes. This continued until the period of Chandradeva's son Madanapala (reigned c. 1104-1113), who was, in all probability, the Kannauj king imprisoned and later released during the period of Ghaznavid sultan Masud III. Despite the regularity of Muslim attacks, which were repulsed by Govindachandra temporarily, the Gahadavalas endeavoured to spread eastward. Govindachandra expanded to the Patna and Monghyr (now Munger) districts in Bihar, and in 1168-1169 southwestern Bihar was being ruled by a feudatory of his son Vijayachandra (reigned c. 1155-1169). Records suggest that Govindachandra had varied relations with an impressive number of Indian and foreign countries. The hostilities with such powers as the Palas, Senas, and the Kalachuris appear to be substantially factual despite exaggeration.

The weakness of the internal structure of the Gahadavala kingdom was finally exposed late in the twelfth century during the invasions of Muizz-ud-Din Muhammad of Ghur. Jayachandra (reigned c. 1170-1194), who held Uttar Pradesh and parts of Bihar, had bitter enmity with the Chahamanas of Rajasthan according to certain sources. He lost the battle and his life at Chandawar (Etawah district, Uttar Pradesh) in an encounter with Muhammad of Ghur. Although the Gahadavalas lingered in Harishchandra's reign (c. 1194?) in Kannauj, Jaunpur, and Mirzapur districts until 1197, the buildup of Muslim expansion in these areas was steady through the early thirteenth century. Gahadavala royalty met an obscure fate, sometime before the middle of the thirteenth century. Around this time the last known Gahadavala escaped to Nagod in central India, after which nothing was heard of the dynasty.

Ganapatya, a member of an esoteric Hindu sect devoted to the worship of the elephant-headed Ganesha (also called Ganapati, "Lord of the People") as the supreme deity. Ganesha was worshipped both by meditating upon his image and by offering him fruit and flowers without meditation. Sect members wore a red circle on their foreheads and branded themselves on the shoulders with the mark of an elephant's face and tusk.

The sect was at its height in about the tenth century and helped to establish Ganesha as an important deity to be propitiated at the beginning of all important undertakings and religious ceremonies. The sect erected temples dedicated to Ganesha, the largest of which is the Ucchi-pillaiyar Kovil, a rock-cut temple in Tiruchirappalli (Tamil Nadu).

Gandhara Art, style of visual art it developed between the first century BC and the seventh century AD in what is now northwestern Pakistan and eastern Afghanistan. The Gandhara region had long been a crossroad of cultural influences. During the reign of the Indian emperor Ashoka (third century BC), the region became the scene of intensive Buddhist missionary activity; and, in the first century AD, rulers of the Kushan empire, which included Gandhara, maintained contacts with Rome. The Gandhara school incorporated many motifs and techniques from classical Roman art, including vine scrolls, cherubs bearing garlands, tritons, and centaurs. The basic iconography, however, remained Indian. The style, of Greco-Roman origin, seems to have flourished largely during the Kushan dynasty and was contemporaneous with an important but dissimilar school of Kushan art at Mathura (Uttar Pradesh, India).

Gandhara's role in the evolution of the Buddha image has been a point of considerable disagreement among scholars. The schools of Gandhara and Mathura each independently evolved its own characteristic depiction of the Buddha in about the first century AD. The Gandhara school, drawing on the traditions of Roman religion, represented the Buddha with a youthful face, dressed in clothes resembling those seen on Roman imperial statues. The schools of Gandhara and Mathura influenced each other, and the general trend was away from a naturalistic composition and toward a more idealized, abstract image. The Gandharan craftsmen made a lasting contribution to Buddhist art in their composition of the events of the Buddha's life into set scenes.

Ganga Dynasty, either of two distinct but remotely related Indian dynasties, the Western Gangas ruled in Mysore State (Gangavadi) from about AD 250 to about 1004 while the Eastern Gangas ruled Kalinga from 1028 to 1434-1435.

The first ruler of the Western Ganga, Konganivarman, created a kingdom by conquest, but his successors, Madhava I and Harivarman, expanded their influence by marital and military alliances with the Pallavas, Chalukyas, and Kadambas. By the end of the eighth century a dynastic dispute had weakened the Gangas. It was Butuga II (c. 937-960) who again rejuvenated the dynasty. He obtained extensive territories between the Tungabhadra and the Krishna rivers, ruling from Talakad (the capital) to Vatapi. Repeated Chola invasions cut the contact between Gangavadi and the imperial capital, and Talakad fell into the hands of the Chola ruler Vishnuvardhana in about 1004. Most of the Western Gangas were Jains, but some patronized Brahminical Hinduism. They encouraged scholarly work in Kannada (Kanarese), built some remarkable temples, and encouraged deforestation, irrigation, and cross-peninsular trade.

The Eastern Gangas arose to intermarry with and challenge the Cholas and Chalukyas in the period when the Western Gangas had been forced to abandon this role. Early dynasties of the Eastern Gangas ruled in Orissa from the eighth century; but Vajrahasta III, who assumed the title of Trikalingadhipat (ruler of the three Kalingas) in 1028, was probably the first to rule all three divisions of Kalinga.

His son Rajraraja I waged war upon the Cholas and the Eastern

Chalukyas and strengthened the dynasty by marrying a Chola princess, Rajasundari. Their son, Anantavarman Codagangadeva, ruled from the mouth of the Ganga River in the north to the mouth of the Godavari River in the south. He began building the magnificent Jagannatha temple at Puri at the end of the eleventh century. Rajaraja III ascended the throne in 1198 and did nothing to resist the Muslims of Bengal, who invaded Orissa in 1206. Rajaraja's son Anangabhima III, however, repulsed the Muslims and built the temple of Megheshvara at Bhubaneswar. Narasimha I, the son of Anangabhima, invaded southern Bengal in 1243. He defeated its Muslim ruler, captured the capital (Gauda), and built the Sun Temple at Konarak to commemorate his victory. With the death of Narasimha in 1264, the Eastern Gangas began to decline. The sultan of Delhi invaded Orissa in 1324, Muslims raided it in 1353, and Vijaynagar defeated Orissa in 1356. Narasimha IV, the last known king of the Eastern Ganga dynasty, ruled until 1425. The "mad king", Bhanudeva IV, who succeeded him, left no inscriptions. His minister Kapilendra usurped the throne and founded the Suryavamsha dynasty in 1434-1435. The Eastern Gangas were great patrons of religion and the arts, and the temples of the Ganga period rank among the masterpieces of Hindu architecture.

Gauda, also known as Gaur, in ancient India, city, country, and a literary style, its first recorded reference is by the grammarian Panini (fifth century BC), and its location is assumed to have been in eastern India.

The name is often used in a wider sense for the western parts of Bengal, as opposed to Vanga (modern Bangladesh). From early times the inhabitants of Gauda were known as sea-farers. In literature, the poetic style *gauda*, or *gaudi*, also known as *prachya* (eastern), is described by Dandin in *Kavyadarsha*—his work on poetics. The name Gauda, in Sanskrit literature, is commonly applied to a country in present-day eastern India. In this sense it occurs fairly widely in the Puranas and other sources. It always seems to have coincided roughly with an area south of the Ganga River in West Bengal.

Gitagovinda, lyrical poem celebrating the romance of Krishna and his beloved, Radha, renowned both for its high literary value and for its expression of religious longing, it is particularly popular among Vaishnavas (followers of Lord Vishnu, of whom Krishna was an incarnation) of India.

The highly original form of the poem, which inspired many later imitations, intersperses the recitative stanzas with 24 eight-line songs. The religious drama of the worshipper's yearning for God is expressed through the idiom of human courtship and love. The *Gitagovinda* is the earliest-known poem dealing with the theme of the divine lovers, Radha and Krishna. Its verses were popular with Chaitanya, the fourteenth-fifteenth-century Bengali saint, and continue to be sung even today at *bhajans* and *kirtans* (gatherings for devotion through song) throughout India. The *Gitagovinda* was also the inspiration for many beautiful miniature paintings of the Rajasthani and Pahari schools in the seventeenth and eighteenth centuries.

The poem was written in Sanskrit by Jayadeva, who was attached to the Bengali court of King Lakshmana Sena (late twelfth century).

Gommateshvara, also called Bahubali, the son of Rishabhanatha, the first Tirthankara, of Jainism, he is most famously depicted as a colossal tenth-century sculpture, which stands on top of a hill at Shravana Belgola, a centre of the Digambara sect in Karnataka. Carved out of a single rock, the figure is 17.5 m tall, one of the largest freestanding images in the world. Every 12 years, the entire statue is ceremonially bathed in curd, milk and *ghee*.

Gorakhnath, also called Gorakshnatha, a Hindu master yogi, commonly regarded as the founder of the Nath, or Kanphata, yogis, an order of ascetics that stresses the physical and spiritual disciplines of Hatha Yoga.

Gorakhnath is traditionally regarded as the disciple of Matsyendranath, who is in turn understood by Nath *yogis* as the first human guru in their teaching succession. Historically, Matsyendranath probably preceded Gorakhnath by at least three centuries. But the connection points to an important transition that Gorakhnath instituted in Tantric or Siddha practice, diverting its erotic, mystical heritage in the direction of austere Hatha Yoga.

Several Sanskrit works are attributed to Gorakhnath, under the title *Gorakh Samhita* ("Collections of Gorakh", thirteenth century?); equally significant is the vernacular poetry attributed to him, anthologized under the title *Gorakh Bani* ("Gorakh's Utterances").

The details of Gorakhnath's life are obscured by the numerous legends that have grown up around his supposedly miraculous powers. Apparently of a low-caste family, Gorakhnath either was born in, or spent a good part of his lifetime in, the Punjab and travelled widely. He was said to have met with such other religious teachers as Kabir and Nanak (though this is chronologically impossible) and to have popularized the practice of *yoga* throughout India.

Grihyasutra, any of the Hindu religious manuals these detail the domestic religious ceremonies performed by the householder over his own fire. The Grihyasutras describe the ceremonies (*samskaras*) that mark each stage of a man's life, from the moment of his conception to his final death rites; the five daily sacrifices (*mahayajna*); seasonal ceremonies; and those observed on special occasions, such as house-building or cattle-breeding. Together with the Shrautasutras (which deal with the grand Vedic sacrifices) and the Dharmasutras (which deal with rules of conduct), they make up the Kalpasutras. The Kalpasutras are collections of brief aphoristic texts that emerged within the different schools of the Vedas (the earliest sacred literature of India).

Gupta Dynasty, rulers of the Magadha State in northeastern India (later Bihar) that flourished from the early fourth to the late sixth century AD, they maintained an empire over northern India and parts of central and western India. The founder was Chandra Gupta I. Development in all spheres took place during the flourishing Gupta era. The decimal system of notation and some great Sanskrit epics were produced in this era. Hindu art and the sciences of astronomy, mathematics, and metallurgy all prospered.

Gurjara-Pratihara Dynasty, either of two dynasties of medieval Hindu India, the lineage of Harichandra ruled in Mandor, Marwar (Jodhpur, Rajasthan), during the sixth-ninth century AD, generally with feudatory status, while the family of Nagabhata ruled first at Ujjain and later at Kannauj during the eighth-eleventh century. Other Gurjara lines existed, but they did not take the surname Pratihara.

The relation of the earlier Harichandra line with the later and more important line of Nagabhata is uncertain. The founder of the later line, Nagabhata I (eighth century), most probably ruled in Malwa, and his grand-nephew Vatsaraja is attested as king of Ujjain in 783. Vatsaraja suffered a great defeat at the hands of the Rashtrakutas. Both he and his son Nagabhata II seem to have accepted Rashtrakuta suzerainty for a time. In the complicated and badly documented wars of the early ninth century—involving the Pratiharas, Rashtrakutas, and Palas—Nagabhata II played an important part. In about 816 he invaded the Gangetic region and captured Kannauj from the local king Chakrayudha, who had the protection of the Pala ruler, Dharmapala. With the power of the Rashtrakutas weakened, Nagabhata II became the most powerful ruler of northern India and established his new capital at Kannauj. Nagabhata II was succeeded by his son Ramabhadra about 833.

After a brief reign, Ramabhadra was succeeded by his son Mihira Bhoja in about 836. Under Bhoja and his successor Mahendrapala (reigned c. 890-910) the Pratihara empire reached its peak of prosperity and power. The extent of its territory rivalled that of the Guptas. Under Mahendrapala, their domain extended from Gujarat and Kathiawar to northern Bengal, though much of it was loosely held under vassal kings.

The Pratiharas were the most important dynasty of medieval northern India, and their disappearance marked a stage in the political decline that accompanied the Muslim conquest.

After the death of Mahendrapala the succession is obscure. The power of the Pratiharas was apparently weakened by dynastic infighting. It was further diminished as a result of a great raid from the Deccan, led by the Rashtrakuta king Indra III, who had ravaged Kannauj in about 916. Under a succession of rather obscure kings the Pratiharas never regained their former influence. Their feudatories became more and more powerful. One by one they threw off their allegiance, until by the end of the tenth century the Pratiharas controlled little more than the Gangetic Doab. Their last important king, Rajyapala, was driven from Kannauj by Mahmud of Ghazni in 1018. He was later killed by the forces of the Chandela king Vidyadhara. A small Pratihara principality apparently survived in the Allahabad district for another generation.

The origin of the Gurjaras is uncertain. Most historians believe the Gurjaras had an indigenous origin. The name Gurjara does not appear before the end of the sixth century.

H

Harappa, was village on the left bank of a now dry course of the Ravi River where one of the world's oldest civilizations existed. It is west-southwest of the town of Sahiwal in the Punjab, in eastern Pakistan.

The excavations revealed that Harappa was similar in plan to Mohenjodaro. There is a citadel resting on a raised area on the western flank of the town and a grid-plan layout of workers' quarters on the eastern flank. The citadel was fortified by a tall mud-brick barricade that had rectangular salients, or bastions, placed at frequent intervals. Between the citadel and the Ravi River there existed barrack-like blocks of workmen's quarters, along with a series of circular brick floors that were used for pounding grain a two rows of ventilated granary buildings, 12 in all, arranged around a podium. The total floor space of the granaries was more than 836 sq m, nearly the same as that of the Mohenjodaro granary in its original form. The whole layout, dominated by the citadel as it was, suggests the close administrative control of the food supplies within convenient proximity to the river-highway of the Ravi. Unfortunately, no intelligible remains survive of the buildings of the çitadel or of the main body of the town itself.

The village stands on an extensive series of mounds in which excavations since 1921 have disclosed the remains of a large city of the Indus civilization, in size second only to Mohenjodaro, which lies about 644 km to the southwest. The English archaeologist Sir John Marshall, initiated and directed the original excavations at the site, beginning in 1921. His findings pushed back knowledge of Indian prehistory to about 3500 BC.

Haribhadra, Haribhadra Suri, is one of the non-canonical Jain authors known for his authoritative works in Sanskrit and Prakrit on Jain doctrine and ethics, who flourished eighth century.

Haribhadra was a Brahmin from Chittor, and he received a thorough education in the Sanskrit classics. On adopting the Jain faith, he entered a Shvetambara order of monks. Haribhadra is best known for his *Saddarshanasamucchaya*, which deals with six philosophical systems of India and his various summaries of Jain thought and practice. He also wrote on logic and on yoga and contributed to Prakrit narrative literature.

Harsha (b. c. 590; d. c. 647), also called Harshavardhana, ruler of a large empire in northern India from AD 606 to 647, he was a Buddhist convert in a Hindu era. His reign seemed to mark a transition from the ancient to the mediaeval period, when decentralized regional empires continually struggled for hegemony.

Harsha was the second son of Prabhakaravardhana, king of Sthanvishvara (Thanesar, in the eastern Punjab). He was crowned at the age of 16 after the assassination of his elder brother, Rajyavardhana, and an encouraging "communication" with a statute of the Buddhist Avalokiteshvara *bodhisattva*. He soon forged an alliance with King Bhaskaravarman of Kamarupa and warred against King Shashanka of Gauda, his brother's assassin. At first he did not assume the title of king but merely acted as a regent. It was only after making his position secure that he declared himself sovereign ruler of Kannauj (in Uttar Pradesh) and formally transferred his capital to that city. Though he never defeated Shashanka, his large army waged incessant war for six years, conquering the "five Indies", believed to be the Vallabhi (now

Valabhi), Magadha, Kashmir, Gujarat, and Sind. His influence extended from Gujarat to Assam, but the area directly under his control probably comprised no more than the modern Uttar Pradesh, with parts of the Punjab and Rajasthan. He attempted to conquer the Deccan (c. 620) but was driven back to the Narmada River by the Chalukya emperor Pulakeshin II. Having brought most of the north under his hegemony, Harsha made little attempt at building a centralized empire but ruled according to the traditional pattern, leaving conquered kings on their thrones and contenting himself with tribute and homage.

Harsha is known mainly through the works of Bana, whose *Harshacharita* ("Deeds of Harsha") describes Harsha's early career. The works of the Chinese pilgrim Hsuan-tsang (Pinyin: Xuanzang) also refer to Harsha, though his opinions are questionable because of his personal friendship and strong Buddhist ties with the king. Hsuan-tsang depicts the emperor as a converted Mahayana Buddhist, though in the earlier part of his reign Harsha appears to have supported orthodox Hinduism. He is described as a model ruler—benevolent, energetic, and just, as well as active in the administration and prosperity of his empire. In 641 he sent an envoy to the Chinese emperor and established the first diplomatic relations between India and China. He established benevolent institutions for the benefit of travellers, the poor, and the sick throughout his empire. Every five years he held an assembly at the confluence of the Ganga and the Yamuna rivers at Prayag (Allahabad), at which he distributed treasures he had accumulated during the previous four years. A patron of men of learning, Harsha sponsored the chronicler Bana and Mayura, a lyric poet. A poet himself, Harsha composed three Sanskrit works: *Nagananda, Ratnavali,* and *Priyadarshika*. Following his death his kingdom broke into factions, with the later Guptas ruling over a portion of it.

Hemachandra (b. 1088, Dhandhuka, Gujarat, western India; d. 1172, Gujarat), Hemachandra Suri, Somachandra, original name Chandradeva, was a Jain teacher of the Shvetambara sect who gained privileges for his religion from Siddharaja Jayasimha, one of the greatest kings of Gujarat. With his eloquence and vast erudition, Hemachandra succeeded in converting the successor king Kumarapala, thus firmly establishing Jainism in Gujarat for all time.

As with the birth accounts of many Indian pundits, Hemachandra's birth is said to have been attended by omens and supernatural occurrences: his mother had 14 dreams foretelling the birth of a wondrous son. When the child was taken to a Jain temple, the priest Devachandra noticed several auspicious signs on his body and he convinced the parents to let him teach the boy.

The Jain thread of doctrine was found in all his writings. When finally he was considered to have become an *acharya* (teacher), Somachandra changed his name to Hemachandra. At the end of his life, in accordance with Jain tradition, he fasted to death.

Chandradeva was ordained in 1110, changing his name to Somachandra. In 1125 he became an adviser to King Kumarapala and wrote the *Arhanniti*, a work on politics from a Jain perspective. A logician and prodigious writer, he produced Sanskrit and Prakrit grammars, textbooks on practically every branch of Indian philosophy and science, and several poems, including the *Trishashtishalaka-purusha-charita* ("Lives of the 63 Great Personages"), a Sanskrit epic depicting the history of the world as envisioned by Jain teachers. Although derivative in many ways, his works have become classics, setting high standards for Sanskrit learning.

Hinayana, the group of more conservative, monastically oriented schools of Buddhism, it maintained a central focus on Gautama Buddha and the normative authority of the words of the Gautama Buddha as they were remembered in the *Sutra Pitaka* and *Vinaya Pitaka*.

The name Hinayana was applied to these schools by the followers of the Mahayana Buddhist tradition in ancient India. The name reflected the Mahayanists' evaluation of their own tradition as superior, surpassing the others in universality and compassion. The only Hinayana school that is still extant is the Theravada (followers of the Way of the Elders). In most Hinayana schools, the future Buddha Maitreya is the only other Buddha that is given serious attention.

Hinduism, refers to the beliefs and practices of Hindus, as expressed in a series of characteristic doctrinal, ritual, social, narrative, and poetic forms. Hinduism, the world's oldest religion is a major world religion, practised by over 700 million people in India, Nepal (where it is the State religion), and by groups dispersed across the world.

Hindus, themselves, refer to their religion in a variety of ways, although the majority accepts the term Hinduism. Those preferring Veda, or Vedic religion, want to embrace an ancient textual core and the tradition of Brahmin learning that preserved and interpreted it. Those preferring *sanatana dharma* ("eternal law") emphasize a more catholic tradition of belief and practice not necessarily mediated by Brahmins. The English term "Hinduism" was coined by British writers in the first decades of the nineteenth century and soon came to designate religious ideas and practices distinctive to India.

The traditions, doctrines, and practice of Hinduism date back well into the third or second millennia BC. Textually, the schools of commentary and debate preserved in epic and Vedic writing can be traced to the second millennium BC. Visually, female terracotta figurines found in excavations of the Indus Valley Civilization (third-second millennia BC) sites, are believed to point to the veneration of goddesses; and *yakshas* (benevolent spirits associated with natural phenomena) and *nagas* (snakelike divinities) were worshipped about 400 BC-AD 400.

Central concepts: Hindu doctrine has been spelt out and debated in a vast textual tradition anchored to the Vedas, the oldest core of Hindu religious utterance. The ultimate cause and foundation, source, and goal of all existence is Brahman. As the All, Brahman either causes the universe and all beings to emanate from itself, transforms itself into the universe, or assumes the appearance of the universe. Brahman is in all things and is the self (*atman*) of all living beings. Hindus believe many things; sometimes the beliefs of one person are in contradiction with the beliefs of another, yet both remain Hindus in the fullest sense. As many Hindus affirm through the prayer "May good thoughts come to us from all sides", truth is of such a nature that it must be sought from multiple sources, not dogmatically stated.

An important dimension drawing Hindus into a single community of discourse is narrative. For at least two millennia, people in almost all corners of India—and now well beyond—have responded to certain prominent stories of divine play and of interactions between gods and humans. These concern major figures in the Hindu pantheon: Krishna and his beloved Radha, Rama and his wife Sita and his brother Lakshmana, Shiva and his consort Parvati (or, in a different birth, Sati), and the goddess Durga or Devi. Many tales focus in different degrees on *dharmic* exemplariness, genealogies of human experience, forms of love, and the struggle between order and chaos, or duty and play. In generating, performing, and listening to these stories. Hindus have often experienced themselves as members of a single imagined family.

A fundamental belief of Hinduism is the doctrine of transmigration and rebirth and the complementary belief in *karma* ("action"—the idea that the soul achieves a happy or unhappy rebirth according to its deeds in the previous life). The whole process of rebirths is called *samsara*. The very meaning of salvation is one's final emancipation (*moksha*) from this morass, an escape from the impermanence that is an inescapable feature of mundane existence. The Bhagavadgita presents three paths (*margas*) to salvation: the path of duties, the path of knowledge, and the path of devotion.

Another strand that contributes to the complex unity of Hindu experience is devotion (*bhakti*), a broad tradition of loving God that is especially associated with the lives and words of vernacular poet-saints throughout India. With its central affirmation that religious enthusiasm is more fundamental than rigidities of practice or doctrine, *bhakti* provides a common challenge to other aspects of Hindu life. At the same time, it contributes to a common Hindu heritage.

Sacred texts: The most important texts are the four collections (Samhitas): the *Rigveda* ("Wisdom of the Verses"), the *Yajurveda* ("Wisdom of the Sacrificial Formulae"), the *Samaveda* ("Wisdom of the Chants"), and the *Atharvaveda* ("Wisdom of the Atharvan Priests"). The works that followed the Samhitas are the Brahmanas (discussions of Vedic ritual), Aranyakas (books studied in the forest), and Upanishads (secret teachings concerning cosmic correlations).

Among the *smriti* texts inspired by the Veda are the Dharmasutra, manuals on *dharma* which contain rules of conduct and rites; and the Dharmashastras, the basis of Hindu law (including the *Manu Smriti*); the Sanskrit epics, the Mahabharata and the Ramayana; and the Puranas, which include 18 great Puranas, and several subordinate Puranas, which detail the myths and legends of the gods.

Together, the components of each of the four Vedas, the Samhitas, Brahmanas, Aranyakas, and the Upanishads, constitute the revealed scripture of Hinduism, or *shruti*, "that which is heard", divine and unchangeable reality. All other works—in which the actual doctrines and practices of Hindus are encoded—are recognized as having been composed by human authors and are thus classed as *smriti*, "that which is remembered", human and possibly imperfect knowledge.

The pantheon: Hindus typically focus their worship on a favourite divinity (*ishtadevata*); they do not insist, however, that there is anything exclusive in that choice. Although a range of deities may be so worshipped, many Hindus worship Vishnu and Shiva. Vishnu is often regarded as a special manifestation of the preservative aspect of the Supreme Reality, while Shiva is considered the manifestation of the destructive aspect. Another deity, Brahma, whose name is a masculine inflection of the neuter noun Brahman, is the creator; he remains in the background. These three deities constitute the *trimurti* ("the one with three forms").

The *trimurti* still figures prominently in Hindu theological writing, but it is virtually absent in practice, since Brahma is rarely worshipped. Much closer to a practical religion is another classical version of the pantheon, in which the Great Goddess (known variously as Devi, Durga, or Shakti) replaces Brahma as the third element in the trinity.

Vaishnavism is the worship of Vishnu and his various *avatars* (personifications). Some of the major Vaishnava groups include the Shri Vaishnavas and Dvaitins ("Philosophical or Religious Dualists") of South India, the followers of the teachings of the philosopher Vallabha in western India, and several Vaishnava groups in Bengal in eastern India, who follow teachings derived from those of the saint Chaitanya.

A pronounced feature of Vaishnavism is the strong tendency to *bhakti*, a passionate love and adoration of God, a complete surrender. The widespread *bhakti* movement seems a natural corollary of the Vaishnava ideal of a loving, personal God and aversion to a conception of salvation that puts an end to all consciousness or individuality.

Shaivism is the worship of Shiva. Shaivites worship different facets of this many-sided god: as Rudra ("the howler"), Shankara ("the auspicious one"), as Pashupati ("Lord of the Cattle"), and as Aghora ("To whom nothing is horrible"). Shaivism includes such diverse movements as the highly philosophic Shaiva Siddhanta and Kashmir schools, the socially distinctive Virashaiva (or Lingayat), ascetic orders such as the *dashnami sannyasis* and Kapalikas and Kalamukhas, and innumerable folk variants.

Shaktism is the worship of goddesses, especially when they are understood as expression or aspects of a single Goddess (Devi) or Great Goddess (Mahadevi). This goddess personifies *shakti* ("power", or "energy"), present throughout the universe and challenges any notion of the feminine as passive or quiescent. Followers of Shakti are often called *shaktas* ("Empowered Ones").

Modes of religious practice: The primary form of worship in the Vedas comprises the chanting of hymns and prescribing sacrifices (*yajnas*) to the deities. For many Hindus, their religion is defined more by what they do than what they think. Thus, "practical" Hinduism may be very different from what the Vedic texts prescribe. Still, among Hindus, *puja*, primarily in the form of image worship, takes place both in small household shrines and in temples. Sometimes worshippers assemble to meditate, to take part in singing and chanting, or to listen to discourse. Central to the *puja* is the giving and sharing of food. Such food is called *prasad* (Hindi: "grace"), reflecting the recognition that when humans make offering to deities, the initiative is not really theirs; they are actually responding to the generosity that bore them into a world rich with life and auspicious possibility.

Life cycle rituals, are still practised by most Hindus, but these sacraments (*samskara*) of refinement and transition are intended to make a person fit for a certain purpose or for the next stage in life by removing taints (sins) or by generating new qualities. In antiquity there was a great divergence of opinion about the number of rites of passage, but in later times 16 came to be regarded as the most important. In modern times, ceremonies relating to the birth of a child, initiation, marriage, and funeral customs are still widely followed.

Tantrism: is the search for spiritual power and ultimate release by means of the repetition of sacred syllables and phrases (*mantras*), symbolic drawings (*mandalas*), and other secret rites elaborated in the texts known as *tantras* ("looms"). Based especially on convictions about divine creative energy (*shakti*) as experienced in the body, Tantrism is a method of conquering transcendent powers and realizing oneness with the divine by yogic and ritual means. It appears in both Buddhism and Hinduism from the fifth century AD onwards, colouring many religious trends and movements.

Festivals and pilgrimages are two of the most remarkable aspects of Indian religious life. Hindu festivals are combinations of religious ceremonies, worship, prayer, music, dances, fasting, and feasting. The functions of these activities are clear from literary sources and anthropological observation: they are intended to purify, avert malicious influences, renew society, bridge over critical moments, and stimulate, celebrate, and resuscitate the vital powers of nature (hence the term *utsav*, meaning both the generation of power and a festival). Pilgrimages to holy rivers, mountains, forests, and cities were already known in Vedic and epic times. It is often said that pilgrimage is a layperson's renunciation; it is physically difficult, it means leaving behind the array of duties and pleasures associated with home and family, and it has for centuries been a major aspect of the lives of many ascetics.

Reforms in attitude: The ancient vision of society classified it into four orders (*varnas*), which were further subdivided into innumerable castes (*jatis*). Discrimination on the basis of caste is a practice dating back to ancient times, and even texts like the *Manu Smriti* were seen to justify low social status, explaining it as the inevitable result of sins in a former life.

The nineteenth and twentieth centuries have been periods of dynamic development within Hinduism, and in Hindu society, and the process has continued even after India's independence.

Reforms in Hinduism began in the nineteenth century. Ramakrishna Paramahamsa, Swami Vivekananda, and Raja Ram Mohun Roy were prominent in attempting to reconcile traditional Hinduism with social reforms and political theories popular at the time. Issues like prohibiting child marriage, banning of *sati*, and allowing the remarriage of widows—all of which are post-Vedic developments—came into the forefront. The Brahmo Samaj (founded 1828), for instance, denounced the caste system, polytheism, and image worship; although it never achieved a significant popularity, the social reforms it proposed were accepted by most of Hindu society by the early twentieth century. The Arya Samaj (founded 1875), on the other hand, achieved far greater social standing, and is still widely followed in India. The Arya Samaj upholds the infallibility of the Vedas, and regards all post-Vedic additions as degenerate. Consequently, it opposes ancestor worship, animal sacrifice, untouchability, child marriage, priestly craft, and temple offerings.

Hindustan, Hindusthan, historically a name for northern India, in contrast to the Deccan, or southern India, this can be defined more precisely as comprising the basin of the five Punjab rivers and the upper Gangetic Plan. Hindustan is sometimes defined as "north of the Vindhya Mountains". It is also used as a synonym for all of India. As a fertile and well-populated corridor situated between walls of mountain, desert, and sea, Hindustan has been regarded as the principal seat of Indian power, containing the bulk of Indian wealth and physical energy.

Hoysala Dynasty, family that ruled from about 1006 to 1346 in the southern Deccan and for a time in the Cauvery (Kaveri) valley, its first kings came from the hills northwest of Dorasamudra (modern Halebid), which became their capital in around 1060. Their followers were hardy, hill-dwelling, Kannada-speaking people. They gradually absorbed Gangavadi (Mysore State, now Karnataka State) and the rich lands beyond the Tungabhadra River towards Dharwad and Raichur. The imperialistic programmes of the Chalukyas of Kalyani helped them, for under the Hoysala rulers Vinayaditya (reigned c. 1047-1098) and his grandson Vishnuvardhana (reigned c. 1110-1141) they gained wide experience as feudatory generals.

Vishnuvardhana won much territory from the tough Kadambas of Hangal, but his weak son, Narasimha I, lost it. Yet Vishnuvardhana's expulsion of the Cholas from the plateau was successful. His grandson Ballala II (reigned 1173-1220) was invited into the plains to help the Cholas. He agreed because what he had won in 1189-1211 from the Chalukya dynasty, beyond the Malprabha and Krishna rivers, had diminished under pressure from the Yadava dynasty of Devagiri. He then extended his domain to the north of Mysore and defeated the Yadavas, making the Hoysalas the dominant power in southern India.

Ballala II's grandson Someshvara (reigned c. 1235-1254) resided in the principality on the Cauvery, given by the Cholas. His son Ramanatha (reigned 1254-1295) was allowed to remain there for some time by the Pandya emperor. When he was evicted, however, his attempt to take the plateau kingdom from his brother, Narasimha III, weakened Hoysala resources. Ballala III (reigned c. 1292-1342), who helped the sultan of Delhi against the Pandyas, brought about the dynasty's downfall by his futile ambitions. The Vijayanagar dynasty succeeded the Hoysalas.

Hoysala architecture and sculpture is especially ornate and intricate, its best examples being at Halebid, Belur, and Somnathpur. The family liberally patronized Kannada and Sanskrit letters.

Hoysala Temple Architecture, style of architecture employed largely in the Karnataka (formerly Mysore) State of southern India. The double-shrine Hoysaleshvara temple at Halebid is a typical example of the twelfth-century Carnatic style. The profusion of carving often tends to obliterate the sense of architectural form, but the enormous skill and labour expended are astonishing. Closely allied to the South Indian style, it developed a distinctive idiom in the mid-twelfth century under the Hoysala dynasty.

The temples of this dynasty are characterized by multiple shrines around a central hall and above all by the extreme exuberance of the sculpture and ornamental decoration. The high plinths of the temples are elaborately covered with horizontal bands of floral and animal motifs, separated from one another by deeply shadowed recesses; a series of divine and semi-divine figures, each under its own foliated canopy, covers the walls. The availability locally of a chloritic schist that is soft when quarried and hardens on exposure to the air contributed to the development of the highly ornate, deeply cut style.

Hsuan-Tsang (b. 602, Chenlu, China; d. 664, China), Pinyin Xuanzang, later known as Tripitika, Buddhist monk and Chinese pilgrim to India who translated the sacred scriptures of Buddhism from Sanskrit into Chinese and founded the Buddhist Consciousness school in China.

Unable to find a solution from his Chinese masters, he decided to go to India to study at the fountainhead of Buddhism. On his journey he travelled north of the Taklamakan Desert, passing through such oasis centres as Turfan, Karashar, Kucha, Tashkent, and Samarkand, then beyond the Iron Gates into Bactria, across the Hindu Kush (mountains) into Kapisha, Gandhara, and Kashmir in northwest India. From there he sailed down the Ganga River to Mathura, then on to the holy land of Buddhism in the eastern reaches of the Ganga, where he arrived in 633.

In India, Hsuan-tsang visited all the sacred sites connected with the life of the Buddha, and he journeyed along the east and west coasts of the subcontinent. The major porition of his time, however, was spent at the Nalanda monastery, the great Buddhist centre of learning, where he perfected his knowledge of Sanskrit, Buddhist philosophy, and Indian thought. While he was in India, Hsuan-tsang's reputation as a scholar became so great that even the powerful king Harsha, ruler of north India, wanted to meet and honour him. Thanks largely to that king's patronage, Hsuan-tsang's return trip to China, begun in 643, was greatly facilitated.

Hsuan-tsang returned to Chang'an, the Tang capital, in 645, after an absence of 16 years. He was accorded a tumultuous welcome at the capital, and a few days later he was granted an audience with the emperor. The emperor was so enthralled by his accounts of foreign lands that he offered the Buddhist monk a ministerial most. Hsuan-tsang, however, preferred to serve his religion, so he declined the Imperial offer.

The monk spent the remainder of his life translating the Buddhist scriptures, numbering 657 items packed in 520 cases, that he brought back from India. He was able to translate only a small portion of this huge volume, about 73 items in 1,330 chapters, but his translations included some of the most important Mahayana scriptures.

Born into a scholarly family, Hsuan-tsang received a classical Confucian education in his youth. Under the influence of an older brother he became interested in the Buddhist scriptures and was soon converted to Buddhism. With his brother he travelled to Chang'an and then to Sichuan (modern Szechwan) to escape the political turmoil that gripped China at that time. While in Sichuan, Hsuan-tsang began studying Buddhist philosophy but was soon troubled by numerous discrepancies and contradictions in the texts. His fame rests mainly on the volume and diversity of his translations of the Buddhist *sutras* and on the record of his travels in Central Asia and India, which, with its wealth of detailed and precise data, has been of inestimable value to historians and archaeologists.

Hun Invasions, a nomadic pastoralist people. The Huns invaded southeastern Europe c. AD 370 and during the next seven decades built up an enormous empire there and in central Europe. The Hephthalites, who invaded Iran and India in the fifth and sixth centuries, and the Hsiung-nu (Xiongnu), known earlier to the Chinese, are sometimes called Huns, but their relationship to the invaders of Europe is uncertain.

The Hun dominion extended from Persia right across to Khotan, the main capital being Bamiyan in Afghanistan. Tormana was the first Indian Hun king of note, and ruled northern India as far as Eran in central India. His son, Mihirakula (reigned 520), appears to have been the closest yet to the popular concept of the fearsome Huns. A Chinese pilgrim travelling through northern India at the time describes him as uncouth in manner and an iconoclast, especially in his hatred for Buddhism. Mihirakula was finally driven out of the plains and into Kashmir where he died about 542. With his death the political impact of the Huns subsided. Yet, in a span of roughly 50 years, the Huns not only managed to hasten the decline of Gupta power but also diminished any scope for creating an imperial structure: all energies of the Gupta kings were constantly devoted towards warding off Hun attacks. The tide of Hun invasions finally receded by the end of the sixth century when the Turks and the Persians attacked them in Bactria.

In the first half of the fifth century during the reign of the Gupta king Kumara Gupta (c. 415-454), there was a perceived threat of Hun invasion from Bactria. For almost a hundred years this remained a threat and successive Gupta kings worked at keeping them from crossing the Hindu Kush mountains into their kingdom. It has been suggested by historians that the resistance put up by the Indians and the Chinese during this period not only weakened the Huns, but was also partly responsible for the ferocity with which they invaded Europe. Towards the end of the fifth century the Huns managed to break through into northern India. Indian Huns, or Hunas, were not independent; they acted as viceroys for a Hun overlord.

I

Indus Civilization, Indus Valley civilization, or Harappan civilization, the earliest known urban culture of the Indian subcontinent was first identified in 1921 at Harappa in the Punjab and then in 1922 at Mohenjodaro, near the Indus River in Sind, both now in Pakistan.

The civilization comprised two large cities, Harappa and Mohenjodaro, and over 100 towns and villages, many of which were relatively small in size. The two cities were each over 5 km in circumference, and their outstanding magnitude suggests political centralization, either in two large States or in a single great empire with alternative capitals, a practice common in Indian history. Or it may be that Harappa succeeded Mohenjodaro, which is known to have been devastated more than once by exceptional floods. The southern region of the civilization in Kathiawar and beyond appears to be of later origin than the major Indus Valley sites. The civilization was literate, and its script, with some 250 to 500 characters, has been partly and tentatively deciphered. The language has been tentatively identified as Dravidian. The nuclear dates of the civilization appear to be about 2500-1700 BC, though southern sites may have lasted later till the second millennium BC.

The Indus civilization apparently evolved from the villages of neighbours or predecessors. It followed the Mesopotamian model of irrigated agriculture with sufficient skill to take advantage of the fertile Indus River valley while controlling the formidable annual floods that simultaneously fertilize and destroy. It obtained a secure foothold on the plain and mastered its more immediate problems. An inevitable sequel to the new civilization with a well-nourished and increasing population was the expansion along the flanks of the great waterways. The civilization subsisted primarily by farming, supplemented by an appreciable but often elusive commerce. Wheat and barley were grown; field peas, mustard, sesame, and a few date stones have also been found, as well as some of the earliest traces of cotton. Domesticated animals included dogs and cats, humped cattle, shorthorns, domestic fowl, and possibly pigs, camels, and buffaloes. The elephant was probably also domesticated, and its ivory was freely used. Minerals, unavailable from the alluvial plain, were brought in sometimes from far afield. Gold was imported from southern India or Afghanistan, silver and copper from Afghanistan or northwestern India (now Rajasthan), lapis lazuli from Afghanistan; turquoise from Iran (Persia), and a jade-like fuchsite from southern India.

Remains of the civilization were found as far as Sutkagen Dor, near the shore of the Arabian Sea, 480 km west of Karachi. Relics were also found at Ropar at the foot of Simla Hills, 1,600 km to the northeast. Later exploration established the civilization's existence southward along the west coast as far as the Gulf of Cambay, 800 km southeast of Karachi. Toward the east it went as far as the Yamuna Basin, 50 km north of Delhi. It is the most extensive of the three earliest civilizations, the other two being those of Mesopotamia and Egypt.

The end of Mohenjodaro is known to have been dramatic and sudden. It was attacked towards the middle of the second millennium BC by raiders who swept over the city and then passed on, leaving the dead lying where they fell. Who the attackers were, is a matter for speculation. However, one thing is clear: the city was already in an advanced stage of economic and social decline before it received the coup de grace. Deep floods had more than once submerged large tracts of it. Houses had become increasingly shoddy in construction and showed signs of overcrowding. The final blow seems to have been sudden, but the city was already dying. For many centuries urban civilization was dead in the northwest of the Indian subcontinent.

In the south, however, in Kathiawar and beyond, the situation appears to have been very different. Here it would seem that there was a real cultural continuity between the late Indus phase and the Copper Age cultures that characterized central and western India between 1700 BC and the first millennium. These cultures form a material bridge between the end of the Indus civilization proper and the developed Iron Age civilization that arose in India in about 1000 BC.

Perhaps the best-known artefacts of the Indus civilization are a number of small seals, generally made of steatite (soapstone), which are distinctive in kind and unique in quality. They depict a wide variety of animals, both real—such as elephants, tigers, rhinoceros, and antelopes—and imaginary, often composite, creatures. Sometimes human forms are included. A few examples of Indus stone sculpture have also been found, usually small and representing humans or gods. There are great numbers of small terracotta figures of animals and humans.

Ishanavarman, chief of the Maukhari family of northern India, originally a feudatory of the Gupta empire, he had declared his independence from the Guptas by the middle of the sixth century and set himself up as a king in the Ganga Valley.

Ishanavarman's only notable successor was Grahavarman, who was defeated and killed by the Guptas soon after his accession and whose capital was occupied. His brother-in-law, Harsha, however, drove out the Guptas around 606 and thus gained control of the Maukhari kingdom. After this, the Maukhari family disappeared into obscurity.

Little is known of Ishanavarman except that during the second half of the sixth century he and his successors were involved in continuous conflict with the kings of the later Gupta line. They seem to have ruled the greater portion of the modern State of Uttar Pradesh and to have had some control over Magadha (southern Bihar State). There is some evidence of Maukhari raids in the Deccan. Their capital was Kanyakubja (modern Kannauj), and they played an important role in the development of this city.

J

Jain Canon, the sacred texts of Jainism whose authenticity is disputed between sects. The *Shvetambara* canon consists principally of 45 works divided as follows: (1) 11 Angas, the main texts—a twelfth has been lost for at least fourteen centuries; (2) 12 Upangas, or subsidiary texts; (3) 10 Prakirnakas, or assorted texts; (4) 6 Cheda-sutras on the rules of ascetic life; (5) 2 Chulika-sutras on cognition and epistemology; and (6) 4 Mula-sutras on miscellaneous topics. Some of these texts are not accepted as authoritative by the non-image worshipping Shvetambara sects.

The *Digambara* sect disputes the authenticity of the entire Shvetambara canon. The Digambaras believe that the original is lost but that the substance of Jain doctrine has been preserved in a variety of religious and philosophical texts written by various leaders and scholars of their community over the centuries.

The Shvetambara works cover a variety of topics, including a list of the Tirthankaras, or Jinas (Jain saviours), exploits and teachings of these figures, and doctrines. Some of the Angas contain supposed dialogues between Mahavira, the most recent Tirthankara, and his followers. Others are said to retain some of the earliest parts of the canon, which appears to have been preserved originally in oral form. The canon is written in the Prakrit dialect, though from the Gupta period onwards (fourth-sixth century AD) Jain writers have used Sanskrit for a wider readership.

Jainism, along with Hinduism and Buddhism, it is one of the three most ancient of India's religious traditions still in existence.

The name Jainism derives from the Sanskrit verb root *ji*, "to conquer". It refers to the ascetic battle that Jain renunciants (monks and nuns) must fight against passions and bodily senses in order to gain omniscience and the complete purity of soul that represents enlightenment in the Jain system. The most illustrious of those few individuals who have achieved this omniscience and purity are called Jina (literally, "Conqueror"), and the laity is called Jain, "Follower of the Conqueror".

Jainism often employs concepts similar to Hinduism and Buddhism, the result of a common background. Nevertheless, Jainism and its followers have always had a sense of their own autonomous identity and the Jain tradition must be regarded as an independent phenomenon, not some variety of Hindu sect or Buddhist heresy as earlier scholars believed.

Jainism has largely been confined to India, although the recent migration of Indians to other, predominantly English-speaking countries has spread its practice to many Commonwealth nations and to the United States. Precise statistics are not available but it seems likely that there are currently approaching four million Jains in India and 100,000 elsewhere.

In its essence, Jainism teaches a path to spiritual deliverance through a disciplined way of life founded upon nonviolence to all living creatures. It also evolved in the course of its history into a developed cultural system that made significant contributions to Indian civilization in areas such as philosophy and logic, art and architecture, mathematics, astronomy and astrology, and literature.

History: Jainism originated around the seventh-fifth centuries BC in the Ganga basin of North India, the scene of intense religious speculation and activity at that time. It was in this region that Buddhism also appeared. The prevailing ideologies common to these new religious perspectives related to asceticism, the abandonment of social action, both ritual and domestic, and the attainment of spiritual knowledge is an attempt to win, by one's own efforts and freedom from repeated rebirth. The authority of the Vedas and ritualistic Brahminic schools were thus rejected.

The community appears to have grown quickly. Jain tradition states that it numbered 14,000 monks and 36,000 nuns at the time of Mahavira's death. From the beginning the community was subject to a number of schismatic movements. The only division to have a lasting effect related to monastic practice. While the

Shvetambaras ("white-robed") claimed that monks and nuns should wear white robes, the Digambaras ("sky-clad", naked) stated that the true monk (but not the nun) should be naked. This dispute gave rise to a further debate concerning whether a soul (*jiva*) can attain liberation from a female body (a possibility the Digambaras deny).

The first Jain figure for whom there is reasonable historical evidence is Parshva, a renunciant teacher, who may have lived in the seventh century and founded a community based upon abandonment of worldly concerns. Jain tradition regards him as the twenty-third Tirthankara (literally, "ford-maker") of the current age (*kalpa*) of the world. A Tirthankara, also called Jina, is a revealer of the Jain religious path (*dharma*) and founder of a community of renunciants and laypeople (*tirtha*) who have achieved freedom from rebirth, thus setting the example that all Jains must follow.

The twenty-fourth and last Tirthankara of this age was Vardhamana, who is known by the epithet Mahavira ("Great Hero"). He is perceived by Jains as the last revealer, in this cosmic age, of the Jain teaching of right knowledge, right faith, and right practice. Although traditionally dated to c. 599-527 BC, Mahavira must be held, as a near exact contemporary of the Buddha whose dates have been reassessed by current research, to have flourished about a century later. The legendary accounts of Mahavira's life preserved by the Jain scriptures form the basis for constructing his biography and enable some conclusions to be formulated about the nature of the early community founded by him.

Mahavira, like the Buddha, was the son of a chieftain of the Kshatriya (warrior) class. At the age of 30, he renounced his princely status to become an ascetic. For a period of twelve-and-a-half years, he followed a path of solitary and intense asceticism, at one point being accompanied by Goshala Maskariputra, later to be founder of the Ajivika sect, at the end of which he gained Enlightenment. Mahavira then converted 11 disciples (called *ganadharas*), all of whom were originally Brahmin exponents of ritual learning. Mahavira is believed to have died at Pavapuri, near modern Rajgir.

A vital factor in consolidating the Shvetambara-Digambara division was the series of councils held to codify and ultimately preserve in writing the Jain scriptures which were maintained orally for a long time after Mahavira's death. Of the councils recorded by Jain history, the last one was held at Valabhi in Saurashtra (in modern Gujarat) in either AD 453 or 456 and was responsible for codifying the Shvetambara canon that is still in use. The Digambara monastic community considered this revision too corrupt to be normative, and the division between the two communities became irrevocable.

During this period, Jainism spread from its place of origin westwards to Ujjain, where it seems to have gained a measure of royal patronage. Much of the early archaeological and inscriptional evidence for early Jainism, especially the laity, comes from the city of Mathura, a vital link on the northwest trade route. During the reign of the Gupta dynasty (AD 320-c. 600), a time of Hindu self-assertion, the Jain community migrated in numbers to central and western India, becoming stronger there than it had been in its place of origin in the Ganga basin.

Early mediaeval developments (AD 500-1100): In fact, there is archaeological evidence in the form of rock caves for the presence of Jain monks in the south of India from before the Common Era; the Digambara sect had for almost two millennia, significant presence in what is now the State of Karnataka. The early mediaeval period was the time of Digambara Jainism's greatest flowering both in that region and in neighbouring Tamil Nadu. The Digambaras gained the patronage of prominent monarchs of three major dynasties during these centuries—the Gangas in Karnataka (third-eleventh century); the Rashtrakutas, whose kingdom was just north of the Ganga realm (eight-twelfth century); and the Hoysalas in Karnataka (eleventh-fourteenth century). Digambara monks are reputed to have engineered the succession of the Ganga and the Hoysala dynasties, thus stabilizing uncertain political situations and securing a guarantee of political protection and support for the Jains. An abundance of epigraphical evidence details an elaborate patronage system through which kings, queens, State ministers, and military generals endowed the Jain community with tax revenues and with direct grants for the construction and upkeep of temples. Most famously, the Ganga general Chamundaraya in the tenth century oversaw the creation of a colossal statue of Bahubali (locally called Gommateshvara; son of Rishabha, the first Tirthankara) at Shravana Belgola.

The Shvetambaras in the north seem to have been less prominently embroiled in dynastic politics than their southern counterparts. But there is evidence of such activity in Gujarat and Rajasthan that helped establish sympathetic kings such as Vanaraja in the eighth century and, in the twelfth century, Kumarapala, whose accession was masterminded by the great Shvetambara scholar and minister of State Hemachandra.

While Mahavira had rejected the claims of that caste hierarchy which privileged Brahmin authority on the basis of innate purity, a formalized caste system nonetheless gradually appeared among the Digambara Jain laity in the south. The Jain caste system differed from the Hindu system in that the Kshatriyas were assigned a place of prominence over the Brahmins and, at least theoretically, connected purity with a moral rather than a ritual source.

Late mediaeval-early modern developments (1100-1800): In the period of their greatest influence (sixth-late twelfth century), Jain monks of both sects to a large extent ceased being wandering ascetics and, perhaps influenced by intense lay patronage, tended to become permanent dwellers at temples or monastic residences. A residue of this can be seen to this day in the Digambara institution of the *bhattaraka*, a cleric who takes monastic initiation but, rather than assuming a life of naked ascetic wandering, continues as an orange-robed administrator and guardian of holy places and temples. Some mediaeval Jain writers saw this compromise with ancient scriptural requirements as both cause of and evidence for the religion's inexorable decline. However, Jainism's gradual slide into a marginalized situation in India can best be ascribed to socio-political reasons.

Various Shvetambara monastic subsects (*gaccha*) appeared on the basis of local and preceptorial association. Invariably, their leaders saw themselves as reforming lax monastic practice. Some of the most important of these subsects are still in existence, such as the Kharatara Gaccha (founded eleventh century) and the Tapa Gaccha (founded thirteenth century). The *gacchas*, which also contained lay followers, often differed markedly from each other over issues of lineage, ritual, and the sacred calendar, with each claiming to represent the true Jainism. According to tradition their leading teachers were also involved in the conversion of Hindu Rajput clans in western India which subsequently became Shvetambara Jain caste groups. All these *gacchas* subscribed to worship of the Tirthankaras in image form.

The Shvetambara Jain community's decline was hastened by the Turko-Afghan Muslim invasion of western and northern India in the twelfth century. An element of persecution was involved at the outset, including the sacking of important shrines, but the most important result for the Jain community with this sudden shift of political control from indigenous to foreign hands was the loss of direct access to sources of power. While there are significant examples of Jain laymen serving as ministers to Muslim rulers and of monks such as Hiravijaya (sixteenth century) instructing the

Mughal emperor Akbar, the Shvetambara community was gradually compelled to redefine itself as an almost exclusively mercantile group which it has remained to this day.

As with the Shvetambaras, the Digambara laity were among the most stringent critics of their community's deteriorating situation. The most significant Digambara reform movement occurred in the late sixteenth century, led by a layman and poet named Banarsidas. This movement attacked what it saw as the emptiness of Digambara temple ritual and the profligacy of the community's clerical leaders and stressed the mystical elements of the Jain path.

In the south Digambara Jainism had, for all its prominence in aristocratic circles, been subjected to attacks by renascent Hindu devotional movements that had arisen in Tamil Nadu as early as the sixth century. With the advent of the Vijaynagar empire in the fourteenth century the Digambara Jains began to lose much of their significant royal support and survived only in peripheral areas of the southwest and in pockets of the north.

Recent Jain History: By the middle of the nineteenth century, the image-worshipping Shvetambara Jain monastic lineages had virtually disappeared. Ritual authority and control of temples were in the hands of quasi-monastic clerics known as *yati*. However, a revival of monastic initiation and learning took place under the auspices of charismatic monks such as Atmaramji and the community of Shvetambara image-worshipping renunciants has expanded. The Tapa Gaccha is numerically by far the dominant subsect. The non-image worshipping Shvetambara sects, the Sthanakvasis and Terapanthis, are smaller in number. The Digambara monastic community also experienced a revival of its ideals in the early twentieth century with the great monk Acharya Shantisagar, from whom virtually all the 120 or so current Digambara monks claim lineal descent.

In the wake of age-old trading links, many Jains from western India settled in eastern African countries, most notably Kenya and Uganda. Political unrest in the 1960s compelled them to relocate firstly to the United Kingdom, where the first Jain temple outside India was consecrated in Leicester, and then increasingly to the United States and Canada where they follow their traditional mercantile and professional occupations with great success. A keen sense of the need to maintain identity has led to the formation in the 1970s and 1980s of trans-sectarian organizations such as the Jain Samaj (Europe) and the Federation of Jain Associations in North America. Through regular English language publications such as *Jain Digest* and *Jain Spirit*, the Jain community outside India has been able to mobilize opinion and present Jain ideals, such as nonviolence, vegetarianism and, most recently, environmentalism, in a modern context to younger members of the community and to others.

In recent years the Shvetambara and Digambara communities in India have devoted much energy to maintaining temples and publishing editions of their religious texts. The Jains have also, as a prosperous social group, been involved in general welfare work such as drought relief in Gujarat in the 1980s, providing relief to Jain widows and the poor, and maintaining shelters for old animals to save them from slaughter, accepted as an act of nonviolence.

The Jain legend: The Jains evolved their own version of legendary history, called the "Deeds of the 63 Illustrious Men" or, by western scholars, "The Universal History". The most important figures within this are, of course, the 24 Tirthankaras, perfected human beings who appear from time to time to preach and embody the Jain religious path. Some of the other protagonists are found in Hinduism, most notably Krishna, regarded by the Jains as a cousin of the twenty-third Tirthankara Arishtanemi, and the hero Rama who, in the 16 major retellings of his story, is treated as a pious, nonviolent Jain. By incorporating yet redefining such important Hindu figures, the Jains were able to remain both part of and separate from the surrounding Hindu world.

Doctrines of Jainism: The Jain conception of reality is complex. It is characterized by arising, change and decay, as opposed to simple permanence (for the Hindus) and impermanence (for the Buddhists). The world is eternal and uncreated. Its constituent elements, the five substances (*dravyas*), are soul, matter, space, the principles of motion and the arrest of motion and, for the Digambaras, time. These also are eternal and indestructible, but their conditions change constantly.

Jain reality is constituted by *jiva* ("soul", "living substance") and *ajiva* ("non-soul", "inanimate substance"). All but *jiva* are without life; the four elements (earth, water, fire, and air) are also inhabited by souls. The essential characteristics of *jiva* are consciousness (*chetana*), bliss (*sukha*), and energy (*virya*). A *jiva* is formless and genderless and cannot be directly perceived by the senses. Like the universe, it is without a point of ultimate origin or end. While the soul assumes the exact dimensions of the body it occupies, it is not identical with that body. On death it assumes the shape of the last physical body which housed it.

The Jain religious goal is the complete perfection and purification of the soul (*jiva*). This can occur only when the soul is in a state of eternal liberation from and non-attachment to corporeal bodies.

All phenomena are linked together in a universal chain of cause and effect. By nature each soul is pure, possessing infinite knowledge, bliss, and power; however, these faculties are restricted throughout time by matter coming in contact with the soul. Liberation of the soul is thus impeded by the accumulation of *karmans*, bits of material generated by a person's actions, that attach themselves to the soul and consequently bind it to physical bodies through many births; this has the effect of thwarting the full self-realization and freedom of the soul.

The non-sentient, non-material substances are the principles of motion and its arrest, space, and time. They are always pure and are not subject to defilement. The principles of motion and its arrest permeate the universe; they do not exist independently but, rather, form a necessary precondition for any object's movement or coming to rest. Space is infinite, all-pervasive, and formless, and provides accommodation for the entire universe. It is divided into occupied (the universe, called *loka*) and unoccupied portions (*aloka*, "non-universe") where nothing exists.

Ajiva is divided into two categories: the non-sentient and material, and the non-sentient and non-material. Matter (*pudgala*) has the characteristics of touch, taste, small, and colour. Its essential characteristic is lack of consciousness. The smallest unit of matter is the atom (*paramanu*). Heat, light, and shade are forms of fine matter.

Time, according to the Jains, is eternal and formless. It is represented as a wheel with 12 spokes (*aras*), the equivalent of ages, six making an ascending arc and six a descending one. In the ascending arc, man progresses in knowledge, age, stature, and happiness, while in the descending arc, he deteriorates. The two cycles joined together make one rotation of the wheel of time, which is called a *kalpa*. These *kalpas* repeat themselves without beginning or end.

Theories of knowledge: According to Jainism, *yoga*, the ascetic physical and meditative discipline of the monk, is the means to the attainment of omniscience and thus to *moksha*, or liberation. *Yoga* is the cultivation of true knowledge of reality, faith in the teachings of the Tirthankaras, and pure conduct; it is thus intimately connected to the Three Jewels (*ratnatraya*) of right knowledge, right faith, and right practice (respectively, *samyagjnana*, *samyagdarshana*, and *samyakcharitra*).

In Jain thought, there are five kinds of knowledge (*jnana*). Of these, *kevala* is the stage of omniscience. *Kevala* is necessarily accompanied by freedom from karmic obstruction. Omniscience is the foremost attribute of a liberated *jiva*, the emblem of its purity; thus, a liberated soul, such as a Tirthankara, is called a *kevalin* ("possessor of omniscience"). However, not all *kevalins* are Tirthankaras: becoming a Tirthankara requires the development of a particular type of *karmic* destiny. All knowledge short of omniscience is flawed.

Ethics is Jainism: Two separate courses of conduct are laid down for the ascetics and the laity. In both cases the code of morals is based on the doctrine of *ahimsa*, or nonviolence. Since thought gives rise to action, violence in thought merely precedes violent behaviour.

Violence in thought, then, is the greater and subtler form of violence, because it arises from ideas of attachment and aversion, grounded in passionate states, which result from negligence or careless behaviour. Jainism enjoins avoidance of all forms of injury, whether committed by body, mind, or speech, and subscribes emphatically to the teaching that "nonviolence is the highest form of religious practice". For Jains, this principle, which manifests itself most obviously in the form of vegetarianism, is the single most important component of their religion's message. Notable in this connection is the friendship and exchange of letters between Mahatma Gandhi and the Jain layman Raychandrabhai Mehta. Gandhi considered his interactions with Mehta to have been important in formulating his own ideas on the use of nonviolence as a political tactic.

The Three Jewels constitute the basis of the Jain doctrinal and ethical stance. Right knowledge, faith, and practice must be cultivated together; none of them can be achieved in the absence of the others. Right faith leads to calmness or tranquillity, detachment, kindness, and the renunciation of pride of birth, beauty of form, wealth, scholarship, prowess, and fame—but only when followed by right practice. Yet, there can be no virtuous conduct without right knowledge, which consists of clear distinction between the self and the non-self. Knowledge of scriptures is distinguished from inner knowledge. Knowledge without faith and conduct is futile. Without purification of mind, all austerities are mere bodily torture. Right practice is thus spontaneous, not a forced mechanical quality.

Attainment of right practice is a gradual process, and a householder can observe only partial self-control; when he becomes a monk, he is able to observe more comprehensive rules of conduct.

Religious practices: All Jain renunciants must exercise the three *guptis* (care in thought, speech, and action) and the five *samitis* (kinds of vigilance over conduct). An essential and regular part of monastic ritual are the *avashyaka* (six obligations, or obligatory actions), practised daily and at important times of the ritual calendar. They are: equanimity; praise of the Tirthankaras; obeisance to the Tirthankaras, teachers, and scriptures; confession; resolution to avoid sinful activities; and "abandonment of the body", which implies standing or sitting in a meditative posture.

It is a tenet of Jain doctrine that no one can achieve liberation in this corrupt time. As a result, Jain renunciants are not so much attempting to gain immediate Enlightenment as aiming for a human rebirth which will bring them nearer to that state. That rebirth is effected through disciplined and meritorious practice that embodies nonviolence to all creatures.

The type of austerities in which a monk engages, the length of time he practises them, and their severity are carefully regulated by his preceptor, who takes into account the monk's spiritual development, his capacity to withstand the austerities, and his ability to understand how they help further his spiritual progress at a given time. The theoretical culmination of a monk's ascetic rigours is the act of *sallekhana*, in which he lies on one side on a bed of thorny grass and ceases to move or take food. This act of ritual starvation is the monk's ultimate act of non-attachment, by which he lets go of the body for the sake of his soul. Jain ideology views this as a positive action of ultimate self-control in which the passions play no part, to be distinguished from the "fool's death" of worldly suicide. While widely followed in ancient and mediaeval times, *sallekhana* is much less common today.

Shvetambaras allow monks to retain minimal possessions such as a robe, an alms bowl, a whisk-broom, and a *mukhavastrika* (a piece of cloth held over the mouth to protect against the ingestion of small insects) which are handed over by a senior monk at the time of initiation. For the non-image worshipping Shvetambara sects, the Sthanakvasis and the Terapanthis, the *mukhavastrika* must be worn at all times. A monk after initiation by a senior teacher must obey the "great vows" (*mahavratas*): avoid injuring any life form, lying, stealing, having sexual intercourse, or accumulating personal possessions.

Among the Digambaras, a full-fledged monk takes the same "great vows" as his Shvetambara counterparts, but remains naked in acknowledgement of a much more intense interpretation of the vow of non-possession. Lower-grade Digambara monks wear a loincloth and keep with them one piece of cloth not more than 1.3 m long. Digambara monks use a peacock-feather duster and water gourd, and beg and eat only once a day, using the cupped palms of their hand as an alms bowl. They regard their interpretation of the Jain monastic vocation as more in accord with the ancient model than that followed by the Shvetambaras.

Both the Shvetambaras and Digambaras allow for the initiation of nuns but; in the former community female renunciants outnumber males by a ratio of approximately three to one. Often women are of great learning and spiritual attainment, still the practical status of Jain nuns is less prestigious than that of monks to whom they are obliged by convention and textual stipulation to defer. In Digambara Jainism, nuns, who wear robes, accept the necessity of being reborn as men before they can advance seriously on the ascetic path (which in that sect is deemed to require nudity).

Religious activity of the common man: Jain literature from earliest times largely portrays the religion as centring on the initiated renunciant and his concerns. But it is clear that from near the very beginning of Jainism there has been a lay community supporting the monastic community and that throughout the religion's history most Jains have followed the lay mode of life. The mediaeval period was a time of particularly intense reflection by both Shvetambara and Digambara monastic intellectuals on the role of the laity. Many treatises were produced from around the fifth century until the seventeenth century discussing the layperson's religious behaviour and vows. According to these writings, laypersons should ideally conform to a pattern of behaviour mirroring the requirements of the ascetic "great vows". However, from a doctrinal point of view, it is held that while following the ascetic path can lead to the destruction of *karman*, the vows of the lay path can only effect the warding off of the influx of new *karman* and thus not radically alter the individual's *karmic* status.

Until very recently, Jainism did not attempt to evolve any particularly distinctive life-cycle rituals to cater for events like birth and marriage, although the ninth century Digambara Jinasena did attempt to legislate in this area. In general, practice has tended to conform to prevailing local custom, provided this does not infringe upon the basic Jain principles.

Typically, a Jain's life is characterized by strict vegetarianism, disciplined business or professional activity, and responsible conduct of family affairs with a view to establishing a sound social reputation, combined with a pious and serious approach to religious matters, especially the requirements of nonviolence. Jains accept that merit generated by pious activity, often involving fasting or disbursement of money for religious or charitable purpose, will have the power not just to enable an individual to advance a little further along the path to final liberation but also to improve his current material situation. The manifest contrast between the great prosperity of the Jain laity and the austere self-denial of the monks and nuns it supports can be explained in this way.

The layman (the focus is invariably upon the male) is enjoined to observe eight primary behavioural qualities (which vary but usually include the avoidance of meat, wine, honey, types of fruits and roots deemed to harbour life forms, and eating at night) and twelve vows: five *anuvratas,* three *gunavratas,* and four *shikshavratas*. The *anuvratas* ("little vows") are vows to abstain from gross violence, falsehood, and stealing; to be content with one's own wife; and to limit one's possessions. The other sets of vows are supplementary in nature, meant to strengthen and protect the *anuvratas*. They involve avoidance of unnecessary travel, harmful activities, and the pursuit of pleasure; fasting and control of diet; offering of gifts and service to monks, the poor, and fellow believers; and voluntary death if the observance of vows proves impossible. Laypersons are enjoined to perform the *avashyaka* at regular intervals.

Image worship: Temple worship is mentioned in early texts that describe gods paying homage to Tirthankara images and relics in heavenly eternal shrines. While Mahavira himself appear to have made no statement regarding the worship of images, it quickly became a vital modality of Jainism as a religious path. Numerous Tirthankara images in the sitting and standing postures dating from the early Common Era have been uncovered in excavations of a Jain *stupa,* or funerary monument, at Mathura.

Worship (*puja*), closely associated with the obligatory rites of the laity, can be offered to all liberated souls, to monks, and to the scriptures. However, amongst the image worshippers (*murtipujaka*) who form the majority of Jinas, the focus is on the icon of the Tirthankara. Though Tirthankaras remain unaffected by offerings and worship and cannot themselves, as individuals who are liberated from rebirth, respond in any way by bestowing aid, such devotional actions serve as a form of meditative discipline for the votary proffering them. Monks and nuns of all sects can only engage in worship in an inward, mental manner, without offering physical worship. The Sthanakvasi and Terapanthi Shvetambara sects completely reject the authenticity of image worship.

Doctrine and Philosophy: The religious merit that accrues from hearing and reading Jain texts encouraged the careful and loving preservation of manuscripts. The Jains have traditionally maintained important libraries throughout India, among the most significant of which are for the Shvetambaras at Khambat, Jaisalmer, and Patan, and for the Digambaras at Karanja and Mudbidri. The miniature paintings on palm-leaf and paper manuscripts preserved in the Jain monastic libraries provide a continuous history of the art of painting in western India from the eleventh century to the present.

Jain canonical scriptures do not belong to a single period, nor is any text free from later revision or additions. The original teachings of the Jinas are said to have been contained in 14 texts, called the *Purvas* ("Prior"), which are now lost. Shvetambaras and Digambaras agree that a time will come when the teachings of the Jinas will be completely lost; Jainism will then disappear from the earth and reappear at an appropriate point in the next time cycle (*kalpa*). The two sects disagree, however, about the extent to which the corruption and loss of the Jinas' teachings has already occurred. Conesquently, the texts for each sect differ.

The Shvetambaras follow an extensive canon (*agama*) as the repository of their tradition, which they believe is based upon compilations of Mahavira's discourses by his disciples. This canon preserves the teachings of Mahavira in an imperfect way, since they have been subject to both interpolation and loss throughout the ages. The number of texts considered to make up the Shvetambara canon has varied over time and by monastic group. Western authors have fixed this number at 45, divided into six groups.

Digambaras give canonical status to two works in Prakrit: the *Karmaprabhrita* ("Chapters on Karman", also called *Shatkhandagama,* ("Scripture of Six Sections") and the *Kashayaprabhrita* ("Chapters on the Kashayas"). The *Karmaprabhrita,* claimed to be based on the now lost *Drishtivada* text, deals with the doctrine of *karman* and was committed to writing by Pushpadanta and Bhutabalin in the mid-second century. The *Kashayaprabhrita,* compiled by Gunadhara from the same source at about the same time, deals with the passions (*kashaya*) that defile and bind the soul.

The Shvetambara and Digambara traditions have produced a voluminous corpus of literature, written in several languages, in the areas of philosophy, poetry, drama, grammar, music, mathematics, medicine, astronomy, astrology, and architecture.

The details of Jain doctrine did not alter much throughout history and no major philosophical disagreements exercised Jain intellectuals. The main concerns throughout the mediaeval period were ensuring that the statements of the scriptures could be demonstrated to be compatible with logic and controverting the rival claims of the Hindus and the Buddhists.

Jain Literature, the original, unadulterated teachings of the Jinas are said to have been contained in fourteen texts, called the Purvas ("Prior"), which are now lost. Shvetambaras and Digambaras agree that a time will come when the teachings of the Jinas will be completely lost; Jainism will then disappear from the earth and reappear at an appropriate point in the next time cycle (*kalpa*). The two sects disagree, however, about the extent to which the corruption and loss of the Jinas' teachings has already occurred. Consequently, the texts for each sect differ.

The Shvetambaras follow an extensive canon (*agama*) as the repository of their tradition, which they believe in, is based upon compilations of Mahavira's discourses by his disciples. This canon preserves the teachings of Mahavira in an imperfect way, as it is thought to be mixed with much that was not said by the Jina. The number of texts considered to make up the Shvetambara canon has varied over time and by monastic group. The Angas contain several dialogues, mainly between Mahavira and his disciple Indrabhuti Gautama, presumably recorded by the disciple Sudharman, who transmitted the teachings to his own disciples.

According to modern scholars, the Acharanga (first chapter) and the Sutrakritanga, among the Angas, and some chapters of the Uttaradhyayana, among the Mula-sutras, are among the oldest parts of the canon. The Cheda-sutra text, Dashashrutaskandha, concludes with the Kalpa-Sutra, which recounts the lives of the Jinas and includes an appendix of rules for a monastic life and a list of eminent monks.

Bhadrabahu, whom tradition credits with being the last Jain sage to know the contents of the Purvas, is asserted to be the author of the Niryuktis, the earliest commentaries on the Jain canonical texts. These concise, metrical commentaries, written in Prakrit, gave rise to an expanded corpus comprising texts called

Bhashyas and Churnis. These were composed between the fourth and seventh centuries and contain many ancient Jain historical and legendary traditions, along with a large number of popular stories brought into the service of Jain doctrine. The Bhashyas and Churnis, in turn, gave rise in the mediaeval period to a large collection of Sanskrit commentaries. Haribhadra, Shilanka, Abhayadeva, and Malayagiri are the best-known authors of such commentaries.

The sacred literature, transmitted orally from the time of Mahavira, was first systematized in a council at Patna about the end of the fourth century BC, and again in two later councils at Mathura and Valabhi in the early third century AD. The fourth and last council, at Valabhi, in the mid-fourth century AD, is considered the source of the existing Shvetambara canon, though some commentators insist that the present version is in accordance with the reading of the Mathura council.

Jain Temples, comprise shrines built by and for the Jain community. The erection of shrines and the donation of religious manuscripts are regarded as pious acts. Most villages or towns inhabited by Jains have at least one Jain shrine; some have become pilgrimage sites. Lists of these shrines have been composed, and the most noteworthy shrines are offered adoration in daily worship.

Several Jain cave temples, dating from as early as the second century BC, have been discovered and excavated. Cave temples are found at Udayagiri and Khandagiri, in Orissa; Rajgir, in Bihar; Aihole, in Karnataka; Ellora, in Maharashtra; and Sittannavasal in Tamil Nadu.

Places of pilgrimage were created at sites marking the principal events in the lives of the Tirthankaras. Parasnath Hill and Rajgir in Bihar and Shatrunjaya and Girnar hills on the Kathiawar Peninsula are among such important ancient pilgrimage sites. Other shrines that have become pilgrimage destinations are Shravana Belgola in Karnataka, Mounts Abu and Kesariaji in Rajasthan, and Antariksha Parshvanatha in Akola district, Maharashtra.

Jataka, refers to any of the extremely popular stories of former lives of the Buddha, that are preserved in all branches of Buddhism.

Many *jatakas* have parallels in the Mahabharata, the *Panchatantra* (animal fables), the Puranas (collections of legends), as well as in non-Buddhist Indian literature. Some turn up again in such places as Aesop's fables. The *jataka* stories have also been illustrated frequently in bas-reliefs of Buddhist shrines (or *stupas*) at Bharhut and Sanchi and monumentally on the great stupa of Java, the Borobudur.

The *jatakas* consist of fairy tales, animal stories and fables (the future Buddha may be incarnate in an animal), ballads, and anecdotes. Each tale begins by noting the occasion that prompted its telling and ends with the Buddha disclosing his identity in the present lives of the characters in the narrative. There is humour in these stories and considerable variety. The future Buddha may appear in them as a king, an outcaste, a god, an elephant—but, in whatever form, he exhibits some virtue that the tale thereby inculcates.

Jayadeva, author of the celebrated Sanskrit poem *Gitagovinda* ("Song of the Cowherd"), which helped to popularize devotional Hinduism flourished in twelfth century Bengal.

Jayadeva has for several centuries been honoured at an annual festival at his birthplace, during which his poem is recited. Songs from the *Gitagovinda* also continue to be sung in temples, during festivals, and at *kirtanas* (communal worship through song).

The *Gitagovinda* describes the love of Krishna, the divine cowherd, for Radha, his favourite among the *gopis* (wives and daughters of the cowherds). The poem presents in dramatic form the lovers' attraction, estrangement, yearning, and final reconciliation through the help of a *sakhi* (confidante). The poem blends recitative stanzas with twenty-four short songs and leans heavily on alliteration, lyricism, and grace of image for its effect.

Born in the village of Kenduli, he was the son of Bhojadeva, a Brahmin, and married to Padmavati. He was attached to the court of King Laxsmanasena (reigned 1178-1205) at Navadvipa (Nabadwip).

K

Kadamba Family, minor dynasty it held sway in an area to the northwest of Mysore city on the Indian subcontinent between the fourth and sixth centuries AD.

The founder, Mayurasharman, said to be a learned Brahmin took up a military career after being insulted by a Pallava official. He soon acquired sufficient territory to bargain with the Pallavas for a feudal principality on the western coast. His son, Kangavarman, who assumed the title Dharmamaharajadhiraja ("Lawful King of Kings"), was probably the king of Kuntala defeated by the Vakataka king Vindhyaseva. His grandson, Kakusthavarman (reigned c. 425-450), was a powerful ruler involved in many marital alliances with the Guptas and other royal families. After his death the southern part of the kingdom was established as an independent principality under his younger son, Krishnavarman. A period of warfare between the two branches of the family followed, during which the junior branch initially triumphed but was quickly forced to acknowledge the suzerainty of the Pallavas first and then the senior branch. The Kadamba kingdom came to an end with Pulakeshin II, the Chalukya king's capture of Banavasi during the reign of Ajavarman.

Kalachuri Dynasty, the best known Kalachuri family in Indian history ruled in central India, with its base at the ancient city of Tripuri (modern Tewar). It originated around the beginning of the eighth century, but little is known of its early history. The dynasty came into the picture only with Kokalla I (reigned c. 850-885). The period between Kokalla I and Kokalla II (reigned c. 990-1015) is marked by a consolidation of Kalachuri power and by their relations with contemporary dynasties. The success attributed to Kokalla I against the Pratiharas, the Kalachuris of Uttar Pradesh, the Guhilas of Marwar, the Chahamanas of Shakambhari, and the kings of Vanga and Konkan appears somewhat exaggerated. Matrimonial relations with the powerful Rashtrakuta family of the Deccan remained uninterrupted for some time. The Kalachuris were at times even involved in Rashtrakuta politics, as in the period of Yuvaraja I (reigned c. 915-945). Between the mid-ninth and the early eleventh centuries the Kalachuris pursued a policy of traditional hostility towards the kingdoms of south Kosala, Kalinga, Gauda, and Vanga. Occasional clashes with the Gurjars, the Chandelas, the Chalukyas of the east coast, the Gujarat Chalukyas, and others are mentioned in their records.

The earliest known Kalachuri family (c. AD 550-620) ruled in northern Maharashtra, Gujarat, Malwa (Malava), and parts of western Deccan. They probably had their capital at Mahismati in the Narmada River valley. Three members of the family—Krishnaraja, Shankaragana, and Buddharaja—are known from epigraphs and coins distributed over a wide area. Although the rise of the Badami Chalukyas ended Kalachuri power in the early seventh century, the dynasty seems to have lingered in the Malwa region until a later date.

These military exploits did not produce any substantial results until the period of Gangeyadeva (reigned c. 1015-1041), who besides achieving success against the traditional rivals, Dakshinakosala and Orissa, pushed northwards to acquire the Varanasi area at the expense of the Palas. He also had substantial success against the

Kalyani Chalukyas. The reign of Gangeyadeva's son, Karna (reigned 1041-1073), represents a high point in contemporary military adventurism. He consolidated his power in the Varanasi-Allahabad area and undertook large-scale military campaigns in eastern, southern, central, and western India. His successes were short-lived, however, and Kalachuri power declined steadily in the period between Yashahkarna (reigned 1073-1123) and Vijayasimha (reigned c. 1188-1209). The neighbouring Gahadavalas, Paramaras, and Chandelas started encroaching on the Kalachuri kingdom. Soon after 1211 Baghelkhand and almost all of Dahalamandala were incorporated into the Chandela kingdom.

Another Kalachuri dynasty rose to power in the Deccan between 1156 and 1181. This family traced its origin to Krishna who was the conqueror of Kalinjar and Dahala in Madhya Pradesh. Its authority in Karnataka was established by Bijjala, who originally served as a feudatory of the Kalyani Chalukyas at Banavasi, Nolambapadi, and Tarddevadi and wrested power from the Chalukya king Taila III. The Kalachuris held power in Karnataka during the reigns of Bijjala's sons, Someshvara and Sankama, but after 1181, Ahavamalla and Singhana, two other sons of Bijjala, gradually surrendered authority back to the Chalukyas. Despite its brevity, the Kalachuri period in Karnataka is historically important because it coincides with the rise of the Lingayat, or Virashaiva, Hindu sect.

Two other Kalachuri families are known to history, namely, the Kalachuris of Sarayupara and the Kalachuris of Ratanpur. The Sarayupara family ruled a territory along the banks of the Sarayu (Ghaghara) River, in the Bahraich and Gonda districts of Uttar Pradesh. The family originated in the late eighth century and lasted until the last quarter of the eleventh century. By then its kingdom extended from the Ghaghara River to the Gandak River and included the towns of Bahraich, Gonda, Basti, and Gorakhpur.

The Ratanpur Kalachuris, who first ruled from Tummana and later from Ratanpur, 26 km north of Bilaspur, were distantly related to, and were feudatories of the Tripuri Kalachuris. Beginning to rule in the early eleventh century, they gained prominence under Jajalladeva I in the early twelfth century. Early historical documents of their rule continue till Pratapamalla (reigned 1188-1217) and are then intermittent until the fifteenth century, by which time the family had split into two branches—Ratanpur and Raipur. No authentic historical document relating to their history after the fifteenth century is known.

Kalibangan, ancient site of the Indus Valley Civilization, northwestern India (now in Rajasthan State), it is of archaeological significance because it contains both pre-Harappan and Harappan remains; and therein can be seen the transition between the two cultures. Although the pre-Harappan culture worked copper and produced pottery, it had no writing system, and its ruins lack the orderly layout and use of baked brick that is found in the later Harappan sites. The Harappan remains include a cemetery and a fortified citadel.

Kalidasa, Sanskrit poet and dramatist, probably the greatest Indian writer of any epoch he flourished in fifth century AD. His six works, identified as genuine, are the dramas *Abhijnanashakuntalam* ("The Recognition of Shakuntala"), *Vikramorvashiyam* ("Urvashi Won by Valour"), and *Malavikagnimitram* ("Malavika and Agnimitra"); the epic poems *Raghuvamsham* ("Dynasty of Raghu") and *Kumarasambhavam* ("Birth of the War God"); and the lyric *Meghadutam* ("Cloud Messenger").

Even though little is known about Kalidasa's person or his historical relationships, a Sinhalese tradition says that he died in Sri Lanka during the reign of Kumaradasa, was ascended the throne in 517. A more persistent legend makes Kalidasa one of the "nine gems" at the court of the renowned king Vikramaditya of Ujjain. Unfortunately, there are several known Vikramadityas (Sun of Valour, a common royal appellation). likewise, the nine distinguished courtiers could not have been contemporaries. It is certain that the poet lived sometime between the reign of Agnimitra, the second Shunga king (170 BC), the hero of one of his dramas, and the Aihole inscription of AD 634, which lauds Kalidasa. He is apparently imitated, though not named, in the Mandasor inscription of 473.

Judged by the Indian tradition as realizations of literary qualities inherent in the Sanskrit language and its supporting culture, Kalidasa has become the archetype for Sanskrit literary composition.

The society reflected in Kalidasa's work is that of a courtly aristocracy, sure of its dignity and power. Kalidasa has perhaps done more than any other writer to wed the older, Brahminic religious tradition, to the needs of a new and brilliant secular Hinduism. The fusion, which epitomizes the renaissance of the Gupta period, did not, however, survive its fragile social base. With the disorders following the collapse of the Gupta Empire, Kalidasa became a memory of perfection that neither Sanskrit nor the Indian aristocracy would know again.

In drama, his *Abhijnanashakuntalam* is the most famous and is usually judged the best Indian literary effort of any period. Taken from an epic legend, the work tells of the seduction of the nymph Shakuntala by King Dushyanta, his rejection of the girl and his child, and their subsequent reunion. The epic myth is important because of the child, for he is Bharata, eponymous ancestor of the Indian nation (Bharatavarsha, "Subcontinent of Bharata"). Kalidasa remakes the story into a love idyll: The characters represent a pristine aristocratic ideal. The girl is sentimental and selfless, alive to little but the delicacies of nature. The king is a strong, resolute hero, first the servant of *dharma* (religious and social law and duties) and protector of the social order. Yet he is tender and suffers agonies over his lost love. The plot and characters are made believable by a change Kalidasa has wrought in the story: Dushyanta is not responsible for the lovers' separation. He acts only under a delusion caused by a sage's curse. As in all of Kalidasa's works, the beauty of nature is depicted with a precise elegance of metaphor that would be difficult to match in any of the world's literatures.

The second drama, *Vikramorváshiyam* (possibly a pun on Vikramaditya), tells a legend as old as the Veda (earliest Hindu scripture), though very differently. Its theme is the love of a mortal for a divine maiden. It is well known for the "mad scene" (Act IV) in which the king, grief-stricken, wanders through a lovely forest apostrophizing various flowers and trees as though they were his love. The scene was intended in part to be sung or danced.

The third of Kalidasa's dramas, *Malavikagnimitram*, is of a different stamp—a harem intrigue, comical and playful, but not less accomplished for lacking any high purpose. The play (unique in this respect) contains datable references, the historicity of which have been much discussed.

Kalidasa's efforts in *kavya* (strophic poetry) are of uniform quality and show two different subtypes, epic and lyric. Examples of the epic are the two long poems, *Raghuvamsham* and *Kumarasambhavam*. The first recounts the legends of the hero Rama's forebears and descendants; the second tells the picaresque story of the god Shiva's seduction by his consort Parvati, the conflagration of Kama (the god of desire), and the birth of Kumara (Skanda) Shiva's son. Kalidasa's mastery of Sanskrit as a poetic medium is nowhere more marked.

A lyric poem, the *Meghadutam*, contains, interspersed in a message from a lover to his absent beloved, an extraordinary series of unexcelled and knowledgeable vignettes, describing the mountains, rivers, and forests of northern India.

Kalpasutra, manuals of Hindu religious practice, which emerged within the different schools of the Vedas, explain the procedures (*kalpa*) of its school as it applies to three different categories: the sacrificial ritual (the Shrautasutras), the domestic ritual (the Grihyasutras), and the conduct of life (the Dharmasutras). *Kalpa* is one of six fields of scholarly discipline known as *vedangas* ("accessories to the Vedas"). They are written in the short aphoristic style of the *sutra* (literally "thread") so that they could be committed easily to memory. As they are regarded to be of human origin, they are considered *smriti* ("tradition") as distinct from the earlier Vedic literature, which is *shruti* ("revelation").

Kanishka, Kaniska, greatest king of the Kushana dynasty that ruled over the northern part of the Indian subcontinent, Afghanistan, and possibly regions north of Kashmir in Central Asia he flourished first century AD.

Through inheritance and conquest, Kanishka's kingdom covered an area extending from Bukhara (now in Uzbekistan) in the west to Patna in the Ganga valley in the east, and from the Pamirs (now in Tajikistan) in the north to central India in the south. His capital was Purushapura (near Peshawar, now in Pakistan). He may have crossed the Pamirs and subjugated the kings of the city-states of Khotan, Kashgar, and Yarkand (now in Chinese Turkistan), who had previously been tributaries of the Han emperors of China. Contact between Kanishka and the Chinese in Central Asia may have inspired the transmission of Indian ideas, particularly Buddhism, to China where it first appeared in the second century AD.

Kanishka himself is believed to have died fighting in Central Asia. Chinese annals refer to one of the Kushana kings who had asked for the hand of a Han princess in marriage and who was defeated by General Ban Chao campaigning in Central Asia at the end of the first century AD. If this be true, then the king can only have been Kanishka or his predecessor, Vima.

Most of what is known about Kanishka is derived from Chinese sources, particularly Buddhist writings. Kanishka was certainly of Central Asian origin since he is depicted as such in a series of portraits of the dynasty discovered at Mathura. He may not have been directly related to the two earlier Kushana kings from the Yuezhi tribe, but it was under him that the dynasty flourished. The Kushana period ranks as one of the significant phases in the cultural development of northern India. When Kanishka came to the throne is uncertain. His accession has been estimated as occurring between AD 78 and 144; his reign is believed to have lasted 23 years. The year 78 marks the beginning of the Shaka era, a system of dating that Kanishka might have initiated. He is chiefly remembered as a great patron of Buddhism.

As a patron of Buddhism, Kanishka is chiefly noted for having convened the Fourth Buddhist Council in Kashmir that marked the beginnings of Mahayana Buddhism. According to Chinese sources, authorized commentaries on Buddhist theology and doctrine were prepared and engraved on copper plates at the council. These texts have survived only in Chinese translations and adaptations. Kanishka was a tolerant king and his coins show that he honoured the Zoroastrian, Greek, and Brahminic deities, as well as the Buddha. During his reign contacts with the Roman Empire led to a significant increase in trade and the exchange of ideas. Perhaps the most remarkable example of the fusion of eastern and western influences in his reign was the Gandhara school of art, in which Greco-Roman classical lines are seen in the images of the Buddha.

Kapila, Vedic sage he is often claimed, along with others (especially Asuri), to be the ancient founder of the system of Samkhya, one of the six schools of Vedic philosophy that flourished in 550 BC.

According to Hindu sources, Kapila was a descendant of Manu, the primal human being, and a grandson of the creator-god Brahma or, alternatively, an *avatar* of Vishnu. The Bhagavadgita pictures him as a recluse associated with yogic adepts (*siddhas*). The Samkhya system attributed to Kapila has had a considerable impact on the Hindu tradition as a whole, especially through its close association with Yoga, as symbolized in Kapila's own renunciant persona. For example, Samkhya forms a notable part of the philosophical background of the Bhagavadgita. In mythology, Kapila is portrayed as an exemplar of yogic stringency. His hermit regimen is said to have produced in him an inner source of such intense heat that he was capable of reducing to ash the 60,000 sons of Sagara.

He is not, however, the author of the text primarily responsible for giving the school its philosophical definition: Ishvarakrishna's *Samkhya-karika* (beginning of the Common Era).

Kashmir Shaivism, also called Pratyabhijna, is an important religio-philosophical system of India that worships Lord Shiva as the supreme reality. The school is idealistic and monistic, as contrasted with the realistic and dualistic school of Shaiva-siddhanta.

Shiva is seen as the sole reality and both the material and

efficent cause of the universe. His power is known in five aspects: *chit* ("consciousness"), *ananda* ("bliss"), *iccha* ("desire"), *jnana* ("knowledge"), and *kriya* ("action"). For the adherents of Kashmir Shaivism, liberation comes about through intense meditation on the Lord and recognition of the identical nature of the individual soul and the Lord.

The principal texts of the school are the Shiva-sutra, said to have been revealed to Vasugupta; Vasugputa's *Spanda-karika* ("Verses on Activity"; eighth-ninth century), Utpala's *Pratyabhijna-shastra* ("Manual on Recognition"; c. 900), Abhinavagupta's *Paramarthasara* ("The Essence of the Highest Truth"), *Pratyabhijnavimarshini* ("Reflections on Recognition"), and *Tantraloka* ("Lights on the Doctrine"), all of the tenth century, and Kshemaraja's *Shiva-sutra-vimarshini* ("Reflections on the Aphorisms on Shiva").

Kautilya, also called Chanakya, or Vishnugupta, was the Hindu statesman and philosopher who wrote a classic treatise on polity, *Artha Shastra*, a compilation of almost everything that had been written in India up to his time on *artha* (property, economics, or material success). He flourished in third century BC.

Kautilya's book became Chandra Gupta's guide. Each of its 15 sections deals with a phase of government, which Kautilya sums up as "the science of punishment". In his book he openly advises the development of an elaborate spy system reaching into all levels of society and encourages political and secret assassinations. Lost for centuries, the book was discovered only in 1905.

Kautilya became a counsellor and adviser to King Chandra Gupta (reigned c. 321-c. 297) of the Maurya Empire of northern India but lived simply himself. He was instrumental in helping Chandra Gupta overthrow the powerful Nanda dynasty at Pataliputra, Magadha.

Compared by many to Machiavelli and by others to Aristotle and Plato, Kautilya is alternately condemned for his ruthlessness and trickery and praised for his sound political wisdom and knowledge of human nature. All authorities agree, however, that it was mainly because of Kautilya that the Maurya Empire, first under Chandra Gupta and later under Ashoka (reigned c. 262-238 BC), became a model of efficient government.

He was born into the Brahmin caste and received his education at Taxila (now in Pakistan). He is known to have had knowledge of medicine and astrology, and it is believed that he was familiar with elements of Greek and Persian learning introduced into India by Zoroastrians. Some authorities believe he was a Zoroastrian or at least was strongly influenced by that religion.

Khajuraho, historical town, ancient name Kharjurvahaka, in northern Madhya Pradesh State, central India, it is a famous tourist and archaeological site, with 25 Hindu and Jain sculptured temples and 3 museums. The original town extended over 21 sq km and contained about 85 temples, built by successive rulers and their ministers. From about the late eleventh century the Chandelas shifted their centre of activity to the hill forts. Between AD 900 and 1150, it was a capital and temple-town under the patronage of the royal family of the Chandela Rajputs, who ruled in the vast region called Jejakabhukti, now the Bundelkhand area of Madhya Pradesh. But Khajuraho maintained its religious importance at least up to the fourteenth century, when the Arab traveller Ibn Battutah visited it in order to see the *yogis* or mendicants. Khajuraho was gradually reduced from a town to a village, and lapsed almost into oblivion.

But in 1838, Captain T.S. Burt, a British engineer, rediscovered the vanished temples amidst a jungle and presented his colourful account in the Asiatic Society of Bengal. Between 1843 and 1847, the local *maharaja* of Chhatarpur executed repair work in the temples. Major General Alexander Cunningham visited the place from 1852 onwards and systematically described the temples in his Archaeological Survey of India reports.

Out of the 25 temples, 10 are dedicated to Vishnu, including his powerful composite form called Vaikuntha, 9 to Shiva, 1 to the sun god, 1 to the esoteric *yoginis* (goddesses), and 5 to the Jain patriarchs of the Digambara sect. A large image of the seated Buddha found here suggests the prevalence of Buddhism too, though on a limited scale. An inscribed image of Hanuman attests to the worship of this monkey god. Khajuraho thus was a religious centre where many cults flourished. The Hindu religious systems of Khajuraho were Tantra-based, but unlike the skull-bearing Kapalika sect (worshippers of Kapalin, the skull bearer, a name of Shiva), they were not extreme Tantric. They were within the orthodox Brahminic fold and were influenced by the Vedic revival and Puranic elements, as inscriptions of temples testify.

The early open-air shrine of the 64 *yoginis* (c. AD 900) is built of rough granite, while the temples are constructed of fine-grained sandstone in the elite Nagara style from the middle of the tenth century. The temples are divided into three groups: (1) the western, which is the biggest and the best, where the royal family built grand monuments, including the Lakshmana or Vaikuntha (inscribed 954),

Vishvanatha (inscribed 999), and Kandariya Mahadeva (c. 1030); (2) the eastern, where merchants built Jain temples, the Parshvanatha (c. 950-970), Adinatha (c. 1075); (3) the southern, where the remains of the Vaidyanatha Shiva temple (34 m long), largest at the site, has been exposed by the Archaeological Survey of India.

Khajuraho monuments are now under the care and supervision of the Archaeological Survey of India (ASI), which has taken up excavation of several mounds, at least 18 of which have been identified. Khajuraho was designated a World Heritage Site by UNESCO in 1986. Modern Khajuraho is a small village, serving the tourist trade with hotels and airport.

Architectural features: Though affiliated to different religious sects, the temples have a cognate architectural style. They are built in the tradition of the central Indian Nagara style of architecture. They are compact unified structures consisting of four or five units: the cella or sanctum (*garbhagriha*), vestibule (*antarala*), large hall (*maha-mandapa*), hall (*mandapa*), and a porch (*ardha-mandapa*). Most of the temples are erected on the east-west axis and get the direct rays of the rising sun. They have no enclosure walls as in the case of the South India and Orissa temples, but have their own separate platforms to demarcate their sacred space.

A highly evolved stage of the Indian temple is seen at Khajuraho. Four large temples are *sandhara*, with built inner ambulatory. At least two of the larger temples, namely the Lakshmana (Vaikuntha) and the Vishvanatha, are five-shrined (*panchayatana*), preserving subsidiary shrines in the four corners of the platform.

The temple is lavishly carved in its interior as well as on its exterior. The ceilings of the temples are carved with intricate geometric and floral designs. The pillar brackets bear high-reliefed sculptures of *vyalas* (griffins) alternating with *apsaras* (celestial maidens). The sanctum doorway is decorated with conventional auspicious motifs: *mithunas* (couples), creepers, and dwarfs. It is guarded by door-keepers (*dvarapalas*), and "purified" by the river goddesses Ganga and Yamuna, sculpted in human form.

The cella of the large temples (Lakshmana, Vishvanatha, Kandariya, Parshvanatha) with its inner ambulatory, resembles on its plan a three-dimensional *yantra* (geometric diagram) with the eight corners guarded by the *dikpalas*. The three cardinal niches represent the manifestations of the main divinity enshrined in the sanctum. The iconic scheme is integrated with the religious cult of the temple.

In addition to the fall platform (*jagati*) on which it stands, the Khajuraho temple has three main divisions on its elevation: basal story (*pitha*), wall (*jangha*), and the roof or spire (*shikhara*). The basal storey contains a series of ornamental mouldings depicting human activities (*narathara*), "masks of glory" (*kirtimukha*), and geometrical designs. The wall section is divided into two or three sculptural zones. It is here that we see lovely figural sculptures—celestial maidens, griffins, couples, divinities including the guardian deities of space (*dikpalas*). The numerous indentations and projections on the ground level are carried upwards to the superstructure of the temple adding to its dramatic effect.

The roofs of the subordinate structures such as the porch and halls are pyramidal in shape, while the tower over the sanctum is curvilinear with graded peaks clustering around it. The architect has emphasized the progressive ascent of superstructures converging to the pinnacle, and has created the semblance of a mountain. Indeed, the inscriptions of Khajuraho compare the temple with Mount Kailash, the abode of Shiva, and Mount Meru, the centre of the Universe. The architectural imagery of the Khajuraho temples helps us to conceive of the temple as a model of the cosmos. The Khandariya Mahadeva, 35 m high, mountain-like with its 84 mini-spires clinging to its central spire, is a masterpiece of Indian temple art.

Sculpture: There is a profusion of figural sculptures on the temples; Cunningham counted 646 figures on the exterior and 226 in the interior of just one temple, the Kandariya Mahadeva. Sculpture is harmoniously integrated with architecture. The unified design of the temple with its horizontal bands of sculpture is perfectly balanced with the rising verticality of the building.

The human body is shown in its sensuous charm in a variety of postures and attitudes. The figures are not muscular as in Greek sculpture; the beauty of the human form is revealed from many angles through apparently diaphanous clothes.

The sculptured figures consist mainly of the divinities—cult icons in the sanctum, multiple manifestations of the principal deity in cardinal and surrounding niches of the halls, and the *dikpalas, matrikas* (divine mothers), *grahas* (planets) and numerous lesser divinities, demi-gods such as flying *vidyadharas, gandharvas* (celestial musicians), *ganas* (dwarfs) in different parts of the temple. There are hundreds of images of divinities holding manuscripts, suggesting the importance of knowledge and learning. Several deities including Vishnu, Shiva, Surya, and Devi sit in yogic positions. One of the most majestic figures is the 2.74 m high icon in the Chaturbhuja Temple.

There are three-dimensional carvings of Nandi, Shiva's bull, and of Varaha, the boar incarnation of Vishnu. The zoomorphic icon of Varaha (c. 950), installed in the western complex of the site is, represented as a cosmic form, carrying more than 650 divinities of the Hindu pantheon on its massive animal body. The mythic composite animal *vyala* is seen in its many varieties, with faces of different animals and birds, combined with the lion's body on all ornate temples. Mythic aquatic creatures, *makaras*, decorate arches and niches.

Khajuraho is neither synonymous with erotic sculpture nor does it illustrate the handbook of love called *Kamasutra*. The erotic theme constitutes not even one-tenth of the total sculpture on the temples but has drawn more attention than it deserves. At Khajuraho, erotic figures are placed on the main wall portion of the temples and therefore they are large and graceful. The artists have made creative use of this already established theme, the conjunction of the opposites, by placing it on the juncture walls of temples, linking the hall for devotees and sanctum of the divinity, to metaphorically convey something beyond the erotic. The surface meaning is erotic, but beneath lies a hidden meaning expressing a subtle yogic-philosophic concept.

One of the favourite motifs of Khajuraho artists is the *apsara* undressing to throw off a scorpion from her body. This was a poetic device to express a fertility theme. Interestingly, one of the Sanskrit words for scorpion is *kharrjura*. The scorpion-bearing *apsara* could be associated with the name of the town Kharjura-vahaka which has two meanings: "The Bearer of the Date-Palm", and "The Scorpion-Bearer". Both sculptors and poets were fond of employing puns and double meanings in their art. The ethos of Khajuraho art is highly sophisticated and Sanskritized.

Apsaras are presented by the Khajuraho artists on all temples of the Nagara style, whether Hindu or Jain. They are shown in various everyday activities such as applying make-up, removing a thorn from the foot, writing a letter, and carrying a baby. The architectural Vastu texts specifically ordain carving of female figures on temple walls. In fact, *apsara* is an ubiquitous theme of Indian art depicted on contemporaneous temples. The *apsaras* of Khajuraho and other mediaeval temples are auspicious art motifs whose origin can be traced to vegetation spirits (*yakshis*) and fertility figures of early Indian art at Sanchi, Bharhut, and Mathura.

The most refined achievement of Khajuraho art, the Kandariya Mahadeva Temple, embodies the symbolism of the *yantra* in its sanctum, the imagery of the cosmic mountain in its multi-turreted spire, and a visual expression of the Shaiva metaphysical system in its iconic scheme. A Shiva *lingam*, the sign of the unmanifest ultimate reality, is in the centre of the sanctum, and graded manifestations of Shiva, emanations and sub-emanations, in the surrounding niches. The temple is an ordered whole in which images are part of an integrated scheme. The Khajuraho temples represent a creative moment in Indian art when artistic talent combined with religious aspirations to produce a meaningful form.

Kharoshti, writing system it was used in northwestern India before c. AD 500. The system probably derived from the Aramaic alphabet while northwestern India was under Persian rule in the fifth century BC. Aramaic, however, is a Semitic alphabet of 22 consonantal letters, while Kharoshti is syllabic and has 252 separate signs for consonant and vowel combinations.

A cursive script written from right to left, Kharoshti was used for commercial and calligraphic purposes. It was influenced somewhat by Brahmi, the other Indian script of the period, which eventually superseded it.

The earliest extant inscription in Kharoshti dates from 251 BC, and the latest from the fourth to fifth century AD.

Kosala, ancient kingdom of northern India, roughly corresponding to the historical region of Oudh (Awadh), in what is now south-central Uttar Pradesh, Kosala extended across both banks of the Sarayu (Ghaghara) River and north into what is now Nepal.

Kosala rose in political importance early in the sixth century BC to become one of the 16 States dominant in northern India. It annexed the powerful kingdom of Kashi. In around 500 BC, during the reign of King Prasenajit (Pasenadi), it was regarded as one of the four powers of the north (perhaps the dominant power). At that time Kosala could command the trade routes of the Ganga River basin. The Buddha, who was born in the Shakya (Sakiya) tribe of northern Kosala (c. 563 BC), often preached at the capital city of Shravasti (Savatthi). He spent the rainy season in Shravasti during the last 25 years of his life.

According to the epic Ramayana, Kosala was ruled by kings descended from the sun. One of these kings was the legendary Rama, whose capital was Ayodhya, near modern Faizabad. He married Sita, princess of Videha, and soon after left on a 14-year exile to the forest along with Sita and his younger brother, Lakshmana. Sita was abducted by Lanka's demon king Ravana. Rama and Lakshmana, along with a monkey- and bear-army led by Hanuman, crossed the sea, entered Lanka, killed Ravana and only then returned victorious with Sita to Ayodhya. Rama was installed as king, and his reign (Ramarajya) is associated till today with peace and prosperity. The warm welcome he received is symbolically celebrated as the festival of lights, Diwali, even today.

In later times Kosala was known as northern Kosala, to distinguish it from a large kingdom to the south known variously as Kosala (also called southern Kosala, or Great Kosala) on the upper Mahanadi River (now in eastern Madhya Pradesh). This latter kingdom, with its capital at Sripura (later Sripur, Raipur), was founded, according to the Ramayana, by Rama's son Kusha and known by this name until the twelfth century AD.

Though there was a matrimonial alliance between Kosala and Magadha, in about 490 BC war broke out between them. As a result, Kosala was weakened and never regained its position of control. Kosala was absorbed into Magadha sometime during the reign of King Ajatashatru (c. 491-c. 459 BC).

Kot Diji, archaeological site in Sind (now in pakistan), excavated in the early decades of the twentieth century, it is recognized as belonging to the early Harappan period. A stone rubble wall surrounding this settlement, appears to date to about 3000 BC.

Kshatriya, Kshattriya, or Ksatriya, second highest in ritual status of the four *varnas*, or social orders, of Hindu India, traditionally the military or ruling class.

The earliest Vedic literature listed the Kshatriya (holders of *kshatra*, or authority), as first in rank, then the Brahmins (priests and teachers of law), next the Vaishya (merchant-traders), and finally the Shudra (artisans and labourers). Movements of individuals and groups from one class to another, both upwards and downwards, were not uncommon; a rise in status even to the rank of Kshatriya was a recognized reward for outstanding services to the rulers of the day.

The legend that the Kshatriya were destroyed by Parashurama, the sixth reincarnation of Vishnu, as a punishment for their tyranny is thought by some scholars to reflect a long struggle for supremacy between priests and rulers that ended in victory for the former. By the end of the Vedic era, the Brahmins were supreme, and the Kshatriya had fallen to second place. In modern times, the Kshatriya *varna* is held to include a broad class of caste groups, differing considerably in status and headed by the aristocratic Rajput lineages.

Kumarajiva (b. AD 343/344; d. 413), Buddhist scholar and seer, famed for his encyclopaedic knowledge of Indian and Vedantic learning, he is recognized as one of the greatest translators of Buddhist scriptures from Sanskrit into Chinese. It was largely due to his efforts and influence that Buddhist religious and philosophical ideas were disseminated in China.

Before his ordination at the age of 20, Kumarajiva studied Theravada Budhdism at Kashgar, China. He was converted to the Madhyamika school of Buddhism by a Mahayanist named Suryasama. Captured by Chinese raiders, he was taken prisoner to China and finally arrived at Chang'an in 401. There he gained the approval of the imperial family and headed a famous school of translators.

Kundalini, in some Tantric forms of Yoga, the cosmic energy that lies within everyone, it is pictured as a coiled serpent lying at the base of the spine. In the practice of Laya Yoga ("Discipline of Dissolution"), the adept is instructed to awaken the *kundalini*, also identified with the deity Shakti, through a series of techniques that combine prescribed postures, gestures, and breathing exercises. In the process the *kundalini* passes upwards through six centres, or *chakras* (Sanskrit: *chakras*, centres of energy). When the *kundalini* arrives at the seventh *chakra*, at the top of the head, the practitioner experiences a feeling of bliss that registers the dissolution (*laya*) of the ordinary self into its external essence, *atman*. This experience is also understood as the primordial union of the male and female cosmic principles, the former being represented by the *lingam* of Shiva and the latter by the *kundalini* for his consort Shakti.

Kuru-Panchala, powerful clan of the later Vedic period, it occupied the upper Doab and the Kurukshetra region.

Kurukshetra was the site of the famous battle fought between the Kauravas and the Pandavas mentioned in the epic Mahabharata. It lasted 18 days and resulted in the annihilation of the Kauravas. The Pandavas took over the capital of Hastinapur and ruled long and well. Some of these events appear to be supported by historic evidence. Recent archaeological evidence at the site of Hastinapur reveals that part of it was washed away (800 BC) by the flooding of the Ganga River, on the banks of which it was situated. This event is referred to in the Puranas as having occurred during the reign of the seventh successor to the king ruling immediately after the war at Kurukshetra. This would suggest 900 BC as the approximate date of the war.

The geographic focus of the later Vedic corpus moves from the Sapta Sindhu region into the Ganga-Yamuna Doab and the territories on its fringe. The areas within this land of the *aryas*, called Aryavarta, were named for the ruling clans. The most powerful among them, commanding the greatest respect, was the Kuru-Panchala, which incorporated the two families of Kuru and Puru (and the earlier Bharatas) and of which the Panchala was a confederation of lesser-known tribes.

Kushana Art. Kusana art produced during the Kushana dynasty from about the late first to the third century AD, it flourished in an area that now includes parts of Central Asia, northern India, Pakistan, and Afghanistan.

At least two major stylistic divisions can be made among the artefacts of the period: imperial art of Iranian derivation and Buddhist art of mixed Greco-Roman and Indian sources. The best examples of the former are gold coins issued by the seven Kushana kings, the Kushana royal portraits (for example, the Kanishka statue), and princely portraits found at Surkh Kotal in Afghanistan. The style of Kushana artworks is stiff, hieratic, and frontal, emphasizing the power and wealth of the individual. There is little or no interest in the realistic rendering of anatomy or drapery, in contrast to the second style, which is typified by the Gandhara and Mathura schools of Kushana art.

Thus, the Kushanas fostered a mixed culture that is best illustrated by the variety of deities—Greco-Roman, Iranian, and Indian—invoked on their coins.

Kushana Dynasty, Kusana ruling line descended from the Yuezhi, a people that ruled over most of the northern Indian subcontinent, Afghanistan, and parts of Central Asia during the first three centuries of the Christian era. The Yuezhi conquered Bactria in the second century BC and divided the country into five chiefdoms, one of which was that of the Kushanas (Guishang). A hundred years later, the Kushana chief Kujula Kadphises (Chiu-Chiu-Chueh) secured the political unification of the Yuezhi kingdom under himself.

The Kushanas became affluent through trade, particularly with Rome, as a large number of their gold coins show. These coins, which exhibit the figures of Greek, Roman, Iranian, Hindu, and Buddhist deities and bear inscriptions in adapted Greek letters, are witness to the toleration and to the fusion in religion and art that prevailed in the Kushana Empire. After the rise of the Sasanian dynasty in Iran and of local powers in northern India, Kushana rule declined.

Under Kanishka I, who flourished in the first century AD, and his successors, the Kushana kingdom reached its height. It was acknowledged as one of the four great Eurasian powers of its time (the others being China, Rome, and Parthia). The Kushanas were instrumental in spreading Buddhism in Central Asia and China and in developing Mahayana Buddhism and the Gandhara and Mathura schools of art.

L

Lalitavistara, dealing with the legendary life of Gautama Buddha, written in a combination of Sanskrit and a vernacular language, the text apparently is a recasting, in the Mahayana ("Greater Vehicle") tradition, of a work from Sarvastivada School. In characteristic Mahayana fashion, an introductory chapter describes the Buddha, deep in meditation and surrounded by a divine effulgence, about to reveal the contents of the text to an assemblage of 12,000 monks and some 32,000 *bodhisattvas* ("those destined to become enlightened"). In the ensuing narrative, the miraculous and mythological elements of the Buddha's conception and birth are emphasized. The *Lalitavistara* is especially sacred in Mahayana circles, and it has inspired a considerable amount of Buddhist art. A version of it appears to have been translated into Chinese in AD 308. Like the *Mahavastu* ("Great Story"), the subject matter of which is the same, the *Lalitavistara* contains later material but also preserves some very ancient passages. It shares with the Hindu Puranas similarities of style as well as the concept of a divine being's earthly activities as "sport", or "play".

Licchavi, Lichchhavi is the name of a people who settled (sixth-fifth century BC) on the north bank of the Ganga River in modern Bihar State, India, with the capital of their republic at Vaishali.

The Licchavis remained influential in northern India and Nepal until about the fourth century AD. In Nepal a Licchavi dynasty is commemorated in a dating system, the Licchavi era, that began in AD 110.

The Licchavis were renowned for their republican government, having a general assembly of the heads of the leading Kshatriya-caste families. They were, for a time, of considerable importance and rivalled the rising power of Magadha, forming a confederacy with other tribal groups (the so-called Vrijjian, or Vajjian, confederacy).

Lingayat, also called Virashaiva, is a member of a Hindu sect with a wide following in South India that worships Shiva as the only deity.

This sect is generally regarded as having been founded by Basava in the twelfth century, but some scholars believe that he furthered an already existing creed. Philosophically, their qualified monism and their conception of *bhakti* (devotion) as an intuitive and loving knowledge of God show the influence of the eleventh/twelfth-century thinker Ramanuja.

The followers take their name ("*lingam*-wearers") from the small representations of a *lingam*, which both the men and women always wear from a cord around the neck, on the left arm, or elsewhere on the body. Lingayats have a set of rites known as the *ashtavarna* ("eight orders") that distinguish them from other Hindus.

Although caste distinctions among Lingayats were eradicated in the early days of the movement, they reappeared in stages as distinctions were made among older and newer converts, and between converts from higher and lower castes. In other respects the movement has modified and reformed Hindu practices such as child marriage and the remarriage of widows. Lingayat priests (Jangama) are not Brahmins, although they are often treated with similar deference.

Lothal, one of the excavated sites belonging to the Indus Valley Civilization that deserves special attention, it is a small settlement built on low-lying ground near a tributary of the Sabarmati River on the west side of the Gulf of Khambhat, in Gujarat State, which appears to have served as a port or trading station.

The most unexpected discovery at Lothal, however, was a great brick basin measuring 219 by 37 m, with 4.5 m-high brick walls that exist to date. This lay east of the settlement, alongside the platform on which the granary block stood. At one end of the basin was a small sluice or spillway with a locking device. According to some researchers this basin was a dock to which ships could be brought from the nearby estuary via an artificial channel that would have been kept clear of silt by the controlled flow of water from the sluice. This view has not been universally accepted. Another view is that it provided a source of fresh water for drinking or agriculture. A cemetery was found outside the perimeter of the wall, west of the site.

Its layout is distinctive: the site is roughly rectangular, measuring about 360 m on the north-south axis and 210 m on the east-west axis. It was surrounded by a massive brick wall, which was probably used for flood protection. The southeastern quadrant takes the form of a great platform of brick with earth filling, rising to a height of about 4 m. On this were built further, a series of further smaller platforms with intersecting air channels, reminiscent of the granary at Mohenjodaro, with overall dimensions of about 48 by 42 m. Behind this block were other buildings including a row of 12 bathrooms with connected drains, also strongly reminiscent of those found on the citadel at Mohenjodaro. Houses and shops evidently took up the remaining enclosed area. Among the significant finds were a bead maker's factory and the shops of goldsmiths and coppersmiths. The main street ran from north to south.

Lotus Sutra, one of the earlier Mahayana Buddhist texts, the Lotus Sutra is regarded by many others as a religious classic of great beauty and power and one of the most important and most popular works in the Mahayana tradition, the form of Buddhism predominant in East Asia.

The *sutra,* composed largely in verse, has a total of 28 chapters and contains many charms and *mantras* (sacred chants). It was first translated into Chinese in the third century AD and became extremely popular in China and Japan, where common belief held that the simple act of chanting it would bring salvation. The twenty-fifth chapter describes the glory and special powers of the great *bodhisattva* of compassion, Avalokiteshvara.

In the Lotus Sutra the Buddha has become the divine eternal Buddha, who attained perfect Enlightenment endless eons ago. His nature as the supreme object of faith and devotion is expressed partly through the language of wondrous powers (for example, his suddenly making visible thousands of worlds in all directions, each with its own Buddha). Here all beings are invited to become no less than the fully enlightened Buddha through the grace of innumerable *bodhisattvas* ("Buddhas-to-be").

Lumbini, grove near the southern border of modern-day Nepal and India it was here that, according to Buddhist legend, queen Maha Maya stood and gave birth to the future Buddha while holding onto a branch of a sal tree. There are two references to Lumbini as the birthplace of the Buddha in the Pali scriptures, the first in a narrative poem attached to the *Nalaka Sutta* and the other in the *Kathavatthu.*

The discovery of an inscription recording the visit of Ashoka, Maurya emperor of India in the third century BC, to the spot he considered the birthplace makes it probable, however, that the legend was established at least as early as the third century BC. The site, which Nepal locates within its national borders, is once again being developed as a place of Buddhist pligrimage. The earliest actual accounts of the birth are in Sanskrit scriptures, the *Mahavastu* and the *Lalitavistara* neither of which can be dated earlier than the first or second century AD.

M

Madhavacharya (b. 1296?; d. 1386?, Sringeri, India), also called Vidyaranya, Hindu statesman and philosopher, he lived at the court of Vijayanagar, a southern India kingdom.

His younger brother, Sayana, the minister of four successive Vijayanagar kings, is famous as a commentator of the Vedas. Madhavacharya, who was a patron of the scholars collaborating in his brother's great work, influenced Sayana's commentaries.

Madhavacharya became an ascetic in 1377 and was thereafter known as Vidyaranya. He was part author of *Jivan-muktiviveka* and *Panchadashi*, works of Vedanta philosophy; *Dhatuvritti*, a treatise on Sanskrit grammar; *Nyayamalavistara*, a work on the Mimamsa system, one of the earliest orthodox systems of Vedic philosophy; and *Parasharasmritivyakhya*, an elaborate comment on the *Parasharasmriti*.

Madhva (b. c. 1199, Kalyanpur, near Udipi, Karnataka, India; d. c. 1278, Udipi), also called Anandatirtha, or Purnaprajna, Hindu philosopher, exponent of Dvaita (dualism).

He believed in eternal damnation, offering a concept of heaven and hell, plus a Hindu purgatory of endless transmigration of souls. Madhva's cult outlawed temple prostitutes and offered figures made of dough as a substitute for blood sacrifices, and its adherents customarily branded themselves on the shoulder with a multiarmed figure of Vishnu.

Madhva set out to refute the nondualistic Advaita philosophy of Shankara (d. c. AD 750), who believed the individual self to be a phenomenon and the absolute spirit (Brahman) the only reality. Thus, Madhva rejected the venerable Hindu theory of *maya* ("illusion"), which teaches that only spirituality is eternal and the material world is illusory and deceptive. Madhva maintained that the simple fact that things are transient and ever-changing does not mean they are not real.

During his lifetime, Madhva wrote 37 works in Sanskrit, mostly commentaries on Hindu sacred writings and treatises on his own theological system and philosophy.

Madhva was born into a Brahmin family, and as a youth,

according to tradition, he disappeared for a short time. After a four-day search, his parents found him engaged in discourse with the learned Vaishnavas (worshippers of Lord Vishnu); later, on a pilgrimage to the sacred city of Varanasi (Banaras), he walked on water, calmed the rough sea, and became a "fisher of men". Similarities between his life story and narratives found in Christian Gospels suggest that he may have been influenced during his youth by a group of Nestorian Christians who were residing at Kalyanpur.

Madhyamika, important school in the Mahayana ("Great Vehicle") Buddhist tradition, its name derives from its having sought a middle position between the realism of the Sarvastivada school and the idealism of the Yogachara school. The most renowned Madhyamika thinker was Nagarjuna (second century AD), who developed the doctrine that all is void (shunyavada). The three authoritative texts of the school are the *Madhyamika-shastra* (Sanskrit: "Treatise of the Middle Way"), the *Dvadasha-dvara-shastra* ("Twelve Gates Treatise") by Nagarjuna, and the *Shataka-shastra* ("One Hundred verses Treatise"), attributed to his pupil Aryadeva.

The basic Madhyamika texts were translated into Chinese by Kumarajiva in the fifth century, and the teachings were further systematized as the Sanlunzong, or Three Treatises, school in the sixth-seventh century by Jizang. The school spread to Korea and was first transmitted to Japan, as Sanron, in 625 by the Korean monk Ekwan.

Buddhism in general assumed that the world is a cosmic flux of momentary interconnected events (*dharmas*), however the reality of these events might be viewed. Nagarjuna sought to demonstrate that the flux itself could not be held to be real, nor could the consciousness perceiving it, as it itself is part of this flux. If this world of constant change is not real, neither can the serial transmigration (rebirth) be real, nor can its opposite, Nirvana. With transmigration and Nirvana being equally unreal, they are one and the same. In the final analysis, reality can only be attributed to something entirely different from all that is known, which must therefore have no identifiable predicates and can only be styled the void (*shunyata*).

Madhyamika thinkers, thus, strongly emphasize the mutations of human consciousness to grasp the reality of that which is ultimately real, beyond any duality. The world of duality could be assigned a practical reality of *vyavahara* ("discourse and process"), but, once the ultimate meaning (*paramartha*) of the void is grasped, this reality falls away. These ideals influenced Hindu thinkers, principally Gaudapada (seventh century) and Shankara (usually dated AD 788-820); the latter is therefore called a crypto-Madhyamika by his adversaries.

Magha, eighth-century Indian writer, Mgaha was a conscious rival of Bharavi, whom he attempted to surpass in every respect. Magha was a master of technique in the strict Sanskrit sense of descriptions; intricate syntax; compounds that, depending on how they are split, deliver quite different meanings; and the full of register of stylistic embellishments. His *Shishupalavadham* ("The Slaying of King Shishupala") is based on an episode of the Mahabharata in which the rival King Shishupala insults the hero-god Krishna, who beheads him in the ensuing duel.

Mahabharata, one of the two major epics of India, it is valued for both its literary and religious qualities. Together with the second major epic, the Ramayana, it is an important source of information about the evolution of Hinduism during the period from about 400 BC to AD 200.

The Mahabharata is an exposition on *dharma* (codes of conduct), including the proper conduct of a king, of a warrior, of a man living in times of calamity, and of a person seeking to attain emancipation from rebirth. Hindus regard the Mahabharata as one of the dharmashastra, teachings on duty and right conduct. The most important part of the Mahabharata is the Bhagavadgita (Book VI), presented as a dialogue between Arjuna and Krishna on the battlefield of Kurukshetra, just as the war between the Pandavas and Kauravas is about to begin. Seeing his friends and kinsmen among those lined up on the other side, Arjuna hesitates. He is recalled to his sense of duty as a warrior by Krishna, who points out to him that the higher way is the selfless discharge of his duty (*dharma*), performed with faith in God, and without desire for personal triumph or gain.

The story revolves around the Bharata dynasty, which ruled the kingdom of Hastinapura. Several years after his wife Ganga (the river in human form) leaves him, King Shantanu falls in love with Satyavati, the daughter of a fisherman. Satyavati's father refuses permission for them to marry because Devavrata (the son of Ganga) would have precedence over Satyavati's son as Shantanu's heir. On hearing this, Devavrata vows he will remain a *brahmacharin* (celibate), and abdicates all his rights to the throne. He is thereafter called Bhishma, or "one who undertakes and fulfils a terrible vow".

Satyavati marries Shantanu and has two sons, Chitrangada and Vichitravirya. After Chitrangada is killed in battle, and Shantanu dies, Vichitravirya (still a minor) is proclaimed king of Hastinapura, with Bhishma as regent.

Bhishma captures the three daughters of the king of Kashi as brides for Vichitravirya. One of them, Amba, declares her love for Shalva, the king of Saubha, and is set free. Shalva, however, rejects Amba, and Bhishma, too, refuses to marry her. Holding Bhishma solely responsible for her humiliation, Amba prays to Lord Shiva to assist her in avenging herself against him. As a result, she is reborn in King Drupada's family as Shikhandi, and is ultimately responsible for Bhishma's downfall.

Meanwhile, the other two princesses, Ambika and Ambalika, marry Vichitravirya, who dies before any children are born to them. Satyavati then asks for Vyasa's assistance for the perpetuation of the dynasty. Through his grace, three children are born, one each to Ambika, Ambalika, and a maid-servant. They are Dhritarashtra (who is blind because his mother Ambika closed her eyes on seeing Vyasa), Pandu (who is pale and weak because Ambalika was pale with fright on seeing the sage), and Vidura (wise and virtuous, the son of the maid-servant who stood fearlessly before Vyasa).

Since Dhritarashtra is blind, Pandu becomes king of Hastinapura. A sage's curse restrains him from begetting children, and Pandu retires to the forest with his wives Kunti and Madri. There, Kunti reveals a boon by which she can invoke the gods and produce sons. She uses the boon and has three sons, Yudhishtira (the son of Dharma, the god of justice), Bhima (the son of Vayu, the wind-god), and Arjuna (the son of Indra, the chief of the gods); Madri invokes the Ashvins, twin horsemen, and bears twin sons, Nakula and Sahadeva. Some years later, Pandu dies and Madri burns herself on his funeral pyre, leaving Kunti to bring up his sons, known collectively as the Pandavas. Kunti and the Pandavas return to Hastinapura, where Vidura (Dhritarashtra's councillor) and Bhishma oversee their upbringing, along with the hundred sons of Dhritarashtra and his wife Gandhari, known collectively as the Kauravas.

Dronacharya, who is skilled in archery, is the guru (preceptor) of the Pandavas and Kauravas. The Pandavas excel at all they are taught, with Arjuna unsurpassed in archery. As the Pandavas earn the love and respect of the elders and the citizens, the jealousy of the Kauravas, especially the eldest, Duryodhana, grows.

Duryodhana attempts to kill the Pandavas in a fire, from which they escape with Vidura's help. Disguised as Brahmins, the Pandavas and Kunti hide in the forest. During this time, Arjuna wins the hand of Draupadi, the daughter of King Drupada; following Kunti's command, all five brothers marry the princess. The Pandavas also meet with their cousin Lord Krishna, who remains their friend and companion thereafter. Along with Draupadi and Kunti, the brothers return to Hastinapura, where, on Vidura's advice, Dhritarashtra divides the kingdom between the cousins. The Pandavas build their new capital at Indraprastha, and Yudhishtira, as king, conducts a great yajna (sacrifice) to proclaim himself emperor.

The *yajna* further arouses Duryodhana's jealousy, and he contrives to bring about the downfall of the Pandavas. With his maternal uncle, Shakuni, he invites the Pandavas to Hastinapura for a game of dice. Shakuni, an expert gambler, plays on Duryodhana's behalf, and soon Yudhishtira loses everything: his kingdom, his wealth, his brothers, himself and, finally, Draupadi. Duryodhana's brother, Dushasana, drags Draupadi to the assembly hall and attempts to disrobe her; which proves impossible, as her garment is miraculously without end. Dhritarashtra, who has been silent all along, restores the Pandavas' freedom and returns their kingdom.

The Pandavas return to their kingdom, but Duryodhana challenges Yudhishtira to another game of dice; etiquette demands that Yudhishtira accept the invitation. This time the stakes are that the loser will be exiled to the forest for twelve years, spending the thirteenth year incognito; if discovered during the thirteenth year, the loser will spend another twelve years in the forest. Yudhishtira loses the game and, along with his brothers and Draupadi, sets out for the forest. After twelve years in the forest, the Pandavas spend their last year of exile in disguise at the court of Virata.

Their exile over, the Pandavas attempt to reclaim their kingdom, but Duryodhana refuses to part with any land. Emissaries are sent to Hastinapura, including Lord Krishna, but return unsuccessful, and both sides prepare for war. The feud culminates in a great battle on the field of Kurukshetra (in modern Haryana State). Bhishma and Dronacharya fight for the Kauravas, although they oppose the war and recognize Yudhishtira's actions as proper *dharma*. Karna, Kunti's son from before her marriage, whose father is the sun god, also joins the Kauravas. The war lasts eighteen days; all the Kauravas are annihilated, and on the victorious side, only the five Pandavas and Krishna survive.

The Pandavas succeed to a kingdom ruined by war. Dhritarashtra, Gandhari and Kunti retire to the forest, where they perish in a fire.

Cursed by Gandhari, Krishna dies at the hands of a hunter who mistakes him for a deer, and the five brothers along with Draupadi and a dog who joins them (Dharma, the god of justice, in disguise), set out for Indira's heaven. One by one they fall on the way, and Yudhishtira alone reaches the gate of heaven. After further tests of his faithfulness and constancy, he is finally reunited with his brothers and Draupadi to enjoy perpetual bliss.

The feud constitutes little more than a fifth of the total work and may once have formed a separate poem, the Bharata. Interwoven with its episodes are the romance of Nala and Damayanti; the legend of Savitri, whose devotion to her dead husband persuades Yama, the god of death, to restore him to life; descriptions of places of pilgrimages; and many other myths and legends.

The poem is made up of almost 100,000 couplets—its length thus being about seven times that of the *Iliad* and the *Odyssey* combined—divided into 18 *parvanas*, or books, to which has been added a supplement entitled Harivamsha ("Genealogy of the God Hari", Krishna-Vishnu). Some sections, such as the Narayaniya (a part of Book XIII), the Anugita (Book XIV), the Bhagavadgita (Book VI), and the Harivamsha are important sources of early Vaishnavite thought. There, Krishna is identified with Lord Vishnu, and other *avatars* (incarnation, personification) are also described. Authorship of the poem is traditionally ascribed to the sage Vyasa (with Ganesha, the elephant-headed god, as his amanuensis), although it may be more accurate to think of the work as having been compiled from existing traditions than as an original composition.

Mahavastu, important legendary life of the Buddha produced as a late canonical work by the Mahasanghika School of early Buddhism and presented as a historical introduction to the *vinaya*, the section of the canon dealing with monastic discipline, its three sections treat the Buddha's former lives, the events from his entering the womb of Queen Maha Maya to his Enlightenment, and his first conversions and the rise of the monastic community.

The life of the Buddha itself is presented as a profusion of miracles and wondrous events. The *Mahavastu* reflects a growth of ideas about *bodhisattvas* ("buddhas-to-be") that was to continue in Mahayana circles, but at the same time, it preserves many ancient stories, traditions, and textual passages. The core of the work may go back to the second century BC, but much material seems to have been added at a later date.

The text is exuberant in style, and in form, a labyrinth. Its central narrative is frequently interrupted by *jatakas* (explanations of present events by incidents in the Buddha's previous lives), *avadanas* (similar tales from the previous lives of others), and doctrinal discourses.

Mahavihara, Buddhist monastery founded in the late third century BC in Anuradhapura, the ancient capital of Ceylon (now Sri Lanka), it was built by the Sinhalese king Devanampiya Tissa not long after his conversion to Buddhism by the Indian monk Mahendra. Until about the tenth century, it was a great cultural and religious centre and the chief stronghold of orthodox (Theravada) Buddhism. Because of the extreme importance of Buddhism in Ceylon, the prestige of the monks of the Mahavihara was such that their power and influence often extended well beyond religion into the realm of secular politics.

The centralized authority and pre-eminence of the Mahavihara, however, gradually disintegrated until, by the eleventh century, it had ceased to be a force in the religious life of Ceylon.

The religious authority of the Mahavihara was first challenged in the late first century BC by a heterodox group of Buddhist monks who broke away and formed the Abhayagiri-vihara. Although an ever-present rival, this monastic order—save for brief periods of royal patronage, notably in the third and seventh centuries—could not permanently usurp the favoured position of the Mahavihara order.

Mahavira (b. c. 599 BC, Kshatriyakundagrama, India; d. c. 527, Pavapuri, traditional dating), last of the 24 Tirthankaras, (the saints who promulgated Jainism), he was reformer of the Jain monastic community. The traditions of the two main Jain sects record that Mahavira became a monk and followed an extreme ascetic life, attaining *kevala*, the stage of omniscience or highest perception. Teaching a doctrine of austerity, Mahavira advocated nonviolence in all circumstances and the acceptance of the *mahavratas*, the five "great vows" of renunciation.

The seventh fifth centuries BC was a period of great intellectual, philosophical, religious, and social ferment in India, a period in which certain members of the Kshatriya caste opposed the cultural domination of the Brahmins, who claimed authority on the basis of their supposed innate purity. In particular, there was growing opposition to the large-scale Vedic sacrifices (*yajna*), which involved the killing of many animals. Unnecessary killing had become objectionable to many thinking people of the time, especially with the spread of the doctrine of continual rebirth, which linked animals and human beings in the same cycle of birth, death, and rebirth.

Economic factors may also have encouraged the growth of the doctrine of nonviolence. The leaders of the anti-Brahmin sects came to be regarded as heretical. Mahavira and his contemporary Siddhartha Gautama, the Buddha, were two of the greatest leaders in this movement.

It is traditionally accepted that Mahavira was born about 599 BC. Many scholars now consider this to be about 100 years too early, as he appears to have been a younger contemporary of the Buddha whose traditional date has now been reassessed. The son of a Kshatriya (member of the warrior caste) family, he grew up in Kshatriyakundagrama, a suburb of Vaishali (modern Basarh, Bihar State), the area of origin of both Jainism and Buddhism. His father was Siddartha, a ruler of the Nata, or Jnatr, clan. According to one Jain tradition, his mother was named Devananda and was a member of the Brahmin (priestly) caste; other traditions name her Trishala, Videhadinna, or Priyakarini, and place her in the Kshatriya caste.

Though the traditions about the life of Mahavira vary according to the two Jain sects—the Shvetambaras ("white-robed") and the Digambaras ("sky-clad"; naked)—he apparently was reared in luxury, though as a younger son he could not inherit the leadership of the clan. According to the Shvetambara sect, At the age of 30, after he had married a lady of the Kshatriya caste and had a daughter, he renounced the world and became a monk. Mahavira used one garment for more than a year, but subsequently he went about naked and kept no possessions—not even a bowl for alms or drinking water. He allowed insects to crawl on his body and bite him, bearing the pain with patience. People frequently shouted at him and hit him because of his uncouth and unsightly body but he endured abusive language and physical injuries with equanimity. He meditated day and night and lived in various places such as workshops, cremation and burial grounds, and under trees. Trying to avoid all sinful activity, he especially avoided injuring any kind of life, thus developing the doctrine of *ahimsa*, or non-violence. He kept numerous fast periods and never ate anything that was expressly prepared for him. Though he wandered about continuously during most of the year, Mahavira spent the four months of the rainy season in villages and towns.

Mahavira's teachings: After 12 years of practising such austerities, Mahavira attained *kevala*, the highest stage of perception. Mahavira may be regarded as the reviver and reorganizer of both Jain doctrine and its monastic order, thus being credited as the founder of Jainism.

Basing his doctrines, according to tradition, on the teachings of the twenty-third Tirthankara, Parshvanatha, a c. ninth- or eighth-century-BC teacher from Banaras (Varanasi, Uttar Pradesh), Mahavira systematized earlier Jain doctrines—along with metaphysical, mythological, and cosmological beliefs—and also established the rules and guidelines of Jain religious life for the monks, nuns, and laity.

Mahavira was given the title Jina, or "conqueror" (conqueror of enemies such as attachment and greed), which subsequently became a synonym for Tirthankara. He died, according to tradition, in 527 BC at Pava in Bihar State, leaving a group of followers who established Jainism, which, with its practice of nonviolence, has profoundly influenced Indian culture.

Mahavira taught that a man can save his soul from the contamination of matter (*karma*) by living a life of extreme asceticism and by practising nonviolence toward all living creatures. This advocacy of nonviolence gradually encouraged his followers, monastic and lay, to become strong advocates of vegetarianism. Mahavira's followers were aided in their quest for salvation by accepting the five *mahavratas* whose formulation has been attributed to Mahavira (although they show connections with contemporary Brahminical practice): renunciation of killing, of speaking untruths, of greed, of sexual pleasure, and of all attachments to living beings and nonliving things. Mahavira's predecessor, Parshvanatha, preached only four vows.

Mahayana, one of the two major Buddhist traditions and the form most widely adhered to in China, Korea, Japan, and Tibet, Mahayana Buddhism emerged in about the first century AD from the ancient Buddhist schools as a more liberal and innovative interpretation of the Buddha's teachings. The Mahayana scriptures were composed mainly in Sanskrit, though in some cases they are known only in their Tibetan and Chinese versions, the original having been lost. Mahayanists distinguished themselves from the more orthodox conservative schools, which they somewhat deprecatingly termed Hinayana. Compasion, the chief virtue associated with the *bodhisattva*, is accorded an equal place with wisdom, the virtue emphasized by the ancient schools. The merit accrued by a *bodhisattva* is considered transferable to others, a concept that led to such devotional movements as the Pure Land Buddhism of China and Japan.

The Mahayana differ from the conservatives, represented in the modern world by the Theravadins of Sri Lanka, Myanmar (formerly Burma), Thailand, Laos, and Cambodia, in their views of the nature of the Buddha and the ideal goal of a Buddhist. While Theravada Buddhists revere the historical Gautama Buddha as a teacher of the truth, Mahayanists attribute to the Buddha a supramundane quality and interpret the historical Buddha as an earthly manifestation of a transcendent celestial Buddha. The ideal goal for a Buddhist in Theravada Buddhism is to become an *arhat* or perfected saint. Mahayanists consider this to be a limited, selfish goal and instead strive to become a *bodhisattva*, a person who has attained the state of Enlightenment but has postponed his Buddhahood in order to work towards the salvation of all others.

Other major schools of Mahayana Buddhism, with a significant modern following, are Zen Buddhism, Nichiren Buddhism, and Tendai.

Mahendra (b. c. 270 BC, Pataliputra, India; d. c. 204 BC, Anuradhapura, Ceylon [now Sri Lanka]), Mahinda, was the propagator of Buddhism in Ceylon. Generally believed to be the son of the Indian emperor Ashoka, he is honoured in Sri Lanka as a founding missionary of that country's major religion.

Mahendra's name has not been found in any of the inscriptions of Ashoka, but his existence and works seen substantiated by the Ceylonese chronicles *Dipavamsha* and *Mahavamsha*. Other evidence consists of the monuments that the Sinhalese raised in his honour at the Buddhist holy city and ancient Ceylonese capital, Anuradhapura.

When Ashoka, a convert to Buddhism from Hinduism, sent Mahendra and Princess Sanghamittha as missionaries to Ceylon about 251 BC, they converted King Tissa and the royal family, who helped them in the conversion of many of the common people. In the tradition of Ashoka, Mahendra did not propagate Buddhism by force but by works of practical piety and benevolence.

Maitraka Dynasty, Indian dynasty it ruled in Gujarat and Saurashtra (Kathiawar) from the fifth to the eighth century AD. Its founder, Bhatarka, was a general who, taking advantage of the decay of the Gupta Empire, established himself as ruler of Gujarat and Saurashtra with Valabhi (modern Vala) as his capital. Bhatarka and his successors were great patrons of religious foundations. Their kingdom was an important centre of Buddhism, and according to tradition, it was in Valabhi that the Shvetambara Jain canon was codified.

The early Maitraka kings were loosely feudatory to the Guptas; they were in fact independent. Under the powerful Shiladitya I (c. late sixth century), the kingdom became very influential. Its rule extended into Malwa and Rajasthan. Later, however, the Maitrakas suffered at the hands of the Chalukyas of the Deccan and of the emperor Harsha of Kannauj. After Harsha's death, the Maitrakas revived, but the Arabs who had established themselves in Sind in AD 712 killed the last Maitraka king, Shiladitya VI, and razed his capital in about AD 780.

Mallas, tribal people they settled in the northern parts of modern Bihar State, India, between the c. sixth and the fourth century BC. Their two most important towns were at Kushinagara (Kusinara) and Pava (located east of modern Gorakhpur). A Malla dynasty ruled Nepal from the tenth century to 1769. The Mallas introduced the first legal and social code influenced by contemporary Hindu practices, and were patrons of the arts and architecture. The Mallas had a republican form of government, with an assembly. They lost their independence around the time of the Buddha and were annexed by the Magadha Empire.

Manjushri, in Mahayana Buddhism, the *bodhisattva* ("Buddha-to-be") personifies supreme wisdom, his name in Sanskrit means "gentle, or sweet, glory". He is also known as Manjughosha ("Sweet Voice") and Vagishvara ("Lord of Speech"). In China he is called Wenshushili, in Japan Monju, and in Tibet Jam-dpal.

His cult spread widely in China in the eighth century. Mount Wutai in Shanxi province, which is dedicated to him, is covered with his temples. Though he is usually considered a celestial *bodhisattva*, some traditions endow Manjushri with a human history. He is said to manifest himself in many ways—in dreams; as a pilgrim on his sacred mountain; as an incarnation of the monk Vairochana, who introduced Buddhism into Khotan; as the Tibetan reformer Atisha; and as the emperor of China.

Although sutras (Buddhist scriptures) were composed in his honour by at least AD 250, he does not seem to have been represented in Buddhist art before AD 400. He is most commonly shown wearing princely ornaments, his right hand holding aloft the sword of wisdom to cleave the clouds of ignorance and his left holding a palm-leaf manuscript of the Prajnaparamita. He is sometimes depicted seated on a lion or on a blue lotus; and in paintings his skin is usually yellow in colour.

Manu, in the mythology of India, he is the first man, and the legendary author of an important Sanskrit code of law, the Manu Smriti. Manu appears in the Vedas as the performer of the first sacrifice. He is also known as the first king, and most rulers of medieval India traced their genealogy back to him, either through his son (the solar line) or his daughter (the lunar line).

In the cosmological speculations of later Hinduism, a day in the life of Brahma is divided into 14 periods called *manvantara*, each of which lasts for 306,720,000 years. In every secondary cycle the world is recreated, and a new Manu appears to become the father of the next human race. The present age is considered the seventh Manu cycle.

In the story of the great flood, Manu combines the characteristics of Noah with those of Adam. The Shatapatha Brahmana recounts how he was warned by a fish, to whom he had done a kindness, that a flood would destroy the whole of humanity. He therefore built a boat, as the fish advised. When the flood came, he tied this boat to the fish's horn and was safely steered to a resting place on a mountaintop. When the flood receded, Manu, the sole human survivor, performed a sacrifice, pouring oblations of butter and sour milk into the waters. After a year there was born from the waters a woman who announced herself as "the daughter of Manu". These two then became the ancestors of a new human race to replenish the earth. In the Mahabharata, the fish is identified with the god Brahma, while in the Puranas ("Ancient Lore") it is Matsya, the fish incarnation of the lord Vishnu.

Manu Smriti, the most authoritative of the books of the Hindu code (Dharmashastra) in India, *Manu Smriti* is the popular name of the work, which is officially known as *Manava-dharmashastra*. It is attributed to the legendary lawgiver, Manu. In its present form, it dates from the first century BC.

The *Manu Smriti* prescribes to the Hindu his *dharma*—that is, the set of obligations that he needs to follow as a member of one of the four social classes (*varnas*) and engaged in one of the four stages of life (*ashramas*). It contains a total of 2,694 stanzas divided into 12 chapters. It deals with cosmogony, the definition of the *dharma*, the sacraments (*samskaras*), initiation (*upanayana*) and study of the Veda, marriage, hospitality, last rites, dietary restrictions, pollution and means of purification, the conduct of women and wives.

The law of kings, leads to a consideration of matters of juridical interest, divided under 18 headings, after which the text returns to religious topics, such as donations, rites of atonement, the doctrine of *karma*, the soul, and hell. The text makes no categorical distinction between religious law and practices and secular law in its treatment. Its influence has been monumental, and it has provided the caste Hindu with a system of practical morality.

Manyakheta, site of a former city, modern Malkhaid, in Karnataka State, India, about 135 km southwest of Hyderabad, it was founded in the ninth century by the Rashtrakuta ruler Amoghavarsha I and became the capital of the dynasty.

In 972 it was devastated by the Paramara ruler Siyaka. After the downfall of the dynasty in the following year, it was taken by the Chalukyas, who adopted it for some time as their capital. Thereafter it never regained its former glory and dwindled to the status of a village.

Matsyendranatha, also called Minanatha, he was first human guru, or preceptor, of the Natha cult, a popular Indian religious movement combining elements of Hinduism, Buddhism, and Hatha Yoga. A form of *yoga* that stresses breath control and physical postures it flourished in tenth century AD, India.

The historical details of Matsyendranatha's life are lost in the legends that have grown up around him. Though an ascetic he succumbed, according to one legend, to the enchantment of two queens of Ceylon and had two sons, Parosenath and Nimnath, who were leaders of the Jain religious sect. His leading disciple, Gorakhnath, is commonly regarded as the founder of the Kanphata Yogis, an order of religious ascetics who stress the practice of Hatha Yoga.

Matsyendranatha's name appears on both the lists of the nine *nathas* ("masters") and the 84 *mahasiddhas* ("great accomplished ones") common to Hinduism and Buddhism. He was given semidivine status by his followers and identified with Avalokiteshvara-Padmapani (a *bodhisattva*, or Buddha-to-be) by his Buddhist followers in Nepal and with the god Shiva by his Hindu devotees. In Tibet he was known as Lui-pa. The name Minanatha ("Fish-Lord") refers, according to one legend, to his receipt of spiritual instruction from Shiva while in the form of a fish and in another legend, to his rescue of a sacred text from the belly of a fish.

Maurya Empire (321-185 BC), in ancient India this refers to a State centred at Pataliputra (later Patna) near the junction of the Son and Ganga rivers. In the wake of Alexander the Great's death, Chandragupta, its dynastic founder, çarved out the majority of an empire that encompassed most of the subcontinent except of the Tamil south. The Maurya Empire was an efficient and highly organized autocracy with a standing army and civil service. This bureaucracy and its operation was the model for Kautilya's *Artha Shastra* ("Treatise on the Aims of Life"), a work of political economy similar in tone and scope to Machiavelli's *The Prince*.

After Ashoka's death the empire shrank because of invasions, defections by southern princes, and quarrels over accession. The last ruler, Brihadratha, was killed in 185 BC by his Brahmin commander-in-chief, Pushyamitra, who then founded the Shunga dynasty which ruled in central India for about a century.

Much is known of the reign of the Buddhist Maurya emperor Ashoka (reigned c. 262-238 BC) from the exquisitely executed stone edicts that he had erected throughout his realm. These comprise some of the oldest deciphered original texts of India. Ashoka campaigned little to expand the realm; rather, his conquest consisted of sending many Buddhist emissaries throughout Asia and commissioning some of the finest works of ancient Indian art.

Megasthenes was the long-time ambassador of Seleukos Nikator of Babylon to the court of Chandragupta Maurya at Pataliputra. Megasthenes compiled an account of the geography, products, institutions, and customs of India as he observed them in the capital city of the Mauryan Empire and in the course of his travels. It was the first authentic, detailed, and connected description of India by a foreign traveller and is therefore regarded as a major source of information on the ancient period in general and the Mauryan era in particular. However, his record has not survived in entirety even though much of it was quoted by later Greek and Latin authors.

Menander (flourished 160 BC?-135 BC?), the greatest of the Indo-Greek kings (second century BC) and the one best known to Western and Indian classical authors, he is believed to have been a patron of the Buddhist religion and the subject of an important Buddhist work, the *Milinda-panha* ("The Questions of Milinda").

Menander was probably the Indo-Greek king who was converted to Buddhism by the holy man Nagasena after a prolonged and intelligent discussion, which has been recorded in the *Milinda-panha*. The style may have been influenced by Plato's dialogues. The wheel engraved on some of Menander's coins is probably connected with Buddhism. Plutarch's statement that when Menander died his earthly remains were divided equally among the cities of his kingdom and that monuments, possibly *stupas*, were to be erected to enshrine them, indicates that he had probably become a Buddhist.

The only inscription referring to Menander has been found in Bajaur, the tribal territory between the Swat and Kunar rivers. A large number of silver and copper coins have been unearthed from this period which attest to both the duration of Menander's reign and the flourishing commerce of his realm.

Menander was born in the Caucasus, but the Greek biographer Plutarch calls him a king of Bactria. Strabo, the Greek geographer and historian, includes him among the Bactrian Greeks "who conquered more tribes than Alexander". It is possible that he ruled over Bactria, and it has been suggested that he aided the Seleucid ruler Demetrius II against the Parthians. His kingdom in the Indian subcontinent consisted of an area extending from the Kabul valley in the west to the Ravi River in the east, and from the Swat valley (in modern Pakistan) in the north to Arachosia in Afghanistan to the south. Ancient Indian writers indicate that he probably led expeditions into Rajputana and as far east along the Gangetic valley as Pataliputra, in the present-day Indian State of Bihar.

Mihirakula, son of Toramana, was the first Hun king in India (early sixth century). Mihirakula, a patron of Shaivism (worship of Lord Shiva), is recorded in Buddhist tradition as being uncouth and extremely cruel. The Gupta rulers, together with Yashodharman of Malwa, seem to have confronted Mihirakula and forced him back to the north. Ultimately his kingdom was limited to Kashmir and Punjab with its capital at Shakala (Sialkot). Hun power declined after his reign. Inscriptions belonging to their reign have been found as far south as Eran (Madhya Pradesh).

Milinda-Panha, to the lively dialogue on Buddhist doctrine with questions and dilemmas posed by King Milinda—Menander, Greek ruler of a large Indo-Greek empire in the late second century BC—and answered by Nagasena, a senior monk. It was composed in northern India in perhaps the first or second century AD (and possibly originally in Sanskrit) by an unknown author, the *Milinda-panha* is the one noncanonical work whose authority was accepted implicitly by such commentators as Buddhaghosha, who quoted it frequently.

The problems discussed are common themes in the Pali canon, beginning with the nonexistence of a soul, and the doctrine is orthodox Theravada. Of the seven books into which the work is divided, the second and third and sections of the first are masterpieces of ancient Indian prose. They deal with basic questions of interest to laypersons and make excellent use of parables. The remainder is a later addition of a more scholastic nature.

It is also one of the few post-canonical works of the Theravada school that was not produced in Ceylon (now Sri Lanka), though its authority there remains unquestioned.

Mimamsa, one of the six orthodox systems (*darshans*) of Indian philosophy and probably the earliest of the six, it is fundamental to Vedanta and has deeply influenced the formulation of Hindu law.

The goal of Mimamsa is to provide enlightenment on *dharma*, which in this school is understood as the set of ritual obligations and prerogatives that, if properly performed, maintains the harmony of the world and furthers the personal goals of the performer. Since, *dharma* cannot be known through either perception or reasoning, one must depend on the Vedas, which are considered eternal, authorless, and absolutely infallible.

The aim of Mimamsa is to give rules for the interpretation of the Vedas and to provide a philosophical justification for the observance of Vedic ritual. Because Mimamsa is concerned with the earlier parts of the Vedas (called the Karmakanda), it is also referred to as Purva-Mimamsa ("Prior Study"), or Karma-Mimamsa ("Study of the Acts"). Vedanta, which deals with the later portion, the Upanishads, is called Uttara-Mimamsa ("Posterior Study"), or Jnana-Mimamsa ("Study of Knowledge").

To find out what one's *dharma* is on specific occasions, examples of direct or implicit command on the Vedic texts must be relied upon. If the command is implicit, one must judge from parallels; if a text fails to detail how a priest proceeds with an action, this detail must be provided from other texts. This concern with precise statement necessitates meticulous examination of the structure of a sentence conveying a command.

The earliest work of the system is the *Mimamsa-sutra* of Jaimini (c. fourth century BC). A major commentary was written by Shabarasvamin (first century BC?), who was followed by a long line of interpreters and teachers, most notably Kumarila Bhatta and Prabhakar (seventh/eighth century AD).

Although it was purely practical in origin, Mimamsa became a powerful intellectual force. Mimamsa, in the person of Kumarila, is traditionally credited with the defeat of Buddhism in India. It has also contributed to the direction, method, and content of Hindu erudition.

Mleccha, people of foreign extraction (non-Aryans) in ancient India, this term was used by the Aryans much as the ancient Greeks used *barbaros*, originally to indicate the uncouth and incomprehensible speech of foreigners and then extended to their unfamiliar behaviour. As a *mleccha*, any foreigner stood completely outside the caste system and the ritual ambience. Historically, contact with them was viewed by the caste Hindu as polluting. *Mlecchas* were found in northwestern India, and there is reason to believe that the people known in Akkadian as Mlakha were the original *mlecchas*.

Mohenjodaro, group of mounds on the right bank of the Indus

River, in Sind province, southern Pakistan, it means "the mound of the dead".

There is no surviving evidence of architectural elaboration, though this may well have been confined to perished timberwork. Stone sculpture, too, is scarce. Among the remains that have been found is the famed "bearded man". This is a bust of a bearded man with an appreciable head and a low forehead, narrowed and somewhat supercilious eyes, a fillet round the brow; and across the left shoulder is a cloak carved in relief with trefoils formerly filled with red paste. Aesthetically the most notable work of figurative art from the city is a famous bronze of a young dancing girl, naked save for a multitude of armlets. Among the innumerable terracotta pieces found, the most expressive are small but vigorous representations of bulls and buffaloes. Female figurines may wear elaborate headdresses, and occasional figurines of small, fat grotesques, male or female, betray a crude sense of humour.

The evidence suggests that Mohenjodaro suffered more than once from devastating floods of abnormal depth and duration, owing not merely to the encroaching Indus but possibly also to a backward flow of the Indus drainage by tectonic uplifts between Mohenjodaro and the sea.

The city of Mohenjodaro is now 3 km from the Indus. It seems to have been protected from the river even in ancient times by artificial barriers as it is today. It was laid out with astonishing regularity into something like a dozen blocks, or "islands", each about 384 m from north to south and 228 m from east to west, subdivided by straight, narrow lanes. The central block on the western side was built up artificially to a dominating height of 6-12 m with mud and mud bricks and was fortified to an unascertained extent by square towers of baked bricks. Buildings on the high summit included an elaborate bath or tank surrounded by a veranda, a large residential structure, a massive granary, and at least two aisled halls of assembly. It is clear that his citadel (for such it evidently was) housed the religious and ceremonial headquarters of the site. In the lower town were a substantial number of courtyard houses indicating a considerable middle class. Most houses had small bathrooms and, like the streets, were well provided with drains and sanitation. Brick stairs indicate at least an upper story or a flat, habitable roof. The walls were originally plastered with mud, no doubt to reduce the deleterious effect of the salts present in the bricks which react destructively to varying heat and humidity.

The archaeological importance of Mohenjodaro was first

recognized in 1922, and subsequent excavations revealed that the mounds contained the remains of what was once the largest city of the Indus civilization. Because of the city's size—about 5 km in circumference—and the comparative richness of its monuments and their contents, it has been generally regarded as the capital of an extensive State.

Moksha, also called mukti, or apavarga, in Hinduism and Jainism, it is the ultimate spiritual goal, designating the individual soul's release from the bonds (*bandha*) of transmigration. The soul, once entered upon a bodily existence, remains trapped in a chain of successive rebirths (*samsara*) until it has reached perfection or the enlightenment that allows its release, or *mok̆sha*. The methods by which release is sought and attained differ from school to school, but most schools consider *moksha* to be a person's highest purpose in life.

Mudra, in Buddhism and Hinduism, it is a symbolic gesture of the hands and fingers used either in ceremonies and dance, or in sculpture and painting. *Mudras* used in ceremony and dance tend to be numerous, complicated, and often esoteric (the hasta-*mudras* of Indian classical dance can express about 500 different meanings, involving not only the hands and fingers but also the wrists, elbows, and shoulders, all in movement). *Mudras* in sculpture and other visual arts, being immobile, are relatively less in number.

The hundreds of *mudras* of Indian dances are described in technical manuals, but, in practice, performers usually limit their gestures or "phrases" (sequences of *mudras*) to those familiar and meaningful to their audiences. The selection may differ from region to region.

In ceremonies, a *mudra* acts as a "visual expression" or "seal", affirming a mystical utterance. A *mudra* can often accompany the spiritual utterance known as *mantra*. Sculptural and other pictorial renderings of the Buddha and Hindu gods and goddesses show them in four basic postures—reclining, standing, walking, and sitting. Different *mudras* or hand gestures appear in any of the postures.

N

Nagarjuna (b. AD 150; d. c. AD 250), Indian monk-philosopher who founded the Madhyamika ("Middle Path") school of Buddhism, Nagarjuna's clarification of the concept of *shunyata* ("emptiness") is regarded by many scholars as an intellectual and spiritual achievement of the highest order.

Something of the Madhyamika philosopher's life and attitude can be gleaned from Nagarjuna's writings. His critical analytic verses and his didactic treatises, letters, and hymns indicate his deep concern to practise "non-attachment" (perceiving the emptiness of all things and hence becoming detached from them) in engagement with people. Through rigorous logical reasoning, as found in the *Madhyamika Karika*, he criticized both Buddhist and Hindu views on existence. Most of his polemics, however, were directed toward the explanations of existence offered by the Buddhist schools of Sthaviravada and Sarvastivada. Nagarjuna's position is closely allied to, and probably dependent on, that found in the early Mahayana literature known as the *Prajnaparamitasutras* ("Perfection of Wisdom Verses"). In the *Prajnaparamita* texts, the notion of *shunyata* is an important term for the wayfarer on the path to Enlightenment and becomes the distinguishing term in the Madhyamika school.

Two basic writings, that are substantially his, are available at present in Sanskrit: *Mulamadhyamakakarika* (more commonly known as *Madhyamikakarika*, "Fundamentals of the Middle Way") and *Vigrahavyavartani* ("Averting the Arguments"), both of which critically analyse false views on existence, the means of knowledge, and the nature of reality.

The earliest available biographical account of Nagarjuna is in Chinese, provided around AD 405 by a renowned Buddhist translator, Kumarajiva. It agrees with other Chinese and Tibetan accounts that Nagarjuna was born in South India into a Brahmin (Hindu priestly caste) family. Present scholarship indicates that Nagarjuna could have lived as early as AD 50 and as late as AD 280. A common consensus gives his dates as AD 150-250.

Nalanda, celebrated Buddhist monastic centre, often spoken of as a university, in northern Bihar State, India, it's traditional history dates to the time of the Buddha (sixht-fifth centuries BC) and Mahavira, the founder of the Jain religion.

According to pilgrims' accounts, from the time of the Guptas, the monasteries of Nalanda were surrounded by a high wall. The excavations revealed a row of 10 monasteries of the traditional Indian design—oblong brick structures with cells opening onto four sides of a courtyard, with a main entrance on one side and a shrine facing the entrance across the courtyard. In front of the monasteries stood a row of larger shrines, or *stupas,* in brick and plaster. The entire complex is referred to on seals discovered there as Mahavihara ("Great Monastery"). A museum at Nalanda houses many of the treasures found in the excavations.

According to a later Tibetan source, Nagarjuna, the second-third century AD Buddhist philosopher, began his studies there. Extensive excavations carried out by the Archaeological Survey of India indicate, however, that the foundation of the monasteries belongs to the Gupta period (fifth century AD). The powerful seventh-century ruler of Kanauj (Kannauj), Harshavardhana, is reported to have contributed to them. During his reign the Chinese pilgrim Hsuan-tsang (Xuanzang) stayed at Nalanda for some time and left a clear account of the subjects studied there and of the general features of the community. I-ching (Yinjing), another pilgrim a generation later, also provided a minute account of the life of the monks. Nalanda continued to flourish as a centre of learning under the Pala dynasty (eighth to twelfth centuries), and it became a centre of religious sculpture in stone and bronze. Nalanda was probably sacked during Muslim raids in Bihar (c. 1200) and never recovered.

Nanda Dynasty, family that ruled Magadha, northern India, between 343 and 321 BC, the Nanda dynasty immediately preceded the dynasty of the Mauryas. Indigenous traditions, both Brahminical and Jain, suggest that the founder of the dynasty, Mahapadma (who was also known as Mahapadmapati, or Ugrasena), evidently had a low social origin—a fact confirmed by classical scholarship. Mahapadma took over from the Shaishunagas not only the reins of Magadhan power but also their policy of systematic expansion. His probable frontier origin and early career as an adventurer helped him to consolidate the empire with ruthless conquests. The authenticity of the Puranic statement that he was the "destroyer of all Kshatriyas" and that he overthrew such disparately located powers as the Ikshvakus, Panchalas, Kashis, Haihayas, Kalingas, Ashmakas, Kurus, Maithilas, Shurasenas, and Vitihotras is borne out by independent evidence. The same evidence also associated the Nandas with conquests in the distant Godavari Valley, Kalinga, and part of Mysore.

The brief spell of Nanda rule, along with the lengthy tenure of the Mauryas, represents the political aspect of a great transitional epoch in early Indian history. The changes in material culture in the Ganga Valley beginning in the sixth-fifth centuries BC, chiefly characterized by settled agricultural technology and growing use of iron, resulted in agricultural production surpluses and a tendency towards the growth of commerce and urban centres. It is significant in this context that in many sources, indigenous and foreign, the Nandas are portrayed as extremely rich and as ruthless collectors of various kinds of taxes. In Alexander's period, Nanda military strength is estimated at 20,000 cavalry, 200,000 infantry, 2,000 quadriga (chariots), and 3,000 elephants. In administration the initiatives of the Nanda State are reflected in references to irrigation projects in Kalinga and the organization of a ministerial council.

The post-Mahapadma genealogy of the Nanda dynasty is perfunctory in the Puranas, which mention only Sukalpa (Sahalya, Sumalya), while the Buddhist text *Mahabodhivamsha* enumerates eight names. Dhanananda, the last of this list, possibly figures as Agrammes, or Xandrames, in classical sources, a powerful contemporary of Alexander the Great. The Nanda line ended with him in about 321 BC, when Chandragupta laid the foundation for Maurya power.

Nataraja, is the name given to Lord Shiva in his form as the cosmic dancer, represented in metal or stone in most Shaiva temples of South India.

The significance of the Nataraja sculpture is said to be that Shiva is shown as the source of all movement within the cosmos, represented by the arch of flames. The purpose of the dance is to release men from illusion, and the place where it is said to have been performed, Chidambaram, called the centre of the universe, is in reality within the heart. The gestures of the dance represent Shiva's five activities (*panchakritya*)—creation (symbolized by the drum), protection (the *abhaya-mudra*), destruction (by the fire), embodiment (by the foot planted on the ground), and release (by the foot held aloft).

In the most common type of images, which include the magnificent Chola bronzes of the tenth-eleventh century, Shiva is shown with four arms and flying locks, dancing on the figure of a dwarf, the Apasmarapurusha (a symbol of man's ignorance; *purusha* meaning "man", and *apasmara* "forgetfulness", or "heedlessness"). The back right hand of Shiva holds the *damaru* (hourglass-shaped drum); the front right hand is in the *abhaya-mudra* (the "fear-not" gesture, made by holding the palm outwards with fingers pointing up); the back left hand carries *agni* (fire) in a vessel or in the palm of the hand; and the front left hand is held across the chest in the *gajahasta* (elephant-trunk) pose, with wrist limp and fingers pointed downwards towards the uplifted left foot. The locks of Shiva's hair stand out in several strands. Interspersed are the figures of Ganga (the Ganga River personified as a goddess), flowers, a skull, and the crescent moon. His figure is encircled by a ring of flames, the *prabhamandala*. In the classic Sanskrit treatises on dance, this form of dance is called the *bhujangatrasa* ("trembling of the snake").

Other dances of Shiva seen in sculpture and painting are the wild *tandava,* which he performs on cremation grounds in the company of his consort Devi, and the evening dance performed on Mount Kailash before the assembly of gods, some of whom accompany him on various instruments.

Natha, religious movement of India whose members strive for immortality by transforming the human body into an imperishable divine body, it combines esoteric traditions drawn from Buddhism, Shaivism, and Hatha Yoga, with occult knowledge.

The Natha cult is made up of *yogis* whose aim is to achieve *sahaja,* defined as a state of neutrality transcending the duality of human existence. This is accomplished through the cultivation of *kaya-sadhana* ("culture of the body"), with great emphasis laid on the control of semen, breath, and thought. Guidance of an accomplished guru is considered essential. The Natha *yogis* and other esoteric orders pass on their traditions through paradoxes and enigmatic verse.

The term is derived from the names of the nine traditional masters, all of which end in the word *natha* ("master", "lord"). Texts do not agree on the lists of the nine. All are believed to have successfully transformed their bodies through yogic discipline into indestructible subtle entities, and, according to popular belief, they reside as demigods in the Himalaya. The nine *nathas* are in many respects similar to the 84 "great perfect ones", the *mahasiddhas,* common to both Hinduism and Buddhism, and their names appear on both lists.

Natya-Shastra, detailed treatise and handbook on dramatic art known as Bharata Natya-Shastra, deals with all aspects of the classical Sanskrit theatre.

The *Natya-Shastra's* many chapters contain detailed treatment of all the diverse arts that are embodied in the classical Indian concept of drama, including dance, music, poetics, and general aesthetics. Its primary importance lies in its justification of Indian drama as a vehicle of religious enlightenment. It is believed to have been written before the third century by the mythic Brahmin sage and priest, Bharata.

Nayanar, any of the Tamil poet-musicians of the seventh and eighth centuries AD, each on of them composed devotional hymns of great beauty in honour of Lord Shiva. The images of the poets Gnanasambandar, Appar, and Sundaramurti (often called "the three") are worshipped in South Indian temples as saints. They were approximately contemporary with their Vaishnava counterparts, the Alvars. The hymns of the Nayanar were collected in the tenth century by Nambi Anar Nambi as *Tevaram* and set to Dravidian music for incorporation into the services of South Indian temples. An inscription of the Chola king Rajaraja the Great (985-1014) records his introduction of the singing of the hymns in the great temple at Thanjavur (Tanjore). Often associated with the Nayanar, though probably slightly later in date, is the superb devotional poet Manikkavasagar, whose hymns are collected as *Tiruvasagam* ("Sacred Utterance").

Nirguna, concept of primary importance in the orthodox Hindu philosophy of Vedanta, which raises the question of whether the supreme being, Brahman, is to be characterized as without qualities (*nirguna*) or as possessing qualities (*saguna*).

The fundamental text of this tenet is the Brihadaranyaka Upanishad definition of Brahman as *neti-neti* ("not this! not that!" 2.3.6). The scriptural texts that ascribe qualities to Brahman, leading to the conception of a qualified Brahman (*saguna*) are, according to the Advaita school, merely preparatory aids to meditations. Others, notably the theistic schools of Vedanta (for example, Vishistadvaita), argue that God (Brahman) is possessed of all perfections and that the scriptural passages denying qualities deny only imperfect ones.

The Advaita (nondualist) school of Vedanta assumes on the basis of selected passages of the Upanishads that Brahman is beyond all polarity and therefore cannot be characterized in the normal terms of human discursive thought. This being the case, Brahman cannot possess qualities that distinguish it from all other magnitudes, as Brahman is not a magnitude but is all.

Nirvana, in Indian religious thought, the supreme goal of the meditation disciplines, the concept is most characteristic of Buddhism, in which it signifies the transcendent state of freedom achieved by the extinction of desire and of individual consciousness.

Liberation from rebirth does not imply immediate physical death; the death of an *arhat* (a perfected person) or a Buddha is usually called the *parinirvana*, or complete Nirvana. In the Mahayana Buddhist tradition, the realization of Nirvana is deferred by the *bodhisattva* ("Buddha-to-be") while he continues, out of compassion (*karuna*), to work for the salvation of others.

According to the Buddhist analysis of the human situation, delusions of ego-centricity and their resultant desires bind man to a continuous round of rebirths and its consequent suffering (*dukkha*). It is release from these bonds that constitutes Enlightenment, or the experience of Nirvana.

Nirvana is conceived somewhat differently within various schools of Buddhism. In the Theravada tradition, it is tranquillity and peace. In the schools of the Mahayana tradition, Nirvana is equated with *shunyata* (emptiness), with *dharma-kaya* (the real and unchanging essence of the Buddha), and with *dharma-dhatu* (ultimate reality).

North Indian Temple Architecture, style of architecture produced throughout northern India and as far south as Bijapur district, it is characterized by its distinctive *shikhara*, a superstructure, tower, or spire. The style is sometimes referred to as *nagara*, a type of temple mentioned in the *Shilpa Shastras* (traditional canons of architecture), but exact correlation of the *Shilpa Shastra* terms with extant architecture has not yet been established.

The typical Hindu temple in northern India, on plan, consists of a small square-shaped sanctuary (called the *garbhagriha*, or "womb-room") housing the main image, preceded by one or more adjoining pillared *mandapas* (porches or halls), which are connected to the sanctum by an open or closed vestibule (*antarala*). The entrance doorway of the sanctum is usually decorated richly with figures of river goddesses and bands of floral, figural, and geometric ornamentation. An ambulatory is sometimes provided around the sanctum. Above the main sanctuary rises a spire (*shikhara*), which is usually curvilinear in outline, and smaller rectilinear *shikharas* frequently top the *mandapas* as well. The whole may be raised on a terrace (*jagati*) with attendant shrines at the corners. If a temple is dedicated to the god Shiva, the figure of the bull Nandi, the god's vehicle, sometimes faces the sanctum, and, if dedicated to the god Vishnu, standards (*dhvaja-stambba*) may be set up in front of the temple.

That the prototype of the North Indian temple already existed in the sixth century can be seen in surviving temples such as the temple at Deogarh in Uttar Pradesh State's Jhansi district, which has a small stunted *shikhara* over the sanctuary. The style fully emerged in the eighth century and developed distinct regional variations in Orissa, central India, Rajasthan, and Gujarat. A classification of North Indian temples is generally made on the basis of *shikhara* types.

The exterior walls are usually decorated with sculptures of mythological and semidivine figures, with the main images of the deities placed in niches carved on the main projections. The interior is also frequently richly carved, particularly the coffered ceilings, which are supported by pillars of varying design.

A development from the simpler to a more elevated and elaborate style is evident in central India. Interiors and pillars are more richly carved than in Orissa. The central Indian style in its most developed form appears at Khajuraho, as seen in the Kandarya Mahadeva Temple (c. eleventh century). There, an overall effect of harmony and majesty is maintained despite the exuberance of sculpture on the outer walls; the rich profusion of miniature shrines on the *shekhari* spire reinforces the ascending movement considerably.

One typical form of the North Indian style is seen in the early temples at Orissa. Its most glorious example is eighth-century Parashurameshvara Temple at Bhubaneshvar, a city that was a great centre of temple-building activity. From the tenth century a characteristic Oriya style developed that exhibited a greater elevation of the wall and a more elaborate spire. The Lingaraja Temple at Bhubaneshwar, of the eleventh century, is an example of the Oriya style in its fullest development. The Sun Temple at Konark, the sanctum of which is badly damaged, is the largest and perhaps the most famous Oriya temple.

Large numbers of temples are preserved in Gujarat, but most of them have been badly damaged. The early eleventh-century Sun Temple at Modhera is one of the finest.

Nyaya, one of the six orthodox (*darshana*) of Indian philosophy, important for its analysis of logic and epistemology. Like the other systems, Nyaya is both a philosophy and a religion; its ultimate concern is to bring an end to man's suffering, which results from ignorance of reality. Liberation is brought about through right knowledge. Nyaya is thus concerned with the means of right knowledge. The major contribution of the Nyaya system is its working out in profound detail the reasoning method of inference.

The Nyaya system—from Gautama through his important early commentator Vatsyayana (c. AD 450) until Udayanacharya (Udayana; tenth century)—came to be called the Old Nyaya (*Prachina-Nyaya*) in the eleventh century when a new school of Nyaya (*Navya-Nyaya*, or New Nyaya) arose in Bengal. The best known philosopher of the Navya-Nyaya, and the founder of the modern school of Indian logic, was Ganesha (thirteenth century).

In its metaphysics, Nyaya is allied to the Vaishesika system, and the two schools were often combined from about the tenth century. Its principal texts are the Nyaya-sutras, ascribed to Gautama (c. second century BC).

The Nyaya theory of causation defines a cause as an

unconditional and invariable antecedent of an effect. In its emphasis on sequence—an effect does not preexist in its cause—the Nyaya theory is at variance with the Samkhya-Yoga and Vedantist views, but it is not unlike modern Western inductive logic in this respect.

Three kinds of causes are distinguished: inherent, or material cause (the substance out of which an effect is produced); non-inherent cause (which helps in the production of a cause); and efficient cause (the power that helps the material cause produce the effect). God is not the material cause of the universe, since atoms and souls are also eternal, but is rather the efficient cause.

The Nyaya school holds that there are four valid means of knowledge: perception (*pratyaksha*), inference (*anumana*), comparison (*upamana*), and testimony (*shabda*). Invalid knowledge involves memory, doubt, error and hypothetical argument.

O

Odantapuri, Uddanadapura, in ancient times a celebrated Buddhist centre of learning (*vihara*), it is believed to have been somewhere near the modern city of Bihar Sharif (Bihar State). It was founded in the seventh century AD by Gopala, the first ruler of the Pala dynasty. Odantapuri served as a model and inspiration for Tibetan Buddhists. Even though the site has never been identified. Tibetan sources indicate that in 749 the Sam-Ye (Bsam-Yas) monastery was modelled upon it and that several distinguished Tibetan scholars studied there. It fell into decline during the eleventh century, and it was probably sacked and destroyed, along with Nalanda, c. 1200, when Muslims under Ikhtiyar-ud-Din Muhammad Bakhtiyar Khalji invaded Bihar.

Om, in Hinduism and other religions of India, is a sacred syllable that is considered to be the greatest of all the *mantras,* or sacred formulae. *Om* mystically embodies the essence of the entire universe. It is uttered at the beginning and end of Hindu prayers, chants, and meditation and is freely used in Buddhist and Jain rituals also. From the sixth century, the written symbol designating the sound is used to mark the beginning of a text in a manuscript or an inscription. *Om* is composed of the three sounds *a-u-m* (in Sanskrit, the vowels *a* and *u* coalesce to become *o*), which represent several important triads: the three worlds of earth, atmosphere, and heaven; the three major Hindu gods, Brahma, Vishnu, and Shiva; and the three sacred Vedic scriptures, Rigveda, Yajurveda, and Samaveda.

The syllable is discussed in a number of the Upanishads, which are the texts of philosophical speculation, and it forms the entire subject matter of one, the Mandukya. It is used in the practice of Yoga and is related to techniques of auditory meditation. In the Puranas the syllable is put to sectarian use; thus the Shaiva mark the *lingam*, or sign of Shiva, with the symbol for *Om*, whereas the Vaishnava identify the three sounds as referring to a trinity composed of Vishnu, his wife Shri, and the worshipper.

P

Padmasambhava (flourished eighth century), also called Guru Rimpoche, Tibetan Slob-dpon ("Teacher"), or Padma 'byung-gnas' ("Lotus Born"), legendary Indian Buddhist mystic who introduced Tantric Buddhism to Tibet and is credited with establishing the first Buddhist monastery there.

The Tibetan Buddhist sect Rnying-ma-pa (the Old Order) claims to follow most closely Padmasambhava's teachings, emphasizing Tantric ritual, worship, and Yoga. Texts basic to the sect's teachings, which were said to have been buried by Padmasambhava, began to be found around 1125. He also had many Tantric books translated from the original Sanskrit into Tibetan.

According to tradition, Padmasambhava was a native of Udyana (now Swat, in Pakistan), an area famous for its magicians. He was a Tantrist and a member of the Yogachara sect and taught at Nalanda, a centre of Buddhist studies in India. He was invited to Tibet in 747 by King Thisrong-detsan and arrived at Samye (Bsan-yas), where he is said to have exorcised demons that were inhibiting the construction of a Buddhist monastery by causing earthquakes. He supervised the completion of the monastery in 749.

Pala Dynasty, ruling dynasty in Bihar and Bengal, India, from the eighth to the twelfth century, the Palas were supporters of Buddhism, and it was through missionaries from their kingdom that Buddhism was finally established in Tibet. Under Pala patronage a distinctive school of art arose, of which many noteworthy sculptures in stone and metal survive. Its founder, Gopala, was a local chieftain who rose to power in the mid-eighth century during a period of anarchy. His successor, Dharmapala (reigned c. 770-810), greatly expanded the kingdom and for a while was in control of Kannauj. Pala power was maintained under Devapala (reigned c. 810-850), who carried out raids in the north, the Deccan, and the peninsula, but thereafter the dynasty declined in power, and Mahendrapala, the Gurjara-Pratihara emperor of Kannauj in the late ninth and early tenth centuries, penetrated as far as northern Bengal. Pala strength was restored by Mahipala I (reigned c. 988-1038), whose influence reached as far as Varanasi (Banaras), but on his death the kingdom again weakened.

Ramapala (reigned c. 1077-1120), the last important Pala king, did much to strengthen the dynasty in Bengal and expanded its power in Assam and Orissa. He is the hero of a Sanskrit historical poem, the *Ramacharita* of Sandhyakara. On his death, however, the dynasty was virtually eclipsed by the rising power of the Senas, although Pala kings continued to rule in southern Bihar for 40 years. The main capital of the Palas appears to have been Mudgagiri (Monghyr, now Munger) in eastern Bihar.

Pali Language, sacred language of the Theravada Buddhist canon, and a Middle Indo-Aryan language of North Indian origin, the history of the Pali language is traced to the time of the Buddha itself. The use of Pali as a Buddhist canonical language came about because the Buddha opposed the use of Sanskrit, a learned language, as a vehicle for his teachings and encouraged his followers to use vernacular dialects. In time, his orally transmitted sayings spread through India to Sri Lanka (c. third century BC), where they were written down in Pali (first century BC), a literary language of rather mixed vernacular origins. Pali eventually became a revered, standard, and international tongue.

Since the underlying fabric of the language reveals many Prakritic trends, it could also be understood by others who do not belong to the speech community of monks. Since Pali is essentially a lingua franca, phonetics in Pali is irregular and arbitrary. Assimilation is an important phonological phenomenon whereby original words change to simple forms. For example, *satya* becomes *sachha, karma* becomes *kamma, dharma* becomes *dhamma*. The peculiarity of the language is its vocabulary. Words appear to have been borrowed from the then existing languages and an element of twist through 'pun' exists in their application. The bulk of the Pali words are Indo-Aryan and it therefore took several words from Sanskrit modified to suit the speech habits of Middle Indo-Aryan. The syntax of the language is inflectional. There also exists a similarity to Sanskrit though a lot of simplification had taken place in grammatical forms.

The language of Pali, due to its high moral, psychological, and disciplinary note, was restricted to the community of monks. The Prakrit underlying Ashokan inscriptions has revealed certain similarities with this language, but the textual language is more refined since it was used among the intellectual circle of monks.

Pali died out as a literary language in mainland India in the fourteenth century but survived elsewhere until the eighteenth. Pali belongs to the Middle Indo-Aryan group of languages that immediately followed the Vedic times. The canonical texts stand close to a living language unlike their commentaries, which appear to be artificial productions. The correct interpretation of the tradition recorded in *Chullavagga* ("Small Grouping") is that each disciple should repeat the teaching in his own dialect.

There are divergent views about where Pali originated. Some believe that it might have originated in southern India. It is also claimed to have originated in the middle to the west of Vindhya mountains based on a pure supposition that the city of Ujjain was the centre of culture at that time. While Pali is also considered by some scholars as the literary form of the Magadhi language, a few others favour Magadha. Rhys David, the doyen of Pali, refers to Kosala as the place of origination of Pali.

The word 'Pali' signifies sacred text. This word was used for the first time by Buddhaghosha, a great commentator of the fifth century AD, as synonymous with the word *patha* (oral recitation). Some scholars derived this word from *pankti* (row), *pariyaya* (to mean as occasion, turn, different discourses and so on), from the root *pal* (to protect), from the name of the city Pataliputra (Pali), the present Patna, and from *palli* (village).

According to tradition, the compilation of the Pali canon began after the death of the Buddha, 100 years later and at the third council, was brought to formal completion. So the canon was handed down orally for nearly 400 years during which period the material grew up continually and was classified into particular collections.

Pali Literature, body of canonical texts and commentaries in the sacred Pali language of Theravada Buddhism. Since that school became the dominant one among many in early Buddhism, the Pali language is often identified with the Buddha's own speech. Most of the canonical literature is exclusively of religious interest, but interspersed in it are works of considerable literary interest.

Of great importance is a huge volume called *jatakas* ("Birth Stories"), recounting some 500 episodes supposedly having occurred in the Buddha's earlier lives. Only those parts in archaic verse are canonical; the prose portion was written later (c. third century AD), probably in Ceylon (now Sri Lanka). The *jatakas* consist of fairy tales, animal stories and fables (the future Buddha may be incarnate in an animal), ballads, and anecdotes. Though their setting is often imaginary, they provide significant material for the historian of society and culture. These short tales abound in moving, delicate, often rustic touches that have made them the delight of the Buddhist world. Their themes are illustrated in bas-reliefs of Buddhist shrines (or *stupas*) at Bharhut and Sanchi and monumentally on the great *stupa* of Java, the Borobudur.

Of considerable literary as well as historical interest is the Pali text *Milinda-Panha* ("The Questions of Milinda"). Milinda is identical to the Greek Menander, the name of a Bactrian Indo-Greek king (c. 140-110 BC) who was sceptical about the verities of Buddhism and was enlightened by the teaching of an elder, Nagasena. The extensive Buddhist erudition that the sage displays is artfully presented in the form of simile and parable, and the work has contributed importantly to the edification of audiences in the countries where Buddhism came to be established. The style, in spite of the repetitions so typical of Buddhist doctrinal texts, is lively and presents the reader with an invaluable picture of contemporary Indian life.

Foremost perhaps are the Buddha's discourses—for example, his sermon "In the Deer Park"—and no doubt deriving from fairly accurate memories. With their straightforward, lively, and incisive style, homely similes, and simple humour, they are excellent examples of the homilies of early Buddhist preaching. Incorporated in the canon, too, are more general works of literature. The *Dhammapada* ("Verses on the Buddhist Doctrine") is a fine example of the moralistic, aphoristic strain in Indian literature, in which virtue is extolled and vice condemned. It has remained a work of considerable diffusion in all Buddhist countries. Much of its popularity is due to its literary style. The Suttanipata collection of the Buddhist canon, composed in a more formal style, contains 55 narrative and didactive poems in the form of dialogues and ballads. They are composed in a metre akin to the Sanskrit *shloka*. Two other works that are of great interest are *Theragatha* and the *Therigatha* ("Hymns of the Senior Monks" and "Hymns of the Senior Nuns"). These, at times, give a vivid insight into the ambience in which a conversion to Buddhism took place. A monk celebrates his newfound freedom in an idyll of the hermit's life. A nun reminisces over the pains of deserting her home and child. She does so without regrets, since she has won the freedom of Buddhism. The prosodic variety of Buddhist lyrics is great; about 30 different metres can be distinguished. Pali poems, with their new metres (often based on a musical phrase), stylistic features, figures of speech, and choice diction, foreshadow classical *kavya* literature in Sanskrit, whose extant specimens date from a later period.

Pallava Dynasty, early fourth-century to late ninth-century southern Indian line of rulers, their members originated as indigenous subordinates of the Satavahanas in the Deccan, moved into Andhra, and then to Kanchi (Kanchipuram in modern Tamil Nadu State, India), where they became rulers.

The Pallavas were the emperors of the Dravidian country and rapidly adopted Tamil ways. Their rule was marked by commercial enterprise and a limited amount of colonization in Southeast Asia, but they inherited rather than initiated Tamil interference with Ceylon (now Sri Lanka).

The Pallavas supported Buddhism, Jainism, and the Brahminical faith and were patrons of music, painting, and literature. Their greatest monuments are architectural, in particular the Shore Temple, various other temples carved from granite monoliths, and the Varaha cave (seventh century) at Mahabalipuram (now Mamallapuram), once a flourishing port. The mother of the Pallava ruler Simhavishnu (mix-sixth century) may have been a Christian. Mahendravarman I wrote (c. 620) the *Mattavilasa-prahasana*, a farce in Sanskrit.

Their geneaology and chronology are highly disputed. The first group of Pallavas was mentioned in Prakrit (a simple and popular form of Sanskrit) records, which tell of King Vishnugopa, who was defeated and then liberated by Samudra Gupta, the emperor of Magadha, in about the middle of the fourth century AD. A later Pallava king, Simhavarman, is mentioned in the Sanskrit *Lokavibhaga* as reigning from AD 436.

In general, the Pallava rulers were ineffective in withstanding military pressure from the western Chalukya dynasty, and their capable feudatories, the Cholas, gradually ousted them from power. Around AD 880 the Pallava dominions passed to the Chola kings.

Pancharatra, early Hindu religious movement its members worshipped the deified sage Narayana (who came to be identified with Lord Vishnu) and, in merger with the Bhagavata sect, formed the earliest sectarian movement within Hinduism. The new group was a forerunner of modern Vaishnavism, or the worship of Vishnu.

The Pancharatra doctrine was first systematized by Shanilya (c. AD 100?), who composed several devotional verses about the deity Narayana; that the Pancharatra system was also known in South India is evident from second-century-AD inscriptions. By the tenth century the sect had acquired sufficient popularity to leave its influence on other groups. It is however criticized by Shankara and other orthodox figures as non-monastic and non-Vedic.

The Pancharatra originated in the Himalayan region perhaps in the third century BC. The cult's name is attributed to a sacrifice continuing for five days and nights (*pancha-ratra*) performed by Narayana by which he obtained superiority over all beings and became all beings.

Panchatantra, collection of Indian animal fables, which has had extensive circulation both in the country of its origin and throughout the world.

In theory, the *Panchatantra* is intended as a textbook of *artha* ("worldly wisdom"); the aphorisms tend to glorify shrewdness and cleverness more than the helping of others. The original text is a mixture of Sanskrit prose and stanzas of verse, with the stories contained within one of the five frame stories. The introduction, which acts as an enclosing frame for the entire work, attributes the stories to a learned Brahmin named Vishnusharman, who used the form of animal fables to instruct the three dull-witted sons of a king.

The original Sanskrit work, now lost, may have come into being at any time between 100 BC and AD 500. It was translated into Pahlavi (Middle Persian) by the Persian royal physician Burzoe in the sixth century. Although this work also is lost, a Syriac translation of it has survived, together with the famous Arabic translation, by Ibn al-Muqaffa (d. AD 760), known as *Kalilah wa Dimnah*, after the two jackals that figure in the first story. The *Kalilah wa Dimnah* led to various other versions, including a second Syriac version and an eleventh-century version in Greek, the *Stephanites kai Ichnelates*, from which translation were made into Latin and various Slavic languages. It was the twelfth-century Hebrew version of Rabbi Joel, however, that became the source of most European versions.

The Fables of Bidpai (after the narrator, an Indian sage, Bidpai, called Vidyapati in Sanskrit). One of the versions reached there as early as the eleventh century.

The seventeenth-century Turkish translation, the *Humayun-namah*, was based on a fifteenth-century Persian version, the *Anwar-e Suhayli*. The *Panchatantra* stories also travelled to Indonesia through Old Javanese written literature and possibly through oral versions. In India the *Hitopadesha* ("Good Advice"), composed by Narayana in the twelfth century and circulated mostly in Bengal, appears to be an independent treatment of the *Panchatantra* material.

Pandya Dynasty. Tamil rulers in the extreme south of India of unknown antiquity, they are mentioned by Greek authors in the fourth century BC.

The Pandya kings were called either Jatavarman or Maravarman. From being Jains they became Shaivites (worshippers of Shiva) and are celebrated in the earliest Tamil poetry. They ruled extensive territories, at times including the Chera (or Kerala) country, the Chola country, and Ceylon (now Sri Lanka) through collateral branches subject to Madura. The "Five Pandyas" flourished from the twelfth to the fourteenth century and eventually assumed control of all the plains of the extreme south as far north as Nellore (1257). However, family quarrels, and Muslim invasions, from 1311, culminating in the foundation of the Madura Sultanate, weakened Pandya influence. By 1312 control over Kerala was lost, and by the mid-sixteenth century all their territories had passed into other hands.

The Roman emperor Julian received an embassy from a Pandya king around AD 361. The dynasty revived under Kadungon in the early seventh century AD and ruled from Madura (now Madurai) or farther south until the sixteenth century. The small but important (ninth-thirteenth century) dynasty of Pandya of Ucchangi, a hill fort south of the Tungabhadra River, may have originated from the Madura family.

Panini (c. between seventh and fourth century B.C.E.), Sanskrit poet and grammarian, he was author of the *Ashtadhyayi*, the earliest standard Sanskrit grammar and authority still in use today, as well as eight other works of four chapters each, containing rules in the form of *sutras* totalling nearly 4,000. His work was continued and critiqued by others, including Patanjali, making it almost a history of the Sanskrit language.

Little is known about Panini's background other than the name of his grandfather Devala, a notable legislator, and that he is also known by his metronymic, Daksheya (son of Dakshi). It is likely that Panini was born at Attock in the Gandhara region of the northwest.

Paramita, in Mahayana Buddhism, it is any of the perfections, or transcendental virtues, practised by *bodhisattvas* ("Buddhas-to-be") in advanced stages of their path towards Enlightenment. The six virtues are generosity (*dana-paramita*); morality (*shila-paramita*); perseverance (*kshanti-paramita*); vigour (*virya-paramita*); meditation, or concentration (*dhyana-paramita*); and wisdom (*prajna-paramita*). Some expand the virtues to 10 by adding skill in the means of helping others (*upaya [kaushalya]-paramitas*), profound resolution to produce Enlightenment (*pranidhana-paramita*), perfection of the 10 powers (*bala-paramita*), and practice of transcendent knowledge (*jnana-paramita*).

Parshvanatha, also called Parshva, in Jainism, the twenty-third Tirthankara, of the present age, Parshvanatha was the first Tirthankara for whom there is some historical evidence, but what is known of his life is intricately interwoven with legend. The four vows that Parshvanatha made binding on members of his community (not to take life, not to steal, not to lie, not to own property) became, with the addition of the explicitly stated vow of celibacy introduced by Mahavira, the five "great vows" (*mahavratas*) of later Jainism. Parshvanatha allowed monks to wear an upper and lower garment, while Mahavira himself gave up clothing. The two sets of views are eventually reconciled, and the followers of Parshvanatha were won over to Mahavira's reforms.

The legends surrounding Parshvanatha emphasize his association with serpents. His mother is said to have seen a black serpent crawling by her side before his birth, and in sculpture and painting he is always identified by a canopy of snake hoods shown over his head. According to accounts in the Jain scripture the Kalpasutra, Parshvanatha once saved a serpent that had been trapped in a log in an ascetic's fire. The snake, later reborn as Dharana, the lord of the underworld kingdom of *nagas* (snakes), sheltered Parshvanatha from a storm sent by an enemy demon.

Pashupata, perhaps the earliest Hindu sect to worship the god Shiva as the supreme deity, it gave rise in turn to numerous sub-sects that flourished in Gujarat and Rajasthan, at least until the twelfth century, and also travelled to Java and Cambodia.

The ascetic practices adopted by the Pashupata included the thrice-daily smearing of their bodies with ashes, meditation, and chanting the powerful syllable "Om". The school fell into disrepute when some of the mystical practices were pushed to excess. Out of the Pashupata doctrine developed two extreme schools, the Kalamukha and the Kapalika, as well as one moderate sect, the Shaivas (also called the Siddhanta school). The Pashupata and the extreme sects were called Atimargika ("schools away from the path") to maintain their distinction from the more rational and acceptable Shaivas, whose development led into modern Shaivism.

The Pashupata sect is mentioned in the Mahabharata. Shiva himself was believed to have been the first preceptor of the system. According to legends contained in later writings such as the Vayu-

Purana and the Linga-Purana, Shiva revealed that he would make an appearance on earth during the age of Lord Vishnu's appearance as Vasudeva-Krishna. The sect takes its name from Pashupati, an epithet of Shiva meaning "Lord of Cattle", which was later extended to convey the meaning "Lord of Creatures".

Shiva indicated that he would enter a dead body and incarnate himself as Lakulin (or Nakulin or Lakulisha, *lakula* meaning "club"). Inscriptions of the tenth and thirteenth centuries appear to corroborate the legend, as they refer to a teacher named Lakulin, who was believed by his followers to be an incarnation of Shiva. On analogy with the Vasudeva cult, some historians place the rise of the Pashupata as early as the second century BC, while others prefer the second century AD as a date of origin.

Patanjali (flourished second century BC, or fifth century AD), also called Gonardiya, or Gonikaputra, was author or one of the authors of two great Hindu classics. The first, Yogasutras is a categorization of yogic thought arranged in four volumes; and the second, the *Mahabhashya* ("Great Commentary"), is both a defence of the grammarian Panini against his chief critic and detractor Katyayana and a refutation of some of Panini's aphorisms.

The Yogasutras seems to span several centuries, the first three volumes apparently written in the second century BC and the last book in the fifth century AD. Authorities therefore tend to credit more than one author writing under this name, although there is wide variance in opinion. There is a possibility that many men used this name, as it was used by the authors of a number of other works on such diverse subjects as medicine, metrics, music, and alchemy. The name itself is obviously a pseudonym, since it denotes no caste and implies divine descent from the Great Serpent, Shesha Naga.

Porus (flourished fourth century BC), was the Indian prince who ruled the region between the Hydaspes (Jhelum) and Acesines (Chenab) rivers at the time of the invasion of the Punjab by Alexander III the Great (327-326 BC). Not known in Indian sources, the name Porus has been conjecturally interpreted as standing for Paurava, that is, the ruler of the Purus, a tribe known in that region from ancient Vedic times. Unlike his neighbour the king of Taxila (Taksashila), Porus resisted Alexander. But with his elephants and slow-moving infantry bunched, he was outmatched by Alexander's mobile cavalry and mounted archers in the battle of the Hydaspes. Impressed by his techniques and spirit, Alexander allowed him to retain his kingdom and perhaps even ceded some conquered areas to him. Thereafter a supporter of Alexander, Porus held the position of a Macedonian subordinate ruler when he was assassinated, sometime between 321 and 315 BC, by Eudamus' agents after the death of Alexander.

Pradakshina is a Hindu and Buddhist rite of circumambulating in a clockwise direction an image, relic, shrine, or other sacred object. Explanations of the rite vary from the delineation of an area for a particular sacred purpose to an attempt to influence the course of events and produce good fortune by imitating the auspicious journey of the sun. Circumambulating in a counterclockwise movement—keeping the left shoulder towards the central object—called *prasavya*, is observed in the funeral ceremonies. The worshipper, by beginning in the east and keeping the sacred object on his right-hand side, proceeds to the south, thus moving in the direction followed daily by the course of the sun. Pilgrimages sometimes consist of circumambulating an entire town, such as the sacred city of Varanasi (Banaras), a 58-km journey, or the Ganga River from source to sea and back, a trip that, when undertaken on foot, requires several years.

Prajapati, one of the creator figures of the Vedic period of ancient India, he came to be identified in the post-Vedic age with Brahma, who gradually surpassed him in importance. Collectively, the Prajapati are the "mind-born" children of Brahma. They are generally considered to number ten, though some authorities reduce them to seven and relate them to the seven great *rishis* (ancient).

The frequent speculations on the creation of the world in the early Vedic literature allude to various primal figures, such as Hiranyagarbha ("Golden Egg") and Vishvakarman ("All-accomplishing"), and the title of Prajapati was applied to more than one such figure. Later it was used to signify one deity, the lord of all creatures. According to one of the stories of creation, Prajapati produced the universe and all its beings after first preparing himself by undergoing *tapas* (ascetic practices); other stories allude to his own creation from the primal waters. His female emanation, who aided him in the creation of other beings, was Vac, the personification of the sacred word, but sometimes his female partner is given as Ushas, the dawn, who is also regarded as his daughter.

Prajnaparamita, body of *sutras* and their commentaries it represents the oldest of the major forms of Mahayana Buddhism, a form that radically extended the basic concept of voidness (*shunyata*). The name Prajnaparamita is also used to denote the female personification of literature or wisdom, sometimes called the Mother of All Buddhas. The main creative period of *Prajnaparamita* thought extended from perhaps 100 BC to AD 150. The best-known work from this period is the *Ashtasahasrika* ("8,000 Verse") *Prajnaparamita*. The first Chinese translation appeared in AD 179. Later, some 18 "portable editions" were forthcoming, the best known of which is the *Vajracchedika-sutra* ("Diamond Cutter Sutra"). Still later, schematic and scholastic commentaries were produced in the *Madhyamika* ("Middle Way") monasteries of eastern India, thus, introducing into the *Prajnaparamita* movement the same confining rationalism against which it had reacted in the first place.

The Chinese traveller Fa-hsien (Faxian) described images of the personified Prajnaparamita in India as early as AD 400, but all known surviving images date from 800 or later. She is usually represented yellow or white in colour, with one head and two arms (sometimes more), the hands in the teaching gesture (*dharmachakra-mudra*) or holding a lotus and the sacred book. Also frequently associated with her are a rosary, sword (to cleave away ignorance), thunderbolt (*vajra*, symbolizing the emptiness of the void), or begging bowl (renunciation of material goods being a prerequisite to the obtaining of wisdom). Images of the deity are found throughout Southeast Asia and in Nepal and Tibet. In Tantric Buddhism she is described as the female consort of the Adi-Buddha (first Buddha).

In the *Prajnaparamita* texts, wisdom (*prajna*), an aspect of the original eightfold path, becomes the supreme perfection (*paramita*), and is considered the primary avenue to Nirvana. The content of this wisdom is the realization of the illusory nature of all phenomena—not only of this world, as in earlier Buddhism, but of transcendental realms as well.

These texts incorporate as aids to meditation, the numerical lists (*matrika*) also found in *Abhidharma* (scholastic) literature. They also supplement their philosophical austerity with the personally appealing figures of mythology.

Prajnapti, in Buddhist philosophy, is the denotation of a thing by a word, the concept of *prajnapti* is especially important in the Madhyamika ("Middle View") and Vijnanavada ("Consciousness-affirming") schools. *Prajnapti* is seen as a fictitious construction unrelated to ultimate reality, or *nisprapancha* (Sanskrit; Pali *nippapancha*: "what is devoid of verbal manifoldness").

According to Madhyamika and Vijnanavada philosophers, the highest reality is non-differential, beyond word and thought. Whatever is differentiated by *prajnapti* is regarded as only nominally existent. Since words denote no reality, empirical knowledge regarding worldly phenomena cannot be held as true in itself. This assertion results from the school's analysis of the process of cognition. When a person sees an object, there is only an immediate awareness that is yet undifferentiated into conceptionc of perceptual judgement expressed in statements such as "This is that". There occurs no analysis of the awareness into subject and object or subject and predicate. Such an analysis is brought about by a conceptual construction, which associates a thing with a name of a conception. This is the cause of illusion, since verbal designation is denied reality, and all empirical knowledge is composed of such judgement.

Prakrit Languages, middle Indo-Aryan languages known from inscriptions, literary works, and grammarian's descriptions, Prakrits are opposed to Sanskrit, from several points of view. First, a distinction is made between correct and incorrect speech forms (*shabda* and *apashabda*). The former are Sanskrit forms which are described by grammarians, chiefly Panini. Such correct elements are part of speech said to be adorned or purified (*samskrita*) by grammar. Starting at least with Katyayana (third to the fourth century BC), grammarians have considered the use of correct forms to lead to merit, thus distinguishing them from coexisting incorrect Middle Indo-Aryan usage. In addition, Patanjali (second century BC) and others consider such incorrect forms as corruptions (*apabhramsha*; "falling away") of acceptable correct forms. The term *prakrita* is derived from *prakriti*, "original matter, source". There are two major views concerning the way in which the two are associated. First, the original matter is considered to be the speech of common people, unadorned by grammar. Thus the Prakrits refer to vernacular usage contrasted with the elevated register of Sanskrit usage. Alternatively, Sanskrit is itself treated as the original source in which Prakrits are considered to occur.

Prakrit vernaculars varied from region to region, and were not only named accordingly but also associated with different groups in literary compositions. One division of literary usage (Kavyadarsha) distinguishes four major groups: Sanskrit, Prakrit, Apabhramsha, and mixed. Of the various Prakrits recognized—such as Shauraseni, Gaudi, Lati—highest status is granted to Maharashtri. Another scheme (for example, Vagbhatalankara, twelfth century) has a fourfold division into Sanskrit, Prakrit, Apabhramsha, and Bhutabhasha. Bhutabhasha, otherwise known as Paisachi, is the language of Gunadhya's *Brihatkatha*, the source of the later *Kathasaritsagara*. There is also a drama composed entirely in Prakrits, Rajasekhara's (ninth and tenth centuries) *Karpuramanjari*. In general, however, dramas employ both Sanskrit and various Prakrits. Treatises on drama, starting from Bharata's (of disputed dates, possibly second century BC) *Natya-Shastra*, specify which language particular groups of persons are to be allowed to use. Sanskrit is the language of refined, educated, upper-class men, while women of equal status and refinement are to use Shauraseni. But the verses sung by them were in Maharashtri. Magadhi is used by men employed in the king's harem, while other servants of a king use Ardhamagadhi. What is particularly noteworthy, however, is that a reversal in usage is allowed when warranted by circumstances. The most famous example of this is the fourth act of Kalidasa's *Vikramorvashiyam*, where Pururavas switches to Apabhramsha in his state of madness at having lost Urvashi. Another example is Malati's switching from Shauraseni to Sanskrit in the second act of Bhavabhuti's *Malatimadhava*. Commentators give various reasons for this. It is meant to show she is to die soon, thus changing her nature, or to demonstrate her learned nature.

The distinction is also associated with cultural differences. Prakrit grammarians grant higher status to Sanskrit by assuring it to be the source language, and formulating rules of change to account for Prakrit forms as derived from the Sanskrit form. This is in consonance with the traditions in which the Vedas have the highest religio-philosophical status. On the other hand, grammarians of the Middle Indo-Aryan language operate with Pali bases as such and do not accord higher status to Sanskrit. This is consonant with the Buddhist tradition, that does not accord the Vedas and Sanskrit such ultimate status. At another extreme, there is the view espoused by Jains, who, as noted by Nami Sadhu (himself a Shvetambara Jain), consider Ardhamagadhi, the language of the Jain canon, to be the source language. Modern scholars usually treat Pali and the languages of the Ashokan inscriptions as distinct early Middle Indo-Aryan as opposed to other Prakrits.

The use of different Prakrits for different personages in drama represents the adaptation to literary convention of different regional varieties that were vernaculars at one time. Apabhramsha also later became a literary vehicle of its own, in poems associated predominantly with Jain authors.

Prakriti and Purusha, also called pradhana, in Indian philosophy, are the two fundamental concepts. The first designates material nature in its germinal state, eternal and beyond perception, while the second denotes the soul or self. *Purusha* is also, in one of the creation myths related in the Vedas, the primal man from whose body the universe was created. He was both sacrificer and victim, and his rite was the prototype for all later Vedic and Hindu sacrifices.

In the dualistic philosophies of Samkhya and Yoga, *purusha* is opposed to *prakriti*, as the two ontological realities. *Prakriti*, a feminine construct, comes into contact with *purusha*, a male construct, and starts on a process of evolution that leads through several stages to the creation of the existing material world. *Prakriti* is made up of three *gunas* ("strands", or constituent cosmic factors) that characterize all nature. In the Samkhyha view, only *prakriti* is active, while the self is incarcerated in it and only observes and experiences. Release (*moksha*) consists in the self's extrication from *prakriti* by the recognition of its total difference from it and non-involvement in it.

Pratihara or Gurjara-Pratihara, was a dynasty that flourished in northern India between c. 750 and 1050 C.E. It ruled first from Avanti in Malwa before moving its capital to the more famous and ancient city of Kanauj. The Gurjara-Pratiharas were neither able to dislodge Arab rule from Sindh nor resist the invasions of Mahmud of Ghazni in the northwest. Moreover, they succumbed in their heartland to the Rashtrakuta expansion from the southwest. The Gurjara-Pratiharas were the last Hindu empire builders of northern India before the Islamic bid for pan-Indian imperial dominance.

Two great Kings, Bhoja (r. 836-885 C.E.) and Mahendrapala (r. 885-914 C.E.), extended their domain from the Himalaya in the north to the Vindhya mountains in the south with outlets on the eastern and western seas. However, they made no lasting contributions to administrative tradition.

Prithviraja III (b. c. 1166; d. 1192), also called Prithviraj Chauhan, was the Rajput warrior king belonging to the clan of the Chauhans of Sapadalaksha who established the strongest kingdom in Rajasthan.

Soon after assuming power, Prithviraja was faced with a rebellion from his cousin, Nagarjuna, who asserted his claim to the Chauhan throne. The revolt was brutally crushed. After demonstrating his mettle, Prithviraja turned his attention to the nearby kingdom of the Bhadanakas, who were a constant threat to the Chauhan-held region around Delhi. (Bhadanaka territory included parts of modern-day Gurgaon, Bhiwani and Hissar in Haryana State, Alwar and Bharatpur in Rajasthan State, and some parts of the Punjab). The Bhadanakas were so comprehensively destroyed sometime prior to 1182 that they cease to find mention in later annals.

Ascending the throne in c. AD 1177, the 11-year-old Prithviraja inherited a kingdom that stretched in the north from Thaneshwar (once the famed capital of the seventh-century ruler Harshavardhan), to parts of Mewar in the south. Within three years of inheriting the throne, young Prithviraja personally assumed reins of the administration. While Prithviraja was trying to consolidate his position, Shihab-ud-Din Muizz-ud-Din Muhammad ibn Sam of Ghur (and Ghazna)—better known as Sultan Muhammad Ghuri—was trying to establish his authority in northern India.

Known for his legendary bravery, Prithvirāja's exploits have been recounted in several books written in the middle ages. His defeat in the second battle of Tarain (1192) at the hands of Muhammad Ghuri, marked a watershed in mediaeval Indian history.

In 1182 Prithviraja defeated King Parmardin Deva Chandela of Jejakbhukti. While the campaign against the Chandelas enhanced Prithviraja's reputation, it added to the number of his enemies. It united the Chandelas and Gahadavalas and forced Prithviraja to increase military expenditure and vigilance on his southeastern frontier.

Prithviraja also turned his sword against the powerful kingdom of Gujarat. In the absence of adequate accounts, little is known about the campaign. In the course of his aggressive campaigns against the Bhadanakas, Chandelas, Chalukyas and Abu Parmars, he probably came into conflict with the ambitions of the Gahadavala ruler of Kannauj, King Jayachand. Jayachand was not only eager to curb Prithviraja's growing ambitions and quest for territorial expansion, but was also keen to avenge his father's defeat by the Chauhans.

While Prithviraja gathered fame as a romantic and dashing general, and a victor of numerous campaigns, Muhammad Ghuri was busy consolidating his empire in India, with the possession of Sind, Multan, and the Punjab to supplement his dominions of Ghazna and Ghur. Towards the end of 1190, Ghuri captured Tabarhindh (Bathinda), which formed a part of Prithviraja's empire. In the meantime, tired of routine pillaging and frequent skirmishes with Ghuri's troops, Govidnaraja, the Chauhan representative looking after Delhi, requested assistance from Prithviraja. Prithviraja immediately marched against Muhammad Ghuri with a strong army.

The rival armies met at Tarain (now in karnal district, Haryana State), 129 km from Delhi. Amidst fierce fighting, Ghuri was seriously injured and was rescued by one of his young warriors. This disaster caused a panic in his army. Leaderless, Ghuri's troops fled from the field and the victorious Prithviraja is said to have pursued the enemy forces for over 60 km.

Tradition, on the other hand, ascribes the immediate cause of their intense and bitter rivalry to the romance between Prithviraja and Jayachand's daughter, Sanyogita (also spelt Samyogita, Sanyukta, and Samyukta). The love of Prithviraja and Sanyogita, and the princess's eventual abduction—with her acquiescence—from the *swayamvara* (ceremony where a princess chose her bridegroom from an invited assembly of kings and princes) has been immortalized to have occurred after the first battle of Tarain in 1191, and shortly before the second and final battle of Tarain between Ghuri and Prithviraja in 1192. However, there has been a prolonged debate amongst historians regarding the historicity of the Sanyogita episode.

Ghuri now turned his attention towards raising a far stronger army, which would help him avenge his defeat of 1191. In 1192 with his preparations complete, Ghuri advanced with 120,000 men to Lahore. From there he continued towards Tarain—the scene of his rout the previous year. Meanwhile, an emissary was sent to Ajmer with a proposal that Prithviraja acknowledge Ghuri's suzerainty. The proposal was met with contempt by the Chauhan king. Instead, he marched to meet his enemy with a vast army that included cavalry, elephants, and a large body of infantry soldiers. As many as 150 Rajputs chiefs are said to have mustered under his banner. Despite the seemingly-invincible Chauhan army, the position of Prithviraja was not as secure as it appeared. Infighting and enmity within Prithviraja's camp had weakened his position.

On reaching Tarain, Prithviraja sent a letter to Ghuri suggesting he should withdraw his forces. The sultan did not reject the letter immediately. Instead, he asked for time to write to his brother in Ghazna and seek permission to withdraw; in the meantime, he agreed to call a truce. The ruse worked. Relying on Ghuri's assurance, the Rajputs relaxed their vigil and are said to have spent the night in celebration. Just before daybreak, Ghuri launched a surprise attack on Prithviraja and his troops. Confusion ensued in the Rajput camp. Although taken by surprise, the Rajputs fought back fiercely. From morning till sunset the battle raged fiercely, and Prithviraja's forces were routed. Prithviraja left the battleground, but was eventually overtaken and captured near Sursuti (modern Sirsa). This is supported by works such as *Prithviraj-Prabandh, Tabaqat-i Nasiri*, and *Hammir-Mahakavya*, which also state that he was put to death after a spell in captivity.

Puranas, in Hindu sacred literature, are a number of popular encyclopaedic collections of myth, legend, and genealogy, varying greatly as to date and origin.

The 18 principal surviving Puranas are often grouped loosely according to whether they exalt Vishnu, Shiva, or Brahma, but each sect made an attempt to include its own teaching in the popular Puranas as a way of influencing the people, and they all deal with similar material. The main Puranas are usually regarded as: (1) the Vishnu-, Naradiya-, Bhagavata-, Garuda-, Padma-, and Varaha-; (2) the Matsya-, Kurma-, Linga-, Shiva-, Skanda-, and Agni-; and (3) the Brahmanda-, Brahmavaivarta-, Markandeya-, Bhavishya-, Vamana-, and Brahma-Puranas. By far the most popular is the Bhagavata-Purana, which in its treatment of the early life of Krishna has had profound influence on the religious beliefs of India. There are also 18 "lesser", or Upapuranas, treating similar material, and a large number of Sthala-Puranas, or Mahatmyas, glorifying temples or sacred places, which are recited in the services of the temples.

Traditionally a Purana treats five subjects: primary creation of the universe, secondary creation after periodical annihilation, genealogy of gods and saints, grand epochs, and history of the royal dynasties. Puranas are connected in subject with the Mahabharata and have some relationship to the law-books (Dharmashastras).

Around this central core has amalgamated much other material of religious concern during the period c. AD 400 to c. 1000, which describes such things as customs, ceremonies, sacrifices, festivals, caste duties, donations, construction of temples and images, and places of pilgrimage. Puranas are written almost entirely in narrative couplets in much the same easy, flowing style as the epic poems, though some scholars judge them poetically inferior to the epics.

Purva-Mimamsa, one of the six schools of early Indian philosophy, it expounded the nature of *dharma* in the form of meritorious acts. It set up a system of exegetical principles to be employed in the interpretation of the Vedas. These were used in the sphere of civil law as well as religious ritual. With Mimamsa referring to the brahmanic philosophy based on the Vedas, the Purva-Mimamsa school is the earlier exposition, and the *uttara* or later school is the Vedanta.

R

Rajatarangini, historical chronicle of early India, written in Sanskrit verse by the Kashmir Brahmin Kalhana in 1148, it is justifiably considered to be the best and most authentic work of its kind. It covers the entire span of Kashmir history, from the earliest times to the date of its composition.

Rajatarangini, which consists, in all, of 7,826 verses, is divided into eight books. Book I attempts to weave imaginary tales of Kashmir kings into epic legends. Gonanda was the first king and a contemporary and enemy of Krishna. Traces of genuine history are also found, however, in references to Ashoka and Jalauka, the Buddhist Kushan kings Hushka, Jushka, and Kanishka, and the Huna Mihirakula. Book II introduces a new line of kings not mentioned in any other authentic source, starting with Pratapaditya I and ending with Aryaraja. Book III starts with an account of the reign of Meghavahana of the restored line of Gonanda and refers to the brief reign of Matrugupta, a supposed contemporary of Vikramaditya Harsha of Malwa. There too, legend is mixed with reality, and Toramana Huna is incorporated in the line of Meghavahana. The book closes with the establishment of the Karkota Naga dynasty by Durlabhaka Pratapaditya II, and it is from Book IV on that *Rajatarangini* takes on the character of a dependable historical narrative. The Karkota line came to a close with the usurpation of the throne by Avantivarman, who started the Utpala dynasty in 855. In Books V and VI the history of the dynasty continues down to 1003, when the kingdom of Kashmir passed on to a new dynasty, the Lohara. Book VII brings the narrative down to the death of King Harsha (1101). Book VIII deals, on the level of extremely dependable details, with the stormy events between the death of Harsha and the stabilization of authority under Kalhana's contemporary Jayasimha (reigned 1128-1149).

In style, the *Rajatarangini* narrative is sometimes considered as versified prose on a massive scale, yet its strong structural appeal made it a model for later historians. In fact, the history of Kashmir was continued, along Kalhana's line, down to some years after the annexation of Kashmir by Akbar (1586) in the following works: *Rajatarangini* (by Jonaraja), *Jainatarangini* (by Shrivara), and *Rajavalipataka* (by Prajyabhatta and Shuka). Neither in style nor in authenticity to these works approximate the quality of Kalhana's *Rajatarangini*.

Kalhana was excellently equipped for the work. He was uninvolved personally in the maelstrom of contemporary politics. Nevertheless, he was profoundly affected by it and stated the following to be his ideal: "That noble-minded poet alone merits praise whose word, like that sentence of a judge, keeps free from love or hatred in recording the past." His access to minute details of contemporary court intrigues was almost direct because his father and uncle were both in the Kashmir court. For the events of the past, Kalhana's search for material was truly fastidious. He delved deep into such model works as the *Harshacharita* and the *Brhhatsamhita* epics. He also used with commendable familiarity the local *rajakathas* (royal chronicles) and such previous works on Kashmir as *Nripavali* of Kshemendra, *Parthivavali* of Helaraja, and *Nilamatapurana*. He displayed surprisingly advanced technical expertise for his age in his concern for unconventional sources. He looked up a variety of epigraphic sources relating to royal eulogies, construction of temples, and land grants. He studied coins, monumental remains, family records, and local traditions.

Rajput, any of about 12 million landowners organized in patrilineal clans and located mainly in central and northern India, especially in former Rajputana ("Land of the Rajputs"), the Rajputs regard themselves as descendants or members of the Kshatriya (warrior ruling) class, but they actually vary greatly in status, from princely lineages, such as the Guhilot and Kachwaha, to simple cultivators. The Rajputs' origins seem to date from a great breakup of Indian society in northern and northwestern India under the impact of the Hephthalites (White Huns) and associated tribes from the mid-fifth century onwards. Following the breakup of the Gupta Empire (late sixth century), invading groups were probably integrated within the existing society, with the present pattern of northwestern Indian society being the result. Tribal leaders and nobles were accepted as Kshatriyas, the second order of the Hindus, while their followers entered the fourth (Shudra, or cultivating) order to form the basis of tribal castes, such as the Jats, the Gujars, and the Ahirs. Some of the invaders' priests became Brahmins (the highest ranking caste). Some indigenous tribes also attained Rajput status, such as the Rathors of Rajasthan and the Chandelas and Bundelas of central India. The Rajputs are divided between the *Suryavanshi* (house of the Sun or solar race) and *Chandravanshi* (house of the Moon or lunar race) and those claiming to come from the great fire pit near Ajmer. Rajput habits of eating meat (except beef) and other traits suggest both foreign and aboriginal origins.

The successful claims to Rajput status frequenty were made by groups that attained secular power. Probably central Asian invaders as well as patrician lines of indigenous tribal peoples were absorbed in this way. There are numbers of Muslim Rajputs in the northwest, and Rajputs generally have adopted the custom of *purdah* (seclusion of women). Their ethos includes an intense pride in ancestry and a mettlesome regard for personal honour. They seek hypergamous marriages (the bride marrying into a social group higher than her own).

The Rajputs emerged into political importance in the ninth and tenth centuries. From c. 800 Rajput dynasties dominated northern India, and the many petty Rajput kingdoms there were among the main obstacles to the complete Muslim domination of Hindu India. After the Muslim conquest of the eastern Punjab and the Ganga valley, the Rajputs maintained their independence in the fastnesses of Rajasthan and the forests of central India. Sultan Ala-ud-Din Khalji of Delhi (reigned 1296-1316) took the two great Rajput forts of Chittaurgarh and Ranthambhor in east Rajasthan but could not hold them. The Rajput State of Mewar under Rana Sanga made a bid for supremacy but was defeated by the Mughal emperor Babur at Khanua (1527). Babur's grandson Akbar took the forts of Chittaurgarh and Ranthambhor (1568-1569) and then made a settlement with all the Rajasthan princes except Mewar. Accepting Mughal overlordship, the princes were admitted to the court and the emperor's privy council and were given governorships and commands of armies. Although damaged by the emperor Aurangzeb's (reigned 1658-1707) intolerance, this arrangement continued until the Mughal Empire itself collapsed in the eighteenth century. The Rajputs then fell victims to the Maratha chiefs until they accepted British suzerainty (1818) at the end of the last Maratha war. After independence (1947) the Rajput States in Rajasthan were merged to form the State of Rajasthan within the Indian Union.

Rakshasa, rakshasa, or (female) rakshasi, in Hindu mythology, it is a type of demon or goblin. *Rakshasas* have the power to change their shape at will and appear as animals, as monsters, or in the case of the female demons, as beautiful women. They are most powerful in the evening, particularly during the dark period of the new moon, but they are dispelled by the rising sun. They especially detest sacrifices and prayer. Most powerful among them is their king, the 10-headed Ravana.

Putana, a female demon, is well known for her attempt to kill the infant Krishna by offering him milk from her poisoned breast; she was, however, sucked to death by the god.

They are vigorously depicted in Rajasthani paintings illustrating the Ramayana. The canons of sculpture instruct the artist to carve them with a terrifying appearance, complete with fearful side tusks, ugly eyes, curling awkward brows, and carrying a variety of horrible weapons.

Not all *rakshasas* are equally evil; some are more akin to *yakshas* (nature spirits), while others are similar to *asuras*, the traditional opponents of the gods. The term *rakshasa*, however, generally applies to those demons who haunt cemeteries, eat the flesh of men, and drink the milk of cows dry as if by magic.

Ramanuja (b. 1017, Sriperumbudur, India; d. 1137, Srirangam, India), also called Ramanujacharya, or Ilaiya Perumal (Tamil: "Ageless Perumal" [God]), thus South Indian Brahmin theologian and philosopher is the single most influential thinker of devotional Hinduism. After a long pilgrimage, Ramanuja settled in Srirangam, where he organized temple worship and founded centres to disseminate his doctrine of devotion to Lord Vishnu and his consort Shri. He provided an intellectual basis for the practice of *bhakti* (devotional worship) in three major commentaries: the *Vedartha-samgraha* (on the Veda), the *Shribhashya* (on the Brahmasutras), and the *Bhagavadgita-bhashya* (on the Bhagavadgita).

The site of Ramanuja's birthplace in Sriperumbudur is now commemorated by a temple and an active Vishishtadvaita school. The doctrines he promulgated still inspire a lively intellectual tradition, and the religious practices he emphasized are still carried on in the two most important Vaishnava centres in southern India, the Ranganatha Temple in Srirangam, Tamil Nadu, and the Venkateshvara temple in Tirupati, Andhra Pradesh.

Like many Hindu thinkers, he made an extended pilgrimage, circumambulating India from Rameswaram (part of Adam's Bridge), along the west coast to Badrinath, the source of the holy river Ganga, and returning along the east coast. Tradition has it that later he suffered from the zeal of King Kulottunga of the Chola dynasty, who adhered to the god Shiva, and withdrew to Mysore, in the west. There he converted numbers of Jains, as well as King Bittideva of the Hoysala dynasty; this led to the founding in 1099 of the town Milukote (Melcote, present Karnataka State) and the dedication of a temple to Shelva Pillai (Sanskrit, Sampatkumara, the name of a form of Vishnu). He returned after 20 years to Srirangam, where he organized the temple worship, and, reputedly, founded 74 centres to disseminate his doctrine. After a life of 120 years, according to the tradition, he passed away in 1137.

He became a temple priest at the Varadaraja Temple at Kanchi, where he began to expound the doctrine that the goal of those who aspire to final release from transmigration is not the impersonal

Brahman but rather Brahman as identified with the personal god Vishnu. In Kanchi, as well as Srirangam, where he was to become associated with the Ranganatha Temple, he developed the teaching that the worship of a personal god and the soul's union with him is an essential part of the doctrines of the Upanishads (ancient speculative texts that are part of Hindu sacred scriptures) on which the system of Vedanta is built; therefore, the teachings of the Vaishnavas and Bhagavatas (worshippers and ardent devotees of Vishnu) are not heterodox. In this he continued the teachings of Yamuna (Yamunacharya; tenth century), his predecessor at Srirangam, to whom he was related on his mother's side. He set forth this doctrine in his three major commentaries.

Ramanuja's chief contribution to philosophy was his emphasis that discursive thought is necessary in man's search for the ultimate verities, that the phenomenal world is real and provides real knowledge, and that the exigencies of daily life are not detrimental or even contrary to the life of the spirit. In this emphasis he is the antithesis of Shankara, of whom he was sharply critical and whose interpretation of the scriptures he disputed. Like other adherents of the Vedanta system, Ramanuja accepted that any Vedanta system must base itself on the three "points of departure", namely, the Upanishads, the Brahmasutras (brief exposition of the major tenets of the Upanishads), and the Bhagavadgita, the colloquy of the god Krishna and his friend Arjuna.

Although Ramanuja's contribution to Vedanta thought was highly significant, his influence on the course of Hinduism as a religion has been even greater. By allowing the urge for devotional worship (*bhakti*) into his doctrine of salvation, he aligned the popular religion with the pursuits of philosophy and gave *bhakti* an intellectual basis. Ever since, *bhakti* has remained the major force in Hinduism. His emphasis on the necessity of religious worship as a means of salvation continued in a more systematic context the devotional effusions of the Alvars, the seventh- tenth-century poet-mystics of southern India, whose verse became incorporated into temple worship. This *bhakti* devotionalism, guided by Ramanuja, made its way into northern India, where its influence on religious thought and practice, has been profound.

Ramanuja's world-view accepts the ontological reality of three distinct orders: matter, soul, and God. Like Shankara and earlier Vedanta, he admits that there is nonduality (*advaita*), an ultimate identity of the three orders, but this nonduality for him is asserted of God, who is modified (*vishishta*) by the orders of matter and soul; hence his doctrine is known as Vishishtadvaita ("modified nonduality") as opposed to the unqualified nonduality of Shankara. Central to his organic conception of the universe is the analogy of body and soul: just as the body modifies the soul, has no separate existence from it, and yet is different from it, so the orders of matter and soul constitute God's "body", modifying it, yet having no separate existence from it. The goal of the human soul, therefore, is to serve God just as the body serves the soul. Anything different from God is but a *shesha* of Him, a spilling from the plenitude of His being. All the phenomenal world is a manifestation of the glory of God (*vibhuti*), and to detract from its reality is to detract from his glory. Ramanuja transformed the practice of ritual action into the practice of divine worship and the way of meditation into a continuous loving pondering of God's qualities; both in turn a subservient to *bhakti*, the fully realized devotion that finds God. Thus, release is not merely a shedding of the bonds of transmigration but a positive quest for the contemplation of God, who is pictured as enthroned in His heaven, called Vaikuntha, with His consort and attendants.

He wrote no commentary on any single Upanishad but explained in detail the method of understanding the Upanishads in his first major work, the *Vedartha-samgraha* ("Summary of the Meaning of the Veda"). Much of this was incorporated in his commentary on the Brahmasutras, the *Shribhashya*, which presents his fully developed views. His commentary on the Bhagavadgita, the *Bhagavadgita-bhashya*, dates from a later age.

Ramanuja's doctrine, which was passed on and augmented by later generations, still identifies a caste of Brahmins in southern India, the Shrivaishnavas. They became divided into two subcastes, the northern, or Vadakalai, and the southern, or Tenkalai.

At issue between the two schools is the question of God's grace. According to the Vadakalai, who in this seem to follow Ramanuja's intention more closely, God's grace is certainly active in man's quest for him but does not supplant the necessity of man's acting towards God. The Tenkalai, on the other hand, hold that God's grace is paramount and that the only gesture needed from man is his total submission to God (*prapatti*).

Ramayana, shorter of the two great epic poems of India, the other being the Mahabharata, the Ramayana was composed in Sanskrit, probably not before 300 BC, and in its present form consists of some 24,000 couplets divided into seven books called *kandas*. Its authorship is generally attributed to the sage Valmiki.

The epic-poem enjoys immense popularity in India, where its recitation is considered an act of great merit. Many of its translations into the vernacular languages are themselves works of great literary merit, including the Tamil version of Kampan, the Bengali version of Krittibas, and the Hindi version, *Ramcharitmanas*, of Tulsidas. Throughout North India the events of the poem are enacted in an annual pageant, the Ram-Lila, and in Kerala, the two epics, the Ramayana and the Mahabharata, even today make up the story repertoire of the Kathakali dance-drama. The Ramayana was popular even during the Mughal period (sixteenth century), and it was a favourite subject of Rajasthani and Pahari painters of the seventeenth and eighteenth centuries.

Traditionally, the Ramayana is considered to be the first narrative poem (*adi-kavya*) in Sanskrit, and Valmiki the first poet (*adi-kavi*). The first book forms a preamble. The sage Valmiki composes the epic in compliance with Brahma's wishes and teaches it to two of his hermit disciples, Lava and Kusha. When the king hears about two boys who travel round the country reciting the epic, he summons them to the palace where they sing the Ramayana before him. Thus initiated, the epic spreads all over the country.

The second book is the *Bala Kanda*, which describes the royal birth of Rama in the kingdom of Ayodhya. King Dasharatha and his three wives have no children. As a result of performing a *putra kameshti yajna* (sacrifice conducted by one desiring a child), four sons are born: Rama to Queen Kaushalya, Bharata to Queen Kaikeyi, and twins Lakshmana and Shatrughana to Queen Sumitra.

When they turn 16, Rama and Lakshmana accompany sage Vishvamitra to his hermitage, to provide him protection against demons and *rakshasas*. Later, the sage takes the princes to Mithila where king Janaka, at his daughter's *swayamvara*, declares his daughter Sita will marry whoever bends a massive bow gifted by Shiva. Rama performs the task with ease, breaking the bow in the process. He marries Sita and returns to Ayodhya.

The *Ayodhya Kanda* is the story of Rama and Sita's life in the palace, the intrigues that deprive Rama of the throne, and his banishment to the forest. Twelve years after Rama's marriage, Dasharatha announces the coronation of Rama as heir apparent. However, Queen Kaikeyi, influenced by her maid Manthara, uses two boons promised to her by the king, and demands the crowning of her son Bharata, and Rama's exile to the forests for 14 years. Dasharatha agrees reluctantly because a promise once made cannot be broken, and soon aftewards, dies of grief.

Meanwhile, Rama, accompanied by Sita and Lakshmana, leaves Ayodhya. When Bharata hears what has transpired, he rushes to Panchkuti, where they are based, outside Ayodhya, and begs them to return. Rama refuses, and Bharata eventually returns to rule Ayodhya as Rama's regent, installing Rama's wooden slippers on the throne.

The *Aranya Kanda* deals with Rama's life in the forest (*aranya*). On the banks of Godavari River, in the Dandaka forest, Rama, Sita, and Lakshmana build a hermitage. After several peaceful years, their tranquility is disturbed with the arrival of the demoness Surpanakha, who takes a fancy to Rama, and on being repulsed, tries to attack Sita. At this, Lakshmana intervenes and cuts off Surpanakha's nose and ears. The disfigured demoness asks her cousin, the *rakshasa* Khara, to avenge her; Khara tries, but is killed by the brothers. Surpanakha then turns to her brother Ravana, the demon-king of Lanka, for help.

Ravana sends the magician-demon Maricha as a golden deer to the hermitage; while Rama and Lakshmana go deeper into the forest in pursuit of the deer, Ravana appears before Sita in the guise of a mendicant and abducts her. On discovering Sita's absence, the brothers leave the hermitage and set about to rescue her.

The *Kishkinda Kanda* marks a turning point in the Ramayana. In their search for Sita, Rama and Lakshmana meet Sugriva from the kingdom of Kishkinda (which belongs to the monkeys), and his minister Hanuman. Rama helps Sugriva become the king of the monkeys and the ruler of Kishkinda. Forging an alliance with the monkeys, and with the help of Ravana's own brother Vibhishana, Rama and Lakshmana attack Lanka, having first built a bridge across the ocean from the mainland to the island kingdom.

The *Sundara Kanda* concerns the exploits of Hanuman in Lanka. Before the bridge is built, Hanuman, with one leap, spans the ocean and, in disguise, searches the city for Sita. He finds her confined to a garden, identifies himself to her, and after passing on Rama's messages to her, sets Lanka on fire and returns to the mainland.

The *Yuddha Kanda* describes the war bewteen Rama and Ravana, the rescue of Sita, and the coronation of Rama. While Rama's monkey-army fights with boulders and trees, Ravana's army of demons is equipped with arrows, swords, and spears. Sorcery and magic tricks by the demons fail to defeat Rama. When Lakshmana is injured, Hanuman flies to the Himalaya and returns with an entire mountain that contains the life-restoring Sanjivini herb. After a fierce battle that rages for several days, Ravana is killed. Vibhishana is crowned king of Lanka, and after Sita undergoes an *agni-pariksha* (test by fire) to endorse her chastity because she had resided in the home of another man, Rama, Sita, Lakshmana, and Hanuman return in the flying Pushpaka *vimana* to Ayodhya. Sage Vashishta crowns Rama king.

The *Uttara Kanda* is considered to be a later addition to the Ramayana, perhaps not written by Valmiki. After some years of prosperity and peace in Ayodhya, Rama learns that the people still question the queen's chastity. Because he believes that despite his personal feelings, a monarch has to be beyond reproach, Sita is sent away to the forest, where she meets Valmiki. At his hermitage Sita gives birth to Rama's twin sons, Lava and Kusha. The family is reunited when the sons come of age, but Sita asks to be received by the earth, which swallows her up.

Some years later, Rama and his brothers, along with many of their subjects, immerse themselves in the Sarayu River.

Rama's reign is the prototype of the harmonious and just kingdom to which all kings should aspire; Rama and Sita set the ideal of conjugal love; Rama's relationship to his father is the ideal of filial love; and Rama and Lakshmana represent perfect fraternal love. Everything in the epic is designed to show harmony, which after being disrupted is at last regained. This accords with the fact that in all but its oldest form (before the first century AD), the Ramayana identifies Rama as an *avatar* (incarnation, personification) of Vishnu.

Alongside the narration of the main story, the Ramayana also contains, in different contexts, a number of legendary episodes, discourses on good governance, the nature of truth, and information on the land, and the people of early India.

Rashtrakuta Dynasty. Hindu dynasty that ruled the Deccan and neighbouring areas of India from c. 755 to 975, these Dravidian farmers were the royal family of Lattalur (Later, Near Osmanabad). They spoke Kannada but also knew the northern Deccan language. Under the Rashtrakutas, who defeated a rival dynasty, the Chalukyas, the Deccan Empire became the second greatest political unit in India, covering the area from Malwa to Kanchi. The importance of the Rashtrakutas during this era is indicated by the fact that a Muslim traveller wrote of the king as being one of the four great rulers of the world (the others being the caliph and the emperors of Byzantium and China).

Several Rashtrakuta monarchs were devoted to learning and the arts. The second king, Krishna I (c. 756-773), built the rock temple of Kailasha at Ellora; another king, Amoghavarsha I, who reigned from c. 814 to 878, was the author of part of the *Kavirajamarga*, the earliest known Kannada poem. Other kings were skilled in the art of war. Dhruva I subdued the Gangas of Gangavadi (Mysore), contained the Pallavas of Kanchi (Kanchipuram), and defeated the king of Bengal and the Pratihara king, who were contending for Kannauj. Krishna II, who succeeded in 878, reacquired Gujarat, which Amoghavarsha I had lost, but failed to retake Vengi. His grandson, Indra III, who came to the throne in 914, took Kannauj and brought Rashtrakuta power to its peak. Krishna III outdid him in northern campaigns (c. 940) and in spectacular occupation of Kanchi and much of the Tamil plains (948-966/67). Khottiga Amoghavarsha IV (968-972) failed to protect the capital, and its devastation destroyed faith in the dynasty. The emperor fled to the Western Ghats, where his line lingered ignominiously, supported by brave Ganga and Kadamba feudatories, until Taila I Chalukya won the succession in c. 975.

Rigveda, collection of hymns, it forms part of the ancient sacred literature of India, known as the Vedas.

The word Veda is cognate with the Avestan "vaeda", the old slavanic "vede", the Latin "video", the old Teutonic "wait", the new English "wit", and the German "Wessen", all of which denote the sense of knowledge, awareness, vision, cognition, learning, and information. The Sanskrit word is derived from the root *vid* which means "to know" or from the root *vidlr* "to obtain". It represents not only a body of knowledge which illumines all things, but a discipline by means of which the fourfold values of life (*purushartha*; pleasures, wealth, integrity and purposefulness in life, and spiritual perfection) are secured. The Veda is both a book and a tradition. The *Mimamsakas* look upon the Veda as having *dharma* as its principal import. *Dharma* is disciplined life at the individual as well as the collective levels.

The values that the Veda advocates are found to be suitable for the development of the individual and also for collective advancement of the group for all time and among all people. The tradition formed in the Vedic corpus has been responsible for the persistent and popular lore (*purana*) which has guided our people both at the urban and rural contexts. The heritage which is very much in evidence throughout the ages comprises of narration of significant events of antiquity (*itihasa*), anecdotal tales suggesting values of life (*akhyayika*), illustrative narrations and the science of good life (*dharma-shastra*), as well as the science of political economy (*artha-shastra*).

The essential message of the Veda is the achievement of a complete and wholesome life through fourfold values (*purushartha*) which are relevant for all people in all ages: material prosperity and well-being (*artha*), satisfaction of all normal urges and impulses (*kama*), purposeful and enlightened living (*dharma*), and absolute freedom from all misery (*moksha*). All the Indian philosophical systems are in fact so many examinations of the values of life, intrinsic and instrumental. The study of the Vedic corpus becomes meaningful only in the context of these values of life.

The religion reflected in the Rigveda is mainly concerned with the propitiation of divinities associated with the sky and the atmosphere. Most important were such gods as Indra, Varuna (guardian of the cosmic order), Agni (the sacrificial fire), and Surya (the sun). The Rigveda is oldest literary work of India, with the most far-reaching influence; the Rigveda has influenced ancient thought and its impact on the Indian mind has been the deepest and most enduring. It not only created Indian culture but also has nourished it all along. It is principally a book of poems, but the elegance of its poetry and the excellence of its imagery, together with the profoundity of its thought, have been regarded as beyond the normal human authorship. It is, therefore, distinguished by its *apaurusheya* ("non-human") origin. The seers to whom the *mantras* (hymns or poems) are traditionally ascribed were inspired and were in a state of transcendental trance when they gave utterance to these sacred poems. The hymns came to them as revelations of reality, as intimations from the unseen but essential aspects of the universe.

There is a hym in the Rigveda which speaks only of two classes of people in the world: the votaries of *rita* and the enemies of *rita*. Both, however, are blessed by the sage Agastya. The idea of *rita* (right, rite) involves the universally valid principles of order, restraint, generosity, and altruistic compassion. It is the law that works for the good of all creatures. The gods and the sages preserve this order; and the right-thinking man must do likewise, and if he does, he is an Aryan. Those whose inclination is for pleasure, power, and possession violate the *rita*, knowingly or unknowingly; and they are non-Aryans.

The Rigveda has 10,552 *mantras* (stanzas) arranged in 1,028 *suktas* (hymns) grouped in 10 *mandalas* (books). There is another arrangement in which the stanzas are arranged in 2,024 *vargas* (sections), grouped in 1,028 *suktas*, and the whole accommodated in 8 *ashtakas*. This Veda is said to have 21 *sakhas* (recessions). Every one of the *mantras* in the Rigvedic corpus is associated with a *rishi* (seer), a metrical form (*chhandas*), and a deity eulogized in the *mantra* *(devata)*. There is a prescription that the three details must necessarily be mentioned while reciting the *mantra* for whatever purpose.

Among other features of Rigvedic religious life, that were important for later generations, were the *munis*. The *muni* was apparently a sort of *shaman* (a religious personage having healing and psychic transformation powers), trained in various magic arts and believed to be capable of supernatural feats, such as levitation. He was particularly associated with the god Rudra, a deity connected with mountains and storm and more feared than loved. Rudra developed into the Hindu god Shiva, and his prestige increased steadily. The same is true of Vishnu, a minor solar deity in the Rigveda, who later became one of the most important and popular divinities of Hinduism.

One of the favourite myths of the Aryans was one that attributed the origin of the cosmos to the god Indra, after he had slain the great dragon Vritra. With time, such tales were replaced by more abstract theories that are reflected in several hymns of the late tenth book of the Rigveda. These speculative tendencies were the beginnings of the persistent effort of Indian philosophers to reduce all things to a single basic principle.

The main ritual activity referred to in the Rigveda is the *soma* sacrifice. *Soma* was a hallucinogenic beverage prepared from a now-unknown plant; recently it has been suggested that the plant was a mushroom and that later another plant was substituted for the agaric fungus, which had become difficult to obtain. The Rigveda contains a few clear references to animal sacrifice, which probably became more widespread later. There is some doubt whether the priests formed a separate class of society at the beginning of the Rigvedic period. If they did so, the prevailingly loose boundaries of class made it possible for a man of non-priestly parentage to become a priest. By the end of the period, however, they had become a separate class of specialists, the Brahmins, who claimed superiority over all the other social classes, including the Kshatriyas, the warrior-kings.

The Rigveda contains little about birth rituals, but the rites of marriage and disposal of the dead were basically the same as specified later in Hinduism. Marriage was an indissoluble bond cemented by a lengthy and solemn ritual centring on the domestic hearth. The funeral rites of the rich included cremation, although other funeral forms were also practised. An interesting reference in one hymn shows that the wife of the dead man lay down beside him on the funeral pyre but was called upon to return to the land of the living before it was lighted. This may have been a survival from an earlier period when the wife committed *sati* (the wife being cremated alive with the husband, seated on his funeral pyre), a custom that was revived in later times.

Rishabhanatha, first of the 24 Tirthankaras, or saving teachers, of Jainism, his name is attributed to the 14 auspicious dreams that were seen by his mother before his birth in which the bull (*rishabha*) appeared first. He is also known as Adinatha ("Lord of the Beginning") and is portrayed in Jain legend as having lived several millions years ago.

Born in the city of Ayodhya, which is also famous as the birthplace of Rama, he attained *moksha* (release from earthly existence) on Mount Kailash in the Himalaya, which is also the legendary home of the Hindu god Shiva. In paintings he is always shown gold in colour (in paintings of the Digambara sect, yellow), and his symbol is the bull.

Rishabhanatha is one of the most honoured of the Jain saints having been the first to preach the Jain faith. Legends also credit him with having taught men the 72 accomplishments (including writing and arithmetic) and women the 64 crafts (including pottery, carpentry, and weaving). He had 100 sons, each of who was 500 bow-shots tall and the most famous of whom was Bharata, the first *chakravartin*, or universal ruler. Rishabhanatha is also said to have instituted marriage, giving of alms, and observing funeral rites.

Rock Edicts, narrative histories and announcements carved into cliff rock, onto pillars, and in caves throughout India by King Ashoka (reigned 265-238 BC). The rock edicts are important sources for the modern understanding of ancient Indian political and religious history, particularly with regard to the influence of the Buddha's teachings on the king and, through him, on the people at large. Ashoka was the most powerful emperor of the Maurya dynasty and a highly influential promulgator of Buddhism. Ashoka's first years as king were marked by his brutal slaughter of thousands of people during the conquest of Kalinga. Having been exposed to the moral teachings (*dharma*) of Buddhism—which are based on the tenets of nonviolence and compassion—Ashoka was moved to deep remorse for his actions. Converted to Buddhism, as a record of his understanding of mortal law, he carved lessons into stone in the hope that he could provide inspiration and guidance to the people of his extensive kingdom.

S

Saddarshana, the six schools of orthodox Indian philosophy formulated from about the beginning of the Christian era through the period of the Gupta Empire, these systems of the Six Schools (Saddarshana) of orthodox philosophy appear in terse *sutras*. The most important of the Six Schools is the Vedanta ("End of the Vedas"), also called Uttara-Mimamsa, or later Mimamsa.

The most renowned philosopher of this school and, indeed, of all Hinduism was Shankara (700?-750?). He was born at Kaladi in Kerala and is said to have spent most of his life travelling through India debating with members of other sects. The Shankaran system has sounded the keynote of intellectual Hinduism down to the present, but later teachers founded subschools of Vedanta, which are perhaps equally important. Shankara was also responsible for the growth of Hindu monasticism, which had been in existence for more than a millennium in the form of hermit colonies. Inscriptions from Gupta times onwards also refer to monk-like orders of Shaiva ascetics, apparently living according to distinctive disciplines and with distinguishing garments and emblems. Shankara founded a closely disciplined Shaiva order, perhaps partly modelled on the Buddhist *sangha*, or order, known as *Dashnami*, which is still the most influential orthodox Hindu ascetic group. The order is composed of 10 brotherhoods and hence called *dashnamis* ("those with 10 names"). Orders became an established institution with wider geographic affiliations. Some of these admitted Brahmins only; others were open to all four classes or even to women; some made a practice of nudity. These Shaiva communities are more inclined to individual asceticism and are less closely organized than the Vaishnava *vairagins* ("the dispassionate") or *gosvamins* ("the masters"). Shankara is also said to have founded the four main monasteries (*maths*) at the four corners of India: Sringeri in Karnataka, Badrinath in the Himalaya, Dwarka in Gujarat, and Puri in Orissa. The abbots of these monasteries control the spiritual lives of many millions of devout Shaiva laymen throughout India, and their establishments strive to maintain the traditional philosophical Hinduism of the strict Vedanta.

According to Ramanuja (c. 1017-1137), a great South Indian thinker of Shrivaishnava persuasion, Brahman (God) is a person with high attributes, the object of an individual's search for the higher knowledge—the only entrance to salvation. Because an absolute creation is denied, God is viewed as the sole cause of His own modifications; namely, the emanation, existence, and absorption of the universe. Although unlimitedly expansive, God is conceived to be essentially different from everything material, the absolute opposite of any evil, free from any imperfection, omniscient, omnipotent, possessed of all positive qualities (such as knowledge, bliss, beauty, and truth), of incomparable majesty, the inner soul of all beings, and the ultimate goal of every religious effort. The universe is considered a real transformation of Brahman, whose "body" consists of the conscious souls and everything unconscious in their subtle and gross states.

The *karma* doctrine is modified as follows: the Lord, having determined good and bad deeds, provides all individual souls with a body in which they perform deeds, reveals to them the scriptures from which they may learn the *dharma*, and enters into them as their internal regulator. The individual acts at his own discretion but needs the Lord's assent. If the devotee wishes to please him, God induces him, with infallible justice and loving regard, to intentions and effort to perform good deeds by which the devotee will attain to him; if not, God keeps him from the goal.

The influence of the Bhakti Movement had earlier led Ramanuja to admit a twofold possibility of emancipation: in addition to the meditative method of the highest insight (*jnana*) into the oneness of soul and God, which destroys the residues of *karma* and propitiates God to win his grace, there is the way of *bhakti*. Those who prefer the former way will reach a state of isolation, the others an infinitely blissful eternal life in, through, and for God, with whom they are one in nature but not identical. They do not lose their individuality and may even meet Vishnu in his Vaikuntha heaven and enjoy delight beyond description. An interesting development of Ramanuja's doctrine of qualified monism is found in the philosophy of Madhva (died c. 1278). This Kannada Brahmin taught a doctrine of dualism according to which God and the soul are eternally distinct.

The system finds its complement in the doctrine of the five *sadakhyas* (five items that bear the name *sat*, "is" or "being") representing the five aspects of that state, which may be spoken of as the experience of "there is" (*sat*) and which had evolved from God's fivefold creative energy (*shakti*). In these, God "dwells" in his aspect called Sadashiva ("the Eternal Shiva"), which is regarded sometimes as a manifestation of and sometimes as identical with the Supreme Being.

Authors of Shaiva Puranas established two ingenious and complementary doctrines to explain the nature and omnipotence of God (the force that rules, absorbs, and reproduces the world and that in performing any one of these acts necessarily performs the other two as well), the existence of the world, and the identity of God and the world. A theory of five "faces", or manifestations—each of which is given mythological names and related *mantras*—is of great ritual significance. It associates Shiva's so-called creative function, with his first face, or aspect; its maintenance and reabsorption with his second and third faces; his power of obscuration, by which he conceals the souls in the phenomena of *samsara* ("cycle of rebirth, or bondage") which his fourth face; and his ability to bestow his grace, which leads to final emancipation Shiva who is the transcendent Brahman.

The faces became the central elements of a comprehensive classification system. They were identified with parts of God's body, regions of the universe, various ontological principles, organs of sense and action, and the elements. The system was used to explain how Shiva's being is the All and how the universe is exclusively composed of aspects or manifestations of Shiva. In his five-fold nature, Shiva was shown to be identical with the 25 (five times five) elements or principles assumed by the prominent Samkhya school of Indian philosophy. The special significance of the number five in Shaivism can be understood as a philosophical elaboration of the time-honoured fourfold organization of the universe. (The four quarters of the sky also play a prominent part in religious practice.) According to this conception, a fifth aspect, when added to the four, is considered the most important aspect of the group because it represents each of the four and collectively unites all of their functions in itself.

Another Shaiva doctrine paints eight "embodiments" of Shiva as the elements of nature (ether, wind, fire, water, earth), sun, moon, and the sacrificer, or consecrated worshipper (also called *atman*). To each of these eight elements corresponds one of Shiva's traditional names or aspects—to the last one, usually Pashupati. The world is a product of these eight forms, consists of them, and can only exist and fulfil its task because the eight embodiments cooperate. Because each individual is also composed of the same eight realities (for example, the light of man's eyes corresponds to that of the sun), Shiva constitutes the corporeal frame and the psychical organism of every living being. The eighth constituent is the indispensable performer of the rites that sustain the gods who preside over the cosmic processes and are really Shiva's faculties.

Although Shaivism is a much more coherent whole than Vaishnavism, there evolved, in different parts of India, some branches with peculiarities of their own. According to the pronouncedly idealist monism of Kashmir Shaivism, an important religio-philosophic school, Shiva manifests himself through a special power as the first cause of creation, and he also manifests himself through a second power as the innumerable individual souls who, because of a veil of impurity, forget that they are the embodiment of the Highest. This veil can be torn off by intense faith and constant meditation on God, by which the soul transmutes itself into a universal soul and eventually attains liberation through a lightning like, intuitive insight into its own nature.

The Shaiva-siddhanta, a prominent religio-philosophic school of Tamil-speaking South India, assumes three eternal principles: God (who is independent existence, unqualified intelligence, and absolute bliss), the universe, and the souls. The world, because it is created by God (efficient cause) through His conscious power (instrumental cause) and *maya* (material cause), is no illusion.

The main purpose of its creation is the liberation of the beginningless souls, conceived as "cattle" (*pashu*) bound by the noose (*pasha*) of impurity (*mala*) or spiritual ignorance, which forces them to produce *karma*. However, they see the *karma* process as a benefit, for as soon as the soul has sufficiently ripened and reached a state of purity enabling it to strive after the highest insight, God graciously intervenes, appearing in the shape of a fully qualified and liberated spiritual guide (guru), through whose words He permits Himself to be realized by the individual soul.

Saka, a term used in ancient India it refers to people from Central Asia known to the Greeks as Scythians and to the Chinese as the Sseu. Sakas settled in the northwestern part of the Indian subcontinent, in the Swat valley, and the area around Taxila, at an indeterminate date and migrated southwards into the Ganges valley, Rajasthan, Malwa, Gujarat, Kathiawar, and Maharashtra, probably because they were pushed out by the Kushans. Chronological information about their early dynasties comes from numismatic sources, as their coins give the name of the ruler and his father and are dated according to the Saka era commencing in 78 C.E.

Later Saka dynasties in the same area took the little of *kshatrapa,* used on their coins of the fourth century C.E., and came to be known as the Western Satraps. They probably owed allegiance to the Gupta Emperors. Samudra Gupta's pillar inscription at Allahabad refers to his successful campaigns in reducing them to vassalage. The Western Satraps appear to have helped repel occasional Sassanian attacks from Iran on Gujarat.

Rudradman I had his capital at Junagarh in the second century C.E. A lengthy pillar inscription in pure Sanskrit describes his exploits in repairing a Mauryan dam and campaigning against the Satavahana armies in the Narmada valley. He ruled over Gujarat, Malwa, the Konkan, and Rajasthan and is described as a handsome man often selected by princesses to be bridegroom.

Samkhya (Samkhya), one of the six orthodox systems (*darshans*) of Indian philosophy, Samkhya adopts a consistent dualism of the orders of matter (*prakriti*) and soul, or self (*purusha*). The two are originally separate, but in the course of evolution *purusha* mistakenly identifies itself with aspects of *prakriti*. Right knowledge consists of the ability of *purusha* to distinguish itself from *prakriti*.

In Samkhya there is belief in an infinite number of similar but separate *purushas* ("selves"), no one superior to the other. *Purusha* and *prakriti* being sufficient to explain the universe, the existence of a god is not hypothesized. The *purusha* is ubiquitous, all-conscious, all-pervasive, motionless, unchangeable, immaterial, and without desire. *Prakriti* is the universal and subtle (unmanifest) matter, or nature, and, as such, is determined only by time and space.

The chain of evolution begins with *purusha,* impinges on *prakriti,* much as a magnet draws unto itself iron shavings. The *purusha,* which before was pure consciousness without an object, becomes focussed on *prakriti,* and out of this is evolved *mahat* ("great one") or *buddhi* ("spiritual awareness"). Next to evolve is the individualized ego consciousness (*ahankara*, "I-maker"), which imposes upon the *purusha* the misapprehension that the ego is the basis of the *purusha's* objective existence.

The *ahankara* further divides into the five gross elements (space, air, fire, water, and earth), the five fine elements (sound, touch, sight, taste, and smell), the five organs of perception (with which to hear, touch, see, taste, and smell), the five organs of activity (with which to speak, grasp, move, procreate, and evacuate), and mind, or thought (*manas*). The universe is the result of the combinations and permutations of these various principles, to which the *purusha* is added.

Largely outside the above system stands the three primal

qualities of matter that are called *gunas* ("qualities"). They make up the *prakriti* but are further important principally as physio-psychological factors. The highest one is *sattva*, which is illumination, enlightening knowledge, and lightness; the second is *rajas*, which is energy, passion, and expansiveness; the third is *tamas* ("darkness"), which is obscurity, ignorance, and inertia. To these correspond moral models: to *tamas* that of the ignorant and lazy man; to *rajas* that of the impulsive and passionate man; to *sattva* the enlightneed and serene man.

Although many references to the system are given in earlier texts, Samkhya received its classical form and expression in the *Samkhya-karikas* ("Stanzas of Samkhya") by Ishvarakrishna (c. third century AD). Vijnanabhikshu wrote an important treatise on the system in the sixteenth century.

Sampradaya, in Hinduism, is a traditional school of religious steaching, transmitted from one teacher to another. In each case the school is named after a distant and perhaps mythological founder, such as Shri (the goddess Lakshmi), from whom it has been transmitted through a succession of teachers to the earthly founders of the sects.

From about the eleventh century onwards, several sects emerged out of Vaishnavism (worship of Vishnu). These sects continue to the present day. They include the Sanaka-sampradaya (also known as Nimbarkas, the followers of Nimbarka); the Shri-sampradaya (or Shrivaishnavas, following the teaching of Ramanuja); the Brahma-sampradaya (or Madhvas, the followers of Madhva); and the Rudra-sampradaya (or Vishnusvamins, the followers of Vishnusvamin).

Samsara, in Indian philosophy, is the central conception of metempsychosis which means cycle of rebirths or bondage. It refers, in Hinduism and Jainism, to the career of the soul, which, once it has fallen from its original state of self-consciousness and bliss, is born as any creature and continues to be reborn until it has found release (*moksha*) from the bonds of its past deeds (*karman*). Buddhism, which does not assume the existence of a permanent soul, accepts a semi-permanent personality core that goes through the process of *samsara*.

The range of *samsara* stretches from the lowliest insect (sometimes the vegetable and mineral kingdoms are included) to Brahma, the highest of the gods, for they also are involved in transmigration. The rank of one's birth in the hierarchy of life depends on the quality of the previous life. After death the soul first goes for a sojourn to heaven or hell until it has consumed most of its good or bad *karma*. Then it returns to a new womb, the remainder of its *karma* having determined the circumstances of its next life. In theory this allows for the possibility of remembering one's previous lives (*jatismara*), a talent that great saints possess or can cultivate. Typical of this belief are the so-called *jataka* stories, in which the Buddha gives accounts of his previous lives.

The Samkhya school of Hindu philosophy has worked out certain details of this transmigration process. It assumes the existence of two bodies, a "gross" one (*sthula*), which is the material body, and a "subtle" one, which is immaterial. When the gross body has perished, the subtle one survives and migrates to another gross body; this subtle body consists of the higher psychomaterial functions of *buddhi* ("consciousness"), *ahankara* ("I-consciousness"), *manas* ("mind as coordinator of sense impressions"), and *prana* ("breath"), the principle of vitality.

Samskara, means any of the personal sacraments traditionally observed at every stage of a Hindu's life, from the moment of conception to the final scattering of his funeral ashes. The observance of the *samskaras* is based on custom as much as on texts such as the Grihya-sutras, the epics, or the Puranas and differs considerably according to region, caste, or family. In modern times the full *samskaras* are not generally performed, despite the efforts of the Arya Samaj, a late nineteenth-century reform movement that tried to revive their popularity. At present the ceremonies most commonly observed are those of name-giving, initiation, marriage, and death.

But the customary rites are required to be performed by the father, in the home, and are to be more carefully observed in the case of male children. A generally accepted list of 16 traditional *samskaras* begins with the prenatal ceremonies of *garbhadhana* (for conception), *pumsavana* (to favour a male birth), and *simantonnayana* ("hair-parting", to ensure safe delivery). The rites of childhood begin before the severing of the cord, with the ceremony of *jatakarman* (birth), followed at a later date by *namakarana* (name-giving), *niskarmana* (the child's first view of the Sun), *annaprashana* (first feeding of solid food), *chudakarana* (first tonsure of the boy's head), and *karnavedha* (piercing of the ears for the wearing of ornaments). The educational *samskaras* can commence as early as the fifth year with the *vidyarambha* (the learning of the alphabet). The *upanayana* (initiation) confers the sacrificial thread on male children of the three upper social classes; the *vedarambha* signals the beginning of the student's study of the Vedas (sacred scriptures); the *keshanta*, or *godana* (first shaving of the beard), marks the approach of manhood, and the *samavartana* (returning home from the house of the guru) or *snana* ("bathing"), the completion of his student life. The sacrament of marriage, the next stage in a man's life, is known as *vivaha*. The final *samskara* to be performed for a man is the *antyeshti*, the funeral rite.

Ṣamudra Gupta (d. AD 380), Indian regional emperor from about AD 330 to 380, he was the epitome of an "ideal king" of the "golden age of Hindu history", as the period of the imperial Guptas (AD 320-510) has often been called. The son of King Chandra Gupta I and the Licchavi princess Kumaradevi, he is pictured as a muscular warrior, poet, and musician who displayed "marks of hundreds of wounds received in battle". In many ways he personified the Indian conception of the hero.

Since he was a member of the influential Brahmin class, it is reasonable to assume that he supported caste distinctions, and the Guptas may have been responsible for the emergence of Brahminism as a theological system as well as a code of social behaviour carried into present Hindu society.

From inscriptions on gold coins and on the Ashoka pillar in the fort at Allahabad, Samudra Gupta is shown to have been especially devoted to Lord Vishnu. He revived the ancient Vedic horse sacrifice, probably at the conclusion of his fighting days, and distributed large sums for charitable purposes during these ceremonies. A special gold coin that he issued commemorated this ceremony, while another showed him playing the harp; all were of high gold content and excellent workmanship.

Samudra Gupta was chosen as emperor by his father over other contenders and apparently had to repress revolts in his first years of rule. On pacifying the kingdom, which probably then reached from what is now Allahabad to the borders of Bengal, he began a series of wars of expansion from his northern base near what is now Delhi. In the southern Pallava kingdom of Kanchipuram, he defeated King Vishnugopa, then restored him and other defeated southern kings to their thrones on payment of tribute. Several northern kings were uprooted, however, and their territories added to the Gupta empire. At the height of Samudra Gupta's power he controlled nearly the whole Gangetic valley and received homage from rulers of parts of east Bengal, Assam, Nepal, the eastern part of the Punjab, and various tribes of Rajasthan. He exterminated 9 monarchs and subjugated 12 others in his campaigns.

Sanchi, historic site, west-central Madhya Pradesh, central India it stands on a flat-topped sandstone hill, rising 90 m above the surrounding country. This is the best-preserved group of Buddhist monuments in India. The region of Sanchi, like the great centres at Sarnath and Mathura, had a continuous artistic history from the third century BC to the eleventh century AD.

The *stupa* is enclosed by a massive stone railing pierced by four gateways on which are elaborate carvings depicting the life of the Buddha, legends of his previous births (*jataka* stories), and other scenes important to early Buddhism (such as Ashoka's visit to the Bo tree). Inscriptions give the names of the donors of the relief; one commemorates the gift of the ivory workers of Vidisha and has given rise to the suggestion that the tradition of working in ivory may have been translated into stone. The Buddha is depicted throughout in symbolic form, by a wheel, an empty throne, or a pair of footprints.

There are three *stupas* at the site. *Stupa* No. 1 is an Ashokan foundation enlarged in succeeding centuries, No. 2, with railing decorations of the late Shunga period (c. first century BC), and No. 3, with its single *torana* (ceremonial gateway) of the last first century BC-first century AD.

Most noteworthy is the Great Stupa (*stupa* No. 1), discovered in 1818. It was probably begun by the emperor Ashoka in the mid-third century BC and later enlarged. Solid throughout, the *stupa* consists of a base bearing a hemispherical dome (*anda*) representing the dome of heaven enclosing the Earth; it is surmounted by a squared rail unit, or *harmika*, the world mountain, from which rises a mast (*yashti*) to symbolize the cosmic axis. The mast bears umbrellas (*chatras*) that represent the various heavens (*devaloka*).

Other features of interest include a commemorative pillar erected by Emperor Ashoka (c. 265-238 BC); an early Gupta temple (temple No. 17), early fifth century, with a flat roof and pillared portico; and monastic buildings ranging over several centuries. Several relic baskets and more than 400 epigraphical records have also been discovered.

Sangam Literature, earliest writings in the Tamil Language, these are thought to have been produced in three *sangams*, or literary academies, in Madurai, India, from the first to the fourth century AD. The Tolkappiyam, a book of grammar and rhetoric, and eight anthologies (*Ettuttokai*) of secular poetry were compiled. The poems are concerned with two main topics, love and the praise of kings and their deeds. Many of them, especially on the latter subject, display great freshness and vigour and are singularly free from the literary conceits of much of the other early and mediaeval literatures of India. Since they are almost entirely secular, these poems are also free from the complex mythical allusions that are such an outstanding feature of most Indian art forms. There are, nonetheless, some instances of religious works in Sangam poetry. *Pattupattu* ("The Ten Long Poems") contains the earliest Indian poem of personal devotion to God, and *Paripadal* contains poems about Vishnu, Shiva, and Murugan.

The eight anthologies are *Kuruntokai, Natrinai, Agananuru, Aingurunuru, Kalittokai, Purananuru, Patirruppattu,* and *Paripadal.* These secular writings are possibly unique in early Indian literature, which is almost entirely religious.

Sangha, Buddhist monastic order, it is traditionally composed of four groups: monks, nuns, laymen, and laywomen. The *sangha* is a part—together with the Buddha and the *dharma* (teaching)—of the Threefold Refuge, a basic creed of Buddhism.

The modern *sangha* is governed by disciplinary rules (*vinaya*) that form part of the sacred canon. Generally, the monastic order is dependent on the lay community for economic support in the form of alms or large gifts of money and property, since Buddhist monks—notably those of the Theravada tradition in Southeast Asia—do not engage in commerce or agriculture.

The *sangha* originated in the group of disciples who renounced worldly life to wander with the Buddha and listen to his teachings. After the Buddha's death his disciples continued to live together as a community, wandering from place to place, living on alms. Every fortnight, at the time of the full and new moon (the *uposatha* days), followers of the Buddha would gather to reaffirm their sense of community and purpose by reciting their basic beliefs, such as the Threefold Refuge and the codes of conduct. The custom of spending the rainy season in one place in a study retreat led gradually to the settling of the community.

Sannyasi, sannyasin, in Hinduism, is a religious ascetic, who has renounced the world, having achieved the fourth *ashram,* or stage, of life. The name *sannyasi* also specifically designates an ascetic who pays particular allegiance to the god Shiva, who is sometimes known as "the great ascetic". The Shaiva ascetics were organized in the eighth century AD by the renowned Hindu teacher Shankara into 10 orders, the *dashnami.*

Sannyasis, and others who are considered to be liberated while still alive, are not cremated (the customary method of disposing of the dead among Hindus) but are generally buried in a seated posture of meditation.

Among the *sannyasis,* the highest stage of achievement is that reached by the *paramahamsa* ("great swan"). This honorific is usually given only after a probation of at least 12 years as an ascetic and only to those *sannyasis* who have achieved full self-knowledge. They are considered free of all worldly rules and duties, such as those pertaining to caste, and are no longer required to carry out image worship or sacrifices but may, if they wish, worship internally only. The most renowned *paramahamsa* of modern times was the nineteenth-century saint Ramakrishna.

Sanskrit Language, meaning processed, cultivated, purified, refined, Sanskrit is traditionally regarded as the language of the gods (*daivi vak, devavani*) and one of the oldest representatives of the Indo-European family. Sanskrit has been in use continuously for perhaps as long as 4000 years for religious purposes. It was first reduced to writing in the first millennium BC, but it has been preserved by rigorous memorization and recitation for perhaps as long as a 1000 years prior to the introduction of writing. It is genealogically related to Persian, Greek, Latin, and almost all of the modern European languages. In South Asia, due to their proximity over thousands of years, the Dravidian, and Austroasiatic groups of languages and Sanskrit have converged.

All the modern Indo-Aryan languages are derived from Sanskrit through the Middle Indo-Aryan languages, the Prakrits, and Apabhramsha. A new trend in the linguistic evolution of Indo-Aryan began around AD 1200. Original Sanskrit words (*tatsama*) for many important things and activities were adopted instead of their derivatives (*tadbhava*)—unlike in the past evolutionary stages. This preference for Sanskrit vocabulary reflects itself in almost all modern Indo-Aryan languages and also in Dravidian languages like Malayalam, Telugu, and Kannada. This phenomenon is also recognized by the Indian Constitution.

The oldest available specimen of Sanskrit is the language of the Rigveda, which may have been composed between c. 1500 and c. 1200 BC. There is a clear continuity between the language of the Rigveda and that of subsequent classical Sanskrit literature. However, the language of the Vedas (*Vaidika* or Vedic as it is called) is characterized by plurality of inflections including declensional, conjugational, and primary derivative formations, as well as some distinct verbal and semantic features.

Vedic literature comprises the four Vedas: Rigveda, Yajurveda, Samaveda, and Atharvaveda, the corresponding Brahmanas (ritual procedures and commentary), Aranyakas, and Upanishads (philosophical treatises) followed by Sutra (aphoristic) literature dealing with the various aspects of Vedic rituals. The other important components of Vedic literature are *shiksa* (phonetics), *kalpa* (the *sutras*), *vyakarana* (grammar, including linguistic description and philosophy of language), *nirukta* (etymology), *chandas* (metrics), and *jyotisha* (astronomy and astrology).

The two great epics, the Ramayana and the Mahabharata, transmitted through oral tradition, were perhaps put to writing beginning as early as 400 BC. This marks the beginning of classical Sanskrit literature as distinct from the Vedic literature. About the same time both types of Sanskrit—Vedic (Vaidika) and Classical (Laukika)—were most scientifically described by Panini in Ashtadhyayi (eight chapters comprising less than 4000 aphorisms—*sutras*). This subsequently served as a model for creative, recreative, philosophical, and scientific writings in classical Sanskrit.

To Sanskrit grammarians, the meaning is implicit and eternally fixed in the root and to know the meaning of the word one has to discover its Sanskrit etymon. In his treatise *Nirukta*, Yaska recognizes four categories of words—nouns, verbs, prepositions, and conjunctions. Panini analyses roots and assigns special meaning to suffixes. Sanskrit is a highly inflected language. It has three genders (masculine, feminine, and neuter), three numbers (singular, dual, and plural), and eight cases (nominative, accusative, instrumental, dative, ablative, genitive, locative, and vocative). Ten conjugational patterns distributed in three numbers and three persons (third person: *prathama*, second person: *madhyama*, and first person: *uttama*) are identified. There are four types of compounds, several types of phonemic and morphophonemic alterations (*sandhi*), causative, desiderative, frequentative, and denominative verbal formations, as well as primary and secondary derivative constituents. As in Greek and Latin, adjectives have to agree with the gender, number, and case-endings of nouns, similarly verbs have to correspond to the tense, mode, voice, number, and person concerned.

Sanskrit is now used for specific purposes. It is listed as one of the current Indian languages in the Eighth Schedule of the Indian Constitution. It is also widely used for creative and recreative writings; in periodicals, conferences, and seminars. Sanskrit is used for conversation in limited circles throughout India.

The discovery of Sanskrit language and literature in the West was directly responsible for creating an awareness about the close genealogical relationship of the languages of the Indo-European family and for the initiation of modern linguistics, comparative

Indo-European linguistics, and comparative mythology. The study of Sanskrit unites scholars from many different countries and cultures, and constitutes a means of uniting what is otherwise divided.

Devanagari is the most commonly used script for Sanskrit especially in printed texts. However, other scripts like Grantha (Tamil), Telugu, Malayalam, Kannada, Maithili, Bengali, Sharada, and Oriya were and are still employed. Quite a few printed texts are also available in Roman. Sanskrit manuscripts and inscriptions are available in Tibetan, Sinhala, Burmese, and other Southeast Asian scripts.

Sanskrit Literature, body of creative writings in Sanskrit including epics (*Mahakavya*), lyric poetry (*Gitiakavya*), prose romances (*Gadyakavya*), folk tales and fables, plays and didactic poetry produced during AD 1000-1800 or even a little earlier. Sanskrit literary tradition, in fact, begins with the Rigveda (c. 1500 to c. 1200 BC) and continues down to the present age.

The collections of Vedic hymns (Samhitas) as well as the two great epics of India—Ramayana and Mahabharata (400 BC) were originally transmitted from generation to generation through oral tradition. This was followed by classical tradition of writing characterized by natural aesthetic elegance and stylistic simplicity. Poets like Kalidasa and Ashvaghosa belong to this period (ending AD 400 or so). The most popular works of Kalidasa are *Abhijnanashakuntalam*, *Kumarasambhavam*, *Vikramorvashiyam*, and *Raghuvamsham*. Sanskrit has also been described in one of the finest grammars ever produced, the *Ashtadhyayi* of Panini. This in turn was the object of a rich commentatorial literature. There was also a long history of work on semantics and philosophy of language called *Vakyapadiya* by Bhartrhari (570?-651?).

The period beginning AD 600 was characterized by the predominance of scholarly temper in creative writings with lesser content and more descriptions of various types. Bharavi's *Kiratarjuniyam* (AD 600) represents the starting point of this tradition of ornate poetry. This epic (*Mahakavya*) describes, in 18 cantos, the story of the Pandavas and Draupadi in exile culminating in a combat between Lord Shiva in the guise of a *kirata* (mountaineer) and Arjuna. This epic impresses with it aesthetic elegance and stylistic sublimity. But the occasional verbal complexities stand in the way of genuine enjoyment. This was followed by Magha's *Shishupalavadham* of about the same time and with the same characteristic features.

The oldest document in the literature of South Asia is the

Rigveda, or Veda of the Stanzas, the fundamental text of Brahminical Hinduism. Not literary but religious-magical in its purpose, it is mostly a compilation of hymns, dedicated to a number of gods of the Vedic religion. They have the regular structure of an invocation. The attention of the god is evoked and a brief account of some of his feats is given to hold his attention. An exhortation for his help concludes the hymn. The poets, of whom little is known, appear to have come at the close of a priestly poetical tradition. They rivalled one another in allusions to obscure exploits. These poets employed a language that was often opaque and at times intended to mystify. Nevertheless, the Rigvedic hymns include lines of great beauty. They may occur in a riddling verse or in poetry addressed to a deity whose beauty inspires the poet to well-turned lines. Nonsacred verses are very rare in the Rigveda, but, when they occur, they can be quite powerful. Although not literary in purpose, the Rigveda had a decisive influence on the form of Sanskrit poetry. Except for narrative verse, the basic unit of all subsequent poems (no matter how many verses they consist of) is the single stanza that contains one complete thought.

The second Veda, the *Yajurveda* (Veda of the Yajus [Formulae]), contains sacred formulae recited by a group of priests at the great Vedic sacrifices. The third, the Samaveda (Veda of the Chants), is in essence an anthology of the Rigveda. More literary interest attaches to the fourth Veda, the Atharvaveda (an *atharvan* was a special priest), which contains hymns, incantations, and many magic charms.

The succeeding literature (1000-700 BC), the *Brahmanas,* such as Aitareya, Satapatha, Samavidhana, and Gopatha, continues not the poetry but the liturgical concerns of the Rigveda. They were written in a dry, expository prose, so that only their narrative portions have any literary interest. Much the same is true of the next layer of the Vedic texts (c. 700 BC) the *Aranyakas* ("Books Studied in the Forest") such as Aitareya Aranyaka and Taittiriya Aranyaka. But the picture changes in the Upanishads (c. 1000-c. 600 BC; "Collections of Esoteric Equations"), namely, *Ishavashyopanishad, Kenopanishad, Kathopanishad, Chandogya Upanishad, Brihadaranyakopanishad.* These prose texts at times convey the actual mode of teaching of a revered sage, in a style that can be strikingly intimate.

While the older Upanishads are in prose, the later ones, dating from around 600 BC, mark a shift back to verse. They are the oldest examples of didactic verse, a genre that later gained enormous popularity.

The most popular Sanskrit epic of the eleventh-twelfth century is Sriharsha's *Naisadhiyacharitam* in 22 cantos. The epic deals with the love story of Nala—the king of Nisadha and Damayanti—the daughter of Bhima, the king of Vidarbha. A swan plays the role of Nala's love-messenger. As is the case with most of the writings of the mediaeval period, the central theme of this epic, too, is derived from the Mahabharata. The epic is full of verbal and semantic embellishments and other scholarly and poetic descriptions and dialogues.

Even though Ratnakara's *Haravijaya* and Sivasvamin's *Kapphinabhyudaya* (ninth century) precede Sriharsha's epic, they surpass it in scholastic flight.

Panditaraja Jagannattha (seventeenth century) is most impressive as a versatile lyricist. His *Bhaminivilasa* is a collection of poems touching the various aspects of life where the poet's sensitivities are manifested aesthetically.

Kalhana's *Rajatarangini*, a historical poem (twelfth century) may also be noted as one of the models of mediaeval literary tradition. The work presents the history of Kashmir from AD 813 to 1150. Jonaraja, Sridhara, and Suka further updated the work in succession (sixteenth century).

Some of the representative epics of the mediaeval period were Mankhaka's *Srikanthacharitam* (twelfth century) dealing with Lord Shiva's story; Vedantadesika's *Yadavabhudaya* (dealing with the exploits of Sri Krishna) of about the same time; Harishchandra's *Dharmasarmabhyudaya* (thirteenth century) dealing with the story of Dharmanatha, the fifteenth Jain Tirthankara; the Bilhana's *Vikramankdevacharitam* (twelfth century).

The period abounds in lyric poetry of both categories—devotional and secular. Utpaladeva's *Shivastotravali*, Jagaddhara-bhatta's *Stutikusumanjali*, Narayanabhatta's *Narayayaniyam*, and Vedantadesika's *Padukasahasram* are some of the poems of the first category. Govardhanacharya's *Aryasaptasati* is composed on the model of Hala's (fifth century) *Gaha Sattasai* in Prakrit, a love poem of 700 stanzas. Jayadeva's *Gitagovinda* is the most popular lyric poem depicting the amorous sentiments of Radha and Sri Krishna. Its *dasavatara* hymn (the 10 incarnations of Lord Vishnu) is very popular all over the country for musical and dance performances.

Some of the major specimens of didactic poetry are Daksinamurti's *Lokoktimuktavali*, Nilakanthadikshita's *Kalividambana*, Jalhan's *Mugdhopadesa*, the three *satakas* (centuries) of Bhartrhari—*Niti Sataka*, *Shringarasataka*, and *Vairagyasataka*—Sridharadasa's

Saduktikarnamrita, and Sarngadhara's *Sargadharaprddhatia*.

Dandin's *Dashakumaracharitam*, Subandhu's *Vasavadatta*, and Banabhatta's *Harsacharitam* and *Kadambari* are the representative prose romances produced during the sixth and seventh centuries. Several plays including some allegorical plays like Gunamisra's *Praboddhachandrodaya* and fairy tales and fables like *Vetalapanchavimsatika* were produced during the period.

Satavahana Dynasty, Indian family belonging to the Andhra *jati*, it was the first dynasty from the Deccan to build an empire in *dakshinapatha* (the southern region). At the height of their power the Satavahanas held distant areas of western and central India.

The accessibility, from the early Satavahana kingdom, of the western coastal ports, which prospered in this period of Indo-Roman trade, and the close territorial proximity with the western Kshatrapas resulted in an almost uninterrupted series of wars between the two Indian kingdoms. The first stage of this conflict is represented by Kshatrapa Nahapana's penetration into Nashik and other areas of the western Deccan. Satavahana power was revived by Gautamiputra Shatakarni (reigned c. AD 106-130), the greatest ruler of the family. His conquests ranged over a vast territorial expanse stretching approximately from Rajasthan in the northwest to Andhra in the southeast and from Gujarat in the west to Kalinga in the east. Some time before 150, the Kshatrapas recovered most of these areas from the Satavahanas and twice inflicted defeats upon them.

The beginnings of Satavahana ascendancy can be dated towards the end of the first century BC, although some authorities trace the family to the third century BC. Initially, Satavahana rule was limited to certain areas of the western Deccan. Inscriptions found in caves, such as those at Nanaghat, Nashik, Karli, and Kanheri, commemorate the early rulers Simuka, Krishna, and Shatakarni I.

Gautamiputra's son, Vashisthiputra Pulumavi (reigned c. 130-159), ruled from the west. The tendency seems to have been to expand to the east and the northeast. Inscriptions and coins of Vashisthiputra Pulumavi are also found in Andhra, and Shivashri Shatakarni (reigned c. 159-166) is known from coins found in the Krishna and Godavari districts. The distribution area of Shri Yajna Shatakarni's (reigned c. 174-203) regional coins is spread over the Krishna and Godavari districts, the Chanda district of Madhya Pradesh, Berar, northern Konkan and Saurashtra.

Shri Yajna was the last important figure in the history of the Satavahana dynasty. He achieved success against the Kshatrapas, but his successors, known mostly from Puranic genealogical accounts and coins, ruled over a comparatively limited area.

Despite the achievements of the northern Mauryas in the Deccan in the fourth-third century BC, it was under the Satavahanas that the historical period proper began in this region. Although there are no clear indications as to whether a centralized administrative system was evolved, an extensive system of currency was introduced throughout the empire. Indo-Roman trade reached its peak during this period. The resultant material prosperity is reflected in the liberal patronage of Buddhist and Brahminical communities, enumerated in contemporary inscriptions.

The "local" character of later numismatic issues and their distribution pattern indicates the subsequent fragmentation of the Satavahana empire. The Andhra region passed on first to the Ikshvaku, and then to the Pallava dynasty. Different areas in the western Deccan experienced the emergence of new local powers such as the Chutus, the Abhiras, and the Kurus. In the Berar region the Vakatakas emerged as a formidable political force in the early fourth century. By this period the breakdown of the Satavahana empire was complete.

Satyasiddhi-Shastra, a treatise in 202 chapters on the doctrine of the void (*shunya*), the work stands as a philosophical bridge between Hinayana, or Theravada, Buddhism, the form predominant in Sri Lanka and Southeast Asia, and Mahayana Buddhism, the tradition predominant in East Asia.

The *Satyasiddhi-Shastra* argues strongly against the absolute existence or ultimate ontological reality of any phenomenon. It was probably written in the early fourth century and was translated into Chinese at the start of the fifth century. In China it gave rise to the Satyasiddhi school, which was considered to be Hinayanist, although the *Satyasiddhi-Shastra* itself was regarded in China as a Mahayana treatise. The text's Sanskrit original has perished, as have all commentaries on the work.

The author, Harivarman, a central Indian Brahmin in origin, studied both Hinayana and Mahayana. The Chinese translation is entitled *Ch'eng-shih Lun* and the Japanese *Jojitsu-ron*.

Saura Sect, Hindu sect widely dispersed throughout India in the Gupta and mediaeval periods, its members worshipped Surya, the sun god, as the supreme deity. Surya was worshipped by Indians from the Vedic period onwards for his help in destroying sins and bestowing blessings. The existence of a sect of sun worshippers is noted in the Indian epic the *Mahabharata*. The Saura, like other sects, interpreted various texts as declaring the supremacy of Surya. Emancipation was believed to be obtained by adoring the sun (just-risen, on the meridian, and setting), by bearing its marks on the body (a circular red *tilaka*, or mark on the forehead), and by chanting his prayer.

Though the Saura is no longer a prominent sect in India, the chanting of the Gayatri mantra, a prayer to the sun, is a part of many observant Hindus' daily routine. Surya also figures as one of the five deities (together with Vishnu, Shiva, Shakti, and Ganesha) worshipped by the Smarta sect.

A relation to the ancient Iranian cult of Mithra is evident as early as the first century AD. Thereafter, North Indian temple images of Surya show him in a typical northern dress, such as boots, and the girdle around the waist known as the *avyanga* (Avestan *avyonhana*). The Magas (the Iranian priests, the Magis) were the special priests of the sun god and were treated in the Hindu caste-structure as Brahmins. The temple constructed at Multan on the banks of the Chandrabhaga River (modern Chenab, now in Pakistan) was an important centre of the cult in the seventh century AD.

Sautrantika, ancient school of Buddhism that emerged in India about the second century BC as an offshoot of the Sarvastivada ("All-Is-Real Doctrine").

The Sautrantikas maintained that though events (*dharmas*) have only momentary existence, there is a transmigrating substratum of consciousness that contains within it seeds of goodness that exist in every person. The Sautrantika sometimes is characterized as a transitional school that led to the development of the Mahayana tradition, and many of its views influenced later Yogachara thought.

The school is so called because of its reliance on the *sutras*, or words of the Buddha, and its rejection of the authority of the *Abhidharma*, a part of the canon.

Seleucus I Nicator (b. 358/354 BC, Europus, Macedonia; d. Aug./Sep. 281, near Lysimachia, Thrace), Macedonian army officer and founder of the Seleucid kingdom.

Seleucus was the son of Antiochus, a general of Philip II of Macedonia, the father of Alexander the Great. Seleucus participated in the conquest of the Persian Empire as one of Alexander's officers, and in 326 he commanded the Macedonian infantry against King Porus of India in a battle on the Hydaspes River. In 324 Alexander ordered a mass wedding ceremony at Susa (in Persia) to put into practice his ideal of uniting the peoples of Macedonia and Persia.

On this occasion Seleucus married Apama, the daughter of Spitamenes, the ruler of Bactria. Of all the Macedonian nobles, he was the only one who did not repudiate his wife after Alexander's death.

In the struggles following the death of Alexander the Great, he rose from governor of Babylon to become king of an empire centring on Syria and Iran.

Shaishunaga Dynasty, ancient ruling family in the Indian kingdom of Magadha, the Shaishunaga line of kings followed the reigns of Bimbisara and Ajatashatru (both contemporaries of the Buddha). The line is generally placed immediately before the Nandas and is dated roughly from the mid-fifth to the mid-fourth century BC.

Shishunaga, or Susunaga, the founder, was of obscure origin and may have initially served as Magadhan viceroy at Kashi (Varanasi). Gradually he came to be associated with the early Magadhan capital Girivraja, or Rajgir, and re-established the city of Vaishali (Basarh in north Bihar). Shishunaga's reign, like that of his Magadhan predecessors, represents a state in the history of the fast expansion of the Magadhan Empire. He successfully fought against Avantivardhana and annexed Avanti to his empire.

The reign of Shishunaga's son Kalashoka is known chiefly for two important events: the meeting of the second Buddhist Council at Vaishali and the shifting of the Magadhan capital to Pataliputra. The end of Shishunaga's line is obscure, as is much of the pre-Mauryan dynastic history of Magadha. Kalashoka's sons, according to traditional lists, were ten in number, but no details about them are known. Kalashoka was brutally murdered, presumably by the founder of the Nanda line, and the Shaishunaga dynasty ceased to rule.

Shaiva Agamas, traditional texts of the Shaivites (worshippers of Shiva).

The sects of Agamic Shaivas (Shiva worshippers who follow their own Agama—"traditional"—texts) encompass both the Sanskritic Shaiva-siddhanta—those who accept the philosophical premises and conclusions of Shaivas in the north—and the southern Lingayats or Virashaivas (from *vira*, literally "hero"; a *lingam* is the Shiva emblem that is worshipped in lieu of images). The Shaiva-siddhanta traditionally has 28 Agamas and 150 sub-Agamas. Their principal texts are hard to date. Most probably they do not antedate the eighth century. Their doctrine states that Shiva is the conscious principle of the universe, while matter is unconscious. Shiva's power, or *shakti*, personified as a goddess, causes bondage and release. Shakti is also the magic Word, and thus her nature can be sought out and meditated upon in *mantras*.

Kashmir Shaivism begins with the *Shivasutra*, or "Lines of Doctrine Concerning Shiva", (c. 850) as a new revelation of Shiva. The system embraces the *Shivadrishti* ("A Vision of Shiva") of Somananda (950), in which emphasis is placed on the continuous recognition of Shiva; the world is a manifestation of Shiva brought about by his *shakti*. The system is called *trika* ("triad"), because it recognizes the three principles of Shiva, Shakti, and the individual soul. Virashaiva texts begin at about 1150 with the *Vachanams* ("Sayings") of Basava. The sect is puritanical, worships Shiva exclusively, rejects the caste system in favour of its own social organization, and is highly structured with monasteries and gurus.

Like much other Hindu sacred literature, this literature is neither well-catalogued nor thoroughly studied. It is only possible to summarize classes of texts within the various traditions.

Shaiva Rites, ritual practices of the Shaivites (worshippers of Shiva). Shaivism, though inclined in doctrinal matters to adoptive inclusivism, inculcates some fundamental lines of conduct: one should worship one's spiritual preceptor (guru) as God himself, follow his path, consider him to be present in oneself, and dissociate oneself from all opinions and practices that are incompatible with the Shaiva creed. Yet some of Shiva's devotees also worship other gods, and the "Shivaization" of various ancient traditions is sometimes rather superficial. Like many other Indian religions, the Shaiva-siddhanta has developed an elaborate system of ethical philosophy, primarily with a view to preparing the way for those who aspire to liberation. Because *dharma* leads to happiness, there is no distinction between sacred and secular duties. All deeds are performed as services to God and with the conviction that all life is sacred and God-centred. A devout way of living and a nonemotional mysticism are thus much recommended. Kashmir Shaivism developed the practice of a simple method of salvation: by the recognition (*pratyabhijna*)—direct, spontaneous, technique-free, but full of *bhakti*—of one's identity with God.

Ascetic tendencies were much in evidence among the Pashupatas, the oldest Shaiva tradition in North India, the last adherents of which now live in Nepal. Pashupatas often gave offence because of their customs and ritual practices. Their Yoga, consisting of a constant meditative contact with God in solitude, required that they frequent burning places for cremated bodies. More extreme groups carried human skulls (hence the name Kapalikas, from *kapala*, "skull") which they used as bowls for liquor into which they projected and worshipped Shiva as Kapalika, "the Skull Bearer", or Bhairava, "the Frightful One", and then drank to become intoxicated. Their belief was that an ostentatious indifference to anything worldly was the best method of severing the ties of *samsara*.

The view and way of life peculiar to the Virashaivas, or Lingayats (*lingam*-bearers), in southwestern India is mainly characterized by a deviation from some common Hindu traditions and institutions such as sacrificial rites, temple worship, pilgrimages, child marriages, and inequality of the sexes. Initiation (*diksha*) is, on the other hand, an obligation laid on every member of the community. The spiritual power of the guru is bestowed upon the newborn and converts, who receive the eightfold shield, which protects devotees from ignorance of the supremacy of God and guides them to final beatitude, and the *lingam*. The miniature *lingam*, the centre and basis of all their religious practices and observances, which they always bear on their body, is God himself concretely represented. Worship is due to it twice or three times a day. When a Lingayat "is absorbed into the *lingam*" (dies), his body is not cremated, as is customary in Hinduism, but is interred, like ascetics of other groups. Those Lingayats who have reached a certain level of holiness are supposed to die in a state of emancipation.

Shaiva Schools, there is a long tradition of Shiva worship going back to the Rudra hymns of the Rigveda, the Shiva-Rudra of the Vajasaneyi-Samhita, the Atharvaveda, and the Brahmanas of the various philosophical systems within Shaivism (religious sect that worships Shiva as the highest deity). Madhava in his *Sarva-darshana-samgraha* referred to three Shaiva systems: the Nakulisha-Pashupata, the Shaiva, and the Pratyabhijna systems. The Shaiva system of Madhava's classification probably corresponds to Shaiva-siddhanta of Tamil country, and the Pratyabhijna is known as Kashmir Shaivism. The Shaiva-siddhanta is realistic and dualistic; the Kashmir system is idealistic and monistic.

Shaiva-Siddhanta, the world and souls are real, and emancipation requires the grace of Shiva. The Shaiva-siddhanta always insisted on the preservation of the individuality of the finite soul, even in the state of emancipation, and rejected Shankara's nondualism.

The source literature of the Shaiva-siddhanta school consists of the Agamas, Tamil devotional hymns written by Shaiva saints but collected by Nambi (c. AD 1000) in a volume known as *Tirumurai, Chiva-nana-potam* ("Understanding of the Knowledge of Shiva") by Meykantatevar (thirteenth century), Shivacharya's *Shiva-jnana-siddhiyar* ("Attainment of the Knowledge of Shiva"), Umapati's *Shivaprakasham* ("Lights on Shiva") in the fourteenth century, and Appaya Dikshita's commentary thereon. This school admits three categories (*padarthas*): God (Shiva or Pati, Lord), the soul (*pashu*) and its bonds (*pasha*), and the 36 principles (*tattvas*). These 36 principles are divided into 3 groups: at the top, in order of manifestation from Shiva, are the 5 pure principles—*shivatattva* (the essence of Shiva), *shakti* (power), *sada-shiva* (the eternal good), *ishvara* (lord), and *shuddha-vidya* (true knowledge); 7 mixed principles—pure *maya*, 5 envelopes (destiny, time, interest, knowledge, and power), and *purusha*, or self; and 24 impure principles beginning with *prakriti* (this list is broadly the same as that of Samkhya). Shiva is the first cause: his *shakti*, or power, being the instrumental cause, *maya* the material cause. This *maya-shakti* is not God's essential power but is assumed by Him; it is *parigraha-shakti* ("assumed power"). The relation of Shiva to his essential power is one of identity. Bonds are of three kinds: *karma*, *maya*, and *avidya*.

Appaya Dikshita's commentary shows the tendency to attempt a reconciliation between the Agama tradition of realism and pluralism with the Advaita tradition. The soul is eternal and all-pervasive, but, owing to original ignorance, it is reduced to the condition of *anava*, which consists in regarding oneself as finite and atomic. Knowledge of its own nature as well as God's is possible only by God's grace.

Shaivism, worship of the god Shiva, with Vaishnavism and Shaktism, it is one of the three principal forms of modern Hinduism. Shaivism includes such diverse movements as the highly philosophic Shaiva-siddhanta and Kashmir schools, the socially distinctive Virashaiva (or Lingayat), ascetic orders such as the *dashnami sannyasis* and Kapalikas and Kalamukhas, and innumerable folk variants.

While scholarly speculation that the worship of Shiva predates Aryan religion has not been conclusive, it is clear that the Vedic god Rudra ("the Howler") had been amalgamated with the figure of Shiva ("Auspicious One") by the period of the later Upanishads. The Shvetasvatara Upanishad treats Shiva as the paramount deity, but it is not until sometime between the second century BC and the second century AD, with the rise of the Pashupata sect, that the sectarian worship of Shiva was recorded.

Shaka, nomadic tribe from Central Asia, also known as Scythian, it disturbed the Bactrian control of Taxila and is referred to in Indian sources as the Shakas. They attacked the kingdom of Bactria and then moved into India.

The Han rulers of China were determined to keep out the Central Asian nomadic tribes (the Xiongnu, Wusun, and Yuezhi) and these tribes were forced to migrate southwards and westwards. A branch of the Yuezhi, the Dayuezhi, moved further west to the Aral Sea, and this displaced the existing Shakas, who poured into Bactria and Parthia. The Parthian king Mithradates II offered resistance, but after his death (88 BC) they swept through Parthia and continued into the Indus Valley. Among the early Shaka kings was Maues, or Moga (first century BC), who ruled over Gandhara. The Shakas moved southwards under pressure from the Pahlavas (Parthians), who ruled briefly in northwestern India towards the end of the first century BC. At Mathura, the Shaka rulers of note were Rajuvala and Shodasa. Ultimately the Shakas settled in western India and Malava (Malwa) and came into conflict with the kingdoms of the northern Deccan and the Ganga Valley—particularly during the reigns of Nahapana, Chastana, and Rudradaman—in the first two centuries AD. Rudradaman's fame is recorded in a lengthy Sanskrit inscription at Junagadh, dating to 150.

Shaka Satrap, also called Kshatrapa, either of two dynasties of satraps in northwestern India ruled with considerable independence on behalf of the Pahlava suzerains. In Indian literature both families are known as the Shakas (from the Indian word for Scythians) but most Western historians know them as the Kshatrapas.

The dynasty of satraps, founded by Chastana in AD 78, ruled for two or three centuries in western India and gave its name to the Shakanripakala, or era of Shaka kings, in Indian history. The rulers of this house can be dated with incomplete accuracy from their coinage. Ptolemy mentions Chastana as ruling into the second century (probably AD 78-110). He extended his holdings at the expense of the Andhras. The wars between the Shakas and the Andhras continued for several generations. The first great Shaka ruler was Rudradaman I, Chastana's grandson, who reigned after AD 130. The direct line of Chastana became extinct in AD 304-305 with the death of Vishvasena, son of Bhartridaman. It is doubtful that the dynasty was important in the fourth century, although one of its members—probably

Rudrasimha III—is recorded as the "Shaka king" killed by Chandra Gupta II when he sacked the Shaka capital in AD 388.

The Kshaharata dynasty was short lived and is known for two rulers, Bhumaka and Nahapana. Their reigns are proved by coinage and by a few surviving inscriptions that appear to fix the year AD 124 as a date in Nahapana's reign. These documents claim that Nahapana ruled over a large area in western India around the Gulf of Cambay, which he could only have won from the Andhras. The possession was, however, brief because the Andhra king Gautamiputra destroyed the Shakas in the latter part of the Shaka year 46 (AD 124-125). A system of dating known as the Shaka era, based on the year AD 78, is still widely used in India in the Hindu calendar, apart from the Gregorian calendar. Its origin has been attributed to the Shakas. So the Shaka year 46 is AD 78 added to AD 46, that is AD 124.

Shakta Tantras. Shaktism in one form or the other has been known since Bana (c. 650) wrote the *Chandi-shataka* (Hundred Couplets to Chandi) and Bhavabhuti, his play *Malati Madhava* (725 AD), both of which refer to Tantric practices. There is no traditional authoritative list of Tantric texts venerating the goddess Shakti, but many texts are extant.

Shaktism is an amalgam of Shaivism and folk mother-goddess cults. The Shaiva notion that not Shiva himself but his *shakti* (creative power) is active is taken to the extreme—that, without Shakti, Shiva is a corpse, and simultaneously that Shakti is the creator as well as creation. In Yoga, great importance is ascribed to *mantras*, which conjure up to the realities with which they are identified.

Another important notion (partly derived from Yoga philosophy) is that these subtle canals through the body which carry esoteric powers connected with the spinal cord, at the bottom of which the Goddess is coiled around the *lingam* as Kundalini. She can be made to rise through the body to the top, whereupon release from *samsara* takes place. Important among the Shakta Tantras are the *Kularnava Tantra* ("Ocean of Tantrism"), which gives details on the "left-handed" cult forms of ritual copulation; the *Kulachudamani* ("Crown Jewel of Tantrism"), which embroiders on ritual; and the *Sharadatilaka* ("Beauty Mark of the Goddess Sharada") of Lakshmanadeshika (eleventh century), which discusses magic.

A temple was erected in honour of the mother goddesses

at Gangdhar, Rajasthan, in AD 423. There, magical rites of a terrifying kind were practised. The temple is described as "loud with the shouts of demonesses, crying in the thick darkness," by the playwright Bhavabhuti, whose drama *Malati Madhava* (about the adventures of the hero Madhava and his beloved Malati) contains a scene depicting secret rites with human sacrifice and ritual cannibalism. The goddess cults eventually centred around Durga, the consort of Shiva, in her fiercer aspect.

Shaktism. "Hinduism" can be divided into three broad, interflowing, overlapping currents: *Vaishnavism,* the worship of the god Vishnu; *Shaivism,* the worship of the god Shiva; and *Shaktism,* the worship of the Goddess as Shakti ("Power"). Shaktism is thus a general term used to designate a wide variety of goddess traditions in South Asia whose general focus is the worship of the Goddess.

As a theological category, the term Shaktism is no doubt helpful, but it is imprecise. It can refer to historically and doctrinally distinct traditions—the mythologies of various goddesses that appear in the mediaeval Puranas to the two major goddess-branches, or "families" (*kula*) of Shakta Tantrism (the *Shri-kula* and *Kali-kula*); also the virtually endless number of local village goddesses, past and present.

As an academic or popular religious category, Shaktism is a reflection of the common Hindu belief that the innumerable goddesses of village and Sanskritic lore are all manifestations of a single Mahadevi, or "Great Goddess". This concept of a Great Goddess is usually held to be ancient but, historically speaking, probably dates back to the mediaeval period when it was used to fuse the wildly disparate local and pan-Indian traditions into an ideologically unifying theology.

Historically, Shaktism has been popular on the geographic peripheries of South Asia, particularly in Kashmir, South India, Assam, and Bengal. Its Tantric symbols and rituals have, however, been omnipresent within the Hindu traditions since at least the sixth century AD. More recently, various forms of traditional, philosophical, and popular Shaktism have entered the West, with traditional immigrant Indian populations, among some ideological academic communities, and with various "New Age" and feminist-oriented traditions, usually in the West under the more popular rubric of Tantrism or Tantra.

Followers of Shakti are often called *shaktas* ("Empowered

Ones"). *Shaktas* not only worship the Shakti as Goddess but also attempt to enhance, control, and transform the Goddess' power-manifestations in the *shakti*, or "energy", of the human body and the living cosmos. Specifically, the Goddess is believed to dwell at the anal base of the human body in the form of a sleeping coiled serpent (*kundalini*). Through complex meditations and sexual-yogic rituals, this "serpent power" can be aroused or awakened. Then, she moves up the central channel (*susumna*) of the subtle body (usually super-imposed upon the spinal column), piercing the various energy centres (*chakras*) located along the way until she enters the final *chakra* at the top of the head and ecstatically unites there with her husband-lover Shiva. This mythological union of the Goddess and the God is experienced psycho-physiologically as an ecstatic-mystical trance whose exploding bliss is said to flow down the entire body in a flood of ecstasy and intense pleasure.

Shankara (b. 700?, Kaladi village?; d. 750?, Kedarnath, India), also called Shankaracharya, philosopher and theologian, was the most renowned exponent of the Advaita Vedanta school of philosophy, from whose doctrines the main currents of modern Indian thought are derived. He wrote commentaries on the Brahma-sutra and the principal Upanishads, affirming his belief in one eternal unchanging reality (Brahman) and the illusion of plurality and differentiation.

A tradition says that Shiva, one of the principal gods in Hinduism, was Shankara's family deity. He was, by birth, a *shakta*, or worshipper of Shakti, the consort of Shiva and the female personification of divine energy. Later he came to be regarded as a worshipper of Shiva or even an incarnation of Shiva himself. His doctrine, however, is far removed from Shaivism and Shaktism. It is ascertained from his works that he had some faith in, or was favourable to, Vaishnavism, the worship of god Vishnu. It is highly probable that he was familiar with Yoga (one of the classical systems of Indian philosophy, as well as a technique to achieve salvation). One study has suggested that in the beginning he was an adherent of Yoga and later becane an advaitin (nondualist). Biographers narrate that Shankara first went to Kashi (Varanasi), a city celebrated for learning and spirituality, and then travelled all over India, holding discussions with philosophers of different creeds. His heated debate with Mandana Mishra, a philosopher of the Mimamsa (investigation) school, whose wife served as a referee, is perhaps the most interesting episode in his biography. It may also reflect a historical fact that there was, a keen conflict between Shankara, who regarded the knowledge of Brahman as the only means to final release, and followers of the Mimamsa school, which emphasized the performance of ordained duty and the Vedic rituals.

There are at least 11 works that profess to be biographies of Shankara. All of them were composed several centuries later than the time of Shankara and are filled with legendary stories and incredible anecdotes, some of which are mutually conflicting. Today there are no materials with which to reconstruct his life with certainty. His date of birth is naturally a controversial problem. It has been customary to assign him the birth and death dates 788-820. But the dates 700-750, based on twentieth-century scholarship, appear to be more acceptable.

Shankara was born into a pious Nambudiri Brahmin family in a quiet village called Kaladi on the Churna (or Purna, Periyar) River, Kerala, southern India. He is said to have lost his father, Shivaguru, early in his life. He renounced the world and became a *sannyasin* (ascetic) against his mother's will. He studied under Govinda, who was a pupil of the seventeenth-century thinker Gaudapada. Nothing certain is known about Govinda, but Gaudapada is notable as the author of an important Vedanta work, *Mandukya-karika*, a commentary in verse on the Mandukya Upanishad, in which the influence of Mahayana Buddhism—a form of Buddhism aiming at the salvation of all beings and tending towards nondualistic or monstic thought—is evident, especially in its last chapter.

More than 300 works—commentative, expository, and poetical—written in the Sanskrit language, are attributed to him. Most of them, however, cannot be regarded as authentic. His masterpiece is the *Brahma-sutra-bhashya*, the commentary on the Brahma-sutra, which is a fundamental text of the Vedanta school. The commentaries on the principal Upanishads that are attributed to Shankara are certainly all genuine, with the possible exception of the commentary on the Shvetasvatara Upanishad. The commentary on the *Mandukya-karika* was also composed by Shankara himself. It is very probable that he is the author of the *Yoga-sutra-bhashya-vivarana*, the exposition of Vyasa's commentary on the Yoga-sutra, a fundamental text of the Yoga school. The *Upadeshasahasri*, which is a good introdution to Shankara's philosophy, is the only non-commentative work that is certainly authentic.

Shankara's style of writing is lucid and profound. Penetrating insight and analytical skill characterize his works. His approach to truth is psychological and religious rather than logical; for that reason, he is perhaps best considered to be a prominent religious teacher rather than a philosopher in the twentieth-century sense. His works reveal that he was not only well versed in the orthodox Brahminical traditions but was also well acquainted with Mahayana Buddhism. He is often criticized as a "Buddhist in disguise" by his opponents because of the similarity between his doctrine and Buddhism. Despite this criticism, he made full use of his knowledge of Buddhism to attack Buddhist doctrines severely or to transmute them into his own Vedantic nondualism, and he tried with great effort to "vedanticize" the Vedanta philosophy, which had been made extremely Buddhistic by his predecessors. The basic structure of his philosophy is more akin to Samkhya, a philosophic system of nontheistic dualism, and the Yoga school than to Buddhism. It is said that Shankara died at Kedarnatha in the Himalaya. The Advaita Vedanta School, founded by him, has always been pre-eminent in the learned circles of India.

It is very likely that Shankara had many pupils, but only four are known (from their writings): Padmapada, Sureshvara, Totaka (or Trotaka), and Hastamalaka. Shankara probably following the Buddhist monastery (*vihara*) system, is said to have founded four monasteries, at Sringeri (south), Puri (east), Dwarka (west), and Badrinath (north). Their foundation was one of the most significant factors in the development of his teachings into the leading philosophy of India.

Shankara would not teach his doctrine to city dwellers. The power of Buddhism was still strong in the cities, though already declining, and Jainism, a nontheistic ascetic faith, prevailed among the merchants and manufacturers. Popular Hinduism occupied the minds of ordinary people, while city dwellers pursued ease and pleasure. There were also epicureans in cities. It was difficult for Shankara to communicate Vedanta philosophy to these people. Consequently, Shankara propagated his teachings chiefly to *sannyasins* and intellectuals in the villages, and he gradually won the respect of Brahmins and feudal lords. He enthusiastically endeavoured to restore the orthodox Brahminical tradition without paying attention to the Bhakti (devotional) Movement, which had made a deep impression on ordinary

Hindus in his age.

Shantirakshita (flourished eighth century, India), was the Buddhist teacher and saint from India who was instrumental in the development of Tibetan Buddhism.

Invited to Tibet by King Thi-srong-detsan (ruled 740-786), Shantirakshita was forced to flee to Nepal after adherents of the nativistic Bon religion blamed him for the outbreak of an epidemic. After his return from Tibet, according to late fourteenth-century accounts, he urged the king to invite the Indian Buddhist teacher Padmasambhava to help him.

Shantirakshita became the first abbot of the monastery at Samye (Bsam-yas), which he headed for 13 years. At the monastery, he and Padmasambhava taught the doctrines of the Buddhist Yogachara sect and Tantric philosophy. He ordained the first seven Tibetan Buddhist monks and is credited with incorporating several elements of Bon, including its pantheon, into the lowest level of Tantric Buddhism and with instituting symbolic worship to take the place of Bon animal sacrifices.

Sharada Script, writing system used for the Kashmiri language by the educated Hindu minority in Kashmir and the surrounding valleys, it is taught in the Hindu schools there but is not used in printing books. The earliest inscriptions in Sharada script, found in Kashmir and northeastern Punjab, are dated AD 804. The Sharada script corresponds letter-for-letter with Devanagari, although it differs greatly in shape, having stiff, thick strokes. Muslims in Kashmir use a Persian-Arabic script, and much Kashmiri literature is written in Sanskrit with the Devanagari script.

Originating in the eighth century AD, Sharada descended from the Gupta script of North India.

Shrautasutra, any of the Hindu ritual manuals, it is used by priests engaged in the performance of the grander Vedic sacrifices, spcially those requiring three fires and the services of many specialized priests.

The manuals are called *shrauta* (from Sanskrit *shruti*, "revelation") because they are based directly on the older Vedic literature considered as a class to be *Shruti*, or revealed. Each Shrautasutra guides the priests of its own particular Vedic school in the performance of specialized functions. The texts deal with such subjects as the laying of the three fires, the full and new moon ceremonies, and the various animal and *soma* sacrifices. The Shrautasutras, together with the Grihyasutras (dealing with domestic ceremonies) and the Dharmasutras (dealing with rules of conduct), make up the Kalpasutras, collections of brief aphoristic texts that emerged within the different schools of the Veda.

Shravasti, city of ancient India, located near the Rapti River, northeastern Uttar Pradesh State, north-central India it was the capital of the kingdom of Kosala Buddhist times (sixth century BC-sixth century AD), and was important both as a prosperous trading centre and for its religious associations. It stood at the junction of three major roads connecting it with the great cities of eastern, northern, and western India. The city has been identified with the twin villages of Saheth and Maheth northwest of Balrampur. Today it is surrounded by a great rampart of earth and brick. Excavations have been undertaken by the Archaeological Survey of India. In the city itself, three main periods have been recognized, ranging from the earliest, characterized by pre-Buddhist painted greyware, to the early wares dating to the final occupation. It was closely associated with the life of the Buddha and with figures significant in later Buddhist history. Its most important religious place was the Jetavana monastery, which was erected in a garden outside the walls of the city and presented to the Buddha by a wealthy banker, Anathapindaka. Other important Buddhist monasteries were the Rajakarama and the Purvarama. Shravasti was also an important centre for the Jains.

Shri-Nathji, is the main cult image of the followers of Vallabha, an important devotional sect of India. It is a unique representation of the god Krishna. The image is enshrined in the main temple of the cult at Nathdwara in Rajasthan State, where it is accorded an elaborate service of worship daily.

The image was first worshipped in Mathura, and, while in flight from the Mughals, the chariot carrying the image broke down at Nathdwara, where it was given protection by the local Rajput chief. Representations of Shri-Nathji, covered with ornaments and garlands of worship, are commonly seen in the homes and shops of devotees throughout North and West India.

According to sect tradition, the image of Shri-Nathji revealed itself to the sect's founder, Vallabha, while he was visiting Mount Govardhana, near Mathura (the image has one hand raised, suggestive of Krishna's lifting of Mount Govardhana to shelter the cowherds from a storm sent by the jealous god Indra).

Shrivaishnava, member of a sect of Hindus, who pay

allegiance to Lord Vishnu and follow the teachings of the philosopher Ramanuja, they are the most numerous in South India. "Shri" refers to Vishnu's consort, also called Lakshmi, to whom Vishnu first taught the doctrine.

The Shrivaishnava is among the most exclusive of the Hindu sects. They worship only Vishnu and his consorts and attendants and do not acknowledge Krishna's youthful companion, Radha. Brahmin members take the lead in the strict observance of caste regulations in such matters as diet and interdining. Shrivaishnava Brahmins are given to scholarly pursuits and have earned for themselves the honorary title of *acharya*, or, in Tamil, *ayyangar*, often spelt *iyengar*.

The sect reached its peak in the late tenth or eleventh century, when the passionate devotional hymns of the Tamil Alvars (a group of mystics) were introduced into the temple service by Nathamuni, called the first *acharya* ("teacher") of the sect. He founded a Sanskrit-Tamil school at Srirangam (Tamil Nadu State), which was then, and continues to be, a great Vaishnava centre in South India. Ramanuja (eleventh/twelfth century), in an exposition of the Vedanta-sutras called *Shribhashya* ("Beautiful Commentary"), gave the sect a philosophical doctrine to fit its views and early literature. *Shribhashya* was the first sectarian commentary ever written on a Hindu sacred text and the model for the many others that followed.

Towards the end of the late fourteenth century, a controversy split the Shrivaishnavas into their present two subsects, the Vadakalai (school of northern learning), which relied more on the Sanskrit scriptures, and the Tenkalai (school of southern learning), which stressed the Tamil hymns of the Alvars.

Shruti, class of literature based on revelation, it is the most revered body of sacred literature in Hinduism. Though *shruti* is considered to be the more authoritative, in practice the *smriti* texts are more influential in modern Hinduism. *Shruti* works are considered divine revelation, heard and transmitted by earthly sages, as contrasted to *smriti*, or that which is remembered. The revealed texts encompass the four Vedas—Rigveda, Yajurveda, Samaveda, and Atharvaveda (the earliest Hindu sacred literature), the Brahmanas (ritual treatises), the Aranyakas ("Books of the Forest"), and the Upanishads (philosophic elaborations on the Vedas that form the basis of much of later Indian philosophy).

Shudra, the fourth and lowest of the traditional *varnas*, or social orders, of Hindu India, comprising artisans and labourers, the term does not appear in the earliest Vedic literature. In its first application, it probably included all conquered peoples of the Indus civilization when they were assimilated as menials to the three-class society of the Brahmins (priests and teachers), Kshatriyas (nobles and warriors), and Vaishyas (merchants).

The Shudra *varna* includes a wide spectrum of endogamous status groups with dominant, landowning groups at one end of the scale and near-untouchables at the other. These variations derive from the Hindu belief that certain behaviour patterns and occupations are polluting, a concept that gave rise to a distinction between "clean" and "unclean" Shudra groups; for example, washers, tanners, shoemakers, sweepers, and scavengers were once relegated to untouchability. As evidence of group mobility in the caste system, some observers have pointed out that many castes claiming Kshatriya and Vaishya status gradually emerged from the Shudra class.

Shudras are not permitted to perform the *upanayana* (initiatory rite), which introduces members of the three upper classes to the study of the Vedas (earliest sacred literature) and gives them their status as *dvija* ("twice-born").

Shunga Dynasty. Indian ruling house founded by Pushyamitra in about 185 BC, it replaced the Maurya dynasty. Pushyamitra assassinated Brihadratha, the last Maurya ruler, at a military parade and assumed royal power. Pushyamitra was a Brahmin, and, though he is said to have persecuted Buddhists, Buddhism still flourished in many areas under his control.

Pushyamitra's reign extended over the cities of Pataliputra, Ayodhya, and Vidisha and perhaps over Jalandhara and Shakala as well. The Maurya system of administering the provinces through princes of royal blood continued, and royal power tended to decentralize in the form of the establishment of nuclear kingdoms within the empire. Pushyamitra conducted several campaigns against the Yavanas, or the Indo-Greeks, who were trying in this period to expand from Bactria into northwestern India.

Pushyamitra, ruled for roughly 36 years. Shunga history thereafter is largely uncertain. Nothing substantial is known about his successor, Agnimitra, the hero of Kalidasa's play *Malavikagnimitram*. According to the Puranas, Agnimitra's successors, in genealogical order, were: Sujyestha (or Vasujyestha), Vasumitra, Andhraka (or Bhadraka), Pulindaka, Ghosha,

Vajramitra, Bhagavata, and Devabhumi (Devabhuti). If the Puranic account is to be believed, the total tenure of Shunga rule was 112 years, and came to an end in about 73 BC.

Shunyata, in Buddhist philosophy, the void that constitutes ultimate reality, *Shunyata* is seen not as a negation of existence but rather as the undifferentiation out of which all apparent entities, distinctions, and dualities arise. The term *shunyata* may also be used as a recognition of *anatta*, or the absence of any self apart from the five *skandhas* (mental and physical elements of existence). Although the concept is encountered occasionally in early Pali texts, its full implications were developed by the second-century AD Indian philosopher Nagarjuna. The school of philosophy founded by him, the Madhyamika (Middle Way), is sometimes called the Shunyavada ("Doctrine That All Is Void").

Siddha, in Jainism, is one who has achieved perfection, by means of right faith, right knowledge, and right conduct. *Siddha* frees himself from the cycle of rebirths and resides in a state of perpetual bliss in the *siddha-shila* at the top of the universe. The *siddha* and the other ascetics constitute the *pancha-paramesthin*, the five chief divinities of the Jains. Their figures are represented on a silver or brass tray called a *siddha-chakra* (saint-wheel), to which great sanctity and magical power are attributed. In the twice-yearly ceremony known as *oli*, the images are washed and anointed, and offerings of rice, sweetmeats, and fruit are made.

In the Digambara sect the saint-wheel is called *navapada* ("nine dignities", or "nine virtues") and consists of the *pancha-paramesthin* plus the Jina (saviour) image, temple, scriptures, and *dharma-chakra* ("sacred wheel of the law").

Silk Road, also called Silk Route, was the ancient trade route linking China with the West. It carried goods and ideas between the two great civilizations of Rome and China. Silk came westwards, while wood, gold, and silver went east. China also received Nestorian Christianity and Buddhism (from India) via this road.

Originating at Xi'an, the 6,400-km road, actually a caravan tract, followed the Great Wall of China to the northwest, bypassed the Takla Makan Desert, climbed the Pamirs (mountains), crossed Afghanistan, and went on to the Levant. From there, the merchandise was shipped across the Mediterranean Sea. Few people travelled the entire route, and goods were handled by a staggered procession of middlemen.

The road now partially exists in the form of a paved highway connecting Pakistan and the Sinkiang Uighur Autonomous Region, China. The old road has inspired a United Nations plan for a trans-Asian highway.

With the gradual loss of Roman territory in Asia and the rise of Arabian power in the Levant, the Silk Road became increasingly unsafe and untravelled. In the thirteenth and fourteenth centuries the route was revived under the Mongols. At that time Marco Polo used the road to travel to China.

Smarta Sect, orthodox Hindu sect, it is composed of members of the "twice-born", or initiated upper classes (Brahmin, Kshatriya, and Vaishya). Its primarily Brahmin followers are characterized by their allegiance to all the gods of the Hindu pantheon and by their adherence to rules of ritual and of conduct laid down in the ancient *sutra* texts.

The Smartas of the North differ somewhat from their counterparts in the South and in Gujarat, in that the nomenclature does not necessarily connote followers of Shankara. Also the number of pure Smarta temples are fewer in the North.

The Smartas may give preference to one deity above the others, and Shiva is highly favoured among them today. But in their worship they pay allegiance to the five major gods—Shiva, Vishnu, Shakti, Surya, and Ganesha—in the *panchayatana puja* ("five-shrines worship").

Smarta Brahmins consider themselves orthodox and have tended to rigidly hold the traditional values of Hinduism. They are active in all branches of learning and have earned the honorary title of *shastri* (Sanskrit: "men of learning"), or, in Tamil, *ayyar* (or *iyer*), which often follows their names.

The name Smarta comes from the Sanskrit *smriti*, a class of texts that are considered to be of human authorship in contrast to the Vedas, which are considered to have been divinely revealed. The *sutras* (brief aphorisms) followed by the Smarta sect form part of the *smriti* literature. Their greatest teacher and, according to some, the founder of the sect was the eighth-century philosopher Shankara, the proponent of Advaita (nondualist) Vedanta. The monastery he founded at Sringeri, in Karnataka (formerly Mysore State), continues to be the centre of the sect, and the head of the monastery. The *jagadguru* ("teacher of the world"), is the spiritual authority of the Smartas in South India and Gujarat and one of the chief religious personages in India.

Smriti. Hindu sacred literature based on human memory, as distinct from Vedic literature, which is considered to be *shruti*, or revealed, *Smriti* literature elaborates, interprets, and codifies Vedic thought. But, being derivative, it is considered less authoritative than the Vedic *shruti*. The texts include the important religious manuals known as the Kalpasutras; the compilations of ancient myth, legends, and history, the Puranas; and the two great epics of India, the Ramayana and the Mahabharata. The latter contains within it probably the single most influential text in Hinduism, the Bhagavadgita. In time the term *smriti* came to refer particularly to the texts relating to law and social conduct, such as the celebrated lawbook, the *Manu smriti* ("Tradition of Manu").

Most modern Hindus, however, have a greater familiarity with *smriti* scriptures.

Soma, in ancient Indian cult worship, an unidentified plant, the juice, of which was a fundamental offering of the Vedic sacrifices. The personified deity Soma was the "master of plants", the healer of disease, and the bestower of riches. The stalks of the plant were pressed between stones, and the juice was filtered through sheep's wool and then mixed with water and milk. After first being offered as a libation to the gods, the remainder of the *soma* was consumed by the priests and the sacrificer. It was highly valued for its exhilarating, probably hallucinogenic, effect.

The *soma* cult exhibits a number of similarities to the corresponding *haoma* cult of the ancient Iranians and is suggestive of shared beliefs among the ancient Indo-Europeans in a kind of elixir of the gods. Like *haoma*, the *soma* plant grows in the mountains, but its true origin is believed to be heaven, from where it was brought to earth by an eagle. The pressing of *soma* was associated with the fertilizing rain, which makes possible all life and growth. In the post-Vedic classical period, *soma* is identified with the moon, which wanes when *soma* is drunk by the gods but which is periodically reborn.

Somadeva. Kashmiri Brahmin of the Shaiva sect and Sanskrit writer who preserved much of India's ancient folklore in the form of a series of tales in verse, he was the court poet to King Ananta of Kashmir. Somadeva was commissioned to compose a cycle of stories to amuse and calm the queen, Suryamati, during a political crisis. Somadeva wrote his monumental work during the two periods of Ananta's interrupted rule, which ended in 1077.

He borrowed from an earlier work, now lost, the *Brihat-katha* ("Great Tale") by the Sanskrit writer Gunadhya, who probably had used Buddhist sources of an even earlier period. Somadeva's work *Katha-saritsagara* ("Ocean of Rivers of Stories") bears a strong resemblance to mediaeval European fairy tales. Magic, demons, bloody orgies, vampires, love, and high adventure abound in the 124 sections, or chapters, known as *taranga* ("waves"). An English translation by Charles H. Tawney, titled *The Ocean of Story,* was published in 1924-1928.

South Indian Bronze, any of the cult images of Hindu divinities, that rank among the finest achievements of Indian visual art, they were produced in a large number from the eighth to the sixteenth century, principally in the Thanjavur and Tiruchirappalli districts of modern Tamil Nadu, and maintained a high standard of excellence for almost 1,000 years.

The images are cast by the cire-perdue, or lost-wax, process. Final sculptural touches are added to the image after it is cast, with the result that hte images are "carved" as well as "modelled". Important collections of South Indian bronzes are housed in the Thanjavur Museum and Art Gallery, in Tamil Nadu, and at the Government Museum in Chennai (formerly Madras), but the largest number of fine images are in the various temples of southern India.

The icons range from small household images to almost life-size sculptures intended to be carried in temple processions. A few Buddhist and Jain images were produced, but the figures mostly represent Hindu divinities, especially various iconographic forms of the gods Shiva and Vishnu, together with their consorts and attendants. Also of outstanding quality are the many images of Shaiva and Vaishnava saints (the Alvars).

During the Pallava period, metal sculpture closely followed the canons of contemporary stone sculpture, and the images were almost invariably frontal, though modelled fully in the round, with arms held symmetrically to either side. A great fluidity of movement is apparent in images of the early Chola period (tenth-eleventh century AD), and the movements and hand gestures of dance are frequently employed. The Chola images are unsurpassed in their elegance and sensitive modelling. During the Vijayanagara period (1336-1565) the ornamentation tended to become more elaborate, interfering with the smooth rhythm of the body, and the postures became more rigid.

South Indian Temple Architecture, also called Dravida style, this style is employed in constructing most Hindu temples in modern Tamil Nadu between the seventh and eighteenth centuries. It was characterized by its pyramidal tower. Variant forms are found in the States of Karnataka (formerly Mysore) and Andhra Pradesh.

The origins of the Dravida style can be observed in the Gupta period. The earliest existing examples of the developed style are the seventh-century rock-cut shrines at Mahabalipuram and a developed structural temple, the Shore temple (c. 700), at the same site.

The South Indian temple consists essentially of a square-chambered sanctuary topped by a spire, and an attached pillared hall (*mandapa*, or *mandapam*), within a rectangular court. The outside walls are segmented and carry niches which house sculpture. The tower above the sanctuary consists of an arrangement of gradually receding levels in a pyramid shape. Each level includes a parapet of miniature shrines. The tower is topped by a cupola and a crowning pot.

The South Indian style is most fully realized in the splendid Brihadishvara temple at Thanjavur, built about 1003-1010 by Rajaraja the Great, and the great temple at Gangaikondacholapuram, built about 1025 by his son Rajendra Chola. Subsequently, the style became increasingly elaborate—the complex of temple buildings enclosed by the court became larger, and a number of successive enclosures, each with its own gateway (*gopuram*), were added. By the Vijaynagara period (1336-1565) the *gopurams* had increased in size so that they dominated the much smaller temples inside the enclosures.

Stupa, solid, domed structure that generally enshrines relics or serves as a focus of Buddhist worship, it is an architectural symbol of the Buddha's *parinirvana*, or death. The hemispherical form of the *stupa* appears to have derived from pre-Buddhist burial mounds in India. As most characteristically seen at Sanchi in the Great Stupa (third-first century BC), the monument consists of a circular base supporting a massive solid dome (the *anda*, "egg", or *garbha*, "womb") from which projects an umbrella (*chatra*). The whole of the Great Stupa is encircled by a railing and four gateways, which are richly decorated with relief sculpture depicting *jataka* tales, events in the life of the Buddha, and popular mythological figures.

Buddhist stupas were originally built to house the earthly remains of the historical Buddha and his associates and are almost invariably found at sites sacred to Buddhism. The concept of a relic was afterwards extended to include sacred texts.

Miniature stupas and pagodas are also used by Buddhists throughout Asia as votive offerings. Stupas were also built by adherents of Jainism to commemorate their saints.

The Indian conception of the stupa spread throughout the Buddhist world and evolved into such different-looking monuments as the bell-shaped *dagaba* ("heart of garbha") of Sri Lanka, the terraced temple of Borobudur in Java, the Lamaist variations in Tibet, and the multi-storied pagodas of China, Korea, and Japan. The basic symbolism, in which the central relic is identified with the sacred person or concept commemorated and also with the building itself, is retained.

Worship of a stupa consists in walking around the monument in the direction taken by the path of the sun (pradakshina). Even when the stupa is sheltered by a building, it is always a free-standing monument.

Sutra, is a brief, aphoristic composition in Hinduism. On the other hand, while in Buddhism it is a more extended exposition, the basic form of the scriptures of both the Theravada ("Way of Elders") and Mahayana ("Greater Vehicle") traditions.

Different from its usages in Hindu literature, the Buddhist sutra denotes a doctrinal work, sometimes of considerable length, in which a particular point of doctrine is propounded and deliberated. The most important collection of the Theravada *sutras* is to be found in the *Sutta* (Sanskrit: Sutra) section of the Pali canon, which contains the discourses attributed to the Gautama Buddha. In Mahayana Buddhism the name *sutra* is applied to expository texts.

The early Indian philosophers did not work with written texts and later often disdained the use of them. Thus, there was a need for explanatory works of the utmost brevity that could be committed to memory. The earliest *sutras* were expositions of ritual procedures, but their use spread. Panini's grammatical *sutras* (fifth-sixth century BC) became in many respects a model for later compositions. All the Indian philosophical systems (except the Samkhya, which had its *karikas,* or doctrinal verses) had their own *sutras,* most of which were preserved in writing early in the Christian Era.

Swastika, equilateral cross with arms bent at right angles, all in the same rotary direction, usually clockwise, the swastika is a symbol of prosperity and good fortune throughout the ancient and modern world. The word is derived from the Sanskrit *svastika,* meaning "conducive to well-being".

In the Buddhist tradition the swastika symbolizes the feet,

or the footprints, of the Buddha. It is often placed at the beginning and end of inscriptions, and modern Tibetan Buddhists use it as a clothing decoration. With the spread of Buddhism, the swastika passed into the iconography of China and Japan, where it has been used to denote plurality, abundance, prosperity, and long life.

In India the swastika continues to be the most widely used auspicious symbol of Hindus, Jains, and Buddhists. Among the Jains it is the emblem of their seventh Tirthankara (saint) and is also said to remind the worshipper by its four arms of the four possible places of rebirth—in the animal or plant world, in hell, on earth, or in the spirit world. The Hindus (and also Jains) use the swastika to mark the opening pages of their account books, thresholds, doors, and offerings. A clear distinction is made between the right-hand *swastika,* which moves in a clockwise direction, and the left-hand *swastika* (more correctly called the *sauvastika*), which moves in a counterclockwise direction. The right-hand *swastika* is considered a solar symbol and imitates in the rotation of its arms the course taken daily by the sun, which in the Northern Hemisphere appears to pass from east, then south, to west. The left hand *swastika* more often stands for night, the terrifying goddess Kali, and magical practices.

It was a favourite symbol on ancient Mesopotamian coinage. In Scandinavia the left-hand swastika was the sign for the god Thor's hammer. The swastika also appeared in early Christian and Byzantine art (where it became known as the gammadion cross, or crux gammata, because it could be constructed from four Greek gammas [T] attached to a common base), and it occurred in South and Central America (among the Maya) and in North America (principally among the Navajo).

In Nazi Germany, the swastika (German: Hakenkruez), with its oblique arms turned clockwise, became the national symbol. In 1910 a poet and nationalist ideologist Guido von List had suggested that the swastika as a symbol for all anti-Semitic organizations; and when the National Socialist Party was formed in 1919-1920, it adopted it. On September 15, 1935, the black swastika on a white circle with a red background became the national flag of Germany. This use of the swastika ended in World War II with the German surrender in May 1945, though the swastika is still favoured by neo-Nazi groups.

Syadvada, in Jain metaphysics, it is the doctrine that all judgements are conditional, holding good only in certain conditions, circumstances, or senses, expressed by the word *syat* (Sanskrit: "may be").

The ways of looking at a thing (called *naya*) are infinite in number. Jains hold that to interpret experience from only one *naya*, or point of view, to the exclusion of others is an error comparable to that of the seven blind men feeling an elephant, each of whom concluded that the part he was holding represented the elephant's true form. The relative pluralism of this position is implicit in the Jain doctrine of *anekantavada*, or the "many-sidedness of reality". According to this doctrine, all statements can be judged as true or not true or as both true and not true and thus inexpressible, depending on the point of view. The combinations of these possibilities can be stated in seven logical alternatives called *saptabhangi*.

T

Tamluk. It is a town, ancient Tamralipti, also called Tamralipta (Pali Tamalitti), in West Bengal State, northeastern India, just south of the Rupnarayan River. Archaeological excavations have revealed a sequence of occupation going back to a period in which stone axes and crude pottery were in use, with continuous settlement from about the third century BC.

A centre for boat traffic on the river, it is an agricultural distribution centre and has chemical factories and general engineering works. It has a surviving Buddhist temple, now dedicated to the Hindu goddess Kali. A number of terracotta figurines were found at the site, most of which are kept in a small museum now. It became a municipality in 1864.

Jain sources identify Tamralipti as the capital of the kingdom of Vanga. It was known as a port. According to the Mahavamsha, an epic history of Ceylon (Sri Lanka), it was the departure point of Prince Vijaya's expedition to colonize Ceylon (500 BC) and for Ashoka's Buddhist missionary expedition to Ceylon 250 years later. Tamralipti was also the port for trade with Southeast Asia. The Chinese pilgrim Fa-hsien (Faxian) visited the city in the fifth century AD, and Hsuan-tsang (Xuanzang) visited it in the seventh century. Hsuan-tsang reported that there were 10 Buddhist monasteries and an Ashokan pillar there, and he referred to Tamralipti as a thriving port for export of indigo, silk, and copper (Sanskrit *tamra*), from which it derived its name.

In ancient times Tamralipti was near the sea. With the advance of the Gangetic delta, Tamluk is now 97 km inland. It is about 32 km from the new port of Haldia on the Hugli (Hooghly) River.

Tantra, one of numerous texts dealing with the esoteric practices of some Hindu, Buddhist, and Jain sects. In the usual classification of Hindu religious literature, *Tantra* refers to a class of post-Vedic Sanskrit treatises similar to the Puranas (mediaeval encyclopaedic collections of myths, legends, and other topics). In this usage *Tantras* are said to encompass theology, yoga, the construction of temples and images, and religious practices; in reality, they tend to deal with such aspects of popular Hinduism as spells, rituals, and symbols. They are distinguished along Hindu sectarian lines between the Shaiva Agamas, the Vaishnava Samhitas, and the *Shakta Tantras.*

The Buddhist *Tantras* are traced to the seventh century or earlier, the *Tathagataguhyaka* being an early and extreme work. The Buddhist *Tantras* were translated into Tibetan and Chinese from about the ninth century onwards, and some texts have been preserved only in those languages, the Sanskrit originals having been lost. Among the Buddhist *Tantras* an important text is the *Kalachakra-tantra.*

The lists of the Shakta *Tantras* differ considerably from one another but suggest that the earliest manuscripts date from about the seventh century. They emphasize the goddess Shakti as the divine female personification of creative power or energy. This view holds that Shiva without his Shakti is like a corpse. In the *Tantras* that deal with yoga, Shakti is identified with the *kundalini,* or the energy that lies coiled at the base of the spine until brought up through the body by yogic disciplines. The *Tantras* also stress the efficacy of *yantras* and *mandalas* (ritual diagrams) and of *mantras* (powerful syllables or sacred formulae). Among the major Shakta *Tantras* are the *Kularnava,* which deals with "left-hand" practices, such as ritual copulation; the *Kulachudamani,* which discusses ritual; and the *Sharadatilaka,* which deals almost exclusively with magic.

Tapas, in Hinduism, is an ascetic practice voluntarily carried out to achieve spiritual power or purification. In the Vedas, *tapas* refers to the "inner heat" creatd by the practice of physical austerities and figured in the creation myths, as a means by which Prajapati (the main creator god) brought the world into existence.

In early Buddhism the monastic life of chastity and poverty was regarded as the only path to Enlightenment. Yet the Buddha renounced the extremes of self-mortification as strongly as he did self-indulgence, in his advocation of the "middle way".

In Jainism, asceticism is seen as a way of preventing new *karma* (effect of good or bad action) from forming, as well as a way of getting rid of the old, and is thus one of the central means of breaking the cycle of rebirths. Jains distinguish between external *tapas*, such as fasting (including the most severe form, fasting unto death), restricting the intake of food, meditating, and living in seclusion, and internal *tapas*, such as contemplation, confession, and repentance of sins.

In later Hinduism the practice of *tapas* was especially associated with yogic discipline as a way of purifying the body in preparation for the more exacting spiritual exercises leading to liberation (*moksha*). Among the austerities mentioned in the sacred literature are fasting, the holding of difficult and often painful bodily postures, vigils kept in the presence of fires or extreme cold, and breath control.

Tat Tvam Asi, in Hindu philosophy, it is the famous expression of the relationship between the individual and the absolute. This statement is frequently repeated in the sixth chapter of the Chandogya Upanishad (c. 600 BC), as the teacher Uddalaka Aruni instructs his son in the nature of the supreme reality. The phrase was given its most literal interpretation by the eighth-ninth-century thinker Shankara of the Advaita (nondualist) school, for whom the statement was one of the great assertions fundamental to his doctrine.

However, the different schools of the orthodox philosophy of Vedanta variously interpreted the identity expressed in this judgement.

Tathagata, one of the titles of a Buddha, the most frequently employed by the historical Buddha, Siddhartha Gautama, when referring to himself. The exact meaning of the word is uncertain; Buddhist commentaries present as many as eight explanations. The most generally adopted interpretation is "one who has thus (*tatha*) gone (*gata*)" or "one who has thus (*tatha*) arrived (*agata*)", implying that the historical Buddha was only one of the many who have in the past and will in the future experience Enlightenment and teach others how to achieve it.

In later Mahayana Buddhism, *tathagata* came to convey the essential Buddha nature hidden in everyone. *Tathagatha* is the "thusness" that makes Enlightenment possible. Having *tathagata* within, one yearns for Enlightenment. As the true state of all that exists, *tathagata* is synonymous with ultimate reality, otherwise indefinable.

Taxila, ancient city of northwestern India, its ruins are about 35 km northwest of Rawalpindi, Pakistan. Its prosperity in ancient times resulted from its position at the junction of three great trade routes: one from eastern India described by a Greek writer, Megasthenes, as the "Royal Highway", the second from western Asia, and the third from kashmir and Central Asia. The city sank into insignificance when these routes ceased to be important and was finally destroyed by the Huns in the fifth century AD.

Literally meaning "The City of Cut-Stone" or "The Rock of Taksha", Takshashila (rendered by Greek writers as Taxila) was founded, according to the Indian epic the *Ramayana*, by Bharata, younger brother of Rama (an incarnation of Lord Vishnu). The city was named after Bharata's son, Taksha, its first ruler. According to tradition, the great Indian epic the *Mahabharata* was first recited at Taxila at the great snake sacrifice of King Janamejaya, one of the heroes of the story. Buddhist literature, especially the *jataka*, mentions it as the capital of the kingdom of Gandhara and as a great centre of learning. Gandhara (Gandarii) is also mentioned as a satrapy or province in the inscriptions of the Achaemenian (Persian) king Darius I in the fifth century BC. As capital of Gandhara, Taxila was evidently under Achaemenian rule for more than a century.

Taxila is known from references to it in Indian and Greco-Roman literary sources and from the accounts of two Chinese pilgrims, Fa-hsien (Faxian) and Hsuan-tsang (Xuanzang).

When Alexander the Great invaded India in 326 BC, Ambhi (Omphis), the ruler of Taxila, surrendered the city and placed his resources at Alexander's disposal. Greek historians accompanying the Macedonian conqueror described Taxila as "wealthy, prosperous, and well governed". Within a decade after Alexander's death, Taxila was absorbed into the Maurya Empire founded by Chandragupta Maurya, under whom it became a provincial capital. But this was only an interlude in the history of Taxila's subjection to conquerors from the west. After three generations of Maurya rule, the city was annexed by the Indo-Greek kingdom of Bactria. It remained under the Indo-Greeks until the early first century BC. They were followed by the

Shakas, or Scythians, from Central Asia, and by the Parthians, whose rule lasted until the latter half of the first century AD.

According to early Christian legend, Apostle Thomas visited Taxila during the Parthian period. Another distinguished visitor was the Neo-Pythagorean sage Apollonius of Tyana (first century AD), whose biographer, Philostratus, described Taxila as a fortified city that was laid out on a symmetrical plan and compared it in size to Nineveh (the oldest and most populous city of the ancient Assyrian Empire).

Taxila was taken from the Parthians by the Kushans under Kujula Kadphises. The great Kushan ruler Kanishka founded Sirsukh, the third city on the site. (The second, Sirkap, dates from the Indo-Greek period.) In the fourth century AD the Sasanian king Shapur II (310-379) seems to have conquered Taxila, as revealed and expressed by the numerous Sasanian copper coins found there. There is little information about the Sasanian occupation, but when Fa-hsien visited the city around the beginning of the fifth century AD, he found it a flourishing centre of Buddhist sanctuaries and monasteries. Shortly thereafter it was sacked by the Huns. Taxila never recovered from this calamity. Hsuan-tsang, visiting the site in the seventh century AD, found the city ruined and desolate, and subsequent records do not mention it. Excavations begun by Sir Alexander Cunningham, the father of Indian archaeology, in 1863-1864 and 1872-1873, identified the local site known as Saraikhala with ancient Taxila. Sir John Marshall continued this work and over a 20-year period completely exposed the ancient site and its monuments.

Archaeology: The structural remains at Taxila include the Bhir mound area, the palace area at Sirkap, the Jandial and Pippala temples, the Giri fortress, the Mohra Moradu and Jaulian monasteries, and the Dharmarajika, Bhallar, and Kunala *stupas* (burial mounds). Different types of masonry used in the monuments indicate their period of origin. The earliest remains are those of the Bhir mound. The palace area, modelled on the same lines as its Assyrian counterpart, has several entrances and outer fortifications. It reveals traces of successive settlements with the oldest parts of the buildings consisting of rubble masonry. A spacious Buddhist temple, several small shrines, and blocks of dwelling houses were uncovered there. The shrine of the double-headed eagle is interesting for its pilasters of the Corinthian order on the front and niches in the interspaces. Other antiquities of the palace area include terracottas and potteries;

small bronze, copper, and iron objects; and beads, germs, and coins of Indo-Greek, Parthian, and early Kushan rulers.

Taxila, besides being a provincial seat, was also a centre of learning. It was not a university town with lecture halls and residential quarters, such as have been found at Nalanda in Bihar. At Taxila, the teacher housed his own pupils, who paid for their board and lodging in cash or in the form of service to the teacher and his family. The Buddhist monasteries also catered to the needs of the students and monks.

The Jandial Temple, set up on an artificial mound, closely resembles the classical temples of Greece. Its ionic columns and pilasters are composed of massive blocks of sandstone. Built in the Scythio-Parthian period, it is probably the temple described by Philostratus in his *Life of Apollonius of Tyana*. Though the Jandial Temple is not Buddhist, the Jaulian remains are. These include a monastery and two *stupa* courts.

The Dharmarajika Stupa, popularly known as the Chir tope, is a circular structure with a raised terrace around its base. A circle of small chapels surround the great *stupa*. Three distinctive types of masonry in the buildings around the main *stupa* suggest the contributions of different periods to the building activity. A silver scroll inscription in Kharoshti and a small gold casket containing some bone relics of the Buddha were found in one of the chapels. The inscription refers to the enshrinement of the relics by a Bactrian named Ursaka from the town of Noacha in the year 136 BC for the bestowal of health on "the great King, Supreme King of Kings, the Son of Heaven, the Kushana" (probably Vima Kadphises, son of the Kushan conqueror Kujala). This site also contained several statues of the Buddha and *bodhisattvas*.

Theravada, is a major form of Buddhism prevalent in Sri Lanka (Ceylon), Myanmar (Burma), Thailand, Cambodia, and Laos. Theravada, like all other Buddhist schools, claims to adhere most closely to the original doctrines and practices taught by the Buddha. Theravadins accept as authoritative the Pali canon of ancient Indian Buddhism and trace their sectarian lineage back to the Elders (Sanskrit: Sthaviras; Pali; Theras), who followed in the tradition of the senior monks of the first Buddhist *sangha* (Buddhist monastic order or community).

Theravada Buddhism tends towards a conservative and orthodox interpretation of the Buddha's teaching. The ideal Theravada Buddhist is the *arhat* (Pali: *arahant*), or perfected saint, who attains Enlightenment as a result of his own efforts. The role of the layman and monk are clearly differentiated by the Theravadins, who do not consider it possible to attain Enlightenment while one is living the life of a layman. Theravadins profoundly revere the historical Buddha as a perfected master but do not pay homage to the numerous celestial Buddhas and *bodhisattvas* that are worshipped in Mahayana temples.

During the early centuries following the death of the Buddha, the community broke up into several sects that, in the beginning, differed little from one another, as far as is known. The first separation occurred in the fourth century BC at the time of the second council, when a group broke away from the Sthaviravadins and became known as the Mahasanghika. A second major schism occurred when the Sarvastivadins (who hold that "all is real") separated from the Vibhajyavadins (adherents of the Doctrine of Distinctions), presumbaly the Sthaviravadins. Those Vibhajyavadins who were distributed geographically in southern India and Sri Lanka became known as the Theravadins (the Pali form of Sthaviravadins). During the reign of Emperor Ashoka (third century BC), the Theravada school travelled to Sri Lanka, where it divided into three subgroups, known after their monastic centres as the Mahaviharika, the Abhayagirika, and the Jetavaniya. The Theravada form of Buddhism gradually spread eastwards, becoming dominant in Myanmar in the late eleventh century and in Cambodia and Laos by the thireenth and fourteenth centuries.

Three Margas, refer to the Paths to Salvation. Although the search of *moksha* has never been the goal of more than a small minority of Hindus, liberation was a religious ideal that affected all lives. *Moksha* determined not only the hierarhical values of Indian social institutions and religious doctrines and practices but also the function of Indian philosophy, which is to discuss what one must do to find true fulfilment and what one has to realize, by direct experience, in order to escape from *samsara* (cycle of rebirths or bondage) and obtain spiritual freedom. While those who have not been reached by formal Indian philosophy have only vague ideas about the doctrines of *karma* and *moksha,* in semi-popular milieus these doctrines gave rise to much speculation.

For the ordinary Hindu, the main aim of worldly life lies in conforming to social and ritual duties, to the traditional rules of conduct for one's caste, family, and profession. Such requirements constitute an individual's *dharma* (custom, law, and duties), one's own part of the broader stability, law, order, and fundamental equilibrium in the cosmos, nature, and society. *Sanatana* (traditional) *dharma*—a term used by Hindus to denote their own religion—is a close approximation to "religious practices" in the West. This traditional *dharma* applies theoretically to all Hindus, but it is superseded by the more particular *dharmas* that are appropriate to each of the four major *varnas*, castes or classes of society: Brahmins (priests), Kshatriyas (warriors), Vaishyas (the common people), and Shudras (servants or the servile group). These four rather abstract categories are further superseded by the more practically applicable *dharmas* appropriate to each of the thousands of particular castes (*jatis*). Thus, religion for Hindus is mainly a tradition and a heritage, a way of life and a mode of thought. In practice, it is the right application of methods for securing both welfare in this life and a good condition thereafter.

Hindus disagree about the way (*marga*) to *moksha*. Three paths to salvation (variously valued but nonexclusive) are presented in an extremely influential religious text, the Bhagavadgita, according to which it is not acts themselves but the desire for their results that produces *karma* and thus attachment. These three ways to salvation are (1) the *karma-marga* ("the path of duties"), the disinterested discharge of ritual and social obligations; (2) the *jnana-marga* ("the path of knowledge"), the use of meditative concentration preceded by a long and systematic ethical and contemplative training, yoga, to gain a supra-intellectual insight into one's identity with Brahman; and (3) the *bhakti-marga* ("the path of devotion"), the devotion to a personal god. These ways are regarded as suited to various types of people.

Tibetan Buddhism, also called Lamaism, it is that distinctive form of Buddhism which evolved from the seventh century AD in Tibet. Based mainly on the rigorous intellectual disciplines of Madhyamika and Yogachara philosophy it utilizes the symbolic ritual practices of Vajrayana (Tantric Buddhism).

By the fourteenth century the Tibetans had succeeded in translating all available Buddhist literature in India and Tibet; many Sanskrit texts that have since been lost in the country of their origin are known only from their Tibetan translations. The Tibetan canon is divided into the Bka'-'gyur, or Translation of the Word, consisting of the supposedly canonical texts, and the Bstan-'gyur, or Transmitted Word, consisting of commentaries by Indian masters.

Buddhism was transmitted into Tibet mainly during the seventh to tenth centuries. Notable early teachers are the illustrious eighth-century Tantric master, Padmasambhava, and the more orthodox Mahayana teacher, Shantirakshita. With the arrival from India in 1042 of the great teacher Atisha, a reform movement was initiated, and within a century the major sects of Tibetan Buddhism had emerged. The Dge-lugs-pa, or One of the Virtuous System, commonly known as the Yellow Hats, the order of the Dalai and the Panchen Lamas, has been the politically predominant Tibetan sect from the seventeenth century until 1959, when the hierocratic government of the Dalai Lama was abolished by the People's Republic of China.

In the second half of the twentieth century Tibetan Buddhism spread to the West, particularly after the subjugation of Tibet to Chinese communist rule sent many refugees, including highly regarded "reincarnated lamas", or *tulkus*, out of their homeland. Tibetan religious groups in the West include both communities of refugees and those consisting largely of occidentals drawn to the Tibetan tradition.

Tibetan Buddhism also incorporates the monastic disciplines of early Theravada Buddhism and the shamanistic features of the indigenous Tibetan religion, Bon. Characteristic of Tibetan Buddhism is the unusually large segment of the population actively engaged in religious pursuits (up until the Chinese communist takeover the country in the 1950s an estimated one-quarter of the inhabitants were members of religious orders); its system of "reincarnating lamas"; the traditional merger of the spiritual and temporal authority in the office and person of the Dalai Lama; and the vast number of divine beings (each with its own family, consort, and pacific and terrifying aspects), which are considered symbolic representations of the psychic life by the religiously sophisticated and accepted as realities by the common people.

Tirthankara, also called Jina ("Victor"), in Jainism it stands for a saviour who has succeeded in crossing over life's stream of rebirths and has made a path for others to follow.

In art, the Tirthankara is represented either standing stiffly in the pose known as *kayotsarga* ("dismissing the body") or seated cross-legged on a lion throne in the posture of meditation, *dhyanamudra*. The images are often carved out of marble or other highly polished stone or are cast in metal, the cold surfaces serving to emphasize the frozen detachment from life. Since the

Tirthankara is a perfect being, there is little to distinguish one from another, except for symbolic colours or emblems. The names of the 24 Tirthankaras are attributed to dreams by their mothers before their births or to some other circumstance surrounding their entry into the world. The word *natha*, "lord", may be added as an honorific to their names.

Mahavira (sixth century BC) was the last Tirthankara to appear. His predecessor, Parshvanatha, lived about 250 years earlier. The other Tirthankaras mentioned in the Jain scriptures cannot be considered historical figures. According to Jain belief, each cosmic age produces its own group of 24 Tirthankaras, the first of whom—if it is an age of descending purity—are giants, but they decrease in stature and appear after shorter intervals of time as the age proceeds.

Images of the Tirthankara are not worshipped as personal gods, capable of giving blessings or interfering with human events. Rather, Jain believers pay them homage as representative of great beings in the hope that they may be filled with a sense of renunciation and the highest virtues and thus encouraged along the path, towards their final liberation.

In order of their appearance, the names, signs, and colours of the Jinas of this age are: (1) Rishabhanatha ("Lord Bull"), or Adinatha ("Lord First"), his emblem the bull, his colour golden; (2) Ajita ("Invincible One"), elephant, golden; (3) Shambhava ("Auspicious"), horse, golden; (4) Abhinandana ("Worship"), ape, golden; (5) Sumati ("Wise"), heron, golden; (6) Padmaprabha ("Lotus-Bright"), lotus, red; (7) Suparshva ("Good-Sided"), the swastika symbol, golden; (8) Chandraprabha ("Moon-Bright"), moon white; (9) Suvidhi, or Pushpadanta ("Religious Duties" or "Blossom-Toothed"), dolphin or *makara* (sea dragon), white; (10) Shitala ("Coolness"), the *shrivatsa* symbol, golden; (11) Shreyamsha ("Good"), rhinoceros, golden; (12) Vasupujya ("Worshipped with Offerings of Possessions"), buffalo, red; (13) Vimala ("Clear"), boar, golden; (14) Ananta ("Endless"), hawk (according to the Digambara sect, ram or bear), golden; (15) Dharma ("Duty"), thunderbolt, golden; (16) Shanti ("Peace"), antelope or deer, golden; (17) Kunthu (meaning uncertain), goat, golden; (18) Ara (a division of time), the *nandyavarta* (an elaborated swastika; according to the Digambara sect, fish), golden; (19) Malli ("Wrestler"), water jug, blue; (20) Suvrata, or Munisuvrata ("Of Good Vows"), tortoise, black; (21) Nami ("Bowing Down"), or Nimin ("Eye-Winking"), blue lotus, golden;

(22) Nemi, or Arishtanemi ("The Rim of Whose Wheel is Unhurt"), conch shell, black; (23) Parshvanatha ("Lord Serpent"), snake green; (24) Vardhamana ("Prospering"), later called Mahavira ("Great Hero"), lion, golden.

Tomara Dynasty, one of the minor early mediaeval ruling houses of northern India, the family is known from scattered sources, and it is impossible to reconstruct its history in any detail. The history of the family spans the period between the reign of Anangapala, who founded the city of Delhi in the eleventh century AD, and the incorporation of Delhi within the Chahamana kingdom in 1164. Puranic evidence gives the early location in the Himalayan region. According to bardic tradition, the dynasty was one of the 36 Rajput tribes. Although Delhi subsequently became decisively a part of the Chahamana kingdom, numismatic and comparatively late literary evidence indicates that such Tomara kings as Anangapala and Madanapala continued to rule as feudatories, presumably until the final conquest of Delhi by the Muslims in 1192-1193.

Trikaya, the concept of *trikaya* applies not only to the historical Buddha, Gautama, but to all other buddhas as well—in Mahayana Buddhism, the concept of the three bodies, or modes of being, of the Buddha: the *dharmakaya* (body of essence), the unmanifested mode, and the supreme state of absolute knowledge; the *sambhogakaya* (body of enjoyment), the heavenly mode; and the *nirmanakaya* (body of transformation), the earthly mode, the Buddha as he appeared on earth or manifested himself in an earthly *bodhisattva*, an earthly king, a painting, or a natural object, such as a lotus.

Trimurti, triad of the three great gods, Brahma, Vishnu, and Shiva in Hinduism. Each god is in charge of one aspect of creation. Brahma is creator, Vishnu is preserver, and Shiva is destroyer. However, sectarian devotees worship only one god as supreme, ascribing all aspects of creation to their single chosen deity. Scholars consider the *trimurti* doctrine an attempt to reconcile different monotheistic approaches with one another and with the philosophic doctrine of ultimate reality (Brahman). The doctrine was given classical expression in Kalidasa's poem *Kumarasambhavam* (fourth-fifth century AD). In *trimurti* symbolism, the three gods are collapsed into a single form with three faces.

Triratna, also called Threefold Refuge, it is the three components of the Buddhist and Jain creeds. One of the three cannot exist exclusive of the others, and all are required for spiritual liberation. The Triratna is symbolized frequently in art as a trident. In Buddhism, the *Triratna* comprises the Buddha, the *dharma* (doctrine, or law), and the *sangha* (the monastic order, or community of believers). From the time of the Buddha, initiation into the order has consisted of the formal recognition of the trinity in the words "I go to the Buddha for refuge, I go to the Doctrine for refuge, I go to the Order for refuge."

In Jainism the three jewels (also referred to as *ratnatraya*) are understood as *samyagdarshana* ("right faith"), *samyagjnana* ("right knowledge"), and *samyakcharitra* ("right conduct").

Trishala, mother of Mahavira, the twenty-fourth and most recent Tirthankara, or saving teacher, of Jainism, Trishala was, like the mother of the Buddha, a member of the Kshatriya, or warrior caste. According to Jain tradition, in common with the mothers of all the 24 Jinas (saints), Trishala had a series of 14 auspicious dreams when she conceived her son.

Trishiksha, in Buddhism, represents the three types of learning required of those who seek to attain Enlightenment. The threefold training comprises all aspects of Buddhist practices. Arranged in a progressive order, the three are: (1) *shila* ("moral conduct"), which makes one's body and mind fit for concentration, (2) *samadhi* ("meditation"), concentration of the mind being a prerequisite to attaining a clear vision of the truth, and (3) *prajna* ("wisdom"), understood not as a collection of empirical knowledge but as intuitive experience of ultimate reality, attained in a state of *samadhi*.

U

Udayagiri, is a hill under Greater Bhubaneshwar, south-central Orissa State, eastern India. Several Jain and Buddhist rock-cut caves and images are located at this village and archaeological site. One of these caves is a double-storeyed cave (Rani Gumpha, Queen's cave) with ornate carvings and ranges of cells cut into three sides of an open courtyard. Inscriptions in the caves date from the second century BC to the tenth century AD.

Udayagiri-Lalitgiri-Ratnagiri Hills, Buddhist complex in eastern Orissa State, eastern India. These three hills in Kendrapata-Jajpur districts (under old Cuttack district) after excavations, reveal extensive ruins of brick pagodas, sculptured stone portals, and esoteric Buddhist images. Hsuan-tsang

(Xuanzang), the Chinese pilgrim traveller, found this area to be the seat of a flourishing Buddhist university called Pushpagiri.

Udayagiri, the largest of these three, has assumed further importance after recent excavations, which revealed the ancient name of this Buddhist monastery as Madhavapura *mahavihara*. The most important is, however, the Ratnagiri Buddhist centre considered by scholars of ancient Indian history as the gem of the complex. The magnificently carved door-jamb of the *vihara* and the superbly finished large Buddha images from perhaps the greatest concentration of the post-Gupta period Buddhist sculptures. Lalitgiri is the earliest of the three belonging to first century AD. The recent excavation as Lalitgiri has brought to light significant archaeological material which upholds it as a great centre of Buddhist attraction.

Ratnagiri, Udayagiri, and Lalitgiri are well-connected with Cuttack by an efficient bus service.

Udayanacharya, Hindu logician he flourished tenth century, near Darbhanga, modern Bihar State, northeastern India he attempted to reconcile the views held by the two major schools of logic out of which developed the Navya Nyaya school of "right" reasoning, which is still recognized and followed in some regions of India.

Of the two schools, the old Nyaya system was concerned with the critical examination of the objects of knowledge by means of logical proof, while the earlier Vaishesika system dealt with particulars—objects that can be thought of and named. Udayanacharya assumed, with the Vaishesika, that the world was formed by atoms, from which physical bodies also derived. But he was equally concerned with the mind and its right apprehension of objets in nature.

His vigorous thinking was set forth in the *Kusumanjali* and the *Bauddhadhikkara*, the latter being an attack on the atheistic thesis of Buddhism. Living in a period of lively controversy with the Buddhists, Udayanacharya defended his belief in a personal God by resorting to the two natures of the world: cause and effect. The presence of the world is an effect that cannot be explained by the activity of atoms alone. A supreme being had to cause the effect and regulate the activity of the atoms; hence, according to Udayanacharya, God exists.

Upanayana, Hindu ritual (*samskara*) of initiation, restricted to the three upper *varnas*, or social orders, it marks the male child's entrance into the life of a student (*brahmacharin*) and his acceptance as a full member of his religious community. The ceremony is performed between the ages of 5 and 24, the wide variance reflecting the different educational requirements of the three upper classes—Brahmins (priests and teachers), Kshatriyas (warriors and rulers), and Vaishyas (merchants and tradesmen).

The actual observance of *upanayana* is increasingly confined to more strictly observant Hindus, particularly those of the Brahmin caste. As a prerequisite to marriage it is sometimes replaced by a simpler and less meaningful ceremony called *janeu* in North India, which takes place on the day of marriage; often both initiation ceremonies are omitted altogether.

After a ritual bath the boy is dressed as an ascetic and brought before his guru, who invests him with a deerskin to use as an upper garment, a staff, and the sacrificial thread (*upavita* or *yajnopavita*). The thread, consisting of a loop made of three symbolically knotted and twisted strands of cotton cord, is replaced regularly so that it is worn throughout the lifetime of the owner, normally over the left shoulder and diagonally across the chest to the right hip. It identifies the wearer as *dvija*, or "twice-born", the second birth understood as having taken place with the imparting by the guru to the student of the Gayatri Mantra, a sacred verse of the Rigveda. The initiation ceremony concludes with the student's kindling of the sacrificial fire and his begging of alms, symbolic of his dependence on others during his *brahmacharin* period.

A corresponding rite among Parsis is *nowzad* (Persian: "new birth"); it invests both six-year-old boys and girls with a thread worn around the waist. Some scholars suggest that this indicates a common and ancient Indo-Iranian origin of the two ceremonies.

Upanishad, any of the speculative texts these contain elaborations in prose and verse of the Vedas, the most ancient Hindu sacred literature. The name Upanishad implies sitting at the feet of the teacher, and the Upanishads, of which approximately 108 are known, record the views of a succession of Hindu teachers and sages who were active as early as 1000 BC and who flourished about 600 BC.

The special philosophical concern of the Upanishads is with the nature of reality. There is a development towards the concept of a single supreme being, and knowledge is directed towards reunion with it. Of fundamental importance to all Hindu thought is the equation in some of the Upanishads of *atman* (the self) with Brahman (ultimate reality). The nature of morality and of eternal life is discussed, as are such themes as the transmigration of souls and causality in creation.

The texts form the basis of much of later Indian philosophy. They represent the final stage in the tradition of the Vedas, so the teaching based on them is known as the Vedanta (Sanskrit: "Conclusion of the Veda"). The older Upanishads may be part of the Brahmanas (commentaries) of their respective Vedas but are distinguished from them both by increased philosophical and mystical questioning and by their diminished concern with Vedic deities and sacrificial rites.

The appearance in Europe in the early nineteenth century of second and third-hand translations of the Upanishads had a profound effect on certain thinkers, notably in Germany. The philosopher Arthur Schopenhauer has fully acknowledged their influence on his thought.

Upasampada, Buddhist rite of higher ordination, by which a novice becomes a monk, or *bhikku,* the ceremony as observed in the Theravada tradition is basically the same as in ancient Buddhism. Ordination is not necessarily permanent and, in some countries, may be repeated in a monk's lifetime.

The ceremony may be performed on any day determined to be auspicious, except during *vassa* (*varsha*), the rainy season retreat. It takes place within the sanctuary, in the presence of monks already ordained. The *pabbajja,* or ceremony of lower ordination to the rank of novice, is repeated even if the candidate has undergone it previously. He dons the garments of a monk and repeats the Triratna ("Threefold Refuge") of the Buddha, the *dharma* (teaching), and the *sangha* (community of believers) and the 10 precepts (basic rules of ethical conduct for a monk); the candidate then stands before the assembly in the company of his sponsoring tutors and is questioned on his fitness to be received into the order. The assembly is questioned three times, and, if there is no objection to his ordination, the candidate is accepted into the priesthood. Female novices are ordained nuns (Pali: *bhikkunis*) in a similar rite.

A candidate for ordination must be at least 20 years old, have the permission of his parents, be exempt from military service, be free from debt and from contagious disease, and have received at least some elementary instruction in Buddhism.

V

Vairagin, in Hinduism, is areligious ascetic who worships principally one or another form of Lord Vishnu. *Vairagins* generally wear white robes, in contrast to the ochre-coloured robes worn by Shaiva ascetics, and are also differentiated by their *tilak* (sect mark on the forehead), which is never made of ash, unlike the Shaivites, and is always vertical in design.

Most *vairagins,* when not wandering or on pilgrimage, reside in monastic communities called *sthanas* ("spots" or "places"); but the naked *naga vairagins,* who are also the militants among the Vaishnava ascetics, form their own groups, called *akharas.* In the past, battles between groups of naked ascetics belonging to different sects centred mainly on bathing and processional rights during pilgrimage assemblies, such as the Kumbha Mela.

Vairochana, also called Mahavairochana, is regarded by many Mahayana Buddhists of East Asia and of Tibet, Nepal, and Java as the supreme Buddha. His characteristic gesture is the *mudra* of the six elements, in which the index finger of the left hand is clasped by the five fingers of the right, symbolizing the uniting of the five elements of the material world (earth, water, fire, air, and ether) with the spiritual (consciousness).

Some Buddhists regard Vairochana, or Mahavairochana, as a being separate from the five "self-born" Dhyani-Buddhas, one of whom is known as Vairochana.

When represented as one of the "self-born" buddhas, as he is in Nepali, Tibetan, and Javanese art, Vairochana occupies the chief position and is often considered to be the progenitor of the other four Dhyani-Buddhas, or the Adi-Buddha himself. In paintings, Vairochana is coloured white and his hands are shown in the *dharma-chakra-mudra* ("teaching gesture"). His consort is Vajradhatvishvari or Tara, his family Moha, his mount the dragon (or lion), his symbol the *chakra* ("wheel"), his *skandha* ("personality component") *rupa* ("matter"), his syllable *a* or *om,* his element space, his sense perception hearing, his sense organ the ear, and his location in the human body the head.

Vaishali, city of ancient India, north of Patna, on the Gandak River, northwestern Bihar State, northeastern India, Vaishali was the capital of the Licchavi republic and was closely associated with the early histories of both Buddhism and Jainism. Roads connected it with Rajagriha to the south and Kapilavastu and Shravasti to the north. According to tradition, in early times the city was surrounded by three walls with gates and watch towers. The site today is marked by two groups of mounds and has been partly excavated by archaeologists. The earliest occupation of the site is associated with black-and-red pottery of probably pre-Buddhist age; it was followed by the northern, black polished ware of early Buddhist times. Vaishali is on the site of a village now known as Basarh.

Mahavira, the founder of Jainism, was born in Vaishali and spent much time there. The Buddha also visited the city on many occasions. Its several important monasteries and shrines were described by the Chinese pilgrim Fa-hsien (Faxian) in the fifth century AD. After the death of the Buddha (c. 483 BC) the second great council of Buddhists was held at Vaishali to provide rules of conduct.

Vaishnava Rites, ritual practices of the worshippers of Vishnu, these comprise five pursuits—purificatory rites, collecting the requisites for worship, acts of worship, study and contemplation of the meaning of the sacred books, and meditative concentration on the Lord's image. Lifelong obligations include the performance of sacrifices and other rites, restraint of the senses, fasting and soberness, worship, recitation of the scriptures, and visits to sacred places. In addition, to those who aspire to liberation, Ramanuja recommends concentration on God, a virtuous way of living, and insensibility to luck and misfortune.

According to Madhva (1199-1278), a faithful observance of all regulations of daily conduct—including bathing and breath control—will contribute to eventual success in the quest for liberation. Devout Vaishnavas are inclined to emphasize God's omnipotence and the far-reaching effects of his grace. They attach much value to the repeated murmuring of his name or sacred formulae (*japa*) and to the praise and commemoration of his deeds as a means of self-realization and of unification with his essence. Special stress is laid on *ahimsa* (nonviolence) as a virtue.

Vaishnava-Sahajiya, an esoteric Hindu cult centred in Bengal it sought religious experience through the world of the senses, specifically human sexual love. *Sahaja* as a system of worship was prevalent in the Tantric traditions common to both Hinduism and Buddhism in Bengal as early as the eighth-ninth centuries. The divine romance of Krishna and Radha was celebrated by the poets Jayadeva (twelfth century), Chandidas, and Vidyapati (mid-fifteenth century), and parallels between human love and divine love were further explored by Chaitanya, the fifteenth-sixteenth century ecstatic teacher, and his followers. The Vaishnava-Sahajiya cult developed from the seventeenth century onwards as a synthesis of these various traditions.

The Vaishnava-Sahajiyas elevated *parakiya-rati* (literally, "the love of a man for a woman who legally belongs to another") above *svakiya-rati* (conjugal love) as the more intense of the two. *Parakiya-rati*, it was said, was felt without consideration for the conventions of society or for personal gain and thus was more analogous to divine love. Radha is conceived as the ideal of the *parakiya* woman, and the Vaishnava-Sahajiyas never attempted (as did some sects of Vaishnavism) to depict her as the wife of Krishna.

The Vaishnava-Sahajiyas were looked upon with disfavour by other religious groups and operated in secrecy. In their literature they deliberately employed a highly enigmatic style. Because of the extreme privacy of the cult, little is known about its prevalence or its practices today.

Vaishnava Samhitas, collections of texts important to Vaishnavites (worshippers of Vishnu), these consist of two groups of texts: *Vaikhanasha Samhitas* and *Pancharatra Samhitas*. The latter group is the prevailing one; more than 200 titles are known, though the official number is 108. Vaikhanasha Samhitas (collections of the Vaishnava school of Vaikhanashas, who were originally ascetics) seem to have embodied the original temple manuals for the Bhagavatas (devotees), which by the eleventh or twelfth century had become supplanted by the Pancharatra Samhitas (collections of the Vaishnava school of Pancharatra, "the System of the Five Nights"). The philosophy of the latter is largely a matter of cosmogony, greatly inspired by both the Samkhya and Yoga philosophies.

Apart from their theology, in which for the first time the notion of *shakti* is introduced into Vaishnavism, they are important because they give an exposition of Vaishnava temple and cult practices. On the philosophical side it is maintained that the supreme god Krishna Vasudeva manifests himself in four coequal "divisions" (*vyuhas*), representing levels in creation. These gods emanate as supramundane patrons before the primary creation is started by their *shakti* (power). In the primary creation Shakti manifests it as a female creative force inspired by the Samkhya philosophy's cosmogony. Practically, stress is laid on a type of incarnation—"iconic incarnation"—in which God is actually present with a portion of himself in a stone or statue, which thus becomes an icon; therefore the icon can be worshipped as God himself.

Vaishnava Schools, the different schools under Vaishnavism, it has a long history, traceable to the Vishnu worship of the Rigveda, the *bhakti* conception of the epics, and the Vasudeva cult of the pre-Christian era. Of the two main Vaishnava scriptures, or *agamas*, the Pancharatra ("Relating to the Period of Five Nights") and the Vaikhanasa ("Relating to a Hermit or Ascetic") are the most important. Though Vaishnava philosophers trace the Pancharatra works to Vedic origin, absolutists such as Shankara refused to acknowledge this claim. The main topics of the Pancharatra literature concern rituals and forms of image worship and religious practices of the Vaishnavas. Of philosophical importance are the *Ahirbudhnya-samhita* ("Collection of Verses for Shiva") and *Jayakhya-samhita* ("Collection of Verses called Jaya"). The most well-known Pancharatra doctrine concerns the four spiritual forms of God: the absolute, transcendent state, known as Vasudeva, the form in which knowledge and strength predominate (known as Samkarshana), the form in which wealth and courage predominate (known as Pradyumna), and the form in which power and energy predominate (known as Aniruddha). Shankara identified Samkarshana with the individual soul, Pradyumna with mind, and Aniruddha with the ego sense. Furthermore, five powers of God are distinguished: creation, maintenance, destruction, favour, and disfavour. *Bhakti* is regarded as affection for God and associated with a sense of his majesty. The doctrine of *prapatti*, or complete self-surrender, is emphasized.

Vaishnavism, also called Vishnuism, it consists of the worship of the god Vishnu and of his incarnations, principally as Rama and as Krishna. With Shaivism and Shaktism, it is one of the major forms of modern Hinduism.

Sectarian Vaishnavism had its beginnings in the cult of Vasudeva-Krishna, who may have been a Yadava tribal leader (c. seventh-sixth century BC). The Vasudeva cult coalesced with others worshipping the deified sage Narayana so that by about the second century AD Vasudeva, Krishna, and Narayana appeared in the celebrated religious poem, the Bhagavadgita, as interchangeable names of Lord Vishnu. The cult of the pastoral Krishna was soon added.

The philosophical schools of Vaishnavism differ in their interpretation of the relationship between individual souls and

God. The doctrines of the most important schools are: (1) *vishistadvaita* ("qualified monism"), associated with the name of Ramanuja (eleventh century) and continued by the Shrivaishnava sect, prominent in South India; (2) *dvaita* ("dualism"), the principal exponent of which was Madhva (thirteenth century), who taught that although the soul is dependent on God it is not an extension of God, that the soul and God are separate entities; (3) *dvaitadvaita* ("dualistic monism"), taught by Nimbarka (twelfth or thirteenth century), according to which the world of souls and matter is both different and not different from God; (4) *shuddhadvaita* ("pure monism") of Vallabha, which explains the world without the doctrine of *maya* (illusion); (5) *achintya-bhedabheda* ("inconceivable duality and nonduality"), the doctrine of Chaitanya, in which the relation between the world of souls and matter on the one hand and God on the other is not to be grasped by thought but is both different and nondifferent.

In addition to these philosophical schools, each of which has its own sectarian following, Vaishnavism also includes a number of popular expressions of devotionalism, which were furthered in the late mediaeval period by the vernacular writings of Ramananda and his disciples and by Vaishnava poets such as Tulsidas in the Hindi area, Mira Bai in Gujarat, and Namdev and Tukaram in the Maratha country.

A major characteristic of Vaishnavism is the strong part played by *bhakti*, or religious devotion. The ultimate goal of the devotee is to escape from the cycle of birth and death so as to enjoy the presence of Vishnu. This cannot be achieved without the grace of God. Vishnu is not only the end (*upeya*) but also the means (*upaya*). For his part, the devotee must cultivate the auxiliary disciplines of *karma*, the path of good works, and *jnana*, the way of spiritual knowledge.

Vaishya, third highest in ritual status of the four *varnas*, or social orders, of Hindu India, it is traditionally described as commoners. The Vaishya were commoners, not servile groups. Their role lay in productive labour, in agricultural and pastoral tasks, and in trading. Their way of life demanded study, sacrifice, and the giving of alms. Early scriptures show that Vaishya could and did rise even to the rank of Brahmin, as in the case of the two sons of Nabhagarishta, mentioned in the sacred work, *Harivamsha*. Legend states that the *varnas* (castes or colours) sprang from Prajapati, a creator god—in order of status: the

Brahmin (white) from his head, the Kshatriya (red) from his arms, the Vaishya (yellow) from his thighs, and the Shudra (black) from his feet. The yellow colour associated with the Vaishya, according to one theory, links them with the south point of the compass.

The Vaishya share with the two higher classes, the priestly Brahmin and the authoritative Kshatriya, the distinction of being *dvija*, or "twice-born", achieving their spiritual rebirth when they assume the sacrificial thread at the *upanayana* ceremony. The Vaishya are credited in history with favouring the rise of the reformist religious beliefs of Buddhism and Jainism.

Vajra, five-pronged ritual object extensively employed in Tibetan Buddhist ceremonies, it is the symbol of the Vajrayana school of Buddhism.

In ritual use, the *vajra* is frequently employed in conjunction with the bell (Sanskrit *ghanta*; Tibetan *dril bu*), the various gestures (*mudras*), when correctly executed, having considerable metaphysical power. The *vajra* (symbolizing the male principle, fitness of action) is held in the right hand and the bell (symbolizing the female principle, intelligence) in the left hand, the interaction of the two ultimately leading to Enlightenment. In art the *vajra* is an attribute of many divinities, such as the celestrial Buddha Akshobhya and his manifestation as a *bodhisattva* ("Buddha-to-be"), Vajrapani ("In Whose Hand is the *Vajra*"). The *vishva-vajra* is a double *vajra* in the shape of a cross with four equal arms.

Vajra, in Sanskrit, has both the meanings of "thunderbolt" and "diamond". Like the thunderbolt, the *vajra* cleaves through ignorance. The thunderbolt was originally the symbol of the Hindu rain god Indra (who became the Buddhist Shakra) and was employed by the eighth-century Tantric (esoteric) master Padmasambhava to conquer the non-Buddhist deities of Tibet. Like the diamond, the *vajra* destroys but is itself indestructible and is thus likened to *shunya* (the all-inclusive void).

The *vajra* is fashioned out of brass or bronze, the four prongs at each end curving around the central fifth to form the shape of a lotus-bud. A nine-pronged *vajra* is less commonly used.

Vajrapani, in one of the celestial *bodhisattvas*, it is the manifestation of the self-born Buddha Akshobhya in Mahayana Buddhist mythology.

Vajrapani is believed to be the protector of the *nagas* (half-man, half-serpent deities) and sometimes assumes the shape of a bird in order to deceive their traditional enemy, the hawklike

Garuda. Because of his association with the rain-controlling *nagas* and with the Hindu god of rain, Indra, he is invoked in times of drought.

Like Indra he holds the thunderbolt and is coloured dark blue or white. His statues are often found in a triad with the Buddha Amitayus (or the *bodhisattva* of wisdom, Manjushri) and the lotus-bearing *bodhisattva* of compassion, Padmapani. In Tibet he assumes ferocious forms to combat demons and to guard the mystical teaching Buddhism, and in Japan he guards the temple doorways.

Vajrayana, also called Tantric Buddhism, it is an important development within Buddhism in India and neighbouring countries, notably Tibet.

Other names for this form of Buddhism are Mantrayana ("Vehicle of the Mantra"), which refers to the use of the *mantra* to prevent the mind from going astray into the world of its fictions and their attendant verbiage and to remain aware of reality as such; and Guhyamantrayana, in which the word *guhya* ("hidden") refers not to concealment but to the intangibility of the process of becoming aware of reality.

In the Tantric view, Enlightenment arises from the realization that seemingly opposite principles are in truth one. The passive concepts *shunyata* ("voidness") and *prajna* ("wisdom"), for example, must be resolved with the active *karuna* ("compassion") and *upaya* ("means"). This fundamental polarity and its resolution are often expressed through symbols of sexuality (*yabyum*).

The historical origin of Vajrayana is unclear, except that it coincided with the spread of the mentalistic schools of Buddhism. It flourished from the sixth to the eleventh century and exerted a lasting influence on the neighbouring countries of India. The rich visual arts of Vajrayana reach their culmination in the sacred *mandala,* a representation of the universe used as an aid for meditation.

Vajrayana, in the history of Buddhism, marks the transition from Mahayana speculative thought to the enactment of Buddhist ideas in individual life. The term *vajra* (Sanskrit: "diamond", or "thunderbolt") is used to signify the absolutely real and indestructible in man, as opposed to the fictions an individual entertains about himself and his nature; *yana* is the spiritual pursuit of the ultimately valuable and indestructible.

Philosophically speaking, Vajrayana embodies ideas of both the Yogachara discipline, which emphasizes the ultimacy of mind, and the Madhyamika philosophy, which undermines any attempt to present a relativistic principle as the ultimate. Dealing with inner experiences, the Vajrayana texts use a highly symbolic language that aims at helping the followers of its disciplines to evoke within themselves experiences considered to be the most valuable available to man. Vajrayana thus attempts to recapture the Enlightenment experience of the Gautama Buddha.

Vajrayogini, female embodiment of the cognitive function leading to Buddhahood, Vajrayana emphasizes experience over speculation but uses the terms of speculative philosophical Buddhism in an imaginative way. This practice means that images taken from the ordinary life of the individual become the means to further a deeper understanding of man's being, which is both action (*upaya*) and knowledge (*prajna*), each reinforcing the other.

In spite of her importance in Vajrayana Buddhism, Vajrayogini does not figure as the main deity of a Tantra (literary work). There are four *sadhanas* (methods of visualization) describing her various forms.

Vajrayogini is usually depicted in a terrifying form, holding in her hands a skull and a dagger, her right leg stretched out, the left one slightly bent (*alidha*). She is surrounded on all sides by cremation grounds, indicating that the ordinary world has become dead in contrast to the rich world of inner life and its vision of reality without distorting fictions. Although she may be visualized alone, she is usually in union (*yab-yum*) with Heruka, who, when he is united with Vajrayogini, is known as Hevajra. As such he is very popular in Tibet, particularly with the Bkabrgyud-pa (a major Buddhist sect), whose tutelary deity he is. As an expression of the multiplicity of psychic phenomena, Vajrayogini may be accompanied by other aspects of herself, such as Vajravairochani ("She Who Reveals"), coloured yellow, like the all-illuminating sun, or Vajravarnani ("She Who Colours"), coloured green, symbolizing the widest range of perception and the fact that man's view is "coloured". In her principal form, Vajrayogini is also known as Vajradakini ("She Who Roams over the Void").

Vakataka Dynasty. Indian ruling house originating in the central Deccan in the mid-third century AD, its empire is believed to have extended from Malwa and Gujarat in the north to the Tungabhadra in the south and from the Arabian Sea in the west to the Bay of Bengal in the east. The Vakatakas, like many of the contemporary dynasties of the Deccan, claimed Brahminical origin. Little is known, however, about Vindhyashakti (c. AD 250-270), the founder of the family. Territorial expansion began in the reign of his son, Pravarasena I, who came to the throne c. 270 and reached the Narmada River in the north by annexing the kingdom of Purika.

Pravarasena's kingdom was partitioned after his death. The main line continued with Rudrasena I (c. 330), his son, Prithvisena I (c. 350), and Prithvisena's son, Rudrasena II (c. 400). In the period of Prithvisena the Vakatakas came into contact with the powerful Gupta family of North India, which was making a bid to expand in the west at the expense of the Western Kshatrapas.

Because of its territorial position, the Vakataka family was recognized as a useful ally so that Prabhavati Gupta, the daughter of Chandra Gupta II, was married to Rudrasena II. In this period, Gupta impact was significant in Vakataka polity and culture. Rudrasena's death was followed by a lengthy regency of Prabhavati Gupta during the minority of her sons Divakarasena and Damodarasena. After the Guptas became involved in a war against the Huns, the Vakataka dynasty was free to expand in central India, and in the period of Narendrasena (c. 450-470), son of Pravarasena II, Vakataka influence spread to such central Indian States as Koshala, Mekala, and Malwa. This power, however, ultimately brought the Vakatakas into conflict with the Nalas and caused a setback to the family. Its power was temporarily revived in the reign of Prithvisena II, the last known king of the line, who acceded to the throne c. 470.

Apart from this senior line was the Vatsagulma (Basim, in Akola district, Maharashtra State) line, which branched off after Pravarasena I and occupied the area between the Indhyadri Range and the Godavari River. The Vakatakas are noted for having encouraged arts and letters.

Valabhi, also called Vallabhipur, city of ancient Indian that was the capital of the Maitraka dynasty in the fifth-eighth centuries AD, it was situated on an inlet of the Gulf of Cambay (Khambhat), northwest of the port of Bhavnagar, in Saurashtra (later Gujarat State), western India. The city is said to have been established about AD 470 by the founder of the dynasty, Senapati Bhatarka, during the period when the Gupta empire was breaking up. It continued as capital until about 780, when it suddenly and unaccountably disappeared from history. It apparently survived the Arab invasions of Saurashtra about 725-735.

The city has now vanished, but it is identified with a village, Vala, where numerous copperplate inscriptions and seals of the Maitrakas have been found.

Valabhi was a celebrated centre of learning, with numerous Buddhist monasteries. It was visited by the Chinese pilgrim Hsuan-tsang (Xuanzang) in the middle of the seventh century and by I-ching (Yiching) at the century's close. The latter described it as equalling the fame of Nalanda in Bihar. According to a Jain tradition, the second Jain council was held in Vallabhi in the fifth or sixth century AD; at this council the Jain scriptures assumed their present form.

Varahamihira (b. 505, Ujjain, India; d. 587, Ujjain), also called Varaha, or Mihira, Indian philosopher, astronomer and mathematician of the sixth century AD, he was born in a village called Kaapitthaka near Ujjain and later lived in the city of Ujjain. Varahamihira has written three famous texts: *Pancha Siddhantika, Brihat-samhita* and *Brihat-Jataka*. The first is a compendium of astronomy encompassing all that was known at the time. The other two are an encyclopaedia and an astrological texts respectively.

Although Varahamihira's writings give a comprehensive picture of sixth-century India, his real interest lay in astronomy and astrology. He repeatedly emphasized the importance of astrology and wrote many treatises on *shakuna* (augury) as well as the *Brihat-Jataka* ("Great Birth") and the *Laghu-Jataka* ("Short Birth"), two well-known works on the casting of horoscopes.

Varahamihira's *Pancha Siddhantika* ("Five Treatises"), is a compendium of Greek, Egyptian, Roman, and Indian astronomy. The five texts are *Paithamaha, Paulisha, Vasishthya, Surya* and *Romaka*. Varahamihira's knowledge of Western astronomy was thorough. In the five sections, his monumental work progresses through native Indian astronomy and culminates in two treatises on Western astronomy, showing calculations based on Greek and Alexandrian reckoning and even giving complete Ptolemaic mathematical charts and tables.

The *Surya Siddhantika* occupies a very important position in the history of Indian astronomy. It is not a work of a single individual but appears to have undergone periodical revisions. It served as a standard astronomical text in different periods of time. Based on actual astronomical observations. Varahamihira revised and brought it up to date.

The present-day Hindu *panchanga* (almanac) is based on the modern version of *Surya Siddhantika*. Varahamihira in his *Pancha Siddhantika* also deals with the astronomical reasons for eclipses and calculations to predict the eclipses. The book contains details on observatories and their construction.

The *Brihat-Jataka* is a treatise on astrology. It contains 26 chapters and gives the descriptions of the 12 zodiacal signs, and their influence on human beings and animals. It also contains many concepts and technical terms of Greek astrology. The *Brihat-samhita* contains extracts from various branches of knowledge prevalent in his time. The *Brihat-samhita* has 100 chapters and contains 4000 stanzas. It covers almost all topics such as astronomy, geography, meteorology, agriculture, economics, botany, engineering, calendar, and politics.

Varanasi, city, also called Banaras, Benares, or Kashi, in southeastern Uttar Pradesh State, north-central India, it is located on the left bank of the Ganga River and is one of the seven sacred cities of the Hindus.

Varanasi has the finest river frontage in India, with miles of *ghats*, or steps, for religious bathing; an array of shrines, temples, and palaces rise tier on tier from the water's edge. The inner streets of the city are narrow, winding, and impassable for motor traffic; the newer, outer suburbs are more spacious and are laid out more systematically. The sacred city is bounded by a road known as Panchakosi; every devout Hindu hopes to walk this road and to visit the city once in a lifetime and, if possible, to die there in old age. More than 1 million pilgrims visit the city each year.

Among the city's numerous temples, the most venerated are those of Vishvanatha, dedicated to Shiva; that of Sankatmochana, dedicated to the monkey-god Hanuman; and that of Durga. The Durga temple is famous for the swarms of monkeys that inhabit the large trees in the vicinity. The Great Mosque of Aurangzeb is another prominent religious building. Two of the more important modern temples are those of Tulasi Manas and the Vishvanatha on the campus of the Banaras Hindu University. The city has hundreds of other temples. At Sarnath, a few miles north of Varanasi, there are ruins of ancient Buddhist monasteries and temples as well as temples built by the Maha Bodhi Society and by Chinese, Burmese and Tibetan Buddhists.

Varanasi has been a city of Hindu learning through the ages. There are innumerable schools and countless Brahmin *pandits*, or learned men, responsible for the continuation of traditional learning. There are also three universities, including the large and important Banaras Hindu University (1915), and more than a dozen colleges and high schools. A university-level Centre for Tibetan Studies has been established at Sarnath.

The city is also a centre of arts and crafts and of music and dance. Varanasi is famous for its production of silks and brocades with gold and silver threadwork, as well as for wooden toys, glass, bangles, ivory work, and brassware. Among the major industries is a railway locomotive manufacturing unit. Population (1991) City 929,270; Metropolitan Area 1,030,863.

Varanasi is one of the oldest continuously-inhabited cities in the world. Its early history is that of the first Aryan settlement in the middle Ganga valley. By the second millennium BC, Varanasi was a seat of Aryan religion and philosophy and was also a commercial and industrial centre famous for its muslin and silk fabrics, perfumes, ivory work, and sculpture. Varanasi was the capital of the kingdom of Kashi during the time of the Buddha (sixth century BC), who gave his first sermon at nearby Sarnath.

The city remained a centre of religious, educational, and artistic activities as attested by the celebrated Chinese traveller, Hsuan-tsang (Xuanzang), who visited it in c. AD 635 and said that the city extended for about 5 km along the western bank of the Ganga River. Varanasi subsequently declined during the three centuries of Muslim occupation, beginning in 1194. Many of the city's Hindu temples were destroyed during the period of Muslim rule, and learned scholars fled to other parts of the country. The Mughal emperor Akbar in the sixteenth century brought some relief to the city's religious and cultural activities.

There was another setback during the reign of the Mughal emperor Aurangzeb in the late seventeenth century, but later the Marathas sponsored a new revival. Varanasi became an independent kingdom in the eighteenth century, and under subsequent British rule it remained a commercial and religious centre. In 1910 the British made Varanasi a new Indian State, with Ramnagar (on the opposite bank) as headquarters but with no jurisdiction over the city of Varanasi. In 1949, after Indian independence, the State of Varanasi became part of the State of Uttar Pradesh.

Varna, any one of the four traditional social classes of Hindu India. The *varnas* have been known since the late-Rigveda hymn

10.90, in which it is declared that the Brahmin (priest), the Kshatriya (nobleman), the Vaishya (commoner), and the Shudra (serf) issued forth at creation from the mouth, arms, thighs, and feet of the primaeval person (*purusha*). The set of four contains several groups of contrasts: the Shudra, surely the aboriginal non-Aryan population, is in contrast with the first three, who are "twice-born" (*dvija*) after undergoing the ceremony of spiritual rebirth (*upanayana*) that initiates them into Aryan manhood. The Shudras live in servitude to the other three. The Vaishyas, in turn, contrast as common people, grazers, and cultivators with the governing classes—the secular Kshatriyas, or barons, and the sacerdotal Brahmins. Brahmins and Kshatriyas themselves contrast in that the former are their priests, while the latter have the actual dominion. In the older description, far greater emphasis is placed on the functions of the classes than or hereditary membership, in contradistinction to caste, which emphasizes heredity over function.

The system of the four classes (*chaturvarnya*) is fundamental to the views the traditional lawgivers held of society. They specified a different set of obligations for each: the task of the Brahmin is to study and advise, the baron to protect, the Vaishya to cultivate, and the serf to serve. History shows, however, that the four-class system was more a social model than a reality. The multitudinousness of castes is explained as the result of hypergamous and hypogamous alliances between the four classes and their descendants. Although the Shudra, in the beginning, clearly comprised the residual class of all non-Aryans, their inclusion in the four-*varna* system bestowed on them a measure of dignity. A move to accommodate still others not so distinguished led to the rather unofficial acceptance of yet a fifth class, the *panchama* (Sanskrit: "fifth"), which include the "untouchable" classes and others, such as tribal groups, who are outside the system and, consequently, *avarna* ("classless").

Vedanta, one of the six systems of Indian philosophy, that forms today the strongest rational basis of Hinduism. The word Vedanta means the concluding portion (*anta*) of the Vedas, which contains the Upanishads, that comprise the knowledge contained in the later Vedic literature as opposed to the ritualistic practices of the earlier part of Vedic literature. That is why Vedanta is also known as Uttara-Mimamsa or "Reflections on the Latter Part of the Vedas".

The Vedanta philosophy springs from interpretations of the

three great texts (*Prasthanatraya*) of Hinduism, the Upanishads, the Bhagavadgita, and the Brahma-sutras. These interpretations by Shankara, Ramanuja, Madhva, and others have resulted in 12 schools of Vedanta of which 3, the Advaita ("monstic") Vedanta of Shankara, the Vishistadvaita ("qualified monism") of Ramanujacharya, the the Dvaita (dualism) of Madhva, are more well known. Among the Upanishads commented upon by the great masters, the older ones like the Chandogya, Brihadaranyaka, Katha, Isha, Kena, and Taittriya deserved greater attention. The Bhagavadgita, the most popular religious text of Hinduism, combines the essence of all the three schools of Vedanta, and has emerged as the scripture for translating Vedic principles in active life. Badarayana wrote the Brahma-sutras, terse aphorisms expounding the Vedanta philosophy and systematizing the teachings of the Upanishads about the fundamental truths of life, existence, and the universe.

Advaita means "non-dual", one without a second; Advaita recognizes Brahman (the Absolute) as the only reality, the one without a second and (*Ekamevadvitiyam*: Chandogya Upanishad), and denies permanent reality to the phenomenal world or to individual souls. The ultimate reality in Vedanta is called Brahman, which is existence (*sat*), consciousness (*chit*), bliss (*ananda*), and the absolute. It has also been described as eternal (*saswata*), immortal (*amrita*), as illuminated reality (*bhrupah*: Chandogya Upanishad) and the exceedingly beautiful or sublime (*atisundaram*—Ashtavakra Gita). The soul inside the individual beings (*jiva*) is called the *atman*. As Absolute Consciousness, Brahman has interpreted everything in this universe as sentient and insentient. Advaita ("non-dualistic") Vedanta, in its most abstract form, owes its first expression to Gaudapada's (seventh-eighth century AD) interpretations (*karikas*) on the Mandukyopanishad. Shankara's (eighth-ninth century AD) commentaries in the *Prasthanatraya*, as also a few independent treatises, elaborated the Advaita philosophy.

The Brahma-sutras define Brahman as the self-willed cause of evolution, sustenance, and dissolution of the universe. Brahman is both the material (*upadana*) and instrumental (*nimitta*) cause of this world, and it has also interpreted phenomenal universe. The three fundamental factors of consciousness are: I exist, I know, and I am blissful. Combining with mind, ego, and intellect, the One Cosmic Consciousness manufactures the feeling of existence, knowledge, and love in individuals. That absolute knowledge of Brahman percolating through the brain of man becomes his intuition, reason, and instinct. Owing to nescience or *avidya* or *maya*, Brahman is called the *atman* or *jiva* in individuals. *Maya* is stated to be *anadi* or beginningless. According to later Vedanta schools, *maya* functions at the cosmic level and *avidya* at the individual level.

Shankara sums up Advaita Vedanta in his well-known dictum: "Brahman alone is real and the world of many is not real. The individual soul is one with supreme Self or Brahman." For Shankara, the action of creation in space-time is not real but only apparent (*vivarta*). He calls it *adhyasa* or *adhyaropa* (superimposition) by the veiling power of *avidya* (nescience or ignorance) or *maya*. The unreality of the world is explained by the well-known Advaita simile of the perception of the snake in a rope (a rope which appears as a snake, an optical illusion). And this superimposition (*ahyasa*) or wrong perception is due to *maya*. *Maya* is a phenomenon that defies description. The snake perceived is neither real (*sat*) nor unreal (*asat*). It is not unreal since at the point of time it is actually perceived. But it is also unreal since it disappears as soon as the substratum, the rope, is perceived as it is. To explain such a peculiar phenomenon Shankara creates a third type of reality which is *sad-asadvilakshana* (different from both the real and the unreal). The cognition (*khyati*) of *maya* is, therefore, precise definition described as *anirvachaniya*, or incapable of any precise definition.

Shankara accepts three degrees of reality. The first, *pratibhashika-satya* ("apparent truth", or "illusory appearance"), is illustrated in the wrong perception of a snake in a rope. The second, *vyavaharika-satya*, is illustrated by our day-to-day sensory experience. And the third is the mystical-intuitive perception of one reality everywhere (*paramarthika-satya*). Gaudapada's interpretation of *Mandukya Karika*, and later Vedantic texts like *Drik-Driya-Vineka* held that Advaita (the nonduality) is the highest reality and that the immanent springs from the transcendent *turiya* which is beyond the senses, it is our consciousness that creates the external world. This idea later crystallized into the theory of *Drishti Srishti Vada* ("Creation is simultaneous with our perception of the reality outside").

Advaita Vedanta equates Brahman (the consciousness) with *atman* (the individual self), and therefore exhorts the seekers of Reality with *mahavakayas* ("great sentences") like *tat tvam asi* ("That thou art") or *aham brahmasmi* ("I am Brahman") in order to attain the state of final fulfilment, infinite bliss, and also immortality beyond the mortal life of man. All Vedanta schools accept the idea of the transmigration of the soul into rebirth according to the desires and fruits of action by the individual, and the goal is to transcend the cycles of birth and death. Among the well-known post-Shankara Advaita philosophers are Sureshvara (ninth century), Padmapada (ninth century), Vachaspati Misra (ninth century), and Madhusudana Sarasvati (sixteenth century).

Shankara established Advaita Vedanta against the contemporary nihilism of the Buddhists, the materialism of the Charvakas, and the ritualism of the early Veda literature (*Purvamimamsa*). Vivekananda established Advaita Vedanta in the face of the scientific materialism and the rationalistic atheism of the nineteenth century; he interpreted Vedanta as a philosophy capable of satisfying modern scientific rationalism through his lectures on *jnana yoga*. Some of the fundamental concepts of Vedanta may be harmonized with modern scientific thought. The Atman-Brahman reality is the outcome of today's particle physics as shown by Fritzof Capra in *Tao of Physics*. Nobel laureate Schrondinger mentioned the same equation as the solution to the problems of consciousness in modern physics in *My View of the World* and *Mind and Matter*. The fundamental uncertainties in defining reality is the outcome of Werner Heisenberg's uncertainty principle. Organic behaviour of microcosmic and subatomic particles is the idea that emerges out of Max Borh's probability wave theory.

The Vishistadvaita Vedanta ("qualified monism") philosophy, which Yamuna (eleventh century) and Ramanuja evolved out of the more ancient teachings, holds the world, which is a transformation (*parinama*) of Brahman, as real and not illusory. It accepts only one reality (Advaita), but with attributes or modes (Vishishta). It accepts three entities, Brahman or Ishvara, *jiva* or *chit*, and *prakriti* or *achit*, as the ultimate realities. Brahman is the absolute, independent reality, whereas the other two are dependent realities.

In Dvaita Vedanta, nature (*prakriti*), the ultimate source of the physical universe, is eternal but insentient. The three *gunas*, the three human attributes or qualities—*sattva* (knowledge and calmness), *rajas* (intense activity and restlessness), and *tamas* (inertia and delusion)—are regarded as its first products. From them emerge in succession the *mahat* (intellect), *ahankara* (egoism), *manas* (mind), the *indriyas* (sensory organs) and the five *bhutas* (elements—earth, water, fire, air, and ether). The Dvaita system postulates an *avyakrita-akasha* or unmodified space, from which this universe evolved as a fundamental and permanent category, coeval with God.

The Dvaita Vedanta system of Madhva (thirteenth century) accepts Brahman as God, the creator-destroyer of this universe, and does not reject this world of sensory experience as *mithya* (illusion) since it is of universal and direct experience. Brahman or God alone is *svatantra* (independent and absolutely free reality) and controls others, including the individual souls and *prakriti* or nature, which are *asvatantra* (dependent categories). The individual self is a reflection of God and gets a faint colouring of some of His attributes.

Ramakrishna, the latest authority on the Vedantic view of reality, accepts all three schools of Vedanta as three gradual stages of man's understanding of the ultimate reality, and they all ultimately culminate in the realization of unity or Advaita which is the final goal. Vedanta is expounded by Ramakrishna and his disciple Vivekananda, therefore, unifies and harmonizes all religious paths to one Godhead and accepts all religions as only different ways and stages of man's approach towards the one Godhead. While Shankara's view accepts the One (Brahman) as real and the Many (the phenomenal world) as unreal, in the Ramakrishna-Vivekananda Vedanta, the phenomenal world is not unreal. It is real and God is in everything. *Maya* is regarded as the energy (*shakti*) of Brahman, "Brahman and Shakti are one". "*Maya* is the energy of the universe, potential and kinetic", says Vivekananda. Many are only manifestations of the One Reality and more emphasis is laid on man's essential divinity (*Jiva Brahma eva na aparah*). Vivekananda puts this idea of man's essential divinity into practice through a philosophy which has given birth to the concept of "Practical Vedanta" based on service to God in the poor, the sinner, the needy, the diseased, and the ignorant.

Vedanta Schools, though Vedanta is frequently referred to as one *darshana* (viewpoint), there are, in fact, radically different schools of Vedanta; what binds them together is common adherence to a common set of texts. These texts are the Upanishads, the Vedanta-sutras, and the Bhagavadgita—known as the three *prasthanas* (the basic scriptures, or texts) of the Vedanta.

The main schools are: Shankara's unqualified nondualism (Shuddhadvaita), Ramanuja's qualified nondualism (Vishistadvaita), Madhva's dualism (Dvaita), Bhaskara's doctrine of identity and difference (Bhedabheda), and the schools of Nimbarka and Vallabha, which assert both identity and difference though with different emphasis on either of the two aspects. From the religious point of view, Shankara extolled metaphysical knowledge as the sole means to liberation and regarded even the concept of God as false; Ramanuja recommended the path of *bhakti* combined with knowledge and showed a more tolerant attitude towards the tradition of Vedic ritualism; and Madhva, Nimbarka, and Vallabha all propounded a personalistic theism in which love and devotion to a personal God are rated highest. Although Shankara's influence on Indian philosophy could not be matched by these other schools of Vedanta, in actual religious life the theistic Vedantic schools have exercised a much greater influence than the abstract metaphysics of Shankara.

The founders of the various schools of Vedanta have all substantiated their positions by commenting on these three source books. The problems and issues around which their differences centre are the nature of Brahman, the status of the phenomenal world; the relation of finite individuals to the Brahman; and the nature and the means to *moksha*, or liberation.

Vedantadeshika (b. 1268, Tuppule, near Kanchipuram, Vijayanagar, southern India; d. 1370, Srirangam, southern India), also called Venkatanatha, leading theologian of the Vishishtadvaita (qualified nondualism) school of philosophy and founder of the Vadakalai, a subsect of the Shrivaishnavas, a religious movement of South India.

Vedantadeshika was born into a distinguished Shrivaishnava family that followed the teachings of Ramanuja, an eleventh-twelfth-century saint. A precocious child, Vedantadeshika was said to have been taken at the age of five to meet the sect's leader, Vatsya Varadacharya, who blessed him, saying he would in time be a great teacher and repudiate all false philosophers. Vedantadeshika married and had a family but lived on alms in order to devote himself fully to his philosophic and literary efforts. He was a prolific writer in both Sanskrit and Tamil; his more than 100 works include commentaries on Vaishnava scriptures, *Nyaya-parishudddhi*, a comprehensive work on Vishistadvaita logic, *Yadavabhyudaya*, and poetic work on the life of Krishna, *Sankalpa-suryodaya*, an allegorical drama, and devotional hymns.

According to Vedantadeshika's interpretation of *prapatti* (surrender to the grace of God), some effort is required on the part of the worshipper to secure God's grace, just as the baby monkey must hold to its mother (the *markata-nyaya*, or the "analogy of the monkey"). This view—together with ritual and linguistic differences—became the basis for the split between the two subsects, the Vadakalai and the Tengalai, who held that God's grace is unconditional and that the human being is as unassertive as a kitten carried by its mother.

Vedas, meaning knowledge, used inclusively for the earliest strata of Indian literature, the earliest Vedic literary productions are the hymns of the Rigveda, the composition of which probably began at the beginning of the second millennium BC, while the latest compositions, the Upanishads, date from the most recent centuries of the first millennium BC. The period of Vedic textual production, then, extended for about 1,500 years, a period which saw considerable development in the language of the texts as well as in many crucial areas of thought, belying the notion that the Vedas represent a single, static, unchanging set of ideas, or contain a single, easily reducible meaning. Like the Rigveda and the Upanishads, virtually all of the surviving Vedic literature is religious in nature. Included are texts on mythology, ritual, and theological speculation. The primary deities represented in the mythology shifted from the great divinities of the Rigveda, including Indra, Agni, Soma, and Varuna, to Prajapati, Brahma, Vishnu, and others of the late Vedic texts. The ritualism, which, from the evidence of the Rigveda, consisted primarily of offerings and formulated to an astonishing precision; and early trends towards abstraction and mysticism grew—though it must be said that seeds of all these changes are to be found in the Rigveda itself. The language of the Vedas also underwent change, from the archaic Vedic dialects of the Rigveda to the language of the Upanishads, which more nearly approximates classical Sanskrit. Indeed, by the close of the first millennium BC, Sanskrit speakers were unable to comprehend much of the language of the Rigveda.

Virtually the entire corpus of Vedic literature consists of oral compositions that were reduced to written form much later than their original composition. In fact, both the reduction of these compositions into coherently sequenced texts and the establishment of the Vedic canon occurred in a period when the texts were still transmitted in exclusively oral form. The individual texts within this Vedic literature, as one may now understand the term, were, from the time of the earliest productions, organic parts of highly developed bardic and priestly traditions, that, in spite of many excellent critically edited texts, continued to be transmitted orally into the twenty-first century.

The composers of the early texts were Vedic-speaking peoples of Aryan descent. They referred to themselves as Arya, "nobility". Though Vedic was an Indo-European language, its speakers were quickly influenced by peoples of the subcontinent who spoke Dravidian or proto-Munda languages. This indigenous influence was not just linguistic; the influence became increasingly evident in the religion, social structure, and material culture represented in the Vedas. On the more recent end of the Vedic temporal spectrum, the authors of the Upanishads and other later texts were thoroughly acculturated within the subcontinent and were inheritors of what were, by then, ancient textual and religious traditions. Like their predecessors, they carefully maintained the textuality of the early bardic and priestly traditions while adapting and reinterpreting them to suit the philosophical and theological goals of their much more settled, urbanized environment.

In the early centuries of the production of Vedic literature the authors were cattle-raiding warriors who employed horse-drawn chariots. However, they also had a pronounced priestly component and a highly developed poetic sensibility. An absence of permanent temples, icons, or images of deities is striking in both the archaeological and literary records, while on the other hand there is ample reference to both temporary ritual structures and the use of everyday items in religious ritual, such as spoons, carts, knives, and ropes—all of which testifies to an early nomadic or migratory lifestyle. By the turn of the first millennium BC or shortly thereafter, however, the texts record a fairly substantial number of cultivated grains, assign specific names to plants and trees, and speak of royal rituals that are necessarily situated in concerntrated cultural strongholds, in bases of social and political power, from which culture radiated centripetally.

Vedic literature, the primary body of Vedic texts is called *shruti,* "that which is heard", indicating the divine revelation of the texts, their status as "heard" rather than composed texts, as well as their status as memorized and recited (hence heard) text, emblematic of an idealized Vedic culture. The composers, or seers, of the Vedic hymns were called *rishis* ("sages") or *kavis* ("poets"). Secondary Vedic literature is called *smriti*, "that which is remembered". This consists of *vedangas*, "limbs of the Veda", which are texts ancillary to the primary *shrutis*. The *vedangas* are pedagogical in nature, designed to assist in the production of Vedic ritual, to guide in proper pronunciation of the texts, and to elucidate grammar, metrics, and etymologies of difficult Vedic words. The *shruti* texts are divided into four text types, in rough chronological order, called Samhita, Brahmana, Aranyaka, and Upanishad. A second fourfold division is according to the Vedic school: Rigveda, Samaveda, Yajurveda, and Atharvaveda. In general, the latter contains at least one representative of the former. For example, the Rigveda contains two nearly identical Samhitas (Shakala and Bashkala), as well as two Brahmans, Aranyakas, and Upanishads. Exceptionally, the Samaveda and Atharvaveda have no corresponding Aranyaka. The Vedic canon is not quite closed: the category of Upanishad has had entrants up to the seventeenth century. The copious numbers of late Upanishads (of all schools) tend to be sectarian and theistic in nature, recasting many of the basic Upanishadic doctrines in terms of a particular non-Vedic deity, such as Krishna, Shiva, or Ganesha. These latter Upanishads usually mimic the diction of the early Upanishads reasonably well, though they have far less connection with the early Vedic textuality. One published collection contains 188 Upanishads of all periods, while there were probably 13 early Upanishads.

Rigveda: The Samhitas ("collections") are the earliest text type of the Vedic schools. These differ in character according to the school. The first of these texts is the Rigveda Samhita, which consists entirely of metrically regulated hymns, largely to various divinities, but with other material as well, including a few hymns with philosophical and sociological themes and a fairly large number with fragmentary descriptions of different sacrificial rituals. The most important of the rituals in the Rigveda is a grand offering of *soma* that produced heightened vision, into sacrificial fires. Based on the linguistic, cultural, and religious content of the Rigveda, it is likely that the earliest hymns date from roughly 1800 BC while the latest are perhaps six or seven hundred years later.

The hymns were gathered into their present Samhita form around the close of the second millennium BC. The Rigveda

Samhita consists of 1,028 hymns (*sukta*) averaging about 10 verses per hymn, and is divided into 10 books called *mandalas*. These *mandalas* are of varying length, the shortest being the second, of 43 hymns, while the longest are the first and tenth, each with 191 hymns, doubtless an intentional gesture on the part of the redactors to confer symmetry on the collection. The core of the Rigveda, which is to say the earliest hymns, are the second to seventh *mandalas*, known as "family books" because they were transmitted from generation to generation (presumably exclusively) within particular clans before the Samhita was collected together. The eighth *mandala* is a hymnology of several (mostly) small clans, while the ninth consists of most of the *soma* hymns, which the editors removed from the family books and placed in one location.

The first ten books are the most recent (determined by close dialectal analysis), the tenth more recent than the first. The first consists of hymns to various deities, not unlike the family books, but are not authored by members of the powerful ancient clans of the second through the eighth *mandalas*. The most important hymns containing theological speculation are found in the first and tenth *mandalas*, indicating a development in the utilization of the hymn form to record more abstract reflection. These include hymns on the nature and importance of the spoken word (*vac*), the divine origin of the social order, as well as meditations on an absolute reality beyond word and deity. Other noteworthy hymns include a lengthy marriage hymn; a series on the nature of death and funerary rites; a touching soliloquy in which the poet expresses remorse over losses in gambling, a rain charm comparing the sound of Brahmins reciting Vedic hymns to frogs croaking in the rain; and one by a young girl, Apala, who secures a portion of her father's *soma* and with it tries to invoke Indra in order to replenish the bald pate of her father, her father's infertile fields, and her own hairless abdomen. Like many stories in the Rigveda, this appears in a somewhat altered form in later Vedic literature. In the Jaiminiya Brahmana, of perhaps 800 BC, Apala appears with a skin rash and has a vision in which she "sees" this Rigvedic hymn. After praising the hymn she finds a *soma* stalk, which she subsequently chews. Indra then approaches her, she recites the hymn, and is cured of her rash.

Samaveda: The Samaveda Samhita is a songbook consisting almost entirely of hymns or random verses from the Rigveda. It is quite likely that it is of nearly the same age as the Rigveda, the adaptations occurring almost immediately. The non-Rigvedic hymns, consisting of about 10 per cent of the collection, resemble the hymns of the Rigveda, but for unknown reasons did not find their way into that collection. The Samaveda is liturgical in character; it is used in *soma* sacrifices, in which selected verses were strung together and chanted in styles very different from the recitation of the Rigvedic hymns. Indeed, the *soma* sacrifices may in no small measure be viewed as songfests featuring extended Rigvedic recitation and Samavedic chant alternating with sacrificial offerings. The Samaveda consists of three surviving rescensions: the closely related Kauthuma and Ranayaniya, and the Jaiminiya (or Talavakara).

Yajurveda: The Yajurveda is the most varied of all the Samhitas because it consists of a fairly large number of rescensions. These are divided into the Shukla (White) Yajurveda and the Krishna (Black) Yajurveda. The former has two branches (Madhyandina and Kanva) while the latter has three surviving branches (Taittiriya, Maitrayani, and Kathaka). The difference between them is that the Shukla Yajurveda separates verses (Samhita) from explanatory material (Brahmana), while the Krishna contains both within the same text. The Yajurveda contains extended speculation on the nature of Vedic ritual, and includes the libretto for the primary officiants of the sacrifices, the *mantras* to be recited at the time of the offerings themselves. Thus, the Yajurveda is the Veda most closely associated with the fundamentals of the sacrifices. The Yajurveda Samhitas were probably the last Samhitas to be composed, dating from the end of the second millennium BC to the earliest centuries of the first millennium BC.

Atharvaveda: The Atharvaveda consists of 20 books (*kanda*) containing a total of 598 hymns and prose passages. Books 1 to 7 contain magical prayers for precise purposes: spells for a long life, cures, curses, and love charms, prayers for prosperity, communion with those who know Brahman, and success in the study of the Veda, charms for kingship, and expiations for civil committed. Books 8 to 12 contain similar texts but also include cosmological hymns that continue those of the Rigveda and provide a transition to the more complex speculations of the Upanishads. For example, the notion of the importance of breath or vital air (*prana*) and speculations on an individual self (*atman*) linked with a universal self, so important in the Upanishads, are first found in the Atharvaveda. Books 13 to 20 celebrate the cosmic principle (*kanda* 13) and present marriage prayers (*kanda* 14), funeral *mantras (kanda* 18), and other magical and ritual formulae. *Kanda* 15 is of great interest because it glorifies the *vratya*, an unorthodox Aryan group that did not study the Veda, yet possessed respected ritualistic and speculative traditions. Indeed, the *vratya* is extolled as lordly and as capable of conferring blessings on a king who receives him as a guest. This section of the Atharvaveda (also 9.2), as well as many Yajurveda passages, explores the significance of hospitality, one of the primary organizing principles of Vedic and later Indian ritual. Another hymn in the Atharvaveda describes and praises human anatomy. Because of this hymn, as well as the general Atharvavedic concern with curing, the classical Indian medical system, Ayurveda, claims descent from the Atharvaveda. However, this claim is not supported by the texts: neither are the principles of Ayurveda found in the Vedas nore are the magical or ritual cures from the Atharvaveda found in Ayurveda. Nevertheless, the practice of systematizing and cataloguing medical remedies commenced with the Atharvaveda.

The *Atharvaveda,* transmitted in two rescensions (Shaunaka and Paippalada) consists almost entirely of hymns composed in many of the same meters as Rigvedic hymns. Beyond that the similarities with the Rigveda end. The Atharvaveda reflects the magico-religious concerns of everyday life—quite different in tone from the more hieratic Rigveda, which glorifies the great gods and records the inspired vision of the poets under the influence of *soma*. Because of its thorough neglect of the sacrifices and general neglect of the great gods, the Vedic priesthood did not often consider the Atharvaveda the equal of the other three Vedas, a status accorded to it only much later. The language is distinctly later than that of the Rigveda, in some places resembling the language of the later Brahmana texts. Thus, it is usually dated at around 1000 BC.

Brahmanas: The Brahmanas, dating from perhaps 900 BC to 700 BC, may be considered the earliest commentaries on the Samhitas. These mostly voluminous prose texts are digests or collections of various views and discourses on the sacrificial rituals. Their goal was not to provide exact descriptions (or prescriptions) of the rituals—that was the aim of the later ritual *sutras* and other ritual handbooks—but to explain the origin, meaning, and purpose of the ritual actions as well as the connections of these actions with the ordinary world. A knowledge of the ritual, its terminology, and technicalities was assumed by the authors, which is the primary reason these texts are often bewildering to modern readers. The notions of ritual intentionality and the distinction between ritual action and ordinary action were such an assumed part of the Vedic ritual discourse that no complex theorizing on the subjects was deemed necessary. Rather, of greatest interest was, first, understanding the ritual as a connecting link between the world and the cosmos and, second, utilizing that knowledge to harness the powers of the cosmos. In other words, the primary epistemological project of the Brahmànas was discovering the connections or homologies (*bandhu*) that linked the different realms, while the primary ontological project was employing that knowledge to bring about personal transformation through ritual action. The personal goals of the rituals ranged from acquisition of cattle and dominion to ensuring an afterlife in heaven. Perhaps the ultimate homology, elaborated in the Shatapatha Brahmana (a text of the Shukla Yajurveda), linked Death, the Year, and Prajapati ("Lord of Creatures"), who merges with the concept of Brahman, the supreme reality and substance of the universe. Through realization of this equation the cosmos is perpetuated: Prajapati, the abstract Brahmanic replacement for the personified Rigvedic Purusha, distributed, which is to say sacrificed, his 1000 parts for the constitution of the cosmos; it is the duty of man to enter the creative matrix through correct understanding and ritual action, therey revivifying Prajapati and completing the creative cycle. The parts of the cosmos utilized in the sacrifices, from the sacrificial arena itself to recited *mantras,* to gestures on the part of the participants, to the sacrificial fee (*dakshina*) paid to the officiants, to offered substances such as rice and *ghee,* all had counterparts in the original integrated body of Purusha/Prajapati, and through the production of Vedic ritual, especially through the burnt oblations conveyed to the gods by Agni, the body of Purusha/Prajapati was made whole again.

Every Veda, including the Atharvaveda whose ritual differs in almost every way from that of the other three Vedas, has Brahmana texts. The most important of these texts are the Aitareya on the Rigveda, the Shatapatha on the Shukla Yajurveda, and the Panchavimsha and Jaiminiya on the Samaveda. Though the Brahmanas of the Krishna Yajurveda are no less important, they were, as mentioned, integrated into the Samhitas and therefore do not appear as separate texts. The exception is the

Taitiriya Brahmana, a rather late text which supplements the explanatory Brahmana passages in the Taittiriya Samhita.

Aranyakas: The Aranyakas, which are found only among the texts of the Rigveda and Yajurveda, are in many ways similar to both the Brahmanas and the Upanishads. They are relatively late, dating from perhaps the eighth to fifth centuries BC. The term *aranyaka* is derived from *aranya* (Sanskrit: "forest"). Aranyakas are texts regarded as so secret, dangerous, and esoteric that they must be studied only by advanced students in the seclusion of the forest. Like the Brahmanas, Aranyakas have as their main subject the explanation of Vedic ritual. More than the Brahmanas, however, the Aranyakas attempt to explain the symbolical and philosophical significance of obscure ritual text passages. Much of the significance of the Aranyakas is that they represent an important transitional stage in the development of Vedic literature. In the Aranyakas, the esoteric explanations of rituals approach independent speculation, paving the way for the more philosophically-based Upanishads and their partial rejection of Vedic ritualism. This is further emphasized by the fact that the Aranyakas were enjoined to be studied not just by ritualists, but often by ascetics, thus demonstrating their divergence from the Vedic ritual, which was explicitly intended for householders.

As a transitional genre with text titles that are often difficult to place, it is not surprising that the contents of the Aranyakas are extremely varied. Included in these self-proclaimed esoteric texts are enumerations of *mantras*, explanation of rituals, mystical identifications and etymologies, legends, references to effects of rituals, descriptions of rituals that were neglected in the Brahmanas, a lengthy description of the details of Veda study (Taittiriya Aranyaka), and meditations on causation and life processes. The structure and style of the Aranyakas are as variegated as their contents, occasionally presenting lists and straightforward descriptions alongside subtle speculative ruminations.

The Aitareya Aranyaka deals at length with an ancient festival called *mahavrata*, containing considerable music, dance, and revelry, preserved as a variant of a normal *soma* sacrifice. Other rituals discussed at length in the Aranyakas include an important variation of the construction of the great fire altar (*agnichayana*) called Arunaketuka (Taittiriya Aranyaka) and a very important rite called *pravargya* (Taittiriya Aranyaka) which is to be performed at least six times prior to the performance of any *soma* sacrifice. Among other topics, the Shankhayana Aranyaka covers topics usually found in the Upanishads, including the internal performance of certain fire sacrifices, the rivalry of the senses, and the permonitions of death.

Upanishads: The most important of the Vedic texts as far as the later Hindu tradition is concerned are the Upanishads, the earliest of which, the *Brihadaranyaka* and *Chandogya*, probably date from the sixth or seventh centuries BC. These texts reveal a full theological advance from the Rigveda's concern for the blessings of divinities and the Brahmana texts' tightly controlled ritual, to an almost exclusive emphasis on speculative and philosophical thought. However, the Upanishads do not leave the earlier texts behind; they continue the tendencies of the Aranyakas to interpret Vedic ritual in a symbolic rather than a literal manner. Much speculation was directed towards the search for harmony and for correspondences between macrocosm and microcosm, with the ultimate goal being a reduction of reality to an all-embracing unity by way of successive equations. The crucial idea was that of Brahman, which tended to become a sort of guiding principle, an approximation of a universal soul, in which the individual soul, or *atman*, is merged. The equation of *atman* (the self) with Brahman (ultimate reality), succinctly expressed in statements such as "thou art that" (*tat tvam asi*, Chandogya), "Brahman is truth, knowledge, infinity" (*satyam jnanam anantam brahma*, Taittiriya), and in the singular all-inclusive syllable "Om" (Chandogya, Taittiriya, Mandukya), became the basis of Hindu metaphysics. The spread by the sixth century BC of the related concepts of the reincarnation of souls, of *karma*, and of the attainment of release (*moksha, apavarga*) from this cycle by meditation rather than through sacrifice marked the end of the Vedic period and the appearance of Hinduism.

Vedangas: The Shrautasutras and other allied texts, namely the Grihyasutras, which prescribe the domestic rites, and the Pitrmedhasutras, which prescribe rites to be performed in honour of deceased ancestors, fall into the *vedanga* category of *kalpa*. The other categories of *vedanga* are phonetics (*shiksha*), metrics (*chandas*), grammar (*vyakarana*), etymology (*nirukta*), and astronomy (*jyotisha*). These texts originated as early as the eighth century BC, and were composed up to probably the third century BC. They were considered recollected (*smriti*), that is, composed and transmitted by humans, rather than "revealed" (*shruti*), and their purpose was to promote better understanding of the language of the *shruti* texts as well as clearer pronunciation and more precise performance of the rituals. Though the extant Vedic texts are listed above, many other texts, both *shruti* and *vedanga*, survive in name only and are presumed lost.

The already knotty problem of Vedic schools becomes even more difficult considering that many of the major schools had a number of ritual subschools associated with them. This is particularly true of the Krishna Yajurveda. In order to perform the major (*shrauta*) rituals, certain types of ritual texts, called Shrautasutras, were employed. Each Vedic school possessed at least one of these texts, which recorded the prescriptions for the performance of these rituals. Because of the broad distribution of the Krishna Yajurveda, and the centrality of the Yajurveda in the Vedic rituals, nine Shrautasutras were composed on this school. One Shrautasutra was composed on the Shukla Yajurveda, two on the Rigveda, one on the Atharvaveda, and nineteen on the Samaveda, of which the three listed bove are the most important.

Vedic Religion, polytheistic and sacrificial religion of the Vedas, is very different from Hinduism.

Mythology: One of the striking themes of Vedic mythology, whether in the hymns of the Rigveda or in the ritualistic Yajurveda texts, was the ever-recurring battle between the gods and the demons, the opposition between good and evil, between creation and destruction. The demons always won the initial skirmishes, but the gods battled back and won in the end, or at least until the next instalment. Many of the battles were parts of creation myths, the most prominent being Indra's (literally) crushing defeat of the serpent demon Vritra, who held the cosmic waters within his coils. Upon smiting Vritra with his thunderbolt (*vajra*), the cosmic waters were released, creating the space between the earth and the vault of heaven (Rigveda 1.32). Like the world of which it was a part, Vedic mythology was grounded in dualities: gods and demons, good and evil, heat and cold, obscuration and resuscitation, earth and heaven, and male and female (*purusha* and *virat*); in the heroic, exemplified by the deeds of Indra; and in a decidedly rural culture in which man, animal—principally cattle, horses, and goats (for sacrifice)—and vegetation subsisted in reasonable harmony. Indeed, there is practically no trace of urban culture in the Vedas (the fired bricks used in the *agnichayana* being a tantalizing exception) and certainly no cultural references to suggest that the Vedas were part of the urban cultures of the Indus Valley from c. 2500-1700 BC.

The Vedas espoused the worship of numerous divinities, most of them male, who were classified as sky, atmospheric, and terrestrial divinities. For example, Surya, the sun god, was a sky deity, as was Indra; Vayu, the god of wind, was an atmospheric deity; while Agni, the god of fire, was a terrestrial deity. The god of highest rank, and the one most often praised in the Rigveda, was Indra, a warlike deity who conquered innumerable human and demon enemies and vanquished the sun, among other epic feats. The next most commonly praised divinities were Agni and Soma. Agni, the priest of the gods and the god of the priests, was the deified sacrificial fire, who carried offered oblations to the gods of the Vedic pantheon. Agni was the fire of the sun, of lightning, of burning wood, which is to say of the sky, the atmosphere, and the earth, and of that which made light for the purpose of religious worship. Soma was simply the deified aspect of the liquid poured in the oblation. In this way Agni and Soma were the deifications of the great forces of fire and water that opposed each other in nature but were equally necessary for human and cosmic sustenance. Another great deity was Varuna, often labelled a king, who was the upholder of the cosmic, ritual, and moral order. Often associated with Varuna, though comparatively minor in the Vedic pantheon, was the benevolent Mitra, who oversaw contracts. Other major divinities were the Maruts, storm gods who assisted Indra in his exploits; the twin Ashvins, aerial "horsemen", the archetypal healers who serve as helpers in time of trouble; Surya, the sun god; and the female Ushas, the dawn. The primary Vedic divinities who became ascendant in later Hinduism were Vishnu, a solar deity who was associated with the sacrifice, and Rudra, a dark and apparently popular deity who gained a place at the sacrificial table only through transgressive deeds, and who later evolved into Shiva. All of these figures, and many other lesser deities and demigods, could serve to illuminate and inspire the poet's vision.

Community (shrauta) ritual: The Vedic communities performed complicated semi-public sacrifices (*yajna*) called *shrauta*, derived from the word *shruti*. This indicates that the *shrauta* rituals employed the primary Vedic texts (*shruti*) in their performances. In its classical conception the objective was to inspire the continuation of the various creative forces operating in nature.

Through a coordinated and extended series of manipulative gestures which were thought to resonate with elemental forces, the cosmos was in whole or in part perpetuated, or even recreated, with the sacrificer, the chief patron (*yajamana*), at the centre. *Shrauta* rituals consisted of: *(a)* coordinated ritual actions performed by representatives of the Rigveda and Yajurveda (and in the case of *soma* sacrifices, representatives of the Samaveda was well); *(b)* recitations of text passages, called *mantras*, from these Vedas; and *(c)* offerings of various substances into a number of fire-places. The latter may be of three kinds: milk products (milk, *ghee*, yogurt) and grain derivatives (rice or barley flour balls), cooked parts of sacrificed animals (including sections of the heart, liver, kidneys, and slices of flesh from the flanks), and *soma*.

The number of officiants ranged from one, the sacrificer himself, in the case of the *agnihotra*, the regular morning and evening offering of milk or rice into the three fires, to four (in addition to the sacrificer) in the case of the milk and grain offerings at the time of the new and full moon (*darsapurnamasa*), to five in the case of independent animal sacrifices (*nirudhapasubandha*), to seventeen in *soma* sacrifices. In the latter case, four represent each of the four Vedas (though in fact the Atharvaveda is not represented) with one serving as honorary supervisor (the *sadasya*). This increasing crescendo of complexity was calendrically derived, from the day to the year as the year represented completeness, wholeness, and was identified with Prajapati, the "Lord of Creatures", the primary deity of the sacrifice.

As part of a one-time initiation (*agnyadheya*) ceremony, the sacrificial patron and his wife (*patni*) vowed to perform at least the daily *agnihotra* and the fortnightly *darsapurnamasa* for 30 years or until one of them died or grew too old and infirm to perform them anymore. Furthermore, they were strongly advised (though not required) to perform a series of seasonal vegetative sacrifices (*chaturmasyas*), a semi-annual independent *soma* sacrifice, and an annual *soma* sacrifice. Each of the latter was more complicated than the former inasmuch as it contained elements of the former ones. Thus, a *soma* sacrifice, which lasted a minimum of five days (but could theoretically be extended for months or years if the sacrificer were a king or wealthy landowner) contained in its simplest form, innumerable, simple *agnihotra*-type oblations, a lengthy series of new and full moon type sacrifices (*ishti*), and three animal sacrifices, in addition to the unique rites of the *soma* sacrifice itself. In the *soma* sacrifice, which ensured the prosperity and well-being of both men and gods, the sacrificer was first consecrated, after which juice was elaborately and ceremoniously pressed three times from the *soma* plant (or its substitute), part being offered into the fire and part consumed by the priests. Each of the three occasions was preceded and followed by lengthy Samavedic chants (*saman, stotra*) and Rigvedic recitations (*shastra*).

The core of the Vedic ritual arena consisted of a long narrow altar (*vedi*), approximately two or three metres in length and two-thirds of a metre in width, stretched in an east-west orientation and strewn with sacred grass (*barhis*). It was on this that that gods were said to come if satisfied with the offerings. The altar was flanked by three fireplaces, the round *ahavaniya* on the eastern end into which oblations to the gods were offered, the square *garhapatya* on the western end into which domestic offerings were made, and the half-moon shaped *dakshinagni* off the southwest side, which served as the receptacle for offerings to the deceased ancestors (*pitr*).

The officiants in a *soma* sacrifice dedicated years, even decades, to learning the recitations and choreography of the rites, while the patron may or may not be learned in Vedic ritual. Indeed, several Vedic texts speak of ignorant sacrificers. In any event, according to the classical doctrine of the Brahmana texts, all the benefits of the rituals were said to accrue to the sacrificer, though the officiants did possess the ability to subvert the rituals. The basic purpose of the sacrifices was ensuring the attainment of heaven (*svarga*) after death, though many among the large number of optional sacrifices (rather than the required ones noted above) had more specific aims, including good health, male progeny, ample rainfall, destruction of enemies, and an abudance of cattle and property.

Several variants of *soma* sacrifices are known for unique performative features, spectacular structures, or ostentatious displays of wealth or power, and could only be performed by kings or wealthy Brahmins. These include the *rajasuya*, the great royal consecration, and the *vajapeya*, a variant of the *rajasuya* intended for a Brahmin sacrificer and featuring a chariot race and an "ascent to heaven" in which the sacrificer and his wife ritually climbed a high tower constructed for that purpose. The *mahavrata* featured dance and musical performances, as well as ritual copulation, within the sacrificial arena. The *agnichayana* featured the construction of a great bird-shaped fire altar constructed of a 1,000 bricks, 200 in each of the 5 layers, that represented the body of Prajapati, and which was the subject of intense speculation in the Brahmana texts. The best known (and probably least performed) of these unique sacrifices was the *ashvamedha*, or "horse-sacrifice", in which a powerful king set loose for a year a specially selected horse, to be followed by 400 warriors. The king then had the right to claim as his own all the property on which the horse stepped, barring challenge from the local king. After a year of wandering, the horse was ritually sacrificed. Among other interesting rites in this sacrifice, the wife of the sacrificer engaged in sex with the dead horse, under the cover of blankets. Human sacrifice (*purusamedha*) is described and alluded to as a former practice but may have been more symbolic than actual. The sacrifice of the mythical giant Purusa, from whose dismembered limbs sprang up the parts of the cosmos and the four major castes, probably served as a model for the conjectured human sacrifices. All of these sacrifices featured enormous fees (*dakshina*) paid to the officiating priests. The basic fee for a *soma* sacrifice, to be distributed among the officiants, was 112 cows, already a considerable sum. But in these grand sacrifices gold, jewels, and ornaments were added.

Domestic ritual: The performance of the classical *shrauta* rituals did occupy considerable space in the literature, but that even in the earliest times they were performed regularly only by kings or learned Brahmins. They were too expensive, complicated, and time consuming for most people engaged in an agrarian lifestyle and economy, or required a greater educational commitment than the family of average means could afford. This bespeaks of a development from the comparatively simple religious ritual of the Rigveda, what scholars call the pre-classical ritual, to the more complicated classical *shrauta* ritual of the Brahmana and later periods. The Rigveda is not organized according to liturgical principles, but according to families of seers, identity of divinities, and length of hymns. This structure, as well as the contents and the very genre of these relatively brief hymns, suggests that the ritual of the Rigvedic people consisted of petitionary worship and simple offerings to the different gods.

It probably became more complicated when *soma* was offered, but not to the degree of the later classical ritual. In the end it was the rituals' progressive complexity and extravagance that led to the exclusivity of the *shrauta* traditions. Yet the very preoccupation with ritualizing that produced the *shrauta* ritual and its overaccumulation of recondite minutiae also legislated a compensatory (and complementary) series of domestic rituals. These were the *grihya* rituals, derived from the word *griha*, "house", because they could be performed at home by the common householder, without an obligation to acquire generally unrealizable material like *soma* or pay exorbitant fees to trained *shrauta* ritualists. The *grihya* rituals were also more manageable because they required a good deal less formal Vedic education and required only one ritual fire.

Though the primary *grihya* manuals, also called *sutras*, were composed in the image of the Shrautasutras, it is likely that the domestic rituals themselves were equally relatively simple, performed individually, and had in mind the welfare of the household. In spite of several formal classifications of domestic rituals presented in the Grihyasutras, they may be reduced to three basic types. First are regular offerings into the sacred fire, modelled on the calendrical schedule of the *shrauta* rituals, but without their increasing levels of complexity. Second are the rites of passage (*samskara*), which tend to be quite numerous, 18 being the usual number. They range from impregnation (*nisheka*) to birth (*jatakarman*) to naming of the newborn baby (*namakarana*) to initiation into Veda study (*upanayana*) to marriage (*vivaha*) and death (*antyeshtikarman*). Third are popular performances, customs, and ceremonies that were formalized in these manuals. These include, for example, the consecration of a new house, ceremonious ploughing at the beginning of the planting season, and an extended series of rites honouring deceased ancestors (the latter were described with even greater specificity in the Pitrmedhasutras, texts dedicated to this purpose that were attached to the Kalpasutras of the different Vedic subschools).

A term that all *grihya* manuals use to refer to their ritual is *pakayajna*, literally "offering of cooked (rice or barley boiled in milk)". This refers to the type of offering made into the sacred fire on all of these occasions, and is employed to contrast *grihya* offerings with the more diverse offerings of the *shrauta* rituals. Despite this general prescription for *pakayajnas*, occasionally more complicated offerings were prescribed, including animal sacrifice. All Vedic schools and subschools had their own *grihya sutras*, though the names were occasionally different from the names of the Shrautasutras. For example, the manual of the followers of the Shukla (White) Yajurveda is the *Paraskara Grihyasutra*, and those of the Kauthuma branch of the Samaveda are the *Khadira Grihyasutra* and the *Gobhila Grihyasutra*, while the texts of the Rigveda retain the names of their Shrautasutras, the *Ashvalayana* and *Shankhayana Grihyasutras*.

Vedic ritual in modern India: The legacy of the Vedas is apparent in several aspects of modern Hinduism. The basic stratification of Vedic society into four social classes (*varnas*)—Brahmins (priests or teachers), Kshatriyas (rulers and soldiers), Vaishyas (traders), and Shudras (non-Aryan serfs)—by and large persisted in later Hinduism. Similarly, offering of oblations to a sacred fire (*homa*) is an important element of much modern Hindu worship, while Vishnu and Shiva, the major deities of classical Hinduism, also figured in Vedic mythology. Most importantly, however, nearly all of later Hindu textuality, including the Mahabharata, the Puranas, many of the Tantras, and virtually all of the "orthodox" philosophical literature, identifies itself as Vedic and places itself distinctly within "Vedic tradition".

In spite of a steady decline in Vedic ritual performance for more than 2,000 years, it persists in some parts of India into the twenty-first century. Indeed, the Vedic sacrificial rituals are the oldest surviving forms of religious practice in the world, with a living and continuous tradition dating back at least 3,500 years. Today there are probably about 100 *ahitagnis*, men who, along with their wives, have established the *shrauta* fires. Most of these *ahitagnis* reside in central Tamil Nadu and coastal Andhra Pradesh and by family tradition follow the Apastamba subsect of the Taittiriya branch of the Krishna (Black) Yajurveda. The purpose of the performances today is largely for its own sake—to keep these performative traditions alive. Very few contemporary performers understand the meaning of the Vedic texts (a situation largely unchanged for the last 2000 years), but they maintain reverence for *shruti* and for that connection with their past which springs to life in ritual performance. While there is a vague sense of the purposes of the rituals mentioned in the Vedic texts, for the most part they have been reinterpreted to suit sectarian Hindu religious thought.

Much more common than the performance of *shrauta* ritual is memorization of Vedic texts. The tradition of memorizing vast sections of text, including the entire Rigveda, Samaveda, and Taittiriya Samhitas is kept alive in Vedic memory schools (*pathashalas*) in central and South India, though these traditions are disappearing quickly under the pressures of modernization. The standardized techniques of memorization, as well as the pedagogy, have remained largely unchanged for thousands of years. Much more common than memorization of Vedic texts is the performance of Vedic domestic rites of passage. These occur virtually everywhere in India, though of course they are limited almost entirely to members of the Brahmin caste, and usually include only the naming ceremony. Vedic initiation (even if the initiate never sees or hears a Vedic text after that, which is increasingly the case), marriage, and death. Many Hindu temple priests are trained to perform these ceremonies, which have by now been altered somewhat to fit sectarian profiles.

Vidisha, town in, west-central Madhya Pradesh State, central India, on the east bank of the Betwa River, it is surrounded by square stone walls, built of materials from the ruined ancient city. The enclosure contains old, Islamic buildings with an air of departed grandeur. In the ninth to twelfth century AD, this ancient city was a prosperous centre of Jainism and Hinduism. The objects of historical interest include the Lohangi Rock and the tomb of Lohangi pir, Pani-ki-Kundi tank, Gumbaz-ka-maqbara, and the Bijamandal Mosque. Formerly called Bhilsa (or Bhelsa), Vidisha is of great antiquity, being mentioned in the Sanskrit epics, the Mahabharata and the Ramayana. Renamed Vidisha in 1956, the modern town is a well-connected agricultural wholesale and retail trade centre and is engaged in flour milling and hand weaving. The town has *dal* [split pulses (legumes)] and oil mills, board and paper mills, and manufacturing units of metal containers and steel trunks. Under the Maurya and Gupta empires the town was a great religious, commercial, and political centre. It fell to the Muslims in 1235. Numerous remains of Buddhist *stupas* nearby, commonly called Bhilsa Topes, date from the third century BC and the first century AD and include the Sanchi group. To the north lies the site of Besnagar, the older town remains, with a list century-BC monolithic pillar. Nearby, on Udayapur Hill, are remains of cave temples dating from the Gupta period (fourth-sixth century AD).

Vidisha has four colleges, including a technological institute, affiliated with Bhopal University.

Vihara, early type of Buddhist monastery consisting of an open court surrounded by open cells accessible through an entrance porch, the *viharas* in India were originally constructed to shelter monks during the rainy season, when it became difficult for them to lead life. They took on a sacred character when small *stupas* (housing sacred relics) and images of the Buddha were installed in the central court.

As the communities of monks grew, great monastic establishments (*mahaviharas*, "great *viharas*") developed that consisted of clusters of *viharas* and associated *stupas* and temples. Renowned centres of learning, or universities, came up at Nalanda, in present-day Bihar State, during the fifth to twelfth centuries and at Nagarjunakonda, Andhra Pradesh, in the third-fourth century.

In western India, the *viharas* were often cut into the rock cliffs. This tradition of rock-cut structures spread along the trade routes of Central Asia (as at Bamian), leaving many splendid monuments rich in sculpture and painting.

Vikramaditya. Vikramaditya was a title assumed by several kings of ancient India, including Chandragupta (r. 380-415 C.E.) and his grandson Skandagupta (r. 455-467) of the Gupta Dynasty, as well as four rulers of the Chalukya Dynasty. The first named, that is Chandragupta Vikramaditya, was third in his line, defeated the Sakas of the northwest, consolidated the Gupta Empire and established his capital at Ujjaini (Ujjain in present-day Madhya Pradesh). He presided over a brilliant court and a period of peace and great cultural florescence. It is likely that Kalidas, the great Sanskrit playwright, received his patronage.

The Vikrama era, or Hindu calendar, is also associated with the legendary ruler whose title means "Sun of Prowess." But this era commences with the year 58 B.C.E. and therefore cannot be linked with any of the historical figures mentioned above.

The accomplishments of this monarch, notably his wisdom and magnanimity, gave rise to a cluster of legends about the "good king Vikramaditya of Ujjaini" who performed heroic and mystical deeds, and whose court was embellished by the *navaratna*, or "nine jewels" of learning. Some of these legends were collected and translated by the nineteenth-century English explorer Richard Burton under the title *The King and the Corpse*.

Vishishtadvaita, one of the principal schools of Vedanta, an orthodox philosophy of India, it grew out of the Vaishnava (worship of Lord Vishnu) devotional movement which was prominent in South India from the seventh century onwards. God has two modes of being, as cause and as product. As cause, he is in his essence qualified only by his perfections; as product, he has as his body the souls and the phenomenal world. There is a pulsating rhythm in these periods of creation and absorption. For Ramanuja, release is not a negative separation from transmigration, or series of rebirths, but, rather, the joy of the contemplation of God. This joy is attained by a life of exclusive devotion (*bhakti*) to God, singing his praise, performing adulatory acts in temple and private worship, and constantly dwelling on his perfections. God will return his grace, which will assist the devotee in gaining release. One of the early Brahmins (class of priests) who began to guide the movement was Nathamuni (tenth century), head priest of the temple at Srirangam (in modern Tamil Nadu State). He was succeeded by Yamuna (eleventh century), who wrote some philosophic treatises but no commentaries.

The most towering figure is his successor, Ramanuja, or Ramanujacharya (master Ramanuja, c. 1017-1137), who wrote commentaries on the Brahma-sutras (the *Shribhashya*, "Beautiful Commentary") and on the Bhagavadgita; and a treatise on the Upanishads, the *Vedarthasamgraha* ("Summary of the Meaning of the Veda"). Ramanuja was the first of the Vedanta thinkers who made the identification of a personal god with the Brahman of the Upanishads and the Vedanta-sutras the cornerstone of his system. As a personal god, Brahman possesses all the good qualities in a perfect degree, and Ramanuja does not tire of mentioning them. He interprets the relationship between the unitary and infinite Brahman and the plural and finite world in a novel way, which, however, has some support in the Upanishads. For him the relation between the infinite and the finite is like that between the soul and the body. Hence nonduality is maintained, while differences can still be stated. Soul and matter are totally dependent on God for their existence, as is the body on the soul.

Vishishtadvaita flourished after Ramanuja, but a schism developed over the importance of God's grace. For the southern, Sanskrit-using school, the Vadakalai, God's grace in gaining release is important, but man himself should make his best efforts. This school is represented by the thinker Venkatanatha, who was known by the honorific name of Vedantadeshika ("Teacher of Vedanta"). The northern, Tamil-using school, the Tenkalai, holds that God's grace alone is necessary.

The influence of Vishishtadvaita spread far to the north, where it played a role in the devotional renaissance of

Vaishnavism, particularly under the Bengal devotee, Chaitanya (1485-1533). In southern India the philosophy itself is still an important intellectual influence.

Vratya, wandering ascetic, member of a sect located principally in the Magadha (South Bihar) region of ancient India, the *vratyas* lived outside the fold of the dominant Aryan society and practised their own forms of austerity and esoteric rites. The *vratya* might have been a source of non-Aryan beliefs and practices introduced into the Vedic religion. Since they are said to speak the language of the initiated, presumably Indo-Aryan, but their observances and practices do not concur with Vedic Brahminism, their ethnic identity remains uncertain.

Vrijji, Pali Vajji, confederacy of the Licchavis and neighbouring peoples in Bihar, India, that existed from the sixth century BC to the fourth century AD, its capital was at Vaishali (in modern Besarh). It was governed as an aristocratic republic. Gautama Buddha is said to have modelled the organizational structure of the Buddhist monastic order, *sangha*, on the government of the Vrijji. In the fourth century BC the marriage of Chndragupta to a Licchavi princess helped establish the Maurya dynasty.

Y

Yadava Dynasty, was ruler of a twelfth to fourteenth century Hindu kingdom of central India in what is the present State of Maharashtra. Originally a feudatory of the eastern Chalukyas of Kalyani, the dynasty became paramount in the Deccan under Bhillama (c. 1187-1191), who founded Devagiri (later Daulatabad) as his capital. Under Bhillama's grandson, Singhana (c. 1210-1247), the dynasty reached its height at the expense of the Hoysalas in the south, the Kakatiyas in the east, and the Paramaras and Chalukyas in the north.

Later rulers continued expansionist wars with varying success. During the reign of the last Yadava king, Ramachandra (reigned 1271-c. 1309), a Muslim army commanded by the Delhi sultan Ala-ud-Din Khalji invaded the kingdom in 1294 and imposed tributary status. A later attempt to throw off the vassalage brought another Delhi army; Ramachandra was imprisoned but was later released and remained loyal to Delhi until his death. In a further attempt, his son and successor died in battle, and the kingdom was annexed by the Khalji Empire in 1317.

Yajna, in Hinduism, is the worship based on rites prescribed in the earliest scriptures of ancient India, the Vedas, in contrast to *puja,* which may include image worship and devotional practices non-Vedic in origin.

A *yajna* is always purposeful, even though the aim may be as general as sustaining the natural order of the universe. Correct performance of the ritual and recitation of the necessary *mantras,* or sacred formulae, is considered essential; and the performer and the objects employed must all be in a high state of purity. Such ritual requirements gave rise to the professional class of priests, the modern Brahmins, who are still required to officiate at all important public *yajnas*. Many orthodox Hindu householders continue to perform the *mahayajnas,* the five daily domestic offerings.

Yajurveda, collection of short formulae that forms part of the Vedas of ancient India. There are two recensions of the Yajurveda. The Krishna, or "Black" Yajurveda, is a mixture of prose and verse and is composed of three distinct books. The Shukla, or "White" Yajurveda, is composed of a single book in verse.

Yakshagana, open-air dance drama popular in Tamil Nadu and Karnataka States of India, it is traditionally performed by men dressed as women, the actors take their cue from the chief narrator who also sits on the stage, along with a chorus of singers and musicians.

The form is comparable to kathakali (from Kerala State) and terukkuttu ("street drama") and kuravanji ("gypsy drama") from Tamil Nadu. The earliest Telugu yakshagana text is *Sugriva Vijayam* (c. 1570) by Kandukuru Rudra Kavi; the earliest in Kannada is probably Shantavira Deshika's *Saundareshvara* (1678). The most celebrated Kannada yakshagana dramatist is the versatile Parti Subba, who flourished around 1800 and is known for his moving episodes and songs from the Ramayana.

The mythological dance-dramas were composed by sixteenth-century Telugu poets, several of whom had based themselves in Thanjavur, Madurai, and Mysore.

Yantra, in Tantric Hinduism and Vajrayana and Tantric Buddhism, it is a linear diagram used as a support for meditation.

One characteristic *yantra* employed in the ritual worship of the goddess Shakti is the *shriyantra* (also called *shrichakra,* "wheel of Shri"). It is composed of nine triangles: five pointing downwards, said to represent the *yoni,* and four pointing upwards, said to represent the *lingam*. The dynamic interplay is understood to be an expression of all the cosmic manifestations, beginning and ending with union at the centre, visualized as a dot (*bindu*).

In its more elaborate and pictorial form it is called a *mandala*. *Yantras* range from those traced on the ground or on paper and disposed of after the rite, to those etched in stone and metal, such as are found in temples. When used along with yogic practices, the components parts of the *yantra* diagram take the believer along the different steps leading to Enlightenment.

Yashodharman, the ruler of Malwa in central India during the first half of the sixth century C.E. He is famous for having defeated the Huna leader, Mihirkula, and driven him back. Yashodharman erected two victory pillars in Mandasore. Their inscriptions credit him with very wide domains and many military victories over his adversaries far and near. Nothing further has been discovered as yet about his antecedents, his successors, or his other achievements.

Yashovarman, is a name or title belonging to several famous Kings of early times. *One* ruled Kanauj in the eighth century C.E., sent friendly emissaries to the Tang Dynasty in China, and was the patron of Sanskrit literati, including Bhavbhuti. *Another* was a ninth-century ruler of Kambuja (present-day Kampuchea) whose numerous stone inscriptions were written in the Sanskrit language, using both the Devanagari script and the more commonly used script of Kambuja, and testified to the close ties between India and Southeast Asian kingdoms at the time. A *third* Yashovarman was a tenth-century Chandella King who battled against the Pratihara armies and built one of the distinctive Vishnu temples at Khajuraho.

Yavana, in early Indian literature, is either a Greek or other foreigner. The word was probably adopted by the Indians of the northwestern provinces from this source, and its earliest attested use in India is by the grammarian Panini (c. fifth century BC) in the form Yavanani, which is taken by commentators to mean the Greek script. At that date the name probably referred to the communities of Greeks settled in the eastern Achaemenian provinces.

From the time of Alexander the Great (c. 334 BC) Yavana came to be applied more specifically to the Greek kingdom of Bactria, and, even more specifically, after about 175 BC, to the Indo-Greek kingdom in the Punjab. Indian sources of that time regarded the Yavanas as a barbarian people of the northwest. From the beginning of the Christian era the word was often used loosely to refer to any foreigner; and at a much later date it was frequently applied to the Muslim invaders of India.

The word appears in Archaemenian (Persian) inscriptions in the forms Yauna and Ia-ma-nu and refers to the Ionian Greeks of Asia Minor, who were conquered by the Achaemenid king Cyrus the Great in 545 BC.

Yoga, one of the six orthodox system (*darshanas*) of Indian philosophy, its influence has been widespread among many other schools of Indian thought. Yogasutras by Patanjali (second century BC?) is its basic text. In the twentieth century, the philosophy and practice of Yoga became increasingly popular in the West. The first important organization for practitioners in the United States was the Self-Realization Fellowship, founded by Paramahamsa Yogananda in 1920. Some 50 years later, instruction emphasizing both the physical and spiritual benefits of Yogic techniques was available through a wide variety of sectarian Yoga organizations, nonsectarian classes, and television programmes in the United States and Europe.

Generally the Yoga process is described in eight stages (*ashtanga-yoga*, "eight-membered Yoga"). The first two stages are ethical preparations. They are *yama* ("restraint"), which denotes abstinence from causing injury (*ahimsa*), falsehood, stealing, lust, and avarice; and *niyama* ("observance"), which denotes cleanliness of body, contentment, austerity, study, and devotion to God. The next two stages are physical preparations. *Asana* ("seat"), a series of exercises in physical posture, is intended to condition the aspirant's body and make it supple, flexible, and healthy. Mastery of the *asanas* is reckoned by the ability to hold one of the prescribed postures for an extended period of time without involutnary movement or physical distractions. *Pranayama* ("breath control") is a series of exercises intended to stabilize the rhythm of breathing in order to encourage complete respiratory relaxation. The fifth stage, *pratyahara* ("withdrawal"), involves control of the senses, or the ability to withdraw the attention of the senses from outward objects to the mind.

The first five stages are called external aids to Yoga; the remaining three are purely mental or internal aids. *Dharana* ("holding on") is the ability to hold and confine awareness of externals to one object of meditation, such as the tip of the nose or an image of the deity. *Dhyana* ("concentrated meditation") is the uninterrupted contemplation of the object of meditation, beyond any memory of ego. *Samadhi* ("self-collectedness") is the final stage and is a precondition of attaining release from the cycle of rebirth. In this stage the meditator perceives or experiences the object of his meditation and himself as one.

The practical aspects of Yoga play a more important part than does its intellectual content, which is largely based on the philosophy of Samkhya. However, unlike Samkhya, Yoga assumes the existence of God, who is the model for the aspirant to spiritual release. Yoga holds with Samkhya that the achievement of spiritual liberation occurs when the self (*purusha*) is freed from the bondages of matter (*prakriti*) that have resulted because of ignorance and illusion. The Samkhya view of the evolution of the world through identifiable stages leads Yoga to an attempt to reverse this order, as it were, so that a person can increasingly detach himself until the self re-enters its original state of purity and consciousness. Once the aspirant has learned to control and suppress the obscuring mental activities of his mind and has succeeded in ending his attrachment to material objects, he will be able to enter *samadhi*, a state of deep concentration that results in a blissful, ecstatic union with the ultimate reality.

The prehistory of Yoga is not clear. The early Vedic texts speak of ecstatics, who may well have been predecessors of the later *yogis* (followers of Yoga). Although Yoga has been made into a separate school (*darshana*), its influence and many of its practices have been felt in other schools.

In course of time, certain stages of Yoga became ends in themselves, notably, the breathing exercises and sitting postures, as in the Yoga school of Hatha Yoga. Patanjali's Yoga is sometimes known as Raja ("Royal") Yoga, to distinguish it from the other schools.

Yoga, in a less technical sense of achieving union with God, is also used, as in the epic poem the Bhagavadgita, to distinguish the alternate paths (*margas*) to such a union.

Yogachara, also called Vijnanavada ("Doctrine of Consciousness"), is an important idealistic school of Mahayana Buddhism. The school emerged in India about the second century AD but had its period of greatest productivity in the fourth century, during the time of Ashanga and Vasubandha. Following them, the school divided into two branches, the Agamanusarino Vijnanavadinah ("Vijnanavada School of the Scriptural Tradition") and the Nyayanusarino Vijnanavadinah ("Vijnanavada School of the Logical Tradition"), the latter subschool postulating the views of the logician Dignaga (c. AD 480-540) and his successor, Dharmakirti (c. AD 600-660). Yogachara attacked both the complete realism of Theravada Buddhism and the provisional practical realism of the Madhyamika school of Mahayana Buddhism. The name of the school is derived from the title of an important fourth or fifth century text of the school, the *Yogacharabhumi-shastra* ("The Science of the Stages of Yoga Practice").

The other name of the school, Vijnanavada, is more descriptive of its philosophical position, which is that the reality a human being perceives does not exist, any more than do the images called up by a monk in meditation. Only the consciousness that one has of the momentary interconnected events (*dharmas*) that make up the cosmic flux can be said to exist. Consciousness, however, also clearly discerns in these so-called unreal events consistent patterns of continuity and regularity; in order to explain this order in which only chaos really could prevail, the school developed the tenet of the *alaya-vijnana*, or "storage consciousness". Sense perceptions are ordered as coherent and regular by a store of consciousness, of which one is consciously unaware. Sense impressions produce certain configurations (*samskaras*) in this unconscious that "perfume" later impressions so that they appear consistent and regular. Each being possesses this storage consciousness, which thus becomes a kind of collective consciousness that orders human perceptions of the world, though this world does not exist. This doctrine was cheerfully attacked by the adherents of the Madhyamika school of Mahayana Buddhism, who pointed out the obvious logical difficulties of such a tenet.

Apart from human consciousness, another principle accepted as real, was the so-called suchness (*tathata*), which was the equivalent of the void (*shunya*) of the Madhyamika school.

The teachings of the Yogachara school were introduced into China by the seventh-century monk-traveller Hsuan-tsang (Xuanzang) and formed the basis of the Fa-hsiang (Faxian) school founded by Hsuan-tsang's pupil K'uei-chi (Kuiji). Because of its idealistic content it is also called Wei-shih (Weishi) ("Ideation Only").

Transmitted to Japan, as Hosso, sometime after 654, the Yogachara school split into two branches, the northern and the southern. During the eighth century it enjoyed a period of political influence and produced such celebrated priests as Gembo and Dokyo. In modern times the school retained the important temples of Horyu, Yakushi, and Kofuku, all located in or near Nara and all treasure houses of Japanese religious art.

Yoni, in Hinduism, is iconic representation of the female sexual organ and the symbol of the goddess Shakti, feminine generative power and, as a goddess, consort of Shiva. The *yoni* is often associated in the iconography of Shaivism together with the *lingam*, Shiva's symbol. The *lingam* is depicted in sculpture and paintings as resting in the *yoni* as a cylinder in a spouted dish. The two symbols together represent the eternal process of creation and regeneration.

Yuga, an age in Hindu cosmology, each *yuga* is shorter than the preceding one, corresponding to a decline in the moral and physical state of humanity. Four such *yugas* (called Krita, Treta, Dvapara, and Kali, or Satya, after throws of declining value in an ancient Indian game of dice) make up a *mahayuga* ("great epoch"), and 2,000 *mahayugas* make up the basic cosmic cycle, the *kalpa*. The first *yuga* (Krita) was an age of perfection, lasting, according to some calculations, 1,728,000 years. The fourth and most degenerate *yuga* (Kali) began in 3102 BC and will last 432,000 years. At the close of the Kali *yuga*, the world will be destroyed by fire and flood, to be recreated after a period of quiescence as the cycle resumes. In a partially competing vision of time, Vishnu's tenth and final *avatar*, Kalki, is described as bringing the present cosmic cycle to a close by destroying the evil forces that rule the Kali *yuga* and ushering in an immediate return to the idyllic Krita *yuga*.

Section Three
The Chronology

Major Dates and Events of Ancient India

B.C.

3000-1500	Indus Valley Civilization
1500-800	Early Vedic Period.
800-500	Later Vedic Period.
560-467	Life and Times of Lord Mahavira.
556-468	Life and Times of Gautama Buddha.
513-485	Reign of Bimbisara in Magadha.
362-321	Nanda Dynasty
326-325	Alexander of Macedon Crosses Indus River.
323	Death of Alexander in Babylon.
321	Accession of Chandragupta Maurya.
321-184	Mauryan Empire.
268-232	Reign of Ashoka.
261	Ashoka captured Kalinga (Orissa) after a sanguinary battle near Bhubaneswar. The great devastation and miserable suffering of the people after the bitter fight brought profound remorse in Ashoka's mind. Since then he took refuge in the Law of Duty and Piety.
259	Ashoka abolished royal hunting of animals, it being contrary to the Buddhist teaching not to take the life of a man or a beast.
251	On the initiative of King Dewanampiya Tissa of Ceylon, Ashoka sent a mission of Buddhism to Ceylon, led by his son Mahendra and daughter Sanghmitra.
250	The third Buddhist Council was held in Pataliputra.

249 Ashoka made a pilgrimage to Lumbini, the birth-place of Buddha, alongwith his preceptor Upagupta and daughter Charumati and erected a 11-metre high monolithic pillar to mark the birth place. His journey was marked by five monolithic pillars on the way.

242 Ashoka made the seven pillar edicts laying down the code of regulations.

240 Emperor Ashoka became a monk and started wearing yellow robe.

232 Ashoka died after a very long reign in the history of India.

220 Simuka established Satavahana (Satakarni) dynasty in Andhra, which ruled till 236 A.D. After a few years he became very wicked. He was dethroned and killed.

209 Kharavela, King of Kalinga, was born. (d. 172 B.C.)

206 Antiochus the Great of Syria invaded North-Western India.

204 Ashoka's son Arahat Mahendra died in Ceylon.

203 Ashoka's daughter Sangamitra died in Ceylon.

185 Coronation of Kharavela took place as the King of Kalinga.

184 Pushyamitra Sunga usurped the Magadha throne and started Sunga dynasty which ruled Magadha till 72 B.C. Pushyamitra was the Commander-in-Chief of the Maurya King Brihadratha, whom he killed while reviewing the army. Pushyamitra was perhaps an Iranian, but with Brahmin orthodoxy. Patanjali II, the celebrated grammarian, was possibly Pushyamitra's contemporary and witnessed the 'Ashwamedh Yajna' performed by Pushyamitra.

180 Menandar, a Greek King, invaded North-Western India and became the Indo-Greek ruler there till 160 B.C.

174 Kharavela annihilated Pithunda and broke the Tamil Confederacy.

173 Kharavela invaded Magadha.

172 Kharavela convened a council of Jain monks, which

	met on Mt. Kumari of Udaygiri Hill in Orissa, and was attended by nearly 3,500 monks.
	Kharavela died. (b. 209 B.C.)
140	Antialkidas, a Greek, became the King of Taxila and ruled till 130 B.C.
80	Malles became the first Saka King of Western India.
72	Devabhuti, the last Sunga King, was killed in an intrigue of his Brahmin Minister Vasudeva, who founded a shortlived Kanva dynasty of Magadha. (ended 27 B.C.)
65	The teachers sent to India by the Chinese Emperor Ming-ti went back to China and Buddhism was introduced there.
57	Vikramaditya, the famous King of Ujjain, ascended the throne by repelling the Saka invaders who earlier overthrew Vikramaditya's father Gardhabhilla. Vikram era started from that date. He built the famous Mahakala Temple in Ujjain which was destroyed by Altamash (Iltutmish) in 1234 A.D.
27	Susarman, the Kanva King of Magadha, was probably killed by Sata Satkarni belonging to Satavahana dynasty. Thus ended the Kanva dynasty of Magadha.
21	The joint Indian mission from mighty kingdoms of Pandya, Chola, and Chera, which sailed from Broach in 25 B.C., was presented to Emperor Augustus in Rome on terms of equality.
A.D.	
10	Huemo Kadphises I, the Kushana Chief, invaded India and established his authority in North-Western India.
45	At the death of Kadphises I at the age of eighty, his son Wimakadphises or Kodphises II succeeded him.
52	Apostle St. Thomas' Mission (Thomas Dadymus) arrived in India by the North-Western route. He was the first person to preach Christianity in India. He established a small church at Mylapur in Madras, known as St. Thomas Church, where he was buried.

67 Kashyapa Matanga is the first Indian scholar to visit China. He settled down at Lo Yang by the Lo river.

68 Ten thousand Jewish refugees with their families emigrated from Jerusalem to the Malabar coast, after the destruction of the second Temple of Jerusalem.

St. Thomas was killed at Mylapur in Madras.

69 Hala, the seventeenth Satavahana King, ascended the throne. Prakrit literature flourished under his patronage.

78 Kanishka ascended the Kushana throne, who extended his authority to Punjab and Uttar Pradesh. He introduced 'Saka' era, probably to commemorate his coronation. His relationship to the previous monarchs Kadphises I or II is not known.

100 Kanishka, with his religious preceptor Parswa, summoned a Buddhist council on the lines of that of Pataliputra.

111 Kushana King Kanishka was suffocated to death with his quilt at the instance of his minister Mathara and other chiefs, since, Kanishka was considered too ambitious and greedy to rule the world. Huvishka succeeded Kanishka as the Kushana ruler.

126 Vilivayakura II Gautamiputra, the Satavahana ruler, expelled the Saka invaders from North-Western Deccan.

138 An Indian embassy was sent to Roman Emperor Antonius Pius.

145 Rudradaman, the Saka king, attacked his son-in-law Pulumayi II of Satavahana dynasty, and grabbed a large portion of his territory.

155 Pandya army of South India invaded Ceylon and captured the capital Anuradhapura.

180 Kushana ruler Huvishka died and was succeeded by Vasudeva during whose regime the Kushana empire started to break up.

200 Chinese monk Chang Yang Sung visited Nicobar Island, which supposedly got its name from the monk's writings 'Lo Jen Quo' or Land of Naked, and

'Nalo Chen Quo' or Land of Cocoanut.

209 Chinese monk Chang Yang Sung arrived at Andaman Island.

226 Kushana ruler Vasudeva died and Kushana power collapsed.

236 Satavahana dynasty virtually extinguished; although a branch line, the Chutus, continued to rule around Vanavasi, a city in South Maharashtra. Abhiras (foreigners) succeeded Satavahanas and ruled for 67 years. Isvarasena was perhaps the founder of this shortlived dynasty called 'Kalchuri'.

305 Ghatotkacha, father of Chandragupta I, established himself as a feudal ruler in Pataliputra.

319 Chandragupta I succeeded his father Ghatotkacha in Pataliputra on February 26 and established Gupta dynasty. The epoch making Gupta era began.

345 Thomas Cana, a merchant from Syria, came to Travancore and founded a Christian colony there.

360 Meghavarna, King of Ceylon, who earlier concluded a treaty of alliance in 352, sent an embassy to Samudragupta's Court in Pataliputra, for the permission to erect a monastery in Bodh Gaya where people could live in comfort. The embassy included one of the brothers of King Meghavarna.

399 Fa-Hsian of China visited India by land route to collect Buddhist manuscripts, texts etc. He left India in 414 by sea route and died in the same year.

401 Buddhist inscriptions of Udaygiri was made.

412 Buddhist inscriptions of Sanchi were made.

431 Gunavarman, the Crown Prince of Kashmir who converted the Javanese to Buddhism, died in Nanking of China.

432 Buddhist inscriptions of Mathura were made.

455 Skandagupta was the last renowned Gupta ruler of Pataliputra. After his death in 480 Gupta empire declined, but lasted for about a century thereafter. The first white Hun attack under Chu-Khan (Konkha) on Gupta empire was repulsed.

457 The famous Jain temple of Girnar in Gujarat with nearly 4,000 steps was built.

465 The Huns under Toramana entered India.

470 Nayan Pal conquered Kanauj slaying its monarch Ajaipal. The race was since then named as Kanauj Rathore. Jaichand was the last monarch of Kanauj.

473 Kesari family obtained the throne of Orissa and held it till 1131.

476 Aryabhatta, the astronomer and mathematician, was born in Kusumapura (Pataliputra). He is supposed to be the inventor of Algebra, and the author of Aryashtaka and Dasagitika.

495 Ballabhi dynasty was esatblished in Gujarat by Senapati Bhattarka, who defeated a foreign tribe called Maitraka, probably of Iranian origin.

500 The Hun leader Toramana established himself in the Central India as a Maharaja.

505 Varahamihir, the astronomer, was born. (d. 587)

510 The Hun leader Toramana was defeated and perhaps died in the battle with Bhanu Gupta of Gupta dynasty of Pataliputra. Toramana was succeeded by his son Mihirkula, who made Sialkot of Punjab his capital. Mihirkula was branded as a blood-thirsty tyrant.

522 Bhaskara I, the great Indian mathematician, was born.

524 Nasirban, King of Persia, attacked Gujarat. The Rajput King lost and fled. His queen gave birth to a child in a cave and he was named Grahaditya or Gaho, who was the 135th ancestor of the Ranas of Udaipur.

528 The combined forces of Isana Varman (Yashodharman), Maukhari King of Malwa and Narasimhagupta Baladitya, King of Magadha, defeated the Hun leader Mihirkula, who retired to Kashmir and captured the throne there. Huns thereafter never seriously threatened India.

542 The Hun Chief Mihirkula died in Kashmir.

587 Astronomer Varahamihir died. (b. 505)

598 Brahmagupta, the astronomer, was born. He developed the usage of 'Shunya' or zero. He was the author of *Brahmasphuta-Siddhanta*.

600 Mahendravarman I established Pallava dynasty in Kanchipuram, which lasted till 894.

605 After the death of Prabhakarvardhana, King of Thaneswar, his son Rajyavardhana II became the King. But he was treacherously killed the next year by Sasanka, King of Gaur (Bengal).

Grahavarman, Maukhari King of Kanauj and husband of Harshavardhana's sister Rajyashree, was defeated and killed by the King of Malwa.

606 Prabhakarvardhana's younger son Harshavardhana took the thrones of Thaneswar and Kanauj at the age of about seventeen years as prince Siladitya. His formal coronation was delayed till 612.

609 Chalukya Prince Pulakesin II came of age. But his uncle Mangalesha, the Regent for the young prince, refused to hand over the kingdom. Pulakesin II by his own prowess waged war on Mangalesha, killed him in battle and declared himself the King. He was the ablest monarch of the dynasty.

Aihole inscriptions were made during the rule of Chalukya (Badami) King Pulakesin II.

612 Harshavardhana's formal coronation took place in October and he took the title 'Rajaputra'.

Harshavardhana held a religious conference in Prayag.

620 Bana wrote 'Harsha-Charita'.

622 The Muslim year 'Hijri' began and is now followed by the Muslims everywhere.

625 Pulakesin II sent an embassy to Persian court of Khusru II.

629 Hiuen Tsang (b. 600) came to India alone by land route. The traveller-pilgrim sojourned in different parts of India and left India in 645 and died in China in 664.

636 The first recorded Arab expedition in India took

place by a naval enterprise under Uthman-ath-Thakafi, Governor of Bahrain. It plundered the West Coast of India, during the rule of Caliph Omar bin Khattab, perhaps without his knowledge.

637 Sasanka, King of Gaur (Bengal), died. It ushered in a political turmoil in Bengal. Anarchy continued until Gopala was made the King of Bengal in 750 by the people themselves.

641 Harshavardhana despatched a Brahmin envoy to Tai Tsung, the second Tang Emperor of China.

642 Chalukya King Pulakesin II of Maharashtra was utterly defeated by Narasimhavarman I, the Pallava King of Kanchipuram, perhaps with the assistance of King of Ceylon.

643 Harshavardhana launched a campaign against Ganjam, which was his last military campaign.

644 Harshavardhana organised 'Kumbh Mela' at Prayag near Allahabad which was perhaps the sixth one.

645 Hiuen Tsang left India.

647 Harshavardhana died.

Tai Sung sent an envoy named Wang Hiuen Tse to Harshavardhana's court. Harshvardhana died before his arrival. Arjuna, an ex-minister of Harshavardhana, usurped his throne. He attacked Tse who escaped to Tibet.

648 Strong-Tsang Gampo, King of Tibet, sent an army with Wang Hiuen Tse, which attacked and captured Trihut of Bihar. Arjuna was caught and taken to Tibet. Trihut was under Tibet's rule till 703.

657 Wang Hiuen Tse again came to India through Nepal and visited sacred spots like Vaisali, Bodh Gaya etc. He returned home through Afghanistan and Pamir.

662 Munjala, the astronomer, wrote *Laghumanasa Ganakatarangini*.

672 Chinese pilgrim I-Tsing reached India. He took up his residence in Nalanda monastery in 675 and returned to China in 695.

710 A small Arab trading vessel from Basra arrived at

the mouth of the Indus and was promptly seized by the local Hindu authorities.

712 Arabs under the command of Muhammad Bin Quasim, attacked and captured Sind. Debal fell in April. Muhammad defeated and killed Dahir, the Hindu King, at Rawar on June 20. He then took the capital Alor in the same month. The widow queen and other women burnt themselves to death to escape dishonour. All males of the age of 17 years and above, who refused to embrace Islam, were killed. But the Arabs lost control in 779. Thereafter Sind continued as a small independent Muslim State.

713 Bappa of Guhila (Gehlote) dynasty of Mewar was born. He belonged to the Surya (Solar) race and theoretically was the 142nd generation from Brahma. Arabs captured Multan.

724 Lalitaditya I Muktapida of Naga or Karnataka dynasty, the most famous of all Kashmir rulers and the builder of renowned Martanda temple, succeeded to the throne of Kashmir.

731 King Yashovarmana of Kanauj sent an embassy to the Emperor of China for his assistance against Yashovarmana's enemies.

735 Bappa's son Guhila captured Chittorgarh throne from Manmori belonging to Paramar dynasty. He established the Guhila dynasty of Mewar.

736 Dhillika, the first city of Delhi, was founded by Anangapal Tuar, the Tomara prince. Tomaras (Tuars) ruled in the Haryana region and they belonged to one of the 36 celebrated Rajput tribes. Tomara rule of Delhi ended in 1151 when Visala Deva, one of the Chauhans of Ajmer, captured Delhi.

740 King Yashovarmana of Kanauj was defeated and slain by Lalitaditya I Muktapida of Kashmir.

746 Vanaraja, Prince of Deo, laid the foundation of Anhilwara Patan of Rajasthan.

750 After a prolonged anarchy in Bengal since the death of Sasanka in 637, people of Bengal selected Gopala as their King. Gopala ruled till 770 and founded Pala dynasty in Eastern India, which lasted for about 450 years. Gopala revived Nalanda University.

760 Krishna I succeeded to the throne of Rastrakutas. His reign is famous for the rock-cut Kailasha temple of Ellora, the most extensive and sumptuous of the rock-cut shrines in India. The size is 84 mt. x 47 mt. and the height is 32.8 mt.

764 Bappa was defeated by the 21st Caliph Al Mansoor. Bappa, after the defeat, departed for Persia (Iran) and perhaps never returned to India.

770 Dharmapala succeeded Gopala in Bengal. He raised the Pala Kingdom to imperial power and virtually became the Emperor of Northern India. He founded Vikramsila University near Bhagalpur.

774 A Jewish colony settled down in Cochin.

779 After Lalitaditya's death in 760, four weak Kings ruled Kashmir. Then Jayapida Vinayaditya ascended the throne of Kashmir. Jayapida revived the glory of Naga (Karnataka) dynasty.

Caliph Mutahid appointed Yaqub ibn Lail's Saffari as the Governor of Sind. From the date Sind became virtually independent of Khilafat.

784 Jinasena completed 'Harivansa Purana' of the Digambar Jains.

788 Adi Sankaracharya was born at Kaladi in Kerala. He founded four 'Mathas' in four corners of India at Sringeri, Puri, Dwarka and Joshi (Badrinath), for the resurrection of Hindu religion. He attained 'Samadhi' at Badrinath in 820.

794 Govinda III, son of Dhruva, became the Rashtrakuta King and was the most remarkable ruler of his dynasty. He expanded his territory over a vast area. He shifted his capital from Nasik to Manyakheta and ruled til 814.

809 Manikya, the Indian physician, was called to the court of Karun-ur-Rashid of Arabia to attend to his illness.

810 Devapala became the King of Bengal. During his reign he deposed the reigning King of Kanauj and

put his own nominee on Kanauj throne. Devapala had 50,000 elephants in his army.

814 Amoghavarsha I, son of Govinda III, became the Rashtrakuta King. He was a devout Jain. But he did not hesitate to cut off one of his fingers and to offer it to Goddess Mahalakshmi to propitiate her to remove the epidemic which was ravaging his kingdom.

816 One Nagabhatta, a descendant of Nagabhata of Gurjara-Pratihara dynasty, captured Kanauj from the nominee of Devapala. Nagabhata's descendants ruled Kanauj till 1017 when Sultan Mahmud of Ghazni captured it.

820 Adi Sankaracharya attained Samadhi at Badrinath.

831 The Chandellas of Bundelkhand or Jejakabhukti first came into notice, when Nanika Chandella overthrew a Parihar chief and became the lord of Bundelkhand.

840 Mihira Pratihara, commonly known as Raja Bhoj, became the King of Gurjara-Pratihara empire. He was a great patron of magic. During his rule, Gurjaras rose to a great height. His rule continued till 885.

855 Avantivarman of Utpala dynasty started his reign in Kashmir. He was notable for his enlightened patronage of literature, his beneficent work like drainage and irrigation schemes.

883 After Avantivarman, Sasankavarman was the next King of Kashmir. He was obsessed for his love for fiscal oppression and plunder of temple treasures.

885 Mahendrapala I, son of Raja Bhoj, succeeded to the Gurjara-Pratihara throne. During his regime, Gurjara-Pratihara empire reached its zenith. He drove the Palas of Bengal out of Magadha.

894 The idol of Sriranganathaswamy of Srirangapatnam was installed.

916 Mahipala, I, the Gurjara-Pratihara King, suffered a severe set-back when Indra III, the Rashtrakuta King of Deccan captured Kanauj and plundered Pratihara territory upto Prayag near Allahabad.

942 Mularaja became the King of Gujarat and founded Solanki dynasty of Anhilwara.

949 The war between Cholas and Rashtrakutas was remarkable for the death of Chola King Rajaditya I on the battlefield. Much bitterness developed between Jainism and orthodox Hinduism.

950 Kshemagupta of Pravagupta dynasty became King of Kashmir and married Didda, daughter of King Simharaja of Laharu. These two are the most notorious couple in Indian history. After Kshemagupta's death in 958, Didda virtually ruled Kashmir. She had no mercy, no scruple, indulged in sex with royal officers and murdered her two grandsons Tribhuvana and Bhimagupta to sit on Kashmir throne in 980.

955 Dhanga, the most powerful Chandella King, sat on the throne. Some of the grandest Khajuraho temples were built during his regime. He joined Jaipal to resist Subuktigin in 977.

967 Dhola Rai, the expelled son of Sova Singh of Gwalior, laid the foundation of the State of Dhandoor, later Amber and now Jaipur.

973 Nurmadi Taila II established Chalukya dynasty in Kalyani of South India. Much of his time was spent in fighting Munja, the Paramar Raja of Dhara, who claimed sixteen victories. On the seventeenth encounter in 995, Munja was caught, forced to beg from door to door and ultimately beheaded.

Al Biruni or Abu Ar Rayhan Muhammad Bin Ahmed was born in Birun of Uzbekistan. His famous history of India 'Tarikh Al Hind' gives a comprehensive survey of India of the 11th century. He also excelled in philosophy, astronomy, physics, chemistry, medicine and Sanskrit. (d. 1048)

977 Chandella King Dhanga of Khajuraho fame and King Jaipal of Lahore, jointly and successfully, opposed Subuktigin.

979 King Jaipal of Lahore encountered Subuktigin at Luckman. A treaty was agreed upon.

981 The 17 mt. high world's biggest monolith statue of

Gomateswara (meaning a handsome man) was erected by King Vira Pandiya on Vindhya Hill at Sravana Belgola for Bahubali, son of Vrishava, the first Tirthankar.

982 Atisa (Dipankar Srijnana), the Buddhist sage of Magadha, was born. He went to Tibet in 1038 and died near Lhasa in 1053.

997 After Taila's death the Chalukya crown was transmitted to his son Satyashraya. During his reign Chalukya kingdom suffered heavily from the invasion by the Chola King Rajaraja I.

1000 Sultan Mahmud of Ghazni, a Turk, haunted on India's border and captured some frontier posts.

1001 Sultan Mahmud of Ghazni made his first real expedition to India and began his crusade against the Hindus. He defeated King Jaipal at Peshawar on November 27. The proud King, unable to withstand the humiliation of defeat, burnt himself to death. His son Anandapal succeeded him. Mahmud's fourteenth and last expedition was in 1026.

1006 Mahmud had his second expedition to India against Raja Bhira Rao and captured the fortress of Bhatia in Bikaner desert.

The same year Mahmud made his third expedition against his subordinate Wali of Multan.

1007 Mahmud was on his fourth expedition to India against Sukpal, a Hindu converted to Islam, whom he made the Governor of some of his conquered territories.

1009 Mahmud's fifth expedition was against Anandapal, son of Jaipal, and captured Nagarkote near Lahore. He carried away 7 tonnes of pure gold, 7 tonnes of jewels and 25 tonnes of gold and silver utensils from the temples in Nagarkote.

In Mahmud's sixth expedition he captured Narain, capital of Matsya.

1010 Mahmud's seventh expedition to India was against Abul Fath Lodi, his own Governor of some of the conquered territories. Raja Bhoj, the renowned King of Paramar dynasty, ascended the throne of Malwa. In 1060 he was defeated by the allied armies of Gujarat and Chedi. This Raja Bhoj is different from that of Gurjara dynasty.

Chola King Rajaraja I consecrates the magnificent Siva temple Brihadeswara at Tanjavur. He also annexed the Maldive Islands.

1012 Rajaraja I and his son Rajendra I jointly ruled the Cholas for 2 years. Rajendra I completed the conquest of Ceylon which his father began.

1013 Mahmud was on his eighth expedition for plunder of India.

1014 Mahmud's ninth expedition was aimed at Thaneswar. He sacked the town and took two lakh Hindu captives from Thaneswar to Ghazni.

1015 In his tenth expedition Mahmud tried to penetrate into Kashmir, but could advance no further than Lohkot (presently Loharin).

1017 Mahmud, in his eleventh expedition, captured Kanauj from the ruler of Gurjara-Pratihara origin, as well as he took Mathura.

Acharya Ramanuja, the Vaishnava philosopher, was born in Sriparambudur in Chinglepet District.

1021 Mahmud advanced into India for the twelfth time to help the King of Kanauj, who was attacked by Nanda, King of Kalanjara. Trilochanapala of Lahore opposed and lost his life in the battle. Mahmud annexed Lahore to Ghazni and thus laid the foundation of future Muhammedan empire in India.

1023 Mahmud invaded India for the thirteenth time. He besieged Gwalior and brought Nanda, the Chandella Raja of Kalanjara, to terms.

The Chola King Rajendra I of Tanjore launched a campaign in North India and attacked Mahipala I of Bengal. Rajendra I prided himself on having advanced as far as the banks of the Ganga.

1026 Mahmud's fourteenth and last expedition in India was mainly aimed at Somnath temple. He plundred and completely destroyed the temple on January 8. In a desperate bid to save their deity, in three days 50,000 defenders sacrificed their lives. The idol was broken into pieces. Some of these pieces were taken to Ghazni where they were placed under the steps of a mosque. Mahmud took away the sandal-wood gates of the city as well. In 1842 Lord Ellenborough, Governor General of India, brought the gates back from Ghazni to India.

1027 The Sun Temple of Modehra in Gujarat was consecrated. It is one of the best Sun Temples from the point of view of stone sculpture and architectural designs. The chief image of the Sun is now missing.

1030 Sultan Mahmud of Ghazni died in his capital on April 30, much to the relief of the people of North India.

1032 Vrishavadeva Jain temple of Dilwara in Mt. Abu was built by Vimal Sah, a Jain merchant of Anhilwara.

1034 Masud, son of Sultan Mahmud of Ghazni, attacked and captured Kashmir.

1038 The mission of Atisa was sent to Tibet during the reign of Mahipala I in Bengal.

1053 Atisa died near Lhasa in Tibet.

1059 Somesvara I, the Chalukya King, fought Rajadhiraja, the Chola King at Koppam in Mysore. Rajadhiraja lost his life in the battle. Somesvara also defeated Raja Karna, the valiant King of Chedi. Somesvara later contacted some incurable disease. To end his suffering Somesvara drowned himself in the Tungabhadra river in 1069.

1063 Nabadwip town of Nadia District was founded by one of the Sena Kings of Bengal, who shifted his capital from Gaur of North Bengal to Nabadwip.

1070 Karnavati was founded by Karnadeva of Gujarat on the present site of Ahmedabad, which got the new name in 1411.

"Katha Sarit Sagar" was written by Somdeva Bhatta.

1076 Vikramaditya VI came to the Chalukya throne of Kalyani. He was the most remarkable ruler of his dynasty.

1077 Chalukya (Eastern) King Koluttunga Chodadeva I sent an embassy of 72 merchants to China.

1089 Utkarsha succeeded his father Kalasadeva of Kashmir, but he committed suicide in the same year. His younger brother Harshadeva became the King of Kashmir. Because of his cruelty, Harshadeva is branded as the "Nero of Kashmir".

Utpala dynasty of Kashmir ended in 1111.

1097 Vijaya Sena succeeded Hemanta Sena, who was a local chief in Burdwan Division. Vijaya Sena captured whole of Bengal and put to an end Pala rule of Bengal by defeating Madanapala.

1099 A great flood and famine devastated Kashmir in this and the following few years.

1114 Bhaskaracharya II, the great mathematician cum astronomer, was born. He wrote three books on astronomy, algebra and arithmetic. His famous book on arithmetic is known as "Lilavati", perhaps named after his daughter.

1120 Udayadya, brother of Vishnuvardhana of the Hoysala dynasty, built the township Srirangapatnam.

1121 Halebid of Karnataka was consecrated.

1143 The most important personality Kumarapala of Solanki or Chalukya dynasty of Saurastra, sat on the throne, succeeding the uncle Jayasimha-Siddharaja. He was an earnest Jain and a patron of the great Jain doctor Hemachandra.

1149 'Rajatarangini', the history of Kashmir in verse, was completed by Kalyana or Kalhana.

1150 Bhaskaracharya II wrote his great work Siddhantasiromoni, of which 'Lilavati' is one of the four parts.

Chodagangadeva, the founder of the Ganga dynasty of Orissa, died. The famous Jagannath Temple of Puri was constructed by him.

1151 Visala-Deva, a Chauhan chief of Ajmer, became the King of Delhi.

1156 The state of Jaisalmer was founded by Jaisal of Bhati tribe, a branch of Yadu race.

1159 Ballala Sena, the most famous of Sena Kings of Bengal, came to power.

1167 The mystic, religious and social reformer Basaveswara passed away. His date of birth is not known. He was born in Bijapur District of Karnataka. At one time he was the Chief Minister of King Bijjala's court, but that did not deter him from spiritual pursuit.

1169 Poet Jayadeva of Kendubilla village in Bengal wrote "Gita Govinda".

1173 Ghiyasuddin sat on Ghazni throne and jointly ruled with his brother Maizuddin. Ghiyasuddin was later known as Muhammad Ghori. Muhammad was the real founder of Muhammedan power in India.

1175 Muhammad Ghori made his first expedition to India, and captured Multan.

Prithviraj II or Rai Pithora abducted Sanyukta, daughter of Jaichand, and married her against Jaichand's wish.

1178 Muhammad Ghori tried to invade Gujarat but was defeated by Bhimadeva, King of Gujarat.

1182 Chandel Raja Paramardideva of Khajuraho was defeated by Prithviraj II Chauhan who captured Mahoba.

1185 The last notable ruler of Sena dynasty of Bengal, namely Lakshman Sena, sat on the throne of Bengal.

Bhaskaracharya II, the great astronomer, died. (b. 1114)

1187 The invincible Daulatabad fort near Aurangabad was built by the Hindu King of Devagiri. It was later named as Daulatabad fort.

1190 Hoysala King of Mysore obtained full independence from the Chalukyas of Kalyani, which came to an end in 1200 A.D.

1191 In the first battle of Tarain Muhammad Ghori was defeated and severely wounded by the combined

Hindu forces, under Prithviraj II Chauhan's leadership.

1192 In the second battle of Tarain, Muhammad Ghori assisted by Qutub-ud-din Aibek, a slave, defeated Prithviraj II, Chauhan who was captured and executed. His city of Ajmer was sacked and inhabitants massacred.

Prithviraj's son was appointed Governor of Ajmer. Muhammad proceeded toward Delhi, but its ruler submitted and Muhammad left Delhi unmolested.

Muhammad left his slave Qutub-ud-din Aibek behind to look after his conquests. Qutubuddin captured Meerut and Delhi.

Section Four
The Bibliography

Important Books on Ancient India

Aggarwal,. V.S., *India as Known to Panini*, Lucknow, 1953.

Aggarwal, Vasudev Sharan, *Paninikaleen Bharata Varsha* (Hindi).

Agni Purana, Anandasarma Sanskrit Series, Poona, 1957.

Agrawal, D.P. and A. Ghose, eds., *Radiocarbon and Indian Archaeology*, Bombay, 1973.

Airi, Raghunath, *Concept of Saraswati in Vedic Literature*, Delhi, 1977.

Aiyar, S.A., *Historical Index to the Study of Indian Temple Architecture*, Bombay, 1972.

Allichin, Bridget, and Raymond Allchin, *Rise of Civilization in India and Pakistan*, New Delhi, 1983.

Altekar, A.S., *Education in Ancient India*, Varanasi, 1965.

Altekar, A.S., *Rashtrakutas and Their Times*, Poona, 1934.

Altekar, A.S., *State and Government in Ancient India from Earliest Times to 1200 AD*, Banaras, 1962.

Aryan, K.C., *The Cultural Heritage of Punjab 3000 BC to 1947 AD*.

Association for Asian Studies, *Bibliography of Asian Studies*, Michigan, 1970 onwards, annually.

Atharva-Veda, The Hymns of Atharvaveda. Translated by Ralph T.H. Griffith, 2 Vols., Banaras, 1968.

Avalon, Arthur and Ellen Avalon, trans. *Hymns to the Goddess*, Madras, 1964.

Banerjea, Jitendra Nath, *The Development of Hindu Iconography*, 2nd ed., Calcutta, 1956.

Banerji, S.C., *Aspects of Ancient Indian Life from Sanskrit Sources*, Calcutta, 1972.

Banerji, Tarasankar, *Indian Historical Research Since Independence*, Calcutta, 1987.

Barua, B.M., *Ashoka and His Inscriptions*, Calcutta, 1946.

Basham, A.L., *The Wonder That Was India*, New York, 1954.

Basham, A.L., (ed.) *A Cultural History of India*, Oxford, 1975.

Beal, Samuel, trans., *Travels of Fa-hien and Sun-Yun, Buddhist Pilgrims from China to India (400-518 AD)*, London, 1964.

Bhandarkar, D.R., *Ashoka*, 3rd ed., Calcutta, 1955.

Bhandarkar, R.G., *Vaishnavism, Shaivism and Minor Religious Systems*.

Bhargava, L.P., *Chandragupta Maurya*, Lucknow, 1935.

Bhargava, Purushottam Lal, *India in the Vedic Age*, 2nd ed., Lucknow, 1971.

Bhattacharya, N.N., *Indian Mother Goddess*, Calcutta, 1971.

Bhattacharya, Narendra Nath, *History of the Shakta Religion*, New Delhi, 1974.

Bhattacharya, N.N., *History of the Tantrik Religion*, 1982.

Bhattacharya, N.N., *The Geographical Dictionary: Ancient and Early Mediaeval India*, New Delhi, 1991.

Bhattacharya, N.N., *Ancient Indian History and Civilization: Trends and Perspectives*, Delhi, 1988.

Bhattacharya, Sachchidananda, *A Dictionary of Indian History*, New York, 1967.

Bhattacharya, S. and Romila Thapar, eds., *Situating Indian History*, Oxford University Press, 1986.

Bhavani, E., *The Dance in India*, Bombay, 1965.

Bloomfield, M., *A Vedic Concordance*, Reprinted, Delhi, 1972.

Bongard-Levin, G., and A. Vigasin, *The Image of India: The Study of Ancient Indian Civilization in the USSR*, Moscow, 1984.

Bose, A.C., *Hymns from the Vedas*, Bombay, 1966.

Brown, Percy, *Indian Architecture*, 2 Vols., Bombay 1965-1968.

Chakravarti, Chintaharan, *Tantras—Studies in Their Religion and Literature*, Calcutta, 1972.

Chakraborti, H.P., *India as Reflected in the Inscriptions of the Gupta Period*, New Delhi, 1978.

Chakraborti, H.P., *Trade and Trade Routes in Ancient India*, New Delhi, 1977.

Chopra, P.N., *India: An Encyclopaedic Survey*, New Delhi, 1984.

Choudhary, Gulab Chanda, *Political History of Northern India from Jain Sources (650-1300 AD)*, Amritsar, 1964.

Choudhury, M., *Tribes of Ancient India*, Calcutta, 1977.

Coomaraswamy, Ananda K., *The Dance of Shiva*, New York, 1957.

Cunningham, A., *Inscriptions of Asoka*, Varanasi, 1961.

Cunningham, Alexander, *The Ancient Geography of India*, Reprinted, Varanasi, 1963.

Dandekar, R.N., *Vedic Bibliography*, Bombay, 1946.

Dandekar, R.N., *Vedic Religion and Philosophy*, Poona, 1965.

Dani, Ahmad Hasan, *The Historic City of Taxila*, Paris, 1986.

Dasgupta, *A History of Indian Philosophy*, Vol. I, Cambridge University Press, 1926.

Davids, T.W. Rhys, *Buddhist India*, Delhi, 1971.

Davies, Collin, *An Historical Atlas of the Indian Peninsula*, Delhi, 1949.

Dayananda Samsthan, *Rigveda Bhasha-Bhashya* (Hindi translation of Rigveda), 2 Vols., Delhi.

Derrett, J.D.N., *Hoysala: A Mediaeval Indian Royal Family*, Oxford University Press, 1957.

Devahuti, D., *Harsha: A Political Study*, Oxford University Press, 1968.

Devi Mahatmya, The Glorification of the Great Goddess. Edited and translated by Vasudeva S. Agrawal, Banaras, 1963.

Dey, N.L., *Geographical Dictionary of Ancient and Mediaeval India*, London, 1927.

Dikshit, K.N., *Pre-historic Civilization of the Indus Valley*, Madras, 1939.

Dikshit, Sadananda K., *The Mother Goddess*, New Delhi, 1957.

Dikshitar, V.R.R., *War in Ancient India*, 2nd ed., 1948.

Dutt, N.K., *Origin and Growth of Caste in India*, Calcutta, 1968.

Embree, Ainslie, ed. *Encyclopaedia of Asian Civilizations*, New York, 1988.

Fabri, Charles L., *An Introduction to Indian Architecture*, Bombay, 1963.

Fairservis, W.A., *The Roots of Ancient India: The Archaeology of Early Indian Civilization*, New York, 1971.

Farguhar, J.N., *An Outline of the Religious Literature of India*, Delhi, 1967.

Fauja Singh, *History of the Punjab from Pre-historic Times to the Age of Asoka*, Patiala, 1977.

Fergusson, J., *History of Indian and Eastern Architecture*, Delhi, 1967.

Frazer, Robert W., *A Literary History of India*, Delhi, 1984.

Ghoshal, U.N., *A History of Indian Political Ideas*, Oxford University Press, 1966.

Ghurye, G.S., *Caste and Race in India*, Bombay, 1969.

Ghurye, G.S., *Indian Acculturation: Agastya and Skanda*, Bombay, 1977.

Ghurye, G.S., *Vedic India*, Bombay, 1979.

Goetz, H., *The Art of India: Five Thousand Years of Indian Art*, New York, 1964.

Gokhale, B.G., *Asoka Maurya*, New York, 1966.

Goldman, R.P., *Gods, Priests and Warriors: The Bhrigus of the Mahabharata*, New York, 1977.

Gordon, D.H., *The Pre-historic Background of Indian Culture*, Bombay, 1950.

Grover, S., *The Architecture of India: Buddhist and Hindu*, New Delhi, 1980.

Gupta, V.P. and Mohini Gupta, *An Encyclopaedia of Punjabi Culture and History*, Delhi, 1999.

Gupta, V.P. and Mohini Gupta, *Mother Goddess: A Global Perspective*, Delhi, 1999.

Gupta, V.P. and Mohini Gupta, *An Encyclopaedia of the Twentieth Century*, Vol. I, Delhi, 2002.

Guruge, Ananda, *The Society of the Ramayana*, New Delhi, 1991.

Havell, E.B., *The Ancient and Mediaeval Architecture of India: A Study of Indo-Aryan Civilization*, London, 1915.

Holroyde, P., *Indian Music: A Vast Ocean of Promise*, London, 1972.

The Hymns of the Rigveda, Translated by Ralph T.H. Griffith, 4th ed., 2 Vols., Banaras, 1963.

India: Archaeological Survey, *Archaeological Remains: Monuments and Museums*, 2 Vols., Delhi, 1964.

Jaiswal, K.P., *Hindu Polity*, Bangalore, 1955.

Jayal, S., *The Status of Women in the Epics*, Delhi, 1966.

Jha, D.N., *Ancient India: An Introductory Outline*, New Delhi, 1977.

Joshi, L.M., *Studies in the Buddhist Culture of India*, Delhi, 1967.

Kalia, D.R. and M.K. Jain, *A Bibliography of Bibliographies in India*, Delhi, 1975.

Kane, P.V., *History of the Dharmshastras*, 5 Vols., Poona, 1930-1965.

Kangle, R.P. (ed.), *The Kautiliyan Arthasastra* (Edited and translated in English), Bombay, 1960-65.

Kanniyan, V., *Scripts in and Around India*, Madras, 1960.

Kapadia, K.M., *Hindu Kingship*, Bombay, 1947.

Kaul, H.K., *Early Writings on India: Books on India in the English Language Published Before 1900*, New Delhi, 1975.

Keith, A.B., *Religion and Philosophy of the Vedas and the Upanishads*, 2 Vols., Harvard University Press, 1925.

Kejariwal, O.P., *The Asiatic Society of Bengal and the Discovery of India's Past, 1784-1838*, Delhi, 1988.

Kelkar, S.V., *History of the Caste in India*, Jaipur, 1979.

Khan, Mohammad Israil, *Saraswati in Sanskrit Literature*, Ghaziabad, 1978.

Kosambi, Damodar D., *Myth and Reality: Studies in the Formation of Indian Culture*, Bombay, 1962.

Kosambi, Damodar D., *The Culture and Civilization of Ancient India*, New Delhi, 1970.

Kosambi, Damodar D., *Introduction to the Study of Indian History*, Bombay, 1975.

Kramirsch, Stella, *The Art of India: Traditions of Indian Sculpture, Painting and Architecture*, Greenwick, 1965.

Kramrisch, Stella, *The Hindu Temple*, Delhi, 1976.

Kramrisch, Stella, *Indian Sculpture*, London, 1981.

Krishnaswami, S., *Musical Instruments of India*, Boston, 1971.

Lach, Donald F., *Asia in the Making of Europe*, 2 Vols., Chicago, 1965.

Lahiri, B., *Indigenous States of Northern India (200 BC-320 AD)*, Calcutta, 1974.

Lahiri, Nayanjot, *The Archaeology of Indian Trade Routes upto 200 BC*, Oxford University Press, 1992.

Lal, B.B. and S.P. Gupta, eds. *Frontiers of the Indus Civilization*, New Delhi, 1984.

Law, B.C., *The Magadhas in Ancient India*, Delhi, 1976.

MacDonell, A.A., *A History of Sanskrit Literature*, Reprinted, Delhi, 1965.

MacDonell, A.A., *The Vedic Mythology*, Reprinted, Varanasi, 1963.

MacDonell, A.A., and A.B. Keith, *Vedic Index of Names and Subjects*, 2 Vols., Reprinted, Delhi, 1951.

Monty, P.K., *Historical Studies in the Cult of the Goddess*, Calcutta, 1966.

Maity, S.K., *Economic Life of Northern India in the Gupta Period*, Calcutta, 1957.

Majumdar, A.K., *Concise History of Ancient India*, 3 Vols., New Delhi, 1980.

Majumdar, R.C. (ed.), *The History and Culture of the Indian People*, 11 Vols., Bombay.

Majumdar, R.C., *Classical Accounts of India*, Calcutta, 1960.

Majumdar, R.C., *Corporate Life in Ancient India*, Calcutta, 1969.

Majumdar, R.C., (ed.) *The Age of Imperial Unity*, Bombay, 1960.

Majumdar, R.C., *The Classical Age*, Bombay, 1954.

Majumdar, R.C. and A.S. Altekar, eds., *The Vakataka and Gupta Age*, Delhi, 1967.

Majumdar, R.C. and A.D. Pusalker, eds., *The Vedic Age*, Bombay, 1953.

Majumdar, R.C., H.C. Roy Chaudhary and K. Datta, *An Advanced History of India*, London, 1950.

Mansingh, Surjit, *Historical Dictionary of India*, Delhi, 1998.

Marg, Bombay, *Buddhist Art: New Studies*, Vol. 39(4), 1986.

Marshall, John, *A Guide to Taxila*, Delhi, 1936.

Marshall, John, *Taxila*, 3 Vols., Cambridge, 1951.

Marshall, John (ed.), *Mohenjo-Daro and Indus Civilization*, 3 Vols., London, 1951.

Masica, Colin P., *The Indo-Aryan Languages*, Cambridge University Press, 1991.

Mayer, J.J., *Sexual Life in Ancient India*, 2nd ed., 1952.

McCrindle, J.W., *Ancient India as Described by Megasthenes and Asian*, Reprinted, Calcutta, 1926.

Mehta, Ratilal, *Pre-Buddhist India*, Delhi, 1985.

Metropolitan Museum of Art, *Indian Sculpture*, New York, 1985.

Mishra, P.K., *The Kadambas*, Allahabad, 1979.

Mitchell, G., *The Hindu Temple: An Introduction to Its Meaning and Forms*, London, 1977.

Mohan, V.M., *The Sakas in India and Their Impact on Indian Life and Culture*, Varanasi, 1976.

Movinder Williams, W., *Religious Thought and Life in India*, 4th ed., London, 1691.

Mookerji, R.K., *The Gupta Empire*, 4th ed., Delhi, 1969.

Motichandra, *The World of the Courtesans*, Delhi, 1973.

Mukerjee, Radha Kamal, *The Culture and Art of India*, London, 1959.

Mukerjee, R.K., *Fundamental Unity of India*, London, 1914.

Mukerjee, R.K., *Ancient Indian Education*, Reprinted, Delhi, 1962.

Mukerjee, R.K., *Chandragupta Maurya and His Times*, Delhi, 1952.

Mukerjee, R.K., *Hindu Civilization*, London, 1936.

Mukherji, B., *Kautilya's Concept of Diplomacy: A New Interpretation*, Calcutta, 1976.

Narain, A.K., *The Indo-Greeks*, Oxford University Press, 1962.

Pal, Pratapaditya, *Indian Sculpture 500 BC-AD 700*, Berkeley, 1986.

Pande, G.S., *Studies in the Origins of Buddhism*, Allahabad, 1957.

Pande, Raj Bali, *Vikramaditya of Ujjayni*, Banaras, 1951.

Piggot, S., *Prehistoric India to 1000 BC*, London, 1962.

Pike, E. Royston, *Ancient India*, London, 1979.

Pradhan, S.N., *Chronology of Ancient India*, Calcutta, 1927.

Puri, B.N., *India as Described by Early Greek Writers*, Allahabad, 1939.

Puri, B.N., *India Under the Kushans*, Bombay, 1965.

Prakash, Buddha, *Rigveda and the Indus Valley Civilization*, Hoshiarpur, 1966.

Ramakrishna Mission, *The Cultural Heritage of India*, 6 Vols., Calcutta, 1986.

Ramaswamy, T.N., *Essentials of Indian Statecraft: Kautilya's Arthasastra for Contemporary Readers*, Bombay, 1963.

Rao, S.R., *Dawn and Devolution of the Indus Civilization*, New Delhi, 1991.

Rao, S.R., *Progress and Prospects of Marine Archaeology in India*, New Delhi, 1993.

Rao, U. Venkata Krishna, *A Handbook of Classical Sanskrit Literature*, Bombay, 1967.

Rawlinson, H.G., *India: A Short Cultural History of India*, London, 1948.

Ray, A., *Villages, Towns and Secular Buildings in Ancient India 150 BC-350 AD*, Calcutta, 1964.

Raychaudhari, H.C., *Political History of Ancient India*, 6th ed., Calcutta, 1953.

Ray, N.R., ed., *Sources of the History of India*, 4 Vols., Calcutta, 1980-1984.

Renou, L., *Vedic India*, Translated from the French by P. Spratt, Delhi, 1971.

Robinson, Francis, ed. *The Cambridge of Encyclopaedia of India, Pakistan, Bangladesh, Sri Lanka, Nepal, Bhutan and the Maldives*, Cambridge University Press, 1989.

Sagar, K.C., *Foreign Influence on Ancient India*, New Delhi, 1992.

Saletore, B.A., *India's Diplomatic Relations with the East (300-1300 AD)*, Bombay, 1960.

Saletore, R.N., *Encyclopaedia of Indian Culture*, 5 Vols., New Delhi, 1981-85.

Sankalia, H.D., *Indian Archaeology Today*, Delhi, 1979.

Sankalia, H.D., *Prehistoric Art in India*, New Delhi, 1978.

Sarkar, S.S., *Ancient Races of the Deccan*, New Delhi, 1972.

Sastri, K.A. Nilakanta, *Age of the Nandas and Mauryas*, Banaras, 1967.

Sastri, K.A. Nilakanta, *Culture and History of the Tamils*, Calcutta, 1964.

Sastri, K.A. Nilakanta, *History of South India from Pre-historic Times to the Fall of Vijayanagar*, 3rd ed., Oxford University Press, 1966.

Sastri, K.A. Nilakanta, *Sources of Indian History with Special Reference to South India*, London, 1964.

Saxena, D.P., *Regional Geography of Vedic India*, Kanpur, 1976.

Sengupta, N., *Evolution of Hindu Marriage with Special Reference to Rituals 1000 BC-AD 500*, Bombay, 1965.

Sengupta, Padmini, *Everyday Life in Ancient India*, Oxford University Press, 1950.

Sen, S.P., ed. *Sources of the History of India*, 2 Vols., Calcutta, 1978-1979.

Sethna, K.D., *Ancient India in a New Light*, New Delhi, 1989.

Sharma, J., *Republics in Ancient India 1500 BC-500 AD*, Leiden, 1968.

Sharma, Ram Sharan, *Aspects of Political Ideas and Institutions in Ancient India*, 3rd rev. ed., Delhi, 1991.

Sharma, Ram Sharan, *Light on Early Indian Society and Economy*, Bombay.

Sidhanta, N.K., *The Heroic Age of India: A Comparative Study*, New Delhi, 1975.

Singh, A.D., *Kalidasa: A Critical Study*, Delhi, 1977.

Singha, R. and R. Massey, *Indian Dances: Their History and Growth*, London, 1967.

Singh, B., *Burial Practices in Ancient India*, Varanasi, 1970.

Singh, S.D., *Ancient Indian Warfare with Special Reference to the Vedic Period*, Leiden, 1965.

Sircar, D.C., *The Shakti-pithas*, Delhi, 1973.

Sircar, D.C., *Ancient India in the Vikramaditya Tradition*, Delhi, 1969.

Sircar, D.C., ed. *Early Indian Numismatics and Epigraphical Studies*, Calcutta, 1977.

Sircar, D.C., *Land System and Feudalism in Ancient India*, Calcutta, 1966.

Smith, Vincent Arthur, *The Early History of India*, 4th rev. ed. Oxford University Press, 1957.

South Asia in Review, Quarterly Review of New Books, Columbia, 1976 onwards.

Srivastava, M.C.P., *Mother Goddess in Indian Art, Archaeology and Literature*, Delhi, 1979.

Strong, John S., *The Legend of King Ashoka*, Princeton University Press, 1983.

Stutley, Margaret, and James Stutley, *A Dictionary of Hinduism 1500 BC-AD 1500*, London, 1977.

Subramanium, N., *Sangam Polity*, Bombay, 1967.

Thapar, B.K., *Recent Archaeological Discoveries in India*, Paris, 1985.

Thapar, Romila, *Ashoka and the Decline of the Mauryas*, Oxford, 1962.

Thapar, *Interpreting Early India*, Delhi, 1992.

Thapar, Romila, *Ancient Indian Social History*, New Delhi, 1978.

Tilak, B.G., *The Arctic Home of the Vedas*, Reprinted, Poona, 1956.

UNESCO, *Conference on History Archaeology and Culture of Central Asia in the Kushan Period*, Paris, 1968.

UNESCO, *Guide to the Sources of Asian History*, Paris.

Upadhyaya, Baldev, *Vedic Sahitya Aur Sanskrit* (Hindi), Varanasi, 1967.

Valmiki, *The Ramayana of Valmiki: An Epic of Ancient India*. Introduction and translation by Robert Goldman Princeton University Press, 1985.

Vats, M.S., *Excavations at Harappa*, 2 Vols., Delhi, 1943.

Vishwa Bandhu (ed.), *Rigveda with Commentaries*, 7 Vols., Hoshiarpur, 1965.

Vyas, S.N., *India in the Ramayana Age*, Delhi, 1967.

Wade, B.C., *Music in India: The Classical Tradition*, New Jersey, 1979.

Wagle, N.K., *Society in the Time of the Buddha*, Bombay, 1966.

Wheeler, Mortimer, *The Indus Valley*, London, 1966.

Wheeler, Mortimer, *The Indus Civilization*, 3rd ed., Cambridge University Press, 1968.

Wheeler, R.E.M., *Civilizations of the Indus Valley and Beyond*, New York, 1966.